MEDIATING MODERNITY

MEDIATING MODERNITY

Challenges and Trends in the Jewish
Encounter with the Modern World

Essays in Honor of Michael A. Meyer

EDITED BY Lauren B. Strauss AND Michael Brenner

WAYNE STATE UNIVERSITY PRESS DETROIT

12 11 10 09 08   5 4 3 2 1

Library of Congress Cataloging-in-Publication Data

Mediating modernity : challenges and trends in the Jewish encounter with the modern world :
essays in honor of Michael A. Meyer / edited by Lauren B. Strauss and Michael Brenner.
p. cm.
Includes bibliographical references and index.
ISBN-13: 978-0-8143-3395-2 (hardcover : alk. paper)
ISBN-10: 0-8143-3395-8 (hardcover : alk. paper)
1. Jews—Identity—History. 2. Jews—History—1789–1945. 3. Enlightenment. 4. Reform Judaism—
History. 5. Meyer, Michael A. I. Strauss, Lauren B. II. Brenner, Michael. III. Meyer, Michael A.
DS143.M356 2008
909'.0976608—dc22

∞

Designed and typeset by Maya Rhodes
Composed in Scala and Meta

Contents

Preface

Lauren B. Strauss and Michael Brenner

Compiling this Festschrift has been a great privilege for both of us. While each of us has a special relationship with Michael Meyer personally, we also recognize his considerable stature as a scholar who has made profound and lasting contributions to his field. As the contents of this volume prove, however, Meyer's field encompasses much more than one topic or method of inquiry. The essays collected here can be classified in such a wide variety of ways—as modern Jewish historiography, German-Jewish intellectual and social history, gender studies, literary criticism, and Zionist history and historiography, to name a few—that the reader quickly realizes that Meyer's influence extends well beyond his own immediate areas of research. But, in truth, that was not the primary reason for our decision to honor him with a collection of essays from his peers. Indeed, the existence of this book is as much a testament to Michael Meyer's character—his incredible work ethic and his personal and intellectual integrity—as to his scholarship.

The response by those we solicited was overwhelming—despite the busy schedules typical of eminent scholars, these colleagues were eager to contribute essays in Michael's honor. One after another, they responded with words of respect and affection, in some cases offering beautiful reflections on decades of intellectual camaraderie and friendship, and in others citing Michael's generosity to them over time as he read drafts, offered advice, steered them in new directions, and promoted their work. The poignancy of such relationships, forged over decades and sometimes across oceans, was brought home to us in the course of editing this volume—particularly with the loss of one of our contributors, the great Israeli literary critic Gershon Shaked. As one of Michael's closest friends and favorite sparring partners, it is perhaps appropriate that one of the last pieces Professor Shaked wrote should be published in this multidisciplinary testament to scholarship and friendship.

This volume would not have been possible without the advice and support of a number of individuals. First, Michael's treasured wife and companion of over forty-six years, Rabbi Margaret J. Meyer (Margie), was enthusiastic from the moment the project was suggested to her, and she tirelessly performed all the subterfuge necessary to keep the book a surprise for its honoree. The Meyers' son (and Lauren Strauss's husband), Jonathan Meyer, was an indispensable sounding board, repeatedly offering computer and editing skills, time, and advice. Rabbi David Ellenson was warm and welcoming in his capacities as Michael's colleague and friend and as president of Hebrew Union College–Jewish Institute of Religion. He made a generous subsidy available to us, and we greatly appreciate his willingness to also write a fine essay despite his many commitments. Our overwhelming gratitude is also due to Kathryn Wildfong, acquisitions editor at Wayne State University Press. She showed immediate and genuine interest in the project, shepherding it through the process of editorial acceptance and production. We have Barbara Selya, managing editor at Hebrew Union College Press, to thank for putting us in touch with Kathy at Wayne State. It is only fitting that this volume is being published by the press that has been Michael Meyer's primary publishing home ever since the publication of his first book, four decades ago.

Finally, as editors of this volume we have each had personal reasons for embarking on this project. Michael Brenner has enjoyed the support and cooperation of Michael Meyer in numerous areas. Their paths first crossed when Meyer agreed to be a member of Brenner's dissertation committee, giving critical support to his study of Jewish culture in Weimar Germany and essential advice on how to transform a dissertation into a book. Later, the two worked together as editor and assistant editor of the four-volume *German-Jewish History in Modern Times*. In this context, two different generations of German Jews joined in their endeavor to look deeper into the German-Jewish past, adopting Meyer's well-known work ethic as they read aloud to each other every sentence of a two-thousand-page manuscript and checked every single footnote. In subsequent interactions at international executive meetings of the Leo Baeck Institute (for which Meyer serves as international president), Brenner discovered another of Meyer's virtues: that of a diplomat, skillfully mediating between different perspectives. All this has been a formative experience for a younger colleague that has influenced and will determine his own research for the rest of his career.

Lauren Strauss, whose impetus for editing this Festschrift stems not only from her family ties to Michael Meyer but also from her professional admiration for him, has been the beneficiary of a "behind-the-scenes" view of his scholarly practices. Meyer's determination to stay abreast of current issues in and out of his immediate field and to stay familiar with the work of colleagues, his desire to master the historical and religious context of subjects that he teaches, and his responsiveness to others no matter how busy his schedule have all inspired Strauss in her academic career and beyond. Though her work in American Jewish history and modern Jewish culture is not directly related to Meyer's areas of expertise, Strauss has often reevaluated and elevated her own standards of intellectual excellence and personal integrity in light of the example she has had before her for many years.

We hope that this collection reflects the fondness and esteem in which its editors and contributors hold their teacher, colleague, and friend.

Modernity through the Eyes of Its Chroniclers

The Scholar as Interpreter and Shaper of Modern Jewish Life

LAUREN B. STRAUSS

In *Ideas of Jewish History*, the landmark collection analyzing the development of modern Jewish historical inquiry through the works of its authors, Michael A. Meyer observed, "For modern Jews, a conception of their past is no mere academic matter. It is vital to their self-definition."[1] In this spirit, the essays collected here, written by over twenty respected scholars on three continents, have contributed not only to a dispassionate study of the Jews as a unique social and religious group but also to the evolving self-perception of Jews who seek a greater understanding of their past—often in the interest of shaping their future.

In the same vein, scholars who pioneered the "scientific study of Judaism" as part of the school of *Wissenschaft des Judentums* in nineteenth-century Germany are often lauded, appropriately, as the first group to embark on serious critical studies of Jewish history and culture. Their intellectual example has inspired generations of historians to confront the world's most geographically diverse and durable people with scholarly tools that attempt to transcend partisanship and instead to offer a cogent picture of the Jewish people's unique experiences. But these historians' individual stories are in many cases as instructive as their writing, highlighting the degree to which the lives of some scholars have been closely bound up with their intellectual output. For some of the *Wissenschaft* historians, writes Meyer, their work "became their way of being Jewish."[2] This intensity of feeling toward one's subject can, in our own time, also be applied to Michael A. Meyer and many of his colleagues, though it is only one of the important ways he and they express their Judaism.

The links between Jewish scholarship and the personal involvement of its practitioners are profoundly illuminated in the present volume. While these articles have been compiled to honor one particular member of the profession, it is in the aggregate of the articles that the relationship of the scholar to his or her material is best illustrated. Here, we include American historians who stand at the helm of modern Jewish religious institutions, Israelis who have come from around the world to realize their lives and careers in the Jewish state, gentile scholars—mostly residing in European countries—who are among the first in the non-Jewish world to study the Jewish experience from a perspective of genuine scholarly interest rather than from anti-semitism or philosemitism, and pillars of the growing field of Jewish studies in the American academy who must continually balance their role as scholar with the expectation of being educators and sometimes spokespeople for the contemporary Jewish community.

The connections between these scholars and the community whose history and culture they study are complex, touching on questions of Jewish self-definition and identity in the modern world and the way the latter is bolstered (and sometimes challenged) by historical data and often used for purposes that reach beyond the concerns of the academy. It would be difficult to find a scholar whose life and career more acutely reflect this tension than Michael A. Meyer, who is both fully involved in contemporary concerns of Jewish life and committed to maintaining his scholarly remove.

As Meyer himself argues in *Ideas of Jewish History* and elsewhere, the work of modern historians of the Jewish experience has often reflected the needs and self-perceptions of the authors and their times almost as much as their subject matter. Thus, for example, *Wissenschaft* scholars' romanticization of Jews in Muslim Spain reflected their own desire to find a model of a Jew who both circulated in non-Jewish society at very high levels and was attractive to non-Jews. Salo Baron's more sociological approach echoed the American values surrounding him, and his anti-"lachrymose conception of Jewish history" stance reflected his desire that the Jew not be seen as a mere victim. Simon Dubnov's writing revealed his personal valuing of Diaspora nationalism, Raphael Mahler's incorporated his own Marxist sympathies, and Zionists like Benzion Dinur gave Israel pride of place in their stories

Lauren B. Strauss

of the Jewish trajectory in modern times. All—no matter how professional and thorough their methods—were undeniably responding to a deeply felt need in their experience of the times.

In Germany, Isaac Marcus Jost was, by all accounts, the first German-Jewish historian to write a comprehensive work of Jewish history. After Jost, German Jewry produced an impressive number of historians who turned to a broad variety of themes of Jewish history, from Leopold Zunz's studies of liturgy and philology, through Heinrich Graetz's magisterial *History of the Jews*, up to Ismar Elbogen's comprehensive *History of the Jews in Germany*, published during its waning hours in 1935. Hardly any other community has reflected so profoundly on its own past. Arguably, Michael Meyer, who was born in Berlin two years after the publication of Elbogen's history, is the last representative of this venerable chain of German-born Jewish historians between the first fruits of enlightenment and the darkening times of destruction.

As with any other historian, the biographical context matters in Meyer's oeuvre as well. Although a product of prewar German Jewry with its Liberal religious traditions and its deep attachment to German culture, he was raised among the German-Jewish émigré community in Los Angeles and brought up as part of American Jewry. Thus, his work is not only shaped by the tradition of *Wissenschaft des Judentums* but is an epitaph to this tradition as well. During the last four decades, he has written on almost every aspect of the rich German-Jewish culture. All of the significant predecessors mentioned earlier, from Jost to Elbogen, have been themselves objects of his studies. Like most of them, he too is deeply embedded both in the study of European history and in the Jewish sources themselves. There has been, of course, a key question driving each of these scholars. For Jost it was the issue of legal integration of the Jews in the societies in which they lived; for Zunz it was his near-obsession to rescue the treasures of the Jewish past; and for Graetz it was the idea of Judaism as the purest representation of the monotheistic idea. If there is any continuous element in the writings of Michael Meyer, a century after these luminaries, it is the ever-present connection between Judaism and modernity. How can the two be reconciled?

In his first major publication, Meyer sought the "origins of the modern Jew."[3] He found them in the period between Moses Mendelssohn and Leopold Zunz, in the Haskalah and in the *Wissenschaft des Judentums*. But the search for these origins would continue to preoccupy him for many decades, through his landmark essay "Where Does the Modern Period of Jewish History Begin?" up to the four-volume *German-Jewish History in Modern Times*, and beyond.[4] What is

Jewish and what is modern, and how do the two come together? These complex questions, to which Michael Meyer has given us some of the most profound answers in the last forty years, remain among the key issues of any occupation with Jewish history. As several contributors to this volume have testified, many of the parameters of questioning and analysis in modern Jewish scholarship—and many of their own ideas—have been inspired by Meyer's work, in particular his continuing struggle to plumb the depths of the connection between modernity and the Jewish experience. Some of the most incisive essays in this volume, in fact, take their course directly from his famous article that compares prevailing views of when modernity began for the Jews. Elisheva Carlebach sheds new light on the Jewish calendar and the issue of its codification, while David Ruderman takes advantage of Meyer's question to present his own ground-breaking work here, proposing a scheme of periodization for early modern Jewish history.

Meyer's early and abiding fascination with the figure of Moses Mendelssohn, and the case he made forty years ago to grant Mendelssohn the title of the world's first modern Jew, have also found echoes in the scholarship that followed his initial work. Mendelssohn's oeuvre has been illuminated from almost every angle, but as Shmuel Feiner asks, can one speculate about his dreams and nightmares? What did he expect from the society around him, and to what extent were his expectations fulfilled? Meanwhile, Mendelssohn's long shadow, which reached far into the twentieth century, forms the subject of Michael Brenner's inquiry. It is well known that both those who created Reform Judaism and those who created modern Orthodox Judaism claimed him as their ideal hero. Less well known is how Mendelssohn's heroic shadow faded away even among German Jews in the early twentieth century. His legacy, however, survives in a variety of realms, not the least of which is his example as biblical translator for a modern age. Richard N. Levy derives inspiration from this aspect of Mendelssohn's tremendous intellect, ruminating on the implications of translation and offering his own forays into this venture.

As with Meyer's predecessors in *Wissenschaft*, his interests are also more than purely scholarly ones. Living at the turn of the twenty-first century, Michael Meyer has continually asked himself not only how previous generations could reconcile Judaism and modernity but also how contemporary Jews can create a kind of Judaism that does not escape from modernity but rather integrates it. Here, the different parts of his biography add up: his German-Jewish birth and American-Jewish upbringing, his dedication to the Hebrew language (whose reemergence is itself one of the great wonders of modern Jewish life), and his adherence to Jewish tradition within the context of Reform

Jewish ideology—along with over forty years of teaching at the intellectual center of Reform Judaism, the Hebrew Union College–Jewish Institute of Religion (HUC-JIR). The present collection counts among its essays a contribution by David Ellenson, who brings his perspective as rabbi, historian, and president of HUC-JIR to bear. Ellenson focuses on Meyer's significant role in clarifying the intent and purpose of Reform Judaism for its adherents and for the rest of the world, pointing both to his personal example and to his scholarship—particularly in his monumental *Response to Modernity*.[5] As Ismar Schorsch, former chancellor of the Conservative movement's Jewish Theological Seminary of America writes here in a personal tribute to his friend and colleague, Meyer "has always resided intellectually in a two-storied dwelling," with Reform Judaism on one level and historical research at its foundation.

Other themes that resonate for Meyer as a Zionist and as a Jew who was forced to leave his native land are also sounded by scholars in this volume, as they work from diverse assumptions about Israel, the premises upon which the State was founded, and the role of displacement as it relates to Jews and modern world history. Perhaps the two most divergent essays dealing with these topics are those by Evyatar Friesel and David N. Myers. Friesel, a German-born Israeli, passionately inveighs against those who, through antisemitism or ignorance, would read Israel and the Jewish people out of history, particularly in discussions of Israel's political realities. Meanwhile, Myers excavates a little-known essay by the late historian Simon Rawidowicz in an effort to better understand both its author and the school of "New Israeli Historicism" that Rawidowicz anticipated decades before its ascendancy. But the close links between Israel's culture and its position in the world are even apparent from less political vantage points. Two essays here—by Arnold J. Band, writing in America, and Richard I. Cohen, in Israel—analyze a fictionalized autobiography by Israeli author Amos Oz and ponder the significance of his memories for a generation of Israelis who grew up in the same milieu. These essays emphasize the extent to which a writer like Oz—not constrained by rules of historical research—has highlighted aspects of Israeli history that he felt were most significant for his life, leaving the scholars to extract historical meaning from the novelist's choices. In Cohen's far-ranging and thought-provoking essay, these choices are set in a context of two other Jewish writers—memoirists rather than novelists—who selectively use history as an instrument to channel their nostalgia as they mature and reflect on their past lives.

The conundrums of the Jewish writer as participant in and shaper of his or her own history do not end there. As literary historian Gershon Shaked makes clear in his posthumously published essay, the evolution of modern Hebrew literature and its analysis have followed many of the same cycles of questioning, deconstruction, and return to traditional modes of scholarship as has the study of Jewish history.[6] It is instructive to note that the connection in this volume between literature and history is by no means limited to writing by Jews or in a Jewish language. As Susannah Heschel demonstrates in her study of Shakespeare's *The Merchant of Venice,* the image of the Jew in literature is powerful even when actual Jews are absent from the society that constructs the image.

Another central aspect of mediating between Judaism and modernity concerns the historian himself or herself. While Meyer's relationship with the State of Israel and his devotion to the Reform movement may form the spiritual center of his Jewish life, it is his active participation in modern Jewish institutions that perhaps most vividly illustrates his commitment to making Jewish scholarship accessible to the world beyond the university walls. As a founder and past president of the Association for Jewish Studies, the American professional organization for those engaged in academic Jewish scholarship, and as international president of the Leo Baeck Institute for the Study of German Jewry, among many other professional commitments too numerous to mention here, Meyer—along with his peers—has seen the field of Jewish studies expand to include innovative spheres of inquiry and methodologies that consistently break new ground. In that spirit, several of the articles presented here introduce new topics—such as Jonathan D. Sarna's unusual pairing of colonial American Jews and mysticism, and Michael Stanislawski's literary-historical inquiry into popular Ashkenazic perspectives on sex and circumcision. Some draw on more recent modes of inquiry as they relate to the study of the Jews; for instance, Paula Hyman evokes postcolonial theory and language about the physicality of the Jewish body to challenge prior perceptions about the place of the Jews in fin de siècle western Europe.

Whatever the methodology and the subject of research, it is still the condition of Jews in their own communities and in relation to the rest of society that reigns as the prevailing concern in this collection, for it is this exquisite tension that is ultimately the central issue posed by modernity. Christhard Hoffmann's valuable contribution views the oft-discussed German Jews of the nineteenth century through the neglected but essential lens of their most important periodical and its longtime editor Ludwig Philippson. According to Philippson, the key to a positive reconciliation between Jews and the surrounding culture was to accentuate the liberal, or "Mosaic," aspects of the religion, and to be open to change. Sometimes the issue explored is that of the

Jews' concern with societal norms—as with the nineteenth-century Cincinnati Jews featured in Karla Goldman's essay, or Marion Kaplan's gender-sensitive comparison of young Jewish men and women in imperial Germany and their professional and sexual development. An adjacent era receives a very different treatment at the hand of Steven M. Lowenstein, who explores the opposing agendas of diverse camps in liberal German-Jewish communities during the Weimar period.

At other times, it is the way in which Jews have been perceived by others that proves instructive, from Peter Pulzer's exposition on German non-Jewish historians and their scholarly treatment of Jews to Avraham Barkai's discourse on the Jewish religion and capitalism. The Christian discussion of the Jews and their ultimate salvation has usually been seen in isolation from other groups, but as Ernst-Peter Wieckenberg demonstrates here, an understanding of the Jews' status in Christian society is enhanced by comparing Christian theological reflections on Jews, Muslims, and heathens. German historian Monika Richarz addresses a more recent legacy of Jewish existence in non-Jewish societies, exploring artist Gunter Demnig's project to memorialize Holocaust victims through inscribed "stumbling stones" embedded in sidewalks throughout Germany. This takes the study of history to a contemporary, extratextual plane that challenges even as it commemorates.

Often, acts of commemoration—as this volume most certainly is, honoring Michael A. Meyer on his seventieth birthday and on the fortieth year since the publication of his first book—are actually opportunities for the participants to paint a composite picture of themselves at that juncture. So we may see in this venture. While it is a genuine tribute to one historian, a major result of this effort is to recognize trends in Jewish academic scholarship in the current era, and to critically consider the role of the historian in drawing the contours of that inquiry. The topics that have been broached, the critical tools utilized, and the schools of thought that appear—and sometimes clash—on these pages paint a portrait that honors the individual whose career has provided the impetus for the volume. But ultimately, this study of the Jewish encounter with modernity does more than honor an individual or illuminate the scholarly questions that lie at the core of each essay. Because each author necessarily brings his or her own experiences to the interpretation of history, such a study becomes a commentary on the intersection of the personal and the academic—from Germany to America, from the Diaspora to Israel, from nearly a century ago to the present day—reflecting the lives and intellects of those who have written here, as well as those who will read their words.

Notes

1. Michael A. Meyer, *Ideas of Jewish History* (New York: Behrman House Press, 1974; Detroit: Wayne State University Press, 1987), xi. Citations are to the Wayne State edition.

2. Michael A. Meyer, *Judaism within Modernity: Essays on Jewish History and Religion* (Detroit: Wayne State University Press, 2001), 13.

3. Michael A. Meyer, *The Origins of the Modern Jew: Jewish Identity and European Culture in Germany, 1749–1824* (Detroit: Wayne State University Press, 1967).

4. Michael A. Meyer, "Where Does the Modern Period of Jewish History Begin?" *Judaism: A Quarterly Journal of Jewish Life and Thought* (Summer 1975): 329–38, reprinted in Meyer, *Judaism within Modernity*, 21–31; Michael A. Meyer, ed., *German-Jewish History in Modern Times*, 4 vols. (New York: Columbia University Press, 1996–98).

5. Michael A. Meyer, *Response to Modernity: A History of the Reform Movement in Judaism* (New York: Oxford University Press, 1988; Detroit: Wayne State University Press, 1995).

6. Professor Shaked's essay was written for this volume during the last weeks of his life. A note of tribute precedes his essay here.

Lauren B. Strauss

| 1 |

PERSPECTIVES ON A SCHOLAR
OF MODERN JEWISH HISTORY

Michael A. Meyer

An Appreciation

ISMAR SCHORSCH

In an academic career spanning some four decades, my friend and colleague Professor Michael A. Meyer has produced an exceptional body of scholarship, which continues to grow apace, in the field of modern Jewish history and thought. Its expanse, I suspect, has everything to do with a rare constancy of institutional affiliation and research agenda. Trained by Hebrew Union College in the sixties, he has remained to grace its faculty in Cincinnati ever since. Concomitantly, his dissertation and first book, *The Origins of the Modern Jew*, in 1967 evinced a deep interest in the early history of Reform Judaism, which would culminate twenty-one years later in his sweeping and masterful history of Reform, *Response to Modernity*. In retrospect, HUC seems to have given him not only his tools and focus but also his center of gravity.

Like Moses Mendelssohn, on whom he has frequently written, Meyer has always resided intellectually in a two-storied dwelling. If devotion to Reform makes up the furnishings of his upper floor, allegiance to the canons of historical research furnishes the lower. In a sober essay titled "Jewish Political Leadership in Nazi Germany," he gave voice to his professional ethos: "This essay . . . neither levels accusations nor offers exculpations but seeks only to arrive at a deepened understanding of motives and actions and the changing milieu in which they found expression."[1] The same can readily be said of his book on Reform, a finely wrought narrative by a consummate historian writing in a spirit of critical empathy rather than blind partisanship.

The historian's craft calls for spadework to precede synthesis, and Meyer has complied in several important ways. He has read widely in the enormously disordered and contentious history of modern Germany, enabling him always to weigh the effect of the German setting on his Jewish subject. In addition, he has scoured the libraries and archives in the United States, Israel, and Germany in search of obscure printed or unpublished materials pertaining to whatever topic has engaged him at the moment. It is that relentless pursuit of the data beyond our ken that infuses his work time and again with such unexpected richness and authority. The passages he chooses to cite from that inexhaustible trove rarely fail to enhance the immediacy and cogency of his argument.

The spadework not only has prepared Meyer for his history of Reform; it has also advanced him to the forefront of contemporary historians of German-speaking Jewry in the modern era. A few years after the publication of his magnum opus, the Leo Baeck Institute invited him to serve as editor of a multivolume history that would survey and synthesize the state of the field after forty years of pioneering research by the institute and others. Under his firm and expert leadership, a team of ten world-class scholars joined to conceptualize and execute the project in four compact volumes under the title *German-Jewish History in Modern Times*. Published in German, English, and Hebrew, the history covers the convulsive period from 1600 to 1945. Meyer's meticulous editorship is largely responsible for the high degree of narrative uniformity and scholarly standards that integrate the panoramic individual volumes into a single majestic canvas, surely the equal of the four-volume history of nineteenth-century Germany by Franz Schnabel before the Second World War or of the three-volume history of modern Germany since the Reformation by Hajo Holborn after the war. The achievement has no parallels in any other area of modern European Jewish history.

Meyer himself authored five of the nine chapters in volume 2, encompassing the years 1780–1871. Though they take up many of the events, issues, and individuals treated by him in his earlier books, these chapters still exude an aura of control, vitality, and elegance that makes them models of scholarly distillation. The canvas is large but uncluttered because it is painted with broad brush strokes. As always, Meyer constructs his narrative tightly and renders it gracefully. Generalizations come along more frequently but are always illustrated with an apposite detail or choice quotation from the most disparate of sources. The equanimity of a mature historian with carefully considered views hovers over its facile prose. In short, Meyer's preeminence as a German-Jewish historian as well as the acclaimed reception of his history of Reform flow directly from the strong influence of the ground floor of his two-storied residence.

On the second floor and at the heart of Meyer's scholarly enterprise lies the history of Reform. Even after the completion of his book, we find him returning ever again to facets of the subject worthy of further exploration. No scholar has done more to give the movement its history. In a secular age prone to marginalizing the study of religion or to accounting for it in largely nonreligious terms, Meyer has an abiding interest in Judaism. I doubt if monetary considerations alone were what prompted him as a freshly minted PhD to translate into English the bulk of Gershom Scholem's essays in *The Messianic Idea in Judaism*. Nor can his interest be attributed to a rabbinic education, for he is not a rabbi as is his beloved wife, Margie, about whose career he is always ready to preen. Notwithstanding, his command of traditional sources is formidable and amply attested by his scholarship.

More specifically, Jewish identity has been the lodestone of his ceaseless labors. Emancipation, whether partial or complete, shifted the locus of Jewish life from the periphery of the body politic to its center and fractured Jewish identity in its wake. As Jews switched languages, altered and expanded the contents of their education, and exploited new economic opportunities, their sense of self and their sensibilities underwent radical change. Meyer has always understood Reform to be a necessary, authentic, and creative religious response to a crisis that was both personal and communal. It is no accident that a form of the word *modernity* recurs in the titles of all three of his books on Reform—*The Origins of the Modern Jew, Response to Modernity,* and *Judaism within Modernity.* Whatever the phenomenon may entail, it had assuredly eroded a once unitary identity to a mere fragment that had now to compete for psychic space with the allurement of possibilities undreamt of. Reform, Meyer has repeatedly stressed, sought to address the chaos of this inner landscape and not to appease German critics or even advocates of emancipation filled with contempt for traditional Judaism.

Significantly, Meyer dedicated his first book to his parents. Beyond the niceties of the gesture, the tribute suggested more deeply the degree to which his study of identities in flux was piqued by his own experience of dislocation. As a child born in Berlin but raised in Los

Angeles, he witnessed and endured the wrenching effects of a change in language, surroundings, and culture on the stability of one's persona. No matter how inchoate, the experience sensitized him to the fate of the individual in times of turbulence.

In *Response to Modernity*, Meyer crafted a stunning classic, worldwide in scope and abounding in empathy and impeccable fairness. An unending spate of unpublished data deepens the analysis. Primarily an intellectual historian, he strives to understand the ideas of his main characters, not to judge or manipulate them. He feels himself into their quandaries and works through the genesis, flow, and meaning of their theology and actions. What emerges unfailingly are captivating précis of often complex worldviews that resonate with clarity, coherence, and plausibility.

Meyer is not an apologist for Reform. In his workshop the adversaries of Reform fare as well as its proponents. His tone throughout is dispassionate and judicious rather than defensive or polemical. If there is a bias, it is structural, that is, in his preference for the concept of modernity to frame his study. Modernity was a sea change faced by Christians and Jews alike, and it induced Meyer to understate the extent to which Reform in Germany was directly and deeply influenced by Christian models and emancipation pressures. What shaped the inner life of German Jews was not only the onrush of modernity but also the protracted and infuriating way in which German states equivocated in their extension of full and equal citizenship to their Jewish subjects. Modernity as an analytical concept is simply insufficient to account for the inescapable, deep-seated unease that was the fate of every German Jew by virtue of his or her persistent outsider status. As late as the First World War, long after the unification of Germany and the final legal emancipation of all its Jews, Meyer points out in his later work on Leo Baeck, some thirty rabbis served as Jewish chaplains in the German army without benefit of any official rank or government pay, in sharp contrast to the status and salary accorded Protestant and Catholic chaplains by the military. Their remuneration came instead from the Jewish community.

Had the emancipation struggle, which set German Jews apart from their Christian neighbors, served as Meyer's overall framework, he might have attributed greater salience to external factors in the emergence of Reform. To be sure, while he recognizes their import on occasion, modernity functions to obscure and dilute the extent to which many innovations were engendered by the desire to eliminate that which Christian intellectuals and bureaucrats found offensive. It is well known, for example, that the sudden upsurge of Reform in the 1840s coincided precisely with a renewed deliberation by a highly conservative Prussian regime on whether to reverse the whole emancipation process. Noticeably, however, the times that Meyer has treated this cascade of Reform initiatives, he has omitted any mention, let alone analysis, of this troubling political context.

If there is one Reform luminary to whom Meyer is particularly drawn it is Leo Baeck. Since 1966 when he devoted one of his earliest published essays to him, Meyer has returned to consider Baeck's life and thought often, most recently as one of the three editors of the superb six-volume German edition of Baeck's collected works. The final seven-hundred-page volume of letters, addresses, and essays, the largest of the set, Meyer edited himself with painstaking expertise. While the items selected are encompassing and enthralling, his splendid introductions to the volume and every section and subsection therein constitute the promising synopsis of the integrated, full-length biography of Baeck that has still to be written. Simultaneously, Meyer worked on an incisive study of Ludwig Meidner, the religiously Orthodox German-Jewish artist who painted portraits of Baeck in 1931 and 1948 and at whose wedding in 1927 Baeck officiated.

Admiration often turns into influence, and the affinities between Meyer and his icon are readily identifiable. As scholars, they are both skillful practitioners of Wilhelm Dilthey's conception of *Geistesgeschichte*, which puts a premium on empathy for comprehending ideas as the conscious expression of concrete, lived experience. As Jews, they share a magnanimity of spirit and deep devotion to the totality of the Jewish people that inure them to any animus toward views of Judaism other than their own. And as theologians, they understand Judaism as a set of religious polarities in creative tension. In the spirit of Kant, both give pride of place to the ethical life grounded in a sacred sense of being commanded as the supreme vocation of Judaism.

What Meyer cherishes most about Baeck is that his life became a glorious embodiment of his faith. That consistent concord between word and deed, belief and behavior also distinguishes Meyer's own life. In a confession of personal faith that he contributed to a *Commentary* symposium in 1996, Meyer revealed his own antimessianic temperament: "the tendency toward apocalypticism in Judaism is largely neutralized by the performance of *mitzvot*, of individual religious commandments. Through commitment to a life of *mitzvot*, whether or not they correspond to the traditional enumeration, we can acknowledge that redemption is not realized suddenly through the fruits of military victory but very gradually, one moral and religious act after another."[2]

That felt testament is a memorable reformulation of what Baeck meant by classical, as opposed to romantic, religion and offers a stirring glimpse of the religious disposition that permeates Meyer's home life and family, his lifelong teaching of rabbinical students, and his illustrious career of engaged scholarship with its uninterrupted flow of essays and books of the highest quality.

Notes

1. Michael A. Meyer, *Judaism within Modernity: Essays on Jewish History and Religion* (Detroit: Wayne State University Press, 2001), 184.
2. *Commentary* (August 1996): 73.

Michael A. Meyer and His Vision of Reform Judaism and the Reform Rabbinate

A Lifetime of Devotion and Concern

DAVID ELLENSON

In conferring the degree of doctor of Hebrew letters honoris causa upon Michael A. Meyer, the Jewish Theological Seminary recognized his prodigious accomplishments in the academic world and concluded their description of him by proclaiming, "Above all, you are a proud and passionate Reform Jew, a concerned participant in the movement's religious welfare and a voice of moderation in determining its future direction. As such you attest again that great scholarship flows from great commitment."

Meyer himself has testified often to his "close professional and personal attachment to Reform Judaism."[1] In an interview that appeared in the *HUC Chronicle* in 2003, Meyer reflected upon the factors that led him to his career in scholarship and service to the Reform movement and attributed these passions, in large measure, to his background. Born in Germany, Meyer arrived in the United States in 1941 at three and one-half years of age. He has observed, "I think my awareness of being one of the *nitzolai haShoah*—those saved from the Holocaust—has deepened my commitment to things Jewish," and he attributes his origins as a Jewish historian to "a combined interest in Judaism and a commitment to Reform Judaism."[2]

Meyer has principally displayed these attachments and interests to the academy and Reform Judaism through his more than four decades long association with the Hebrew Union College–Jewish Institute of Religion (HUC-JIR). He received his doctorate from HUC-JIR under the direction of Fritz Bamberger and Ellis Rivkin, and he has taught at all four campuses—Los Angeles, Cincinnati, Jerusalem, and New York. Meyer continues to teach medieval and modern Jewish history, Jewish historiography, history of Reform Judaism, and the intellectual history of Zionism at HUC-JIR and feels himself "in accord with the school's goals."[3] Indeed, he feels "a special satisfaction in teaching rabbinical students, with whom I share values and through whom I can have some influence on the Reform movement and the religious lives of individuals."[4] Through his lectures and seminars as well as his writings, Meyer has been a preeminent interpreter of the Reform movement for his students, and he has self-consciously attempted to transmit a compelling and authentic vision of modern Judaism for them. It is a vision that recognizes and captures the full complexity of directions that inform the modern Jewish world as well as the full panoply of issues that are involved in the education of Reform rabbis for the contemporary Jewish situation.

Meyer recognizes that societal developments in recent years have meant that "the rabbinate has shifted from the rabbi as the one who deals with Jewish issues to the rabbi who is largely a pastoral counselor."[5] Nevertheless, he continues to challenge his students academically and hold them, in view of his sense of "responsibility as a Jewish historian dedicated to the tradition of *Wissenschaft des Judentums*—the impartial, scientific study of the Jewish past," to the highest traditions of a modern scholarly rabbinate.[6] Such knowledge is a prerequisite for their claim to authenticity and authority. Without a significant knowledge of Jewish sources and history, Meyer believes that the modern rabbi has no legitimate claim on the title.

Furthermore, the academic enterprise itself is crucial for Reform rabbis to grasp the role they occupy in the future growth and development of Judaism. Reform, Meyer points out, "represents that branch of Judaism that has been the most hospitable to the modern critical temper while still endeavoring to maintain continuity of faith and practice with Jewish religious tradition." He quickly adds, "Reform Judaism can scarcely be comprehended by reference only to its current spectrum of beliefs and practices," and an understanding of the dynamic flow of Jewish history and texts is required if the rabbi is to comprehend the "dynamic tensions" that mark Reform and its approach to Judaism.[7] The Reform rabbi must grasp how Jewish self-understanding and the reconceptualization of Judaism that has emerged

David Ellenson

for Jews in the wake of that modern self-understanding "has been a response to their new situation, . . . a modernity that, even as it threatens to swallow up the faith of a diminishing minority, also offers the possibility for differentiation, development, and renewal."[8]

At the same time, an emphasis on knowledge and the self-understanding and awareness that scholarship provides is not sufficient to capture the complete dimensions of the tasks Meyer believes confront Reform Judaism and the Reform rabbi. For inasmuch as Meyer sees Reform as a dynamic manifestation of Jewish religious tradition, he envisions Reform as part of a broader and overarching landscape of Jewish fate and solidarity. Meyer naturally applauds the fact that today "the Reform Movement is moving in the direction of greater depth in religion and Jewish education than in the past." However, he demands that the movement "recapture the awareness of broader Jewish destiny." Reform must "cope with new challenges, including the large number of mixed couples in Reform congregations who require a sense of Jewish peoplehood." As a corollary to this, the movement "also has to strengthen its relationship to Israel, which," in his view, "regrettably has weakened since the 1970s." Meyer therefore concludes, "It is up to us on the faculty at HUC-JIR to create a readiness to meet these challenges among our students."[9]

Meyer has promoted this vision to help his students and the leaders of the movement to envision what Reform might become. His vision of Reform Jewish education in general and rabbinical education in particular is a rich and bold attempt to resolve the conflict between the values of modernity with its commitment to critical thought on the one hand and the notion of religious commitment and communal sensibility that is so central to Judaism on the other. In his seminal and provocative essay "Reflections on the 'Educated Jew' from the Perspective of Reform Judaism," Meyer offers a fuller description of and richer insight into his approach to Reform Judaism. At the outset of this essay, Meyer writes that Judaism is marked by the presence of polarities throughout its history and that Judaism involves "living in the tensions they create." In our age, there are values "external to Judaism" we seek to integrate into our lives, and Judaism seeks to transmit these values along with those of "the Jewish heritage" to its adherents. The challenge is to live between these two polarities. Consequently, Meyer contends that his Judaism "flows from an idea of Judaism that recognizes and affirms the value of modernity, represented especially by personal autonomy, while insisting upon the priority of Jewish religious faith."[10]

Meyer continues by casting a critical eye on both Judaism and the certainties of modern life. Jews today live within the "multiple tensions of autonomy and obligation, integration and separation, peoplehood and religion, dispassionate knowledge and life-determining commitment." The task is to incorporate "personally configured elements of Jewish traditions into individual lives." However, he believes those choices should be influenced by "educating toward core Jewish values" that create "Jewish religious lives that stand under the authority of an obligating God." Reform Judaism believes that truth comes from a multiplicity of sources and believes in universalism. At the same time, it recognizes that "an untrammeled universalism" can destroy "the bonds that unite Jews with one another."[11]

Meyer expands on the danger this trend poses to contemporary Judaism in general and Reform in particular in a companion essay, "Will the Center Hold?" which he published in *Conservative Judaism.* Indeed, this latter essay highlights and illuminates the position Meyer advances in his essay "The 'Educated Jew.'" In "Will the Center Hold?" Meyer states that American Judaism, until recently, with its "strong collective emphasis upon people and community," had "resisted the disintegrative forces of extreme individualism." However, he writes that American Judaism today is "adapting itself to a greater degree than ever before to an American individualism—at apparent cost to Jewish solidarity."[12] Increasing individualization has given rise to what Steven Cohen and Arnold Eisen, in their influential book *The Jew Within,* have labeled "the sovereign self." To be sure, notions of selfhood and autonomy have always been present in Reform. However, Meyer believes, "heightened personalism has come at the expense of trans-personal memories and loyalties. For the younger generation of American Jews, the Holocaust and the State of Israel play diminished roles in their self-understanding as Jews." Furthermore, Prophetic Judaism itself "is in eclipse." This disturbs Meyer considerably, and he is upset that just 9 percent of the Jews Eisen and Cohen surveyed for their book "regarded concern for social justice as essential to being a good Jew."[13]

From this, Meyer concludes that "the non-judgmentalism that dominates our culture has a twofold effect on American Jewry: it inhibits Jews from arguing for the greater virtue or higher truth of their own tradition and it makes them reject any attempt, whether by rabbis, relatives, or friends, to subject their own personally chosen form of Judaism to any objective standard." Jews "are reluctant to accept external sources of authority," and Meyer cites the Cohen finding that 75 percent of intermarried young people who were brought up in the Conservative movement either leave the movement as adults or do not join themselves as further evidence of the significant test that confronts Reform Judaism and the Reform rabbis who are his students,

David Ellenson

for these Jews, when they do move on from the Conservative move-ment and when they do affiliate, do so in overwhelming numbers with the Reform movement.[14] The future of Judaism in America is thus contingent, to a large extent, upon the success Reform rabbis will have in instilling communitarian religious values and commitments in per-sons who have rejected them in their previous affiliations. The magni-tude of this challenge is clearly immense.

Nevertheless, Meyer argues that despite these "powerful indi-vidualist trends in American society," Jewish religious leadership in general, and the Reform rabbi in particular, must still "advocate for the acceptance of divine commandment, not alone in the area of ritual mitzvoth, but also . . . in [the realm] of moral commandments. . . . The encounter with reasserted individualism must result in a gradual pro-cess of absorption which does not sacrifice principle or integrity." This process "could be free to incorporate the legitimate quest for personal meaning, bringing it under the canopy of unconditional and ongoing commitment to people, faith, and divinely imposed obligation."[15]

Meyer thus asserts that while there is always a "need to maintain openness" in Reform, the task of "establishing and upholding a clear sense of [Jewish] self" is more difficult than ever. In contemporary American society, Jewish identity is "no longer hidden." However, its "borders have been rubbed away." Meyer therefore believes that "under these circumstances the dominant thrust of Jewish education must be inward," with an emphasis upon particularity. We need "Jewishly edu-cated Jews." Reform should be a tradition that "aims to direct life, not merely enhance it," and that can only be done when there is an effort to instill in Jews "what it is like to live within the circle [of Judaism]." Instilling a sense of identification with the Jewish tradition and Jewish people must be the first task of the rabbi and the prime goal of Jewish education. As Meyer succinctly phrases it, "Choice follows [only] after commitment." Meyer thus modifies the previous Reform emphasis upon autonomy as the foundation for Reform Judaism. Instead, he opts to construct a contemporary concept of autonomy upon a more communitarian vision of the self that allows for Jewish commitment to precede "choice."[16]

To be sure, Meyer states, "Historical honesty would require the recognition that, by and large, liberal values have emerged from out-side religious traditions, that they are the product of modernity, not re-ligiosity," and he says, yet again, that Reform Judaism recognizes this conflict. However, the assignment of the Reform rabbi is to uphold and instill a communitarian Reform religious ideal of the self—the notion of a "Jewish covenantal self"—in Reform Jews. Reform rabbis must strive to instill behaviors and commitments to a way of life in modern Jews. As Meyer phrases it, Reform Jewish education "must lead to Halakhah, whether that term is understood literally or metaphorically." He understands this to mean "the inclusion of recurrent specifically Jewish acts within the routine of personal and family life (Halakhah in a broad sense), and the application of values drawn from Jewish sources to life decisions within both the private and public spheres." The challenge is to make Judaism "the primary source of ultimate meanings" for the Reform Jew. The teacher, and by extension the rabbi, must be "model Jews," and there must be "ethnic awareness" as well as "religious knowledge" that complement Jewish behaviors.[17]

For all his devotion to the peoplehood component of Judaism, Meyer cautions that a Judaism that rests on the ethnic pillar alone is not viable. In the Diaspora, he observes, "ethnic Judaism is speedily being devoured by an absorbent American culture." Furthermore, "in Israel it is being transformed from Jewish to Israeli." Meyer therefore concludes that only a Reform Judaism that "nurtures religious belief and religious practice can sustain Jewish identity in the long run." The rabbi must be capable of making the texts of the tradition "vehicles for conveying religious and ethical messages" to a contemporary Jewish audience as he prepares and charges his students to do the same.[18]

It is in light of this religious thrust in his thinking that one can properly grasp the central place the State of Israel occupies in Meyer's Reform Jewish thought. He points out that Reform Judaism in America and Europe promoted a notion of "religious mission" that "attributed a new historical significance to the lives of newly emancipated Jews." Zionism, on the other hand, "placed the Jewish people alongside other national entities seeking liberation and independence." The former addressed the individual, the latter the collective. Yet, he claims, "We are Jews whose Judaism is modulated by our commitment to two propositions (i.e., Zionism and Reform) which we today claim complement rather than contradict one another."[19]

Meyer explains his stance regarding the complementarity of contemporary Zionism and Reform in the following way. He acknowledges that the classical Zionist argument that links exile with persecution has never held well in the United States, and it does so even less today. After all, American Jews "are not strangers," and they participate in every facet of American life. Yet, Meyer, in a powerful and emotional statement, delineates the many reasons that the United States remains "*galut*-exile" for the Reform Jew. He argues that it "remains *galut* because in at least one sense it is not our country. . . . America is not a country whose atmosphere is pervaded by Judaism. . . . America is *ga-*

lut because in its beneficent atmosphere our numbers are destined to diminish. . . . America is *galut* because it is gradually swallowing us up as Jews. Finally, America is *galut* because, according to Jewish conception, the end of exile cannot occur until the messianic age. As long as we and the world about us remain unredeemed we dwell in exile from the messianic vision of moral perfection. In this sense of the word, all Israel, all the world, and even God remain in exile."[20]

It is the particular and universal hope for *ge'ulah,* for redemption, that makes exile bearable. Meyer believes that "for the Jewish people the establishment of the State of Israel has been a collective act of redemption." Yet, Reform religious zionism is "an unrealized messianism." Unlike many Orthodox religious Zionists who hold land as primary, Reform religious Zionism looks to the "commandment" as the category that "holds messianism in check."[21] Here Meyer draws upon the thought of Leo Baeck, who, while a non-Zionist, taught that "when man . . . wishes to give his life direction and lead it toward a goal, then he is always confronted with the commandment, the task, that which he is to realize. The foundation of life is the mystery; the way of life is the revealed. The one is from God, the other to be achieved by man. . . . Life dwells only where both are present."[22]

Meyer, echoing and extending Baeck, writes, "We can speak without apology about our own particular redemption, which consists of building the earthly Zion. We can justly call individual acts of *aliyah* redemptive acts."[23] This Zionist vision is integral to Reform and is not just historical or cultural Judaism. He thus concludes, "*Tzion,* as opposed to *tzionut,* is the goal of Judaism even as Sinai is its fountainhead. It is the object of our physical and spiritual ascent as individuals and as a people. It is the goal of our *tikvah,* our hope, and the object of our *mitzvot.*" Israel remains our *moked,* our focus, not our *merkaz,* our center.[24]

For Meyer, the Jewish task is to transform Israel and ultimately the world, and he has devoted a lifetime of scholarship and religious vision to making these ideas and commitments fundamental to the creation and contours of a Reform Judaism that honors the totality of its dynamic and evolving heritage. He has done this through his years of devotion to the HUC-JIR and its students, as well as his years of service to the Reform Jewish movement that sustains the institution with which he has been associated throughout his life. His vision of Reform Judaism is demanding and challenging, and the ability of his students to carry it forth and actualize it will surely inform and shape the destiny of the Jewish people and the Reform movement as Judaism advances into the next century.

Notes

1. Michael A. Meyer, *Judaism within Modernity: Essays on Jewish History and Religion* (Detroit: Wayne State University Press, 2001), 11.
2. Jean Bloch Rosensaft, "Michael A. Meyer: Four Decades at HUC-JIR," *HUC Chronicle* 62 (2003): 22.
3. Michael A. Meyer, introduction to *Hebrew Union College-Jewish Institute of Religion at One Hundred Years,* ed. Samuel E. Karff (Cincinnati: Hebrew Union College Press, 1976), 3.
4. Rosensaft, "Michael A. Meyer," 22.
5. Ibid., 24.
6. Meyer, introd. to *HUC-JIR at One Hundred Years,* 3.
7. Michael A. Meyer, *Response to Modernity: A History of the Reform Movement in Judaism* (New York: Oxford University Press, 1988), vii.
8. Meyer, *Judaism within Modernity,* 18.
9. Rosensaft, "Michael A. Meyer," 28.
10. Michael A. Meyer, "Reflections of the 'Educated Jew' from the Perspective of Reform Judaism," *CCAR Journal* (Spring 1999): 8.
11. Ibid., 8–9.
12. Michael A. Meyer, "Will the Center Hold? Conservative Judaism Reexamined," *Conservative Judaism* 54, no. 1 (2001): 5–7.
13. Ibid.
14. Ibid., 8–12.
15. Ibid., 15.
16. Meyer, "Educated Jew," 10–13.
17. Ibid., 15.
18. Ibid., 17.
19. Michael A. Meyer, "Setting Zion before Us," *Journal of Reform Zionism* 2 (March 1995): 5.
20. Ibid., 7.
21. Ibid., 7–8.
22. "Leo Baeck," in *Contemporary Jewish Thought: A Reader,* ed. Simon Noveck (Clinton, Mass.: B'nai B'rith Department of Jewish Education: 1964), 195.
23. Meyer, "Setting Zion before Us," 7.
24. Ibid., 8.

| 2 |

Between Tradition and Modernity

Michael A. Meyer's Periodization of Modern Jewish History

Revisiting a Seminal Essay

DAVID B. RUDERMAN

One of the interesting ironies of Michael A. Meyer's brilliant and prolific career is the fate of a small essay he published in the semi-academic journal *Judaism* in 1975. Appearing to be a mere spin-off of research Meyer had completed in the previous year leading to his important anthology *Ideas of Jewish History*, the article was simply titled "Where Does the Modern Jewish Period of History Begin?" As a recent graduate of the Hebrew University in 1974, I was immediately drawn to the essay as a wonderful distillation of the variety of interpretations to which I had been exposed in my studies both in Jerusalem and in the United States. Having recently sat in the lectures of some of the luminaries Meyer had discussed, namely, Ettinger, Katz, and Scholem, I noted that this modest publication seemed to encapsulate precisely the challenges of understanding the modern period, especially the prominent articulations of the so-called Jerusalem school of historiography to which I had been richly exposed, or some might say, with which I had been indoctrinated. Meyer's essay quickly became required reading for all of my students at the University of Maryland, my first academic position. And as I subsequently learned, most of my other colleagues both in the Diaspora and in Israel similarly adopted this accessible and succinct essay as required reading in introducing students to modern Jewish history.

In many respects, Michael Meyer's article was a specific extension and elaboration on the opening sentence to the preface of *Ideas of Jewish History*: "For modern Jews a conception of their past is no mere academic matter."[1] Meyer's major point was to show how narratives of the modern period in Jewish history were intertwined with ideological and theological positions of their exponents. Assigning a specific date with which to begin the modern Jewish experience was a subjective exercise, grounded in basic assumptions on the part of each author about the nature of Jews and Judaism in contemporary times. From Jost, Krochmal, and Graetz to Dubnov, Dinur, Scholem, and Baron, each had attempted to periodize modernity in an often arbitrary, idiosyncratic, and ultimately unsatisfactory way. Each historian's choice of event to initiate the period, whether the Enlightenment or political emancipation or the beginning of a consciousness of return to the Land of Israel, involved privileging one or more factors over others. There was no way of determining a uniform modern period for all Jews of variegated economic and social backgrounds or geographic location. And given the futility of such an exercise, there was no real value in periodizing at all. Meyer's summary was valuable in illustrating what his larger book had shown, namely, that history and ideology were intimately linked and that all reconstructions of modernity could not hope to capture the actual meaning of this elusive experience. Meyer's solution was to suggest instead a focus on the evolution of a process called modernization while pragmatically proposing the opening of a modern Jewish history survey course with the seventeenth century. The latter could represent no more than a convenient starting point in which to chart the unfolding of a cluster of economic, social, political, and religious factors usually associated with the rise of modernity.

Most recently, Moshe Rosman has also stressed the importance of Meyer's essay, not only as an indicator of the preoccupation with periodization that seemed to afflict students of Jewish history of the 1970s, but also as a kind of closing epithet that seemed to facilitate the decline of this preoccupation altogether. For Rosman, after the appearance of this article, there was little interesting left to be said about the subject. Students of modern Jewish history no longer needed to worry about the essential meaning of long periods of time and large geographical spaces in Jewish history but could concentrate instead on narrower fields of inquiry and specialized studies analyzing individual subjects. The bigger picture had now given way to the "tyranny of specialization."[2]

David B. Ruderman

That Michael Meyer's article played such a decisive role as Rosman suggests in closing a prolonged debate of some 150 years may be a bit of an overstatement. But there is no doubt that it well reflected a critical moment at the apex of a stimulating conversation among Jewish historians that surely has lost much of its intensity thirty years later. But has the need to periodize also lost its élan with the passage of so many years? Is there really nothing interesting that can be said on the subject in our own era and from our own perspective? And was Meyer right that there is no real value in periodizing in the first place?

Rosman himself pointed to an important development in conceptualizing the modern era that emerged exactly a decade after the Meyer article: the publication of Jonathan Israel's *European Jewry in the Age of Mercantilism, 1550–1750*.[3] The book clearly marked a significant moment in the emergence of a field that we can appropriately call early modern Jewish studies. For the first time a well-known historian had skillfully attempted to define what had been denied or ignored or taken for granted by most previous researchers in the field: that the period from the late-sixteenth to mid-eighteenth century represented a unique epoch in the history of Jewish society and culture, to be distinguished from the end of the Middle Ages on the one hand and from the modern on the other. Despite the visible differences among Jews living in western and eastern Europe and in the Ottoman Empire, Israel offered a plausible argument for placing their disparate histories under the rubric of a common early modern Jewish experience.

Israel's book was noticed precisely because he approached his subject with the broad strokes of a general European historian, with a range and mastery of detailed information few of his peers possess and with the relative ease to move from economic and political to intellectual history in order to demonstrate a common relationship among all three. But the book was flawed in one major respect: it did not adequately examine the cultural and intellectual history of Jews living in this era. For Israel, the principal driving forces in transforming early modern Jewish society were external factors present in European society as a whole, namely, mercantilism and a revolution in European thought.[4] While for Israel the Renaissance and the Reformation had more limited effect in changing the relations between Jews and Christians, the so-called intellectual crisis of the seventeenth century had a lasting effect. Because of the new secular philosophy articulated most forcefully by Spinoza, a general critique of religion, and the new biblical scholarship, Christianity as a cultural force was on the decline and the foundations of a new secular culture were clearly emerging. The elements of Jewish culture that interested Israel were primarily those that intersected with these trends in western society in general.

Stated differently, Israel's depiction of early modern Jewish culture rested on two strongly held premises: that the decline of religion and its authority over Christian and Jewish populations was ultimately a liberating force that represented the primary factor in creating a secularized modern world and that Jewish intellectual history is essentially derivative, representing no more than a Jewish version of a universal European trend. Furthermore, from the perspective of early modern Europe as a whole, Jewish intellectual history is interesting only in the ways it contributes to and is informed by non-Jewish society. On its own terms and in its engagement with its own tradition and intellectual past, it exhibits little intrinsic significance.

This is not the place to offer a full critique of both premises regarding the liberalizing force of secularism and the assumption that Jewish intellectual history in early modern Europe can be defined solely or even primarily in its relation to the so-called European intellectual crisis of the seventeenth century. Israel's reconstruction of Jewish intellectual and cultural history is clearly in need of revision both because of the explosion of new scholarship Israel never considered and because of his limited perspective in approaching his subject. What I would instead like to stress here is the significant contribution of Israel's insight that an early modern period of Jewish history does exist and needs to be compared and contrasted with the concept of a modern period proper. Michael Meyer's negative conclusions about establishing the beginnings of modernity might have been mitigated considerably if he had been in a position to consider Israel's notion and how it serves to clarify modernity as well. This also leads me to champion the project of periodization for Jewish historians and to argue that with all its limitations, it remains a useful activity still worthy of the best of historical thinking.

Periodization schemes, with all their flaws, imprecisions, and imperfections, still remain critical in interpreting the past. Any attempt at periodization invites the detailed criticisms of specialists eager to discredit any facile generalizations regarding their hallowed scholarly turf. We undoubtedly live in an age where periodization schemes have gone out of fashion, as both Meyer and Rosman would emphasize, since they suggest an effort to essentialize or to even perceive historical development in teleological terms, and it is much easier and more certain to focus on the particular than the sweeping explanations of larger historical units. Yet thinking about the past cannot, in the final analysis, be sufficiently satiated with microhistories and specific con-

David B. Ruderman

textualizations of limited events and places alone. Because the historian lives in the present and his or her questions are ultimately shaped by it, one is required to think beyond one's data and specific expertise and to search for larger patterns no matter how elusive they may appear to be. Meyer was certainly right that the grand schemes he examined were all inadequate and subject to the critical scrutiny of specialists, but there still remains, to my way of thinking, something exciting and meaningful in their very efforts to visualize a panoramic view of the past rather than merely its minute details. That historians of our own age have hesitated to propose similarly grandiose structures is surely a reflection of a contemporary mood of timidity and insecurity that marks our historical profession, battered by the "linguistic turn," by postmodernism, and by other challenges to the very idea that historians can offer any reliable guide to the past in the first place. Avoiding the big picture is surely a safer path for most scholars who emerge unscathed from the inevitable criticisms broad reconstructions of the past readily elicit. But big pictures surely have their critical place in all reflection on the past.

In turning to early modern Jewish history in particular, the challenge of periodizing is certainly not made easier by the state of the field among European or world historians. As Randolph Starn has pointed out, early modernity represents a patent but flawed remedy for the problem of periodizing the time between medieval and modern history, touted as a kind of democratic alternative to the previously utilized terms, Renaissance and Reformation, and the high culture they appeared to suggest. This indeterminacy, he adds, confers the aura of innovation on an agenda that by now is as conventional as anything previously said about the Renaissance. And he concludes, "Early, partly, sometimes, maybe modern, early modern is a period for our period's discomfort with periodization."[5]

But the effort, I contend, is still worth making. In describing an early modern Jewish culture, I do not intend to homogenize its various components. Rather, I wish to merely underscore the links of a global Jewish community where constant movements of people and ideas served to connect in some way each of its parts and to reinforce an awareness among its variegated constituents of the existence of a larger Jewish community transcending formal local boundaries and neighborhoods. My project also is not to move modernity back to an early starting point such as the seventeenth century, a preoccupation of several of the historians Michael Meyer discussed, such as Scholem and Baron. I wish to claim only that early modernity represents for Jewish history an epoch in its own right with an integrity of its own, neither medieval nor modern. And unlike Jonathan Israel, I would suggest that early modernity begins as early as the close of the fifteenth century and extends to the end of the eighteenth.[6]

I have considered five elements that might allow me to speak about the period as a whole. Each element needs to be examined over the entire period and across regional boundaries to assess its significance as a marker of a newly emerging Jewish cultural experience. These categories overlap, but to my mind, they offer us a most promising beginning in speaking about a common early modern Jewish culture.

The first element we might consider is that of mobility, social mixing, and hybridity. What I have in mind are both large-scale migrations like those of 1492 and 1497 as well as the movement of smaller groups and even individual scholars. The notion of the refugee scholar, the displacement, adjustment, and reorientation that being "on the move" implies, is well known as a phenomenon of twentieth-century culture but surely constitutes a critical dimension of this period in particular. Within Jewish culture, the expulsion of Spanish Jewry has long been viewed as a watershed in the physical dislocation and cultural transformation it engendered. Certainly for the large numbers of Jews exiting the Iberian Peninsula at the end of the fifteenth century, the process of migration, of establishing new roots, of mixing with other resident Jewish populations especially in the Ottoman Empire, and the creative tensions the new environments engendered are all matters of great consequence for historians of this era. As Moshe Idel has recently argued, mobility was a key factor in the shaping of kabbalistic writing and praxis in the sixteenth century. Mobility was also a critical dimension in the lives of Converso intellectuals in the sixteenth and seventeenth centuries who migrated to Italy, southern France, Amsterdam, Hamburg, and London, even returning to Spain and Portugal when the opportunity arose. Ashkenazic Jews were similarly in motion during the same period, traveling to Italy to study medicine, migrating to southern France and Amsterdam in search of better economic conditions, or crossing the continent on their way to the Land of Israel. They also moved eastward from Poland to the Ukraine after its annexation in 1569. From the sixteenth century, Jewish scribes, book dealers, and itinerate preachers were constantly traveling in search of new markets and new audiences.[7]

The ultimate effect of mobility on cultural formation has not yet been systematically studied, but it is clear that it is multifaceted: from the accelerated pace of writing in many languages to the emergence of new forms of literary creativity in law, mysticism, belles lettres, medicine, history and biography, homiletics, and more; the concentration of Jews in itinerant professions such as medicine, performing arts, and trade; the production of custom books meant to acknowledge and to enshrine in memory regional differences liable to be forgotten; and the internal conflicts and transcommunal structures erected to address diversity and controversy such as the printing of a universal code of Jewish law, the *Shulḥan Arukh* and its accompanying *Mappa*, the merger of the Sephardic and Ashkenazic traditions.[8]

A second element in describing early modern Jewish culture is communal cohesion accompanied by the growing laicization of communal authority. Earlier historians, including Jonathan Israel, have long recognized the importance of powerful Jewish communal structures in the early modern period. In the Netherlands and Italy, in Germany, in the Ottoman Empire, and especially in eastern Europe, Jewish communities appear to have become more elaborate and complex as agencies representing their Jewish constituencies before host governments and as providers of educational and social services to their individual members. This powerful surge of communal development stands in sharp contrast to the decline and deterioration of communal structures in the modern period. At the same time, these elaborate communal structures did not necessarily bode well for the rabbinic leadership of the community, who often found themselves in conflict with powerful lay leaders. They were often run by a small number of affluent families in an oligarchic and even despotic manner. In Italy, for example, despite the prominence of individual rabbis, the latter were generally beholden to the communities they served and to the wealthy families who dominated communal life, including the many confraternities enriching the social and cultural life of the ghettos. The prominence of wealthy merchants in shaping communal affairs also marked the collective life of Amsterdam, Hamburg, and London Jewries. The governing hierarchy of these communities scrupulously controlled the management of communal affairs and demonstrated a heightened sensitivity to the projection of a proper image and to proper collective demeanor before governmental authorities. In the Ottoman Empire, no chief rabbinate ever existed and the authority of the rabbis was always circumscribed by the dictates of Muslim law. Despite the temporarily growing power of the rabbis in the seventeenth century, their authority ultimately declined. Jewish communal life was weakened by the creeping penetration of merchant colonies of Conversos in Ottoman port cities such as Smyrna, and economically powerful magnates continued to hold considerable power.

The elaborate Jewish self-government of Poland-Lithuania emerging by the sixteenth century was strictly under lay, not rabbinic, control. Communal rules and ordinances were not enacted by halakhic authorities but by lay leaders who virtually controlled the Jewish communities. Some rabbis exercised power because of their exceptional expertise in Jewish law and their strong personalities, but more often than not, they also derived their authority by virtue of their own affluence, either gained through birth or proper marriage, thus allowing them to become part of the oligarchic power structure themselves.

The implications of this general picture seem clear. The seeds of the crisis over rabbinic authority, usually associated with the late seventeenth and eighteenth centuries, can already be located in the sixteenth century, at the very inception of powerful communal structures and at the very pinnacles of Jewish self-government and internal political life. The rabbinate was certainly not a spent institution in early modern Europe; it had not yet been drained of all its considerable legal and moral resources to direct the religious lives of the constituencies it served; and it certainly did not see itself in crisis until the very end of this period. But its power had been eclipsed, and rabbis reluctantly were obliged to function within a new reality of sharing leadership with lay leaders for generations to come.[9]

The third element, and perhaps the most significant in defining an early modern Jewish culture, I have simply called "knowledge explosion," and by this I primarily mean the effect of the printed book. Although Jews "on the move" explain in part the possibility of a shared cultural experience between disparate Jewish communities at great physical and psychological distance from one another, books "on the move" explain much more. Before print, no one could have conjured up the seemingly absurd merger of two legal traditions on one page as captured in the printing of the aforementioned *Shulḥan Arukh* (1578–80). And no one could have imagined the extraordinary layout of multiple commentaries from different eras and regions surrounding the core text of the Talmud and simultaneously appearing on the same page with it, or those of the rabbinic Bible, first published by the Christian printer Daniel Bomberg, in Venice in the first decades of the sixteenth century. As Elhanan Reiner has shown, the migration of these and other Hebrew books printed in Venice into eastern Europe created a crisis for the rabbinic elites of Poland-Lithuania. The printed text soon arrested the creative and open process of a fluid scribal culture, making the text canonical and not subject to accretions and modifications. The text, not the teacher, became the ultimate word, thus diminishing the authoritative capacity of the rabbi as exegete. In this new market of books originating in Venice, Amsterdam, and Constantinople, Ashkenazic readers were exposed to the classics of the Sephardic library, while eventually Sephardic readers became aware of Ashkenazic writing. Printing thus shattered the isolating hold of

David B. Ruderman

potent localized traditions and attitudes as one community became increasingly aware of a conversation taking place long distances away.[10]

Another effect of the printing revolution was the emergence of secondary elites—preachers, teachers, scribes, cantors—who exploited the printing press to publish cheap books and to publicize themselves and their views. This dissemination of new publications ultimately shattered the exclusivity and hegemony of the rabbis, opening up new reading audiences. Books printed in Yiddish and Ladino, two Jewish languages that emerged in the early modern era in this new age of print, accelerated even more the wide dissemination of books and authors and the growing literacy of less educated males and females.

Besides reading and writing in Hebrew, Ladino, and Yiddish, an increasingly larger number of Jews read and wrote in western languages as well. Jewish authors felt the need to address Christian readers beyond their immediate community of coreligionists or Conversos whose primary language was Spanish or Portuguese. Christians also sought out books in Hebrew, and the book revolution accelerated considerably the market of Hebraica written both by Jews and by Christians and purchased by both communities. Print also represented a critical factor in modifying the very notion of what constitutes appropriate Jewish knowledge. Jewish intellectuals in dynamic cultural environments such as Mantua, Venice, Amsterdam, and Prague were bombarded with new books in print and, like other readers, were encouraged to expand their cultural horizons, to integrate and correlate the vast range of sources and ideas now available to them with those of their own intellectual legacy.

The knowledge explosion, although primarily engendered through print, was also precipitated through the unprecedented entrance of Jews and Conversos into the university, starting with Padua in the sixteenth century. Exclusively studying medicine, the students found the university an enriching and life-transforming experience both in the sense of the formal knowledge acquired and in the socializing process that inevitably emerged as Jews invaded what had previously been almost an exclusively Christian space. While print ultimately was the primary agent in bringing individual Jewish communities closer together and offering a modicum of uniformity among diverse local cultural traditions, the emerging Jewish medical community, graduates of medical schools eventually throughout much of Europe, also served to shape a common Jewish culture and a common Jewish identity.[11]

I would call the fourth element of an early modern Jewish culture a crisis of authority, accompanied by the threat of heresy and enthusiasm, the latter term associated especially with trends prevalent across the larger European landscape during the seventeenth and eighteenth centuries. In contrast to Jonathan Israel, I would define this as less a crisis precipitated by Spinozism and more one engendered by the messianic movement of Shabbetai Zevi, called Sabbateanism, although both discrete phenomena are also connected in several ways, as I shall indicate.

Shabbetai Zevi's declaration of his messiahship in 1665–66 engendered an enormous reaction among followers and detractors alike. He was ultimately incarcerated and converted to Islam but, nevertheless, remained the focus of messianic aspirations within the Jewish communities of the Ottoman Empire and throughout Europe well into the eighteenth century. The phenomenon of this strange messianic figure became the basis of a new antinomian and nihilistic ideology constructed especially by Nathan of Gaza and Abraham Cardoso, which challenged the very foundations of normative Judaism and rabbinic Judaism already in decline centuries earlier, as I have suggested.

This is not the place to review the various historical reconstructions of Sabbateanism beginning with the highly influential one of Gershom Scholem and the revisions of his students and colleagues. I will stress only one recent development in the growing literature on Shabbetai Zevi and his movement: that of challenging Scholem's insistence on seeing the roots of Sabbateanism as primarily an internal matter based exclusively on Lurianic kabbalah and generally isolated from the larger European context where it belongs. Several recent historians have underscored the reception of Shabbetai Zevi within the Christian world, its intertwined connections with apocalyptic anticipations of seventeenth-century Christians, and the obvious and explicit connections between Sabbateanism and Converso messianism. These latter connections are most obvious in the writings of the Sabbatean leader Abraham Cardoso, former Converso and leading publicist of the movement, in his attempt to portray Shabbetai Zevi as a Converso himself living with two separate identities and constructing a syncretistic messianic ideology based on elements of both religions.

By the first decades of the eighteenth century, with the fading memory of Shabbetai Zevi, the rise of another messianic movement in Poland associated with the infamous Jacob Frank, and the decline of Sabbateanism within the Ottoman orbit, the history of this movement and subsequent witch hunt to root out Sabbatean iconoclasts in all corners of the European world can better be explained by recourse to the notions of enthusiasm and antienthusiasm. When the Sabbatean prophet Nehemiah Hayon evoked an unprecedented alarm among a remarkably impressive number of rabbis writing from all over Europe, the charges surrounding him had less to do with his personal connection with Shabbetai Zevi and his ideology and more to do with his pretension to understand the divine essence as expressed in a Trinitarian form, that is, to understand the Godhead exclusively through his own innate powers. Similarly, the other great internal schisms associated with Sabbateanism in the eighteenth century, the accusations leveled against Moses Hayyim Luzzatto and Jonathan Eybeshutz, were primarily concerned with their explicit or implicit challenge to the authoritative structure of the rabbinate and the anxiety they and their followers generated over this perceived diminution of its actual power. Sabbateanism, then, in its later eighteenth-century dimensions, was simply a code word, a convenient label for enthusiasm, heresy, and the undermining of rabbinic authority.

Sabbateanism and anti-Sabbateanism and its vigilant rabbinic crusaders as pan-European phenomena underscore more than anything else the shaping of a truly early modern Jewish culture through books, emissaries, and a vast network of communication between advocates and detractors. Whatever else Sabbateanism engendered among early modern Jews, it created a real sense of their relationship to one another, their need to address either positively or negatively a predicament commonly shared by all and transcending regional boundaries. One might even speak about the emergence of a common front of "orthodoxy" engendered by the anxiety created by Sabbatean heretics throughout the entire continent. Ironically, the Europe-wide rabbinic crusade to vilify Nehemiah Hayon and the publication of his heretical book in the early decades of the eighteenth century ultimately revealed not only a united front against a perceived enemy of the faith but a common culture and a common fate. Sabbateanism left no doubt in the minds of its opponents that a threat to one rabbi or community was ultimately a threat to the entire fabric of Jewish faith and institutional life.

There is little evidence to suggest an equivalent contemporary reaction on the part of the Jewish community to the heresy of Benedict Spinoza as compared to that of Shabbetai Zevi. However, the common conditions under which Shabbetai Zevi and Benedict Spinoza emerged in the second half of the seventeenth century and the common results they achieved need to be stressed. Both were patently linked to the Converso experience; Sabbateanism and Spinozism in general were nurtured in Amsterdam itself; and both generated ideologies that challenged the legitimacy of rabbinic norms and rabbinic authority. In the end, both converge in interesting ways, although it is impossible to weigh them equally as factors in the collapse and deterioration of rabbinical authority at least before the late eighteenth century. The connections between this Jewish crisis and those larger social and institutional crises of European society as a whole also appear to be quite opaque. Nevertheless, Jews and Christians living in early modern Europe, most notably their religious and political leadership, seem to have shared a common perception of living through a genuine crisis that they could neither control nor arrest.[12]

The fifth and final element in my presentation of the constituent parts of a transnational Jewish culture in early modern Europe I term "the blurring of religious identities" or "mingled identities." By this I mean not only the phenomenon of the Conversos and their conspicuous presence throughout much of Europe but also three other discrete but related groupings: individual Jewish converts to Christianity, Christian Hebraists, and Sabbatean syncretists intent on forging a Jewish-Christian identity.

The religious and cultural ambiguity of Jewish self-definition first became an acute problem in early modern Europe with the reintegration of Conversos into Jewish life in Italy, northern Europe, and the Ottoman Empire. For new Christians who attempted to return to Judaism in the seventeenth century, their rite de passage was neither simple nor complete. They retained consciously or unconsciously identifiable attitudes and associations with their distant past, both religious notions and ethnic loyalties, which, in most cases, they could not fully dislodge. For new Christians who exited the Iberian Peninsula but hesitated to publicly acknowledge the Jewish faith, lingering in a transitional state between Christianity and Judaism, their religious and ethnic perceptions of themselves were even more complex. For some, it was possible, even desirable, to return to Spain and Portugal if opportunity permitted.

Viewing the Converso phenomenon alongside the other aforementioned groups: individual converts, Sabbateans, and Christian Hebraists, one cannot help noticing the recurrent and conspicuous boundary crossings between Judaism and Christianity in early modern Europe, or as Richard Popkin labeled them, "Jewish Christians" or "Christian Jews." When Jewish identity became a matter of choice rather than imposed communal will, when a growing secular lifestyle for some severely attenuated religious commitments and the time one spends in either synagogue or church, when certain Christians attempted to recover their spiritual roots through their study of Judaism while certain Jews found social and intellectual relations with Christians more attractive than ever, the possibilities for Jewish-Christian syncretistic thinking and praxis seemed unlimited. Decades before the eighteenth-century enlightenment, Jews and Christians were

David B. Ruderman

encountering one another in public and private places, in intellectual forums, and in radical and spiritualist movements. Certain Conversos were actually shaping a personal identity drawn simultaneously from both faith communities. Sabbateanism in particular, in its Frankist and other radical forms, could easily be conjoined with radical Christian ideologies like those of the Rosicruscians, Swedenburgians, and Freemasons.

The full history of these boundary crossings is still to be told. We have considerable inquisitional testimonies about Conversos who could adopt and discard different religious identities either out of conviction, or lack of it, or for economic motives. There is scattered evidence of Jewish collaboration with radical Christian groups, rich documentation of Jewish converts and their ambiguous identities in early modern Germany, Great Britain, and elsewhere, and complex writings of Christian Hebraists, especially kabbalists, who appropriated esoteric Jewish notions in reconstructing their own Christian identities. This fluid and ambiguous state of religious affiliation among all of these groups and their constantly changing combinations and collaborations represent a central feature of early modern Jewish culture. These new expressions of religious and cultural identity surely reflect the weakened and fragile state of the Jewish and Christian communities and their religious leadership by the seventeenth century as well as the prominent search for spiritual meaning among members of both faiths in an unstable social and political climate.[13]

Here, then, are those five elements that might allow us to describe the early modern period as a meaningful chronological unit for Jewish cultural history. Each of these factors can be located across the continent, including the Middle East, albeit with considerable variations among specific periods and places with regard to the number of people affected by each of them. Despite these apparent differences, they still might allow us to consider how Jewish communities in early modern Europe from Krakow to Venice to Amsterdam and Smyrna were linked in fascinating ways and how Jews living in this era were communicating with one another and were more conscious of their connections with one another—economically, socially, and religiously—than ever before. Through a thorough examination of these markers across time and space, it might be possible to grasp more fully the unique nature of the Jewish cultural experience in early modern Europe, an experience both unique to the Jewish communities across the continent and shared with other European peoples.

Through the project of describing an early modern Jewish culture, historians of the modern Jewish experience can better understand their own period in comparison with that which preceded it.

Mapping early modern Jewish culture provides an invaluable context and perspective for appreciating what was actually different about modernity and what represented a significant break from the past. Perhaps we are in a better position than Michael Meyer was in 1975 to grasp more clearly the lines of continuity and discontinuity that mark the transition from premodernity to modernity among Jews and when one period might plausibly be deemed to close as another opens. By introducing the "early modern" as a distinct era in its own right, rather than as a mere seedbed for anticipating later modern developments, modernity, in all its various dimensions and phases, might be apprehended more definitively and more precisely.

NOTES

1. Michael A. Meyer, ed., *Ideas of Jewish History* (New York: Behrman House Press, 1974), xi.
2. Moshe Rosman, "Defining the Postmodern Period in Jewish History," in *Text and Context: Essays in Modern Jewish History and Historiography in Honor of Ismar Schorsch*, ed. Eli Lederhendler and Jack Wertheimer, 95–130 (New York: Jewish Theological Seminary of America, 2005).
3. Jonathan Israel, *European Jewry in the Age of Mercantilism, 1550–1750*, 3rd ed. (London: Littman Library of Jewish Civilization, 1998). The book was first published by Oxford University Press in 1985, revised in 1989, and then revised and updated in 1998 by the Littman Library of Jewish Civilization. I cite from this later edition.
4. So, e.g., Israel states in his preface to the third edition, "Also central is the proposition that it was less the internal dynamics of Jewish life and culture than the external tensions and contradictions in the wider European world around the Jews which formed the principal driving force behind the changes within Jewish society in this period. This external dynamic, I argue, is best conceived of as a duality—a set of economic changes on the one hand and a set of intellectual and cultural shifts on the other." Israel, *Age of Mercantilism*, v–vi.
5. Randolph Starn, "The Early Modern Muddle," *Journal of Early Modern History* 6 (2002): 296–307.
6. In what follows I draw heavily from several essays of mine where I have already offered a preliminary sketch of my notion of early modern Jewish culture. This sketch also adumbrates a larger project in which I am presently engaged. See David Ruderman, "The Ghetto and Jewish Cultural Formation in Early Modern Europe: Towards a New Interpretation," in *Jewish Literatures and Cultures: Context and Intertext*, ed. Anita Norich and Shahar Pinsker (forthcoming); David Ruderman, "Mingled Identities: Jews, Christians, and the Changing Notions of the Other in Early Modern Europe," in *Europa, America, y el Mundo: Tiempos Historicos*, ed. Roger Chartier and Antonio Feros, 25–39 (Madrid:

David B. Ruderman

Fundación Rafael del Pino, 2006); and especially, David Ruderman, "Jewish Culture in Early Modern Europe: An Agenda for Future Study," in *Rethinking European Jewish History*, ed. Jeremy Cohen and Moshe Rosman (forthcoming).

7. I cite only a limited bibliography here: Yosef H. Yerushalmi, "Exile and Expulsion in Jewish History," in *Crisis and Creativity in the Sephardic World, 1391–1648*, ed. Benjamin R. Gampel, 3–22 (New York: Columbia University Press, 1997); Moshe Idel, "On Mobility, Individuals, and Groups: Prolegomenon for a Sociological Approach to Sixteenth-Century Kabbalah," *Kabbalah* 3 (1998): 145–73; Sophia Menache, ed., *Communication in the Jewish Diaspora: The Pre-Modern World* (Leiden: Brill, 1996).

8. See Elhanan Reiner, "The Ashkenazic Elite at the Beginning of the Modern Era: Manuscript versus Printed Text," in *Jews in Early Modern Poland-Polin*, vol. 10, ed. Gershon David Hundert, 85–98 (London: Littman Library of Jewish Civilization, 1997).

9. See, e.g., Israel, *European Jewry*, 151–69; Robert Bonfil, *Rabbis and Jewish Communities in Renaissance Italy*, trans. Jonathan Chipman (New York: Oxford University Press, 1990); Mordecai Breuer, *Rabbanut Ashkenaz bi-mai Ha-Beinayim* (Jerusalem: Zalman Shazar Center, 1976); Israel Halperin, with revisions and expansions by Israel Bartal, *Pinkas Va'ad Arbah Arzot*, 2nd ed. (Jerusalem: Mossad Bialik, 1990); Israel Halperin, *Yehudim ve-Yahadut be-Mizrah Eropah* (Jerusalem: Magnes Press, 1968); Joseph Hacker, "The Boundaries of Jewish Autonomy: Jewish Self-Jurisdiction in the Ottoman Empire from the 16th through 18th Centuries" [in Hebrew], *Temurot ba-Historiah ha-Yehudit ha-Hadasha . . . Sefer Yovel le-Shmuel Ettinger*, ed. S. Almog et al., 349–88 (Jerusalem: Zalman Shazar Center, 1988); Yaron Ben-Naeh, "Ha-Hevrah ha-Yehudit Be-Arei Ha-Impiri'ah Ha-Ottomanit ba-Me'ah ha-17 (Istanbul, Salonika ve-Izmir)" (PhD diss., Hebrew University, 1999), 166–203; Adam Teller, "The Laicization of Early Modern Jewish Society: The Development of the Polish Communal Rabbinate in the Sixteenth Century," in *Schöpferische Momente des europäischen Judentums in der frühen Neuzeit*, ed. Michael Graetz, 333–49 (Heidelberg: Universitätsverlag C. Winter, 2000); and Yosef Kaplan, *An Alternative Path to Modernity: The Sephardic Diaspora in Western Europe* (Leiden: Brill, 2000).

10. A rich study of the published books read by eastern European Jews is that of Jacob Elbaum, *Petihut ve-Histagrut: Ha-Yezirah ha-Ruhanit ha-Sifrutit be-Polin uve-Arzot Ashkenaz be-Shalhe ha-Meah ha-Shesh Esreh* (Jerusalem: Magnes Press, 1990).

11. Besides the Reiner essay mentioned in note 8, see Elhanan Reiner, "Transformations in the Polish and Ashkenazic Yeshivot during the Sixteenth and Seventeenth Centuries and the Dispute over Pilpul" [in Hebrew], in *Ke-Minhag Ashkenaz ve-Polin: Sefer Yovel le-Chone Shmeruk*, 9–80 (Jerusalem: Zalman Shazar Center, 1989); Elhanan Reiner, "A Biography of an Agent of Change: Eleazar Altschul of Prague and his

Literary Activity," in Graetz, *Schöpferische Momente*, 229–47; Zeev Gries, "Printing as a Means of Communication among Jewish Communities during the Period after the Expulsion from Spain" [in Hebrew], *Da'at* 21 (1992): 5–17; Amnon Raz-Krakotzkin, "Print and Jewish Cultural Development," *Encyclopedia of the Renaissance*, 6 vols. (New York: Scribner's, 1999), 5:161–69; David Ruderman, *Jewish Thought and Scientific Discovery in Early Modern Europe* (New Haven: Yale University Press, 1995; repr., Detroit: Wayne State University Press, 2001).

12. See esp., Gershom Scholem, *Sabbatai Sevi: The Mystical Messiah, 1626–1676* (Princeton: Princeton University Press, 1973); Gershom Scholem, *Meḥkarei Shabta'ut*, ed. Yehudah Liebes (Jerusalem: Am Oved, 1991); Yehudah Liebes, *Sod ha-Emunah ha-Shabeta'it* (Jerusalem: Mossad Bialik, 1995); Matt Goldish and Richard Popkin, eds., *Jewish Messianism in the Early Modern World* (Dordrecht: Kluwer Academic Publishers, 2001), 77–90; Jacob Barnai, *Shabta'ut: Hebetim Ḥevrati'im* (Jerusalem: Zalman Shazar Center, 2000); Elisheva Carlebach, *The Pursuit of Heresy: Rabbi Moses Hagiz and the Sabbatian Controversies* (New York: Columbia University Press, 1990); and Matt Goldish, *The Sabbatean Prophets* (Cambridge: Harvard University Press, 2004).

13. See Robert Bonfil, "Dubious Crimes in Sixteenth-Century Italy: Rethinking the Relations Between Christians, Jews, and Conversos in Pre-Modern Europe," in *The Jews of Spain and the Expulsion of 1492*, ed. Moshe Lazar and Stephen Haliczer, 299–310 (Lancaster, Calif.: Labyrinthos, 1997); Kaplan, *Alternative Path to Modernity*; Richard Popkin and Gordon Weiner, eds., *Jewish Christians and Christian Jews* (Dordrecht: Kluwer Academic Publishers, 1994); Allison Coudert, *The Impact of the Kabbalah in the Seventeenth Century: The Life and Thought of Francis Mercury van Helmont (1614–1698)* (Leiden: Brill, 1999); Elliot Wolfson, "Messianism in the Christian Kabbalah of Johann Kemper," in Goldish and Popkin, *Jewish Messianism*, 138–87; Elisheva Carlebach, *Divided Souls: Converts from Judaism in Germany, 1500–1750* (New Haven: Yale University Press, 2001); David Graizbard, *Souls in Dispute: Converso Identities in Iberia and the Jewish Diaspora, 1580–1700* (Philadelphia: University of Pennsylvania Press, 2004); and Mercedes García Arenal and Gerard Wiegers, *A Man of Three Worlds: Samuel Pallache, a Moroccan Jew in Catholic and Protestant Europe* (Baltimore: Johns Hopkins University Press, 2003).

When Does the Modern Period of the Jewish Calendar Begin?

Elisheva Carlebach

"Where Does the Modern Period of Jewish History Begin?" For generations of students in the eponymous courses it begins with a reading of Michael A. Meyer's essay by that title. Few scholars have contributed as richly to our understanding of the encounter of Judaism with modernity and its attainments and costs for Jews and Judaism. This essay on the Jewish accounting for time and its first encounters with modernity is, then, appropriately dedicated to Professor Meyer.

There is no Jewish equivalent to any of the great modern experiments to liberate the western calendar from its religious moorings. Neither the French Revolutionary example nor the equally radical and unsuccessful attempts to reconfigure the Russian Revolutionary calendar ever served as models for Jewish modernizers. This could not necessarily have been predicted from early modern auguries. The reform of the western Christian calendar barely seems worthy of a high ranking among the many momentous upheavals of that century. But what may seem like a mere technical adjustment in hindsight's long perspective loomed seismic to contemporaries. Sixteenth-century Europeans conducted intense deliberations for decades over the introduction of a revised calendar. The gradual drift that separated Easter from true spring had grown to a ten-day difference. In 1582 Pope Gregory XIII prepared the Catholic world for a momentous change: in October of that year, ten days would be dropped from the calendar. It would take two centuries for all western Europeans to adopt the new calendar. Regardless of where they stood on the matter, every person from priest to peasant would be affected by the change; none could remain indifferent. It is against this backdrop of heightened awareness of calendar as sign of denomination and identity that we can frame some of the diverse challenges to the traditional Jewish calendar. Regardless of whether the impulse derived from rationalism, humanism, or messianism, the figures we follow all acted in a world in which the calendar could no longer be taken for granted as an immutable reflection of the laws of nature. Its assumptions and workings, even if defended, were subjected now to a level of existential questioning as they had not been for centuries.

The calendar played a central role in one of the notable rabbinic controversies of the sixteenth century, the fierce dispute over the revival of rabbinic ordination, *semikha,* initiated in the Land of Israel. The historian Jacob Katz has correctly emphasized the messianic impulse behind Safed rabbi Jacob Berav's (1474–1546) campaign to unite the rabbinate and revive the ancient chain of apostolic ordination toward the goal of establishing a Jewish high court, a Sanhedrin.[1] Less attention has been paid to one of the crucial arguments offered by his implacable opponent, Jerusalem rabbi Levi ibn Ḥaviv (c. 1483–1545). It is true that ibn Ḥaviv and Berav differed fundamentally over their vision of the messianic order. Berav believed that Jews should begin taking steps to prepare for history's denouement, while ibn Ḥaviv did not think it necessary for Jews to usher in the messiah by building an infrastructure before his advent. Rather, he argued, "Jerusalem will be [re]built in an instant and afterward we can install a Sanhedrin."[2] Ibn Ḥaviv's concerns had far more practical consequences than an argument about the sequence of events in the messianic age. The most compelling and significant reason for his opposition was his opinion that if a Sanhedrin existed, it would perforce be invested with the power to sanctify the New Moons by direct sighting. This would render the fixed calendar that had served so well through the medieval period obsolete. Each month could only be proclaimed once the moon made its appearance; Jews would not know the exact dates of their holidays in advance. Such a change would throw world Jewry into chaos and confusion, resulting in the opposite of Berav's stated goal. Rather than providing leadership in times of crisis and a center in times of dispersion, the establishment of a Sanhedrin while Jews still remained scat-

Elisheva Carlebach

tered in a state of exile would shatter the tenuous unity that remained to them. (Berav denied that his proposed Sanhedrin would have this power.) Ibn Ḥaviv believed that he was defending the Jewish calendar as it had been calculated and transmitted for over a millennium from the threat of a utopian impulse that might have led to temporal and religious anarchy.

Another sixteenth-century challenge to the Jewish calendar came from a different quarter entirely. Sixteenth-century humanist scholar Azariah de' Rossi subjected the traditional Jewish chronology to a systematic and critical examination in the third section of his monumental Me'or Eynaim (The Light of the Eyes).[3] De' Rossi's questioning of the anno mundi chronology undermined the entire Jewish calculation system, which was based on a theoretical point in time as the moment of creation. De' Rossi maintained that the reckoning of the calendar from that starting point in time known as bahara"d, the pivot of traditional rabbinic chronology, was erroneous. Despite de' Rossi's protestations to the contrary ("It is obvious that given that what is past is past, the fixing of the months and festivals and the intercalation of the years is not affected by whether the figure is actually more or less"), his argument could potentially have rendered all religious observances based on the calendar null and void.[4] De' Rossi remained adamant about this argument and repeated it in a second book, Matsref la-kesef, published posthumously.[5] Yet ultimately, despite the controversy surrounding his work, his strictures did not have the slightest influence on any practical aspect of calendar calculation or chronology.[6]

In the seventeenth century, former Marranos such as Uriel d'Acosta criticized rabbinic calendar observances that had no basis in Scripture. The author of Kol Sakhal (Voice of a Fool), presumably Leone Modena, produced the most original and thoroughgoing critique of the Jewish calendar since the medieval Karaite schism. He subjected many aspects of rabbinic interpretation of biblical tradition to withering scrutiny, some of it echoing Christian or Karaite criticism, some anticipating later Reform challenges to the rabbinic calendar. The "fool" attacked rabbinic observances such as the second day of holidays observed only in the Diaspora, yom tov sheni shel galuyot.[7] Modena advocated a return to the biblical practice of celebrating the New Moon as a festival but only for one day. He ridiculed the rituals related to the Blessing of the New Moon and found fault with many rabbinically mandated observances related to the holidays. He singled out for derision the deḥiyyot, the deferment of the New Moon, particularly the one invoked on account of Hoshana Rabbah, which he argued caused Jews to observe the biblically mandated holidays on the wrong date. While no single element was novel, in its totality, Modena's critique would have returned the calendar to its scriptural foundations. This would not simply have had the effect of diminishing the number of days for religious observance; it would have undermined the entire Jewish calendar since so many of its elements derive from rabbinic readings of and elaborations on biblical texts.[8] But no one heeded the voice of the "fool," and the calendar remained intact.

By the eighteenth century, the growing secularization of Jewish life led many Jews to dilute or ignore aspects of traditional calendar-related observance. The debate over observance of the *yom tov sheni* in the nineteenth century is well known. Even traditionalists abandoned certain local fasts, instituted in the medieval period, as no longer consonant with the age of emancipation.[9] Yet the calendar itself, unlike the liturgy, never became the focus of a fundamental, sustained modern critique.[10] In what follows, we will examine one possibly unique attempt by a modernizer to subject the traditional calendar to rationalist critique and a traditionalist response.

Radical maskil and Kantian philosopher Lazarus Bendavid (1762–1832) is the only one of his cohort, so far as I know, to devote an entire work to the Jewish calendar and its traditional chronology.[11] Bendavid belittled the Jewish claim to an original, divinely ordained system of calculation, crediting the ancient Persian and Babylonian calendars for it. It was simply not credible, he argued, that Jews just happened upon the same precise fraction of time in their calculations as ancient Greeks and Babylonians did for their lunations.[12]

He historicized the traditional Jewish chronology as a relatively recent invention and averred that students of the Bible alone would never be able to satisfactorily answer the question of when historical time began.[13] The current Jewish New Year observed in Tishrei, Bendavid argued, had been instituted when the Jews returned from the Persian-Babylonian exile and consecrated the new Temple that month.[14] Yom Kippur, with its rituals of mortification, was the day when ancients manumitted their slaves.[15] Passover, Jubilees, and sabbatical years were forgotten until the second Temple period when Hezekiah discovered the lost Torah scroll.[16]

Bendavid's polemic is distinctive not only for the attention he paid to a subject neglected by most other modernizing Jews of his time but also for the mocking and scornful tone he adopted. The sound of the shofar, the ram's horn blown during the High Holy Day season, he compared to the "lowing of a cow."[17] He characterized midrashim concerning the time of creation as "nonsense."[18]

Yet, for all his sarcasm, Bendavid did not advocate abandonment or even fundamental reform of the Jewish calendar. Just the reverse, Bendavid supported an old, discarded method of calculating the *keviot*

       Elisheva Carlebach

(signs that determine the settings of the year) of each year based on a 247-year perpetually returning cycle (thirteen repetitions of the *maḥzor katan*, the 19-year lunar cycle). This 247-year cycle, attributed to Rabbi Nachshon Gaon, had been proven inaccurate by 905 parts and had been discarded as the basis for Jewish calendar calculations before Moses Maimonides' time. Bendavid mocked rabbis who rejected it.[19]

Bendavid's scornful tone and mocking asides provoked an angry traditionalist response from Meyer Moses Kornick, a scholar and mathematician.[20] Kornick, who had corresponded with Rabbis Akiva Eger and Moses Sofer as well as contemporary Christian savants published synoptic calendar tables that were highly regarded in scholarly circles, both Jewish and non-Jewish.[21] In his *Davar be-itto* (A word in its time) Kornick responded to the substance and tone of Bendavid's work: "Behold the new treatise [on the Jewish calendar] by the philosopher Lazarus Bendavid of Berlin, which comes to contradict the accounting of the years of the children of Israel. . . . I said, 'It is time to act . . . now, . . . to reply to him appropriately.'"[22] Although he wrote the book in Hebrew, Kornick rendered into German his announcement that the book was a response to Bendavid.[23]

Kornick accused Bendavid of writing the treatise not for the scientific objective of promoting knowledge but for a confluence of petty ulterior motives. First, he alleged, Bendavid intended to impress the gentiles, "the nations and their officers," with his great expertise in Hebraic scholarship. Bendavid accused the Jews and besmirched their reputation on a matter in which they were blameless. He mocked the Jewish sages whose wisdom, as found in the Talmud, embraced all the sciences. Their hearts, in Kornick's view, were "as wide as an auditorium," and the divine spirit was manifest in them. He noted that Bendavid's focus on the Jewish calendar itself was an unprecedented attack and marveled that Bendavid had ventured to erect a stumbling block for the masses in a subject on which he demonstrated such great ignorance and lack of comprehension.

As one who had devoted a lifetime to studying the formulae used to calculate the world's calendars, Kornick easily pointed out Bendavid's various deficiencies in understanding the Jewish calendar. But Kornick went far beyond highlighting errors in definition and calculation (e.g., the varying definitions of a rabbinic hour) committed by Bendavid. He responded as well to Bendavid's attack on the entire tradition that the calendar had come to signify in their exchange. His defense encapsulated the message conveyed by centuries of *sifre ibbur*, literature of the Jewish computus. Kornick's traditionalist polemic argued the following points:

1. The science of time among Jews is of divine origin. "Moses had difficulty with the [laws of] *kiddush ha-ḥodesh* [sanctification of the New Moon] until the Lord Blessed be He showed him the moon at the time of its renewal, because Moses and Aaron did not acquire that supernal science by [means of] their own mind and investigations. Rather, the *sod ha-ibbur* [secret of the intercalation] and the roots of its science came by way of prophecy, as it is impossible for the human species to acquire it. From there the tradition unfolded in the manner of the other Torah commentaries and minutiae of the mitzvot, as it says, 'And the sons of Issachar knew the *yod'ei bina l'ittim* [wisdom of time], etc.' They fixed the months and intercalated the years through their wisdom, and in accordance with their tradition. They knew many secrets in the science of the seasons and constellations which could not be known through the ordinary methods of human investigation."[24]

2. The Jewish calendrical system was appropriated by the nations of the world, not the reverse. "It has always been thus in Israel, they have known the wisdom of time. There have been great experts in the science of astronomy . . . as they received it transmitted orally from one to the other, reaching back to Moses." Kornick cited many medieval authorities on the precedence of Israel in the astronomical sciences. "I call upon reliable witnesses to the effect that the science of astronomy emerged first in Israel, and when the nations of the world ruled over us, it passed into their hands."[25] While not all the authorities he cited in fact supported this position, David Gans's *Neḥmad ve-na'im* opens with a classic statement of it: "I will reveal what I have found in other books concerning the pedigree of this science [the calendar] from Adam until today. I have found in the books of Josippon ben Gorion that Adam was a very wise person and great astronomer. . . . Abraham our forefather transmitted this science to his son and grandson, Isaac and Jacob. The Egyptians got the science of numbers and engineering, together with astronomy from Jacob and his sons when they descended to Egypt, in addition to what they had always received from Abraham, and as a result of the travails of exile the wisdom was forgotten from the children of Israel and it remained in the hands of the magicians of Egypt. The Greeks received it from the sorcerers of Egypt . . . the Babylonians received it from the Egyptians and the Greeks. [Although it may seem as though astronomy originated among the gentiles] the matter is otherwise. The principal knowledge in this field emerged first among our nation."[26]

3. Elements of the calculation remain esoteric and are not accessible to the Jewish masses or to non-Jews, a position embedded in the

phrase *sod ha-ibbur*. "As matters pertaining to *sod ha-ibbur* are profound, requiring great thought and exacting calculations, they have hidden this precise mode of calculation, and did not transmit it except to those who had ordination, and to unique individuals, the pious ones of the generation such as the prophets, the Sanhedrin, and not to the masses of Israel. They would intercalate as they saw the need, according to the signs that had been transmitted to them. That was the custom . . . until several years after the destruction of the second Temple when ordination was abolished. . . . When the authorities decreed the death of ordainer and ordained (Sanhedrin 14), Hillel the Nasi and the Bet Din together with the Sages of Israel . . . reckoned the intercalations for us. That is the way we do it in all Israel until this day, until the coming of our redeemer, [may he come] speedily in our days."[27]

4. The addition of the *yom tov sheni*, while no longer technically necessary, is a rabbinic *gezerah* (decree) that remains in force. "Although it is true that our calculations are now accurate and we do not need to add the second day, it is a *takanat ḥakhamim* that we guard carefully the custom of our forefathers as 'times are a *gezerah*' as it says in [BT] Betzah 4b."[28]

5. The Jewish calculation system continued to be accurate and valid, whereas the civil calendar needed reconfiguration. "The wise men among the gentiles marveled at our reckoning of the *moladot* [mean lunar conjunction], that it was never repudiated in any of its respects, and that it is accurate and does not deviate for any time or period. . . . Nothing has changed from their days until our own, and each remains valid from generation to generation."[29]

6. The perfection of the calendar testified to the truth of the entire tradition. "And this is a clear proof, to which there can be no retort that the Torah is divine, for we have succeeded with this marvelous calculation to fix our holidays at the seasons appropriate to them for all the time the world will exist. . . . You can draw a parallel from this to all the other precepts in the Torah, until even the most defiant cannot avoid admitting that it is impossible that the matter came from the human mind or human science, even the wisest in the world, for it is the 'finger of God.' Concerning that which our sages have said, 'It is a mitzvah to calculate the seasons and constellations etc.' [Its purpose is] to raise the honor of the Torah in the eyes of the nations and to prevail over their opinions that they should admit that the Torah is divine, and all its words are wise and profound. For the great astronomer Batholomeus [Ptolemy] admitted that this is a divine matter, and this proves that there was prophecy in Israel. Thus it compels human opinion to admit that all its laws are divine."[30]

7. The science of Jewish calendar calculation was becoming a lost art. "Despite all this, there are hardly any seekers of this wisdom among our nation."[31]

Kornick concluded with a plea that the study of the calendar's structure be revived among the Jews. In addition to the reasons cited, he proffered two more arguments. In the first place, the printed calendars were riddled with errors: "The majority depend on the calendar that is printed each year, and its preparation is a matter both great and exacting; sometimes the calculation of the *tekufa* and the *molad* is wrong, and there is no one to take care to correct it. Such is the case with the calendar for [the year] 5578 to come [which corresponds to 1818], that was published in Fürth. It is mistaken in its *tekufot* and *moladot* and its *seder ha-dorot* [chronograph] and this shames us in the eyes of the gentiles. Sometimes errors have fallen in the *kevi'ot* of the year, and even if the error was caught after some time, nevertheless, the damage is great to those who travel to distant places, and those who cross the seas, who rely on the calendar in their hands like an inscribed code of law; it would be better to print the calendars with the assent of the sages of our generation, as it was in the days of old."[32]

A second, more compelling reason Kornick urged a return to study of calendar reckoning was that an individual who calculated his own calendar fulfilled the mitzvah of sanctifying the New Moon. "It is worthwhile to publicize the matters that are already known: that in order to fulfill the mitzvah according to Maimonides at the beginning of 'Hilkhot Kiddush ha-ḥodesh' . . . and so it says in the book *Yesh Nohalin:* 'Do not rely on the prepared calendar, only calculate for yourself, for a mitzvah in its own time is beloved.'"[33]

Kornick took special pains to rebut Bendavid's attempt to revive the 247-year cycle (RMZ in Hebrew letter equivalent, thirteen cycles of the 19-year metonic cycle, *maḥzor katan*). In doing so, he defended the honor of R. Mordechai Yaffe, the author of the Levush, who had already rejected it:

> Regarding what he said about the calendar of 247 cycles (*luaḥ rm"z*), it is true up to a certain point, and can be found in the *evronot* [calendar calculation manuals] and in the *Levush ha-ḥur* of the great genius Mordechai Yaffe, who was an illustrious Torah scholar, had many disciples, and was expert in many sciences. Many of those who see his works will be astonished [see *Sifte yeshenim*].[34] This Bendavid has gone on to mock him undeservedly, calling his book "*Levush ha-shaḥor*," and so he has written to me.[35]

Know, my friend, that the Lord cares more about the honor of the righteous than his own honor. . . . He [Bendavid] undoubtedly heard it incorrectly, and so he erred in a matter that even children know, that the word *ḥur* comes from *ḥiver*, which is *weiss* in German. What he wrote about the 247 cycle is also incorrect; indeed it says there that this sign does *not* return perpetually. Yet he [Bendavid] wrote, after "exposing" it, that it could become a perpetual calendar thus misleading the public. It is worthwhile to publicize his arguments and their refutations even in German to expose him to the scientists among the nations, whose entire desire is to reveal hidden wisdom, and they love truth. They will look into his lines and will investigate with their minds whether his words have any benefit. It is a mystery why a great philosopher who is expert in other sciences should try his hand in matters in which he does not have adequate knowledge. My heart is content to know that any person to whom God has given a portion of this science will see that the truth is with me.[36]

Kornick accused Bendavid of reviving ancient arguments against the rabbinic tradition: "For he has gathered the words of the ancients, believers, and non-believers, along with the arguments of the Sadducees and Boethusians, Karaites and those who deny and oppress Israel, as though he wanted to wage war against the upholders of Torah. He believes in his heart that none among us can refute his words. . . . I have done this in order to remove an obstacle from the public, so that they will not God forbid violate the festivals, and because of the fools who believe anything."[37]

This exchange between Bendavid and Kornick is one of the sharpest concerning the value of the traditional Jewish calendar calculation and chronology to take place in the nineteenth century. That the calendrical system remained remarkably impervious to foundational challenges suggests some limits of the modernizing enterprise. No modernizing Jewish ideology advocated the total abandonment of the Jewish calendar in favor of the western civil calendar. None advocated any fundamental changes that were not essentially returns to ancient practices. Despite the tendentiousness of some of Kornick's arguments, he seems to have intuited the centrality of the calendar to Jewish identity, even to the most rational of modernizers.

To return to our initial question perhaps we must not ask *when* the modern period of the Jewish calendar began, but *whether* it ever did.

Notes

1. Jacob Katz, "Maḥloket ha-semikha ben R. Ya'akov Berav ve-ha-Ralbakh," *Halakha ve-kabbalah* (Jerusalem: Magnes, 1986), esp. 232. English translation, "The Dispute between Jacob Berab and Levi ibn Habib over Renewing Ordination," in *Binah: Studies in Jewish History,* ed. Joseph Dan, 3 vols. (New York: Praeger, 1989), 1:119–41, and in Jacob Katz, *Divine Law in Human Hands: Case Studies in Halakhic Flexibility* (Jerusalem: Magnes Press, 1998), 146–70.

2. Levi ibn Haviv, *Sefer she'elot u-teshuvot* (Venice: [Giovanni di Gara], 1555), 277a.

3. Azariah de' Rossi, *The Light of the Eyes.* Trans. Joanna Weinberg (New Haven: Yale University Press, 2001).

4. Ibid., 482–83.

5. See the useful annotations in the selections in Reuven Bonfil, ed., *Kitvei Azariah min ha-adumim* (Jerusalem: Mossad Bialik, 1991), 377–420.

6. See Weinberg's discussion of the reception history of *Me'or Eynaim* in de' Rossi, *Light of the Eyes,* xix–xxii. On the controversy over *Me'or Eynaim,* see Meir Benayahu, "Ha-pulmus al *Sefer me'or enaim* le-rabi Azariah min ha-adumim," *Asufot* 5 (1991): 213–65, chronology, 217–18.

7. Meyer has already noted the ways in which Modena's critique anticipated and differed from later Reform: see Michael A. Meyer, *Response to Modernity: A History of the Reform Movement in Judaism* (Oxford: Oxford University Press, 1988), 397n27. For Modena's critique, see Talya Fishman, *Shaking the Pillars of Exile: "Voice of a Fool," an Early Modern Jewish Critique of Rabbinic Culture* (Stanford: Stanford University Press, 1997), 137. For further discussion of *yom tov sheni,* see Leo Depuydt, "Ancient and Medieval Sources and Mechanism of the Calendrical Practice of 'Yom Tov Sheni Shel Galuyyot,'" in *Life and Culture in the Ancient Near East,* ed. R. Averbeck, M. Chavalas, and D. Weisberg, 435–70 (Bethesda, Md.: CDL Press, 2003); Hirsch Jakob Zimmels, "The Controversy about the Second Day of the Festival," in *The Abraham Weiss Jubilee Volume,* 139–68 (N.p.: N.p., 1964); Meir Benayahu, *Yom Tov sheni shel Galuyot* (Jerusalem: Yad Harav Nissim, 1987); and Jacob Katz, "The Orthodox Defense of the Second Day of the Festivals," in Katz, *Divine Law in Human Hands,* 255–320.

8. On the Blessing of the New Moon, see Fishman, *Shaking the Pillars,* 135, regarding the *deḥiyyot,* 140.

9. See the discussion of fasting to commemorate the events during the Crusades in Zvi Benjamin Auerbach of Halberstadt, *Naḥal Eshkol* (Halberstadt: H. Meyer, 1865–67), 2:16: "Those [fasts] had been instituted eight hundred years ago at a time of persecution and there was no relief until the new era; it was voluntary and they did not accept it anew." The fast did not wither for lack of piety but because of the principle that at a time when religious coercion had ceased, maintaining the fast was voluntary. Auerbach deemed such a fast inconsonant with the age of emancipation.

10. David Nieto's defense of the Jewish calendar emerged out of a different context than the one treated here. I hope to discuss it more fully elsewhere.

11. Lazarus Bendavid, *Zur Berechnung und Geschichte des jüdischen Kalendar: aus den Quellen geschöpft* (Berlin: Nicholaischen Buchhandlung, 1817).

12. Ibid., 6.

13. Ibid., 15. Bendavid also belittled the Christian chronology, accusing Christians of manipulating the years so that Christ should appear near the four thousandth year from Creation, a method he characterized as "der Beweis nach dem Bedarf."

14. Ibid., 17.

15. Ibid., 18.

16. Ibid., 23.

17. Ibid., 20.

18. Ibid., 34.

19. Meyer Moses Kornick, in *Davar be-itto* (Breslau: Leyb Sulzbach, 1817), describes another exchange with a Berlin Jew who showed him tables based on the 247-year cycle (7).

20. Alternative spellings include Kornik or Kurnik. See Isidore Singer and M. Seligsohn, "Kornik (Kurnik), Meir ben Moses," *The Jewish Encyclopaedia* (New York: Funk and Wagnalls, 1901–6), 562. Kornick was born in Glogau, where he later served as rabbi; he died in 1826.

21. Kornick's *System der Zeitrechnung in Chronologischen Tabellen* (Berlin, 1825), a concordance of Julian, Gregorian, Jewish, and Islamic calendars, formed the basis of Jahn's *Tafeln* (Leipzig, 1856). It was highly praised by Isidore Loeb in his *Tables du Calendrier Juif* (Paris: Durlacher, 1886). Max Simon published a brief overview of the Jewish computus: "Neue einfache Methode zur Vergleichung jüdischer und Christlicher Daten," *Magazin für die Wissenschaft des Judenthums* 18 (1891): 288–95. He explained that although Kornick's esteemed tables were sold out at booksellers they still could be found with the scholars who rely upon the tables for their research. Simon cautioned that the trust in this exemplary work must be tempered by the knowledge that he found sixty errors in print in the work, for which he proceeded to append a correction table, "Zu Meier Kornicks System der Zeitrechnung in chronologischen Tabellen" (296).

22. Kornick, *Davar be-itto*, 3.

23. Ibid., title page.

24. Ibid., 3.

25. Ibid. Among his sources for this position Kornick cited Moses Maimonides, *The Guide of the Perplexed* (trans. Shlomo Pines [Chicago: University of Chicago Press, 1963], 175); Isaac Israeli, *Yesod Olam*; Abraham Bibago, *Derekh Emunah* (Constantinople, 1522), ch. 3; Azariah de' Rossi, *Me'or Eynaim*, chaps. 2, 40; *Shiltei ha-gibborim*, 8th path; David Gans, *Neḥmad ve-na'im* (Jessnitz: Israel bar Avraham, 1743), intro.; and *Ya'arot Dvash*, section 2. Some of the sources Kornick cited do not really

maintain this or, in the case of de' Rossi, maintain the opposite of what Kornick attributes to them. Needless to say, Kornick does not cite Abraham ibn Ezra and other medieval Jews whose opinions on this matter openly conflicted with his.

26. Gans, *Nehmad ve-na'im*, 8a–8b.

27. Kornick, *Davar be-itto*, 3–4.

28. Ibid., 3.

29. Ibid., 11.

30. Ibid., 14.

31. Ibid.

32. Ibid.

33. Ibid.

34. Shabtai Meshorer/Bass, *Sefer sifte yeshenim* (Amsterdam: Tartas, 1680), a seventeenth-century bibliographical work.

35. The substitution of the word *shahor*, black, for *chur*, pale, is a play on the Hebrew root and a dysphemism intended as an insult to Yaffe.

36. Kornick, *Davar be-itto*, 27.

37. Kornick then implied that Bendavid risked displeasing the conservative Prussian monarchs by attacking traditional Judaism: "I am certain that he would admit it too, as happens to those who accuse us when we are innocent, against the wishes of the state, and the mighty King, may he be exalted, renowned in all four corners of the world; may his government be raised for all generations, who is benificent to all his subjects who take shelter in his lands. He is like an eagle hovering over his young, . . . over his young long may he and his offspring rule, and may all his endeavors succeed, MIGHTY KING FRIEDRICH WILHELM III." Ibid., 26–27.

5

The Controversy over the Salvation of the Jews, Turks, and Heathens in the Second Half of the Eighteenth Century

A Theological Path to Tolerance?

ERNST-PETER WIECKENBERG
TRANSLATED BY MARK LOTITO

Can the Jews, Turks, or heathens be saved? This was indeed an old question, but it was freshly posed in the eighteenth century. That the best minds of the time occupied themselves with it, and not uncommonly quarreled bitterly over the respective answers, cannot be dismissed as a historical curiosity. The question must have had in itself a meaning, one that we no longer recognize today. The following article deals with a historical reconstruction of this issue.

It began in a seemingly harmless way, namely, with the question of whether Jews, Turks, or heathens could be virtuous. This also was not new, but it was posed with a new urgency. In eighteenth-century Europe, the number of writings that took up this question and attempted to answer with images of good, noble, virtuous Jews, Turks, or heathens increased in a way that was previously almost unimaginable.

Books on the noble, virtuous savage fill entire libraries. The image of the *bon sauvage* was old; however, in the eighteenth century, for the first time, it moved to the center of the anthropological discourses of philosophers and theologians, travel writers, and novelists.[1] It was frequently invoked in the sense of a societal critique, but there were other reasons as well. The noble savage was religious; indeed, he was living proof that no peoples of the earth manage without religion.

From this observation, arguments against atheism would be allowed to triumph.[2] At the same time, this lay close to another idea, namely, that all men possess a common religious and moral core.[3] This could be put to use in the dispute, dreaded by Orthodox Lutherans, over "important" and "less important" religious truths.

Noble Turks (or Orientals) had emerged already in the German literature of the Middle Ages, in Wolfram von Eschenbach, for example, but the centuries of continual Ottoman threat to the Christian West had contributed to an image of the "terrible Turk." In the eighteenth century, however, the number of works in which virtuous Muslims appeared rapidly increased. Antoine Galland's translation *Les mille et une nuits* (1704–17), which circulated across Europe, probably accomplished more for the spread of a new image of virtuous Orientals than any other philosophical, historical, or literary work.

Whoever employed the image of the noble savage or Turk may have done so with the intention of promoting tolerance, but wherever virtuous Jews were presented, the appeal for tolerance was bound inextricably to it. Michael A. Meyer has impressively presented the history of this sometimes clear, sometimes veiled request for tolerance, dedicating particular attention to three works: the *Lettres Juives* of Marquis d'Argens (1735–38, German 1763–66), Christian Fürchtegott Gellert's novel *Leben der Schwedischen Gräfin von G . . .* (1747–48), and Gotthold Ephraim Lessing's comedy *Die Juden* (written 1749, published 1754).[4] In Lessing's play, the baron, who was saved by a Jew from highwaymen and who recognized in his rescuer a magnanimous man, cries out, "O how worthy of esteem the Jews would be if they were all like you!" To which the Jew replied, "And how worthy of love the Christians if they possessed all your qualities!"[5] That was the courageous design for a future in which a Jew could dare to speak with a Christian so openly and self-confidently.

Reality, however, looked quite different, and the Göttingen theology professor Johann David Michaelis immediately registered his protest. In a review published in *Göttingische Anzeigen von Gelehrten Sachen* (1754), he stated that it would be very unlikely for one to find so noble a character among the Jews. This was aimed at Lessing's comedy, but Michaelis had in mind both of the German books, for he explicitly wrote, "One cannot, therefore, read this comedy without being obligated to set next to it the poetic account, with the same ultimate goal, of the honest Jew in Herr Gellert's *Schwedischer Gräfin*."[6] Similar criticisms were repeatedly expressed by the Hamburg pastor Johann Melchior Goeze, a correspondent of Michaelis and like him an advocate of "rational orthodoxy." In 1782, in his last statement on Lessing's play, he wrote, "The apology Lessing wrote for the Jews in his comedy, which bears that title, probably has as its characters the Jews who dwell beyond the River Sambatyon."[7] With this, Goeze played on the legend of the Ten Lost Tribes of Israel, who lived on both sides of the Sambatyon (the Sabbath River), and thus refers to the noble Jew as if he were from a fairy-tale land.[8] Michaelis, like Goeze, misunderstood; Lessing's play was not based in reality, but rather it was the design for a world in which there was no more prejudice.[9]

In such judgments, a Christian anti-Judaism is undoubtedly expressed, which is not entirely understandable without taking into account its theological dimension. Lutheran Orthodoxy of that time held as irrefutable that the religious truths of its confessions were logical conclusions drawn from biblical revelation. Intellectually, it followed that the only ones who could attain salvation were those who acknowledged their faith in these teachings.[10] Now, however, orthodoxy had to deal with Enlightenment theologians who attached increasingly less meaning to theological truths and preached a doctrinally weaker "Christianity of virtue." The leading mind of this theology of virtue, Johann Joachim Spalding, defined morally good conduct as the actual essence of Christianity: "The only universal indication of whether we are truly good Christians and pleasing to God is the consciousness of a proper governing attitude, which actively proves itself constant and steadfast through good conduct toward God and man."[11] Whoever spread the news that there might be virtuous Jews knocked, so to speak, at the gate of the Lutheran doctrinal fortress and demanded that it open at least a crack for those who belong to other religions.

In 1721 Christian Wolff had delivered a formal address at the University of Halle, "De Sinorum philosophia practica," in which he explained that the ancient Chinese had been capable of developing a model understanding of virtue.[12] With this he had overstepped the bounds of what was permissible for his theological colleagues, and they succeeded in influencing the Prussian court against him: Wolff was banished from the land under threat of capital punishment. The view that Jews could be virtuous published by Gellert and Lessing a quarter century later no longer aroused the same indignation, but it was still a challenge to Lutheran Orthodoxy.

If Michaelis and Goeze presented their objections to the image of the virtuous Jew in a comparatively moderate way, then presumably the reason for doing so was that they thereby sought to open a discussion with Enlightenment theologians, or neologists, as they were soon called. The Orthodox proceeded against them with all their strength, for according to their view, whoever held to the idea that an individual could live in a God-pleasing way if he only conducted himself virtuously rejected the central doctrine of Lutheran theology, that justification is only possible through faith. Furthermore, if one could by some means convict advocates of this view of heresy, then at the same time the assertion that there might be virtuous Jews would be deprived of its disruptive force. Men like Goeze sought to label the theology of virtue as heresy by accusing its adherents of Pelagianism or Socinianism. This was not entirely unjustified, since Pelagius (350/4–420) and also Fausto Sozzini (1539–1604) had held the view that "the justification of man takes place in the obedient imitation of Christ."[13]

The chances for orthodoxy to assert itself deteriorated as Enlightenment theologians seized on the teaching of the *Apokatastasis panton*—translated into German most often at that time as *Wiederbringung Aller* and today frequently also as *Allversöhnung*.[14] The teaching of apokatastasis—that the will of God for all to be saved (*Heilswille Gottes*) would finally reach even to the last of sinners—was supported by many of the Church fathers, and particularly by Origen.[15] The Church had pronounced it a heresy at the Synod of Constantinople (543) and at the Fifth Ecumenical Council (553). The most important argument brought against this teaching was that it contradicted the doctrine of eternal punishment in hell.[16]

The attempts to completely suppress the teaching of apokatastasis had never been successful, but its history in the early modern period is still to be written. In the eighteenth century, it seemed to follow two directions. The adherents of the first, inspired by messianic and chiliastic ideas, supported a teaching of apokatastasis in the emphatic sense of the word. The adherents of the second assumed a temporal boundary for punishment in hell and awaited the eternal bliss of all, after improvement through chastisement.[17] However, there were also many aspects of overlap, and the struggle against the doctrine of eternal punishment in hell was almost always, regardless of particular interpretations, a confession of apokatastasis.[18]

It is difficult to say who merits the title of the first to have derived a claim for religious tolerance from apokatastasis.[19] Jean Jacques Rousseau, for example, in his novel *Emile* (in the confession of the Savoyard vicar) had already suggested this connection. A year later in his letter to Christophe de Beaumont (1763), Rousseau explicitly stated, "I believe that a man upright in any religion, who adds to this a sincere heart, can be saved." Upon this he then based a formulation of tolerance.[20] However, it is possible that scarcely any work accomplished more for this sort of claim to religious tolerance than the novel *Bélisaire* (1767), by the French writer Jean François Marmontel.[21] The fifteenth chapter of the novel in particular caused a tremendous sensation. There, the blind eponymous hero of the novel, a former general, unfolds his teaching on virtue in a discussion with Emperor Justinian

Ernst-Peter Wieckenberg

and the young Tiberius. "The good man is bound with God," says Bélisaire, "he is certain that God loves him."[22] From this, it followed for
Bélisaire that the heathen will also be taken up to heaven, and finally
a vision of tolerance follows that only gives the government the right
to make decisions about those things that are harmful or useful to
the common good, and not about that which the individual believer is
obliged to hold as true or false.[23] "Each man is answerable for his soul.
It also lies with him, and entirely with him alone, to make a choice,
which involves his eternal damnation or salvation."[24]

Already in February 1767, a few days after its publication, the
novel was banned by the censors, but its spread could no longer be
stopped. That Voltaire defended Marmontel with satires may have contributed to the success of the work in France and across Europe. In the
same year as the first edition, a German translation was published in
Leipzig, additional printings followed, and pirated copies provided for
an even wider circulation of the book.

Marmontel's book seemed to embody the theology of virtue and
the sentimentalism closely bound to it; however, his theological teaching could not stand up to philosophical or theological critique. In Germany, Johann August Eberhard took up the task of providing a philosophical and theological basis for apokatastasis in his two-volume
*Neue Apologie des Sokrates, oder Untersuchung der Lehre von der Seligkeit
der Heiden* (1772–78), and there he explicitly refers to Marmontel as
the one who stimulated him to pursue his own study.

In order to prove that the teaching of the damnation of the heathen is absurd, Eberhard pursues two questions in the first part of his
book: "Is this exclusion of such a large number of people proper to
the wisdom and goodness of God, and are the grounds on which one
builds this doctrine as firm as they are made out to be?"[25]

In answering the first question, Eberhard proceeds from two
petitiones principii. The first is that God is essentially perfect. From
this principle concerning the nature of God, it becomes for Eberhard
absolutely without doubt that sins cannot be ascribed to one who did
not himself commit the sins, and hence the doctrine of original sin is
invalid. The second principle is that God cannot impose any punishment on the sinner that could not be alleviated or cancelled through
self-improvement. Punishments, in so far as they are perfect, must
"apply even to the best of sufferers, and consequently as soon as the
improvement takes place they must be eased."[26] Eberhard answers the
second question by examining the doctrines that support the teaching
of the eternal damnation of the heathen, and he attributes them to
flaws in biblical exegesis.

In the second part of the book, Eberhard argues on behalf of non-Christians' moral conduct. On the one hand, he shows through anthropological and philosophical reasons that heathens are capable of morally good conduct, and on the other he provides evidence from ethnological and historical sources that testify to the genuine virtuousness of their conduct. The result of his explanation is that "God cannot reject the virtuous souls of the heathen, even less so can he condemn them eternally."[27] The consequence of this is an appeal for tolerance.

The book was theologically courageous, for the author knew full well that it would bring him trouble. Not even Frederick II could assert himself against Eberhard's opponents so that he might receive the position intended for him as preacher in Charlottenburg.[28] Eberhard's friends were even more surprised that Gotthold Ephraim Lessing subjected the *Apologie des Socrates* to a critique.[29] Lessing had resolved soon after his appointment as librarian in Wolfenbüttel to publish under the title *Zur Geschichte und Litteratur: Aus den Schätzen der Herzoglichen Bibliothek zu Wolfenbüttel* treatises that dealt with unknown books and manuscripts from the library. In connection with this, he came across the unpublished introduction of his predecessor Leibniz to Ernst Soner's *Demonstratio theologica et philosophica, quod aeterna impiorum supplicia non arguant Dei justitiam sed injustitiam* (Theological and philosophical demonstration that the eternal punishment of unbelievers argues not for the justice but rather the injustice of God). The appearance of Eberhard's *Neue Apologie des Socrates* offered Lessing the possibility of presenting Soner's text and at the same time of defending Leibniz against Eberhard's reproach that he was conforming to orthodoxy by philosophically justifying his espousal of the doctrine of eternal punishment in hell. His treatise, "Leibnitz von den ewigen Strafen," appeared in January 1773 in the *Ersten Beitrag* of the new series.[30]

Karl Aner received this defense with "a certain surprise," because he would have gladly seen Lessing on the side of Eberhard, and he explained this in a psychological way: "Lessing could not be orthodox Lutheran; instead he became orthodox Leibnizian. And as his father did not tolerate the slightest casting of a shadow over Luther and his work, so it grieved Lessing the son that Eberhard interpreted as diplomacy Leibniz's vote [for the eternity of the punishments of hell]."[31] Lessing's contemporaries hardly reacted with more understanding. Christian Gottlob Heyne reproached the treatise as "a little too dialectically clever," and Friedrich Nicolai made no secret of his annoyance.[32] Indeed, Lessing's brother Karl had at hand his own interpretation of the publication: "Your view of eternal punishment in hell is philosophy; it is heresy to both the orthodox and the heterodox."

Ernst-Peter Wieckenberg

And yet he added, "However who is to thank you for this Christian or ingenious volte? Reason or Christianity?"[33] This seems to indicate a certain disconcertedness even on his part. Lessing answered, not without a bit of sharpness, "If Herr Eberhard does not understand me better than you appear to understand me, then he has understood me miserably. So have I really, do you think, wanted to court the Orthodox with my thoughts about eternal punishment? You think I have not considered that they neither are, nor could they be, pleased with this? What concern are the Orthodox to me? I despise them just as much as you; only I despise our modern clergy still more, they are much too little theologians, and not nearly enough philosophers."[34] With this, he hinted at an idea, which he would set forth more clearly in later years, for example in a letter to his brother dated February 2, 1774: "With Orthodoxy, it was, thank God, somewhat possible to cope; there was a dividing wall set up between it and philosophy, behind which each could go along its way, without the other to hinder. But what is one supposed to do now? This dividing wall has been torn down, and under the pretext of making us rational Christians, we are turned into the most irrational philosophers."[35]

None of the interpretations presented to this point has been able to remove the enigma that in his treatise Lessing—by arguing about "truths," which are divorced from reason—rejected the views developed in this letter. Or did he only pretend to do this? Did he want the letter of February 1774 to his brother to be understood as a set of reading instructions for the treatise? The hypothesis then presents itself that Lessing, following Pierre Bayle's theoretical reflections, was trying in practice to show that "rational" discussions about truths of faith, as Eberhard conducted them and as he himself appeared to take them up, must of necessity lead to an insoluble dilemma.[36] If reason were to presume to judge a teaching as true or as false, to which faith alone could grant or deny the designation as "truth," then contradictory views might seem to be conclusively established. Certainly, there is no direct indication that Lessing wanted his writing to be understood in this way, unless his remarks are read in the sense that it is for him not a matter of "defending the truth" of eternal punishments but rather more a matter of Leibniz's "attitudes and arguments in the case of his defense."[37]

If Lessing's writing is not read in this way, then it remains in itself contradictory. But it is possible that it might simply be so, since during his entire life Lessing was not able to resolve the contradictions of his own thoughts about orthodoxy and neology, reason and revelation.[38] The result was that no religious party was able to constructively use his refutation of Eberhard. Eberhard indeed believed, or at least asserted, that the differences between his position and Lessing's were basically minor; however, he did not know how to capitalize on this.[39] On the other hand, the orthodox obviously distrusted the defense— through Lessing of all people—of one of their most important tenets of faith. Goeze, for example, did not take note of it at all. He furthermore advocated with his old arguments the assertion that the teaching of apokatastasis is to be condemned.

There is no doubt that was misrepresented in Otto Weber's statement that "The teaching of a universal reconciliation with God notoriously paralyzes the Church's creative power and zeal for missions."[40] In contrast to the salvation promised through the teaching of universal reconciliation, he set conversion as the only way for Jews, Turks, and heathens to attain eternal bliss. For example, in 1782 he wrote a work titled *Beweis, daß . . . allein die Missionen, die Mittel gewesen sind, und noch sind, die Erkäntnis der christlichen Lehre auf dem Erdboden auszubreiten*. In this treatise, Goeze defended missions while refuting the teaching of the eternal salvation of the heathen. However, one must counter the widespread notion that he pleaded for an aggressive intolerance toward the Jews and that he even held the "eradication of unbelievers" as "the highest duty of the Lutheran state."[41] On the contrary, Goeze condemned in the harshest possible terms the "malicious hatred of religion," and he wrote, "I wish that Christian authorities would inflict particularly harsh and unremitting punishment upon such unchristian behavior. For the irrational hatred of religion, as well as the spirit of persecution that arises from it, are true vomit from hell."[42] Even if Goeze and many other Orthodox Lutherans wanted to deny Jews open practice of their religion, and they also made no secret of their aversion toward them, they were still against expulsion and forced conversion. Therefore, their appeal for missionizing no longer possessed the same fervor with which the pastors of Hamburg, as late as 1699, had called upon the Senate to hasten the conversion of the Jews, arguing that at the last judgment they would be able to complain that nothing had been done for the well-being of their souls.[43]

Lessing and the Orthodox Lutherans, with Goeze as their chief representative, were not able to stop the advance of apokatastasis. Friedrich Nicolai's novel *Sebaldus Nothanker* (1773), with its polemic against the doctrine of eternal punishment in hell, reached thousands of readers. In the second edition of his book, *Wahrheit der Christlichen Religion*, the Göttingen theologian Gottfried Leß—who had previously sided with Goeze in an expert report during the dispute in Hamburg over the morality of the theater—confessed his adherence to the teaching of apokatastasis and in almost poetic tones made known his "happy and delightful hopes for the state of the eternal souls of our fellow redeemed heathen, Jews and Muslims, to the honor of our universally charitable religion."[44] This may have caused a breakthrough for this way of thinking, and at the very least, it was an event with great symbolic effect. Like his predecessors, through the extension of his religious system to apokatastasis, Leß concluded that Christianity was obligated to tolerance.[45] If Goeze was incensed at this change in Leß's thinking, then it aggravated him even more that in 1784 his Hamburg colleague Johann Heinrich Moldenhawer openly supported apokatastasis.[46] In several publications, Goeze attempted to silence this opponent.[47] He died in 1786 and thus was spared from seeing Johann Otto Thieß—who had been rejected by him as a candidate for the Hamburg church—present a book with the title *Über die biblische und kirchliche Lehrmeinung von Ewigkeit der Höllenstrafen* (1791), in which he left the decision of what view to support to the personal choice of the individual theologian.[48]

It is striking that Eberhard and other Enlightenment supporters of apokatastasis made at most scant reference to their predecessors among the Pietists. This might arise from the tendency of Enlightenment thinkers, as Charles Kors and Paul J. Korshin have shown, to conceal the "pre-Enlightenment" sources of their ideas.[49] A noteworthy example of this is Wilhelm Abraham Teller's critical treatment of the doctrine of original sin, which suppressed the long history of its disintegration. Certainly, the neologist supporters of apokatastasis had motives understandably stemming from religious politics: they had to remove the basis for any possible accusation of religious fanaticism, and they skillfully did this by presenting their teaching as the product of their own rational thinking. It also cannot be ignored that by speaking of the eternal salvation of the heathen they no longer thought so much about preserving the teaching of apokatastasis, with its promise grounded in salvation history, as they did about destroying the old doctrine of the eternity of punishment in hell.[50] In any case, however, they might have been familiar with many Pietist affirmations of apokatastasis.

Nearly all Pietists shared the conviction that, in accordance with the biblical promise, the Jews would all be converted at the coming of the messianic kingdom.[51] From this conviction, a great esteem for the Jews arose among them, which diverged decidedly from the attitude of Lutheran Orthodoxy, and even while it was firmly grounded in salvation history, it also differed from the attitude of neology. In spite of such common convictions among the Pietists, they held a variety of religious-political stances toward the Jews. Two general tendencies prevailed: one whose representatives saw their Christian duty in making missionary efforts to prepare for the coming of the kingdom of

God and a second, radically Pietist view, whose adherents renounced every attempt at conversion in the chiliastic expectation of a universal conversion of the Jews at the beginning of the end of times.[52] However, the radical Pietist direction, which could open the "historical possibility for a Jewish acculturation and emancipation without forced assimilation" was also, as Hans-Jürgen Schrader has stated, not politically effective, because they based their high esteem and concern for the Jews primarily on biblical grounds and on salvation history.[53]

"Here the Enlightenment was eventually able to succeed," writes Schrader, and in this respect he refers above all to Christian Wilhelm Dohm's efforts at political reform.[54] There were also theological attempts to go beyond the apolitical nature of Pietist ideas of tolerance and, in the argument over apokatastasis, to establish a politically effective demand for tolerance. The theologian Johann Christoph Döderlein made an attempt at this through his now little-noticed tract *Giebt uns die Bibel Hofnung zu einer künftigen allgemeinen Judenbekehrung?* (1781). Döderlein, at that time professor of theology at Jena, was a supporter of a moderate Enlightenment position, which was critically opposed to Lutheran Orthodoxy as well as to every hint of Pietist fanaticism.[55]

In his tract, Döderlein asked the question "whether and how far prophecies entitle us to await an impending universal conversion of the Jews."[56] With this he reacted against the chiliastic ideas of the radical Pietists, erasing their expectations based on the culmination of salvation history. By posing concrete questions, he transferred conversion from that future moment down to the earthly present. Should conversion be considered in such a way that the Jews "would also be permitted to unite in name with the Christians and to integrate [*nationalisieren*] into the Church?" Would the conversion of the Jews come to pass in such a way that they "would represent their own Christian— perhaps even entirely superior—party?"[57] In reality, he saw "no reason why the conviction of an approaching universal conversion of the Jews should be necessary, or even useful and important for the peace and improvement of mankind."[58] That could have been an implicit request to treat the Jews with tolerance, but Döderlein drew from his reflections a different, and surprising, conclusion: "I will prophesy nothing: however, only this much must be granted to me, that the Jews can convert, even though they neither pay homage to the bishop of Rome nor subscribe to our Lutheran Confessions."[59]

It is difficult to determine whether with this Döderlein expressed a widespread view, or whether he alone held to it. What is quite certain, though, is that his "prophecy" did not remain unnoticed. Goeze reacted angrily to it; others accepted it with approval.[60] Whatever

Ernst-Peter Wieckenberg

Döderlein's ideas about the uniting of Christians and Jews without conversion might have been, his tract reads like an invitation to the *Sendschreiben*, which in 1799 David Friedländer addressed to Provost Wilhelm Abraham Teller in Berlin.[61] Whether Friedländer was aware of Döderlein's tract is difficult to establish. It cannot be ruled out, however, since he was associated with Nicolai and many Berlin collaborators on the *Allgemeine deutsche Bibliothek*, and thus with a circle that was better informed than almost any other about new publications in Germany.[62] The depth of Friedländer's familiarity with Enlightenment theology is demonstrated still more in his tract published by Traugott Krug, *An die Verehrer, Freunde und Schüler Jerusalem's, Spalding's, Teller's, Herder's and Löffler's* (1823).[63]

Friedländer's open letter "Sendschreiben an seine Hochwürden, Herrn Oberconsistorialrath und Probst Teller zu Berlin, von einigen Hausvätern jüdischer Religion" amounted to a question of whether a conversion of the Jews to Protestantism was possible. The notion was that nothing more would be demanded from them than an acknowledgment of common fundamental truths, and therefore would be only a change in name and not of belief.[64] These aspects have been treated elsewhere at length.[65] What seems to have been overlooked, however, is that the *Sendschreiben* makes use of important ideas that had been expressed in the debates over apokatastasis. Thus, it is highly likely that Friedländer was influenced by Eberhard's thoughts.

Friedländer sought to construct a bridge between Judaism and Christianity by describing the fundamental truths that applied, as far as he was concerned, to both religions. By doing so, he reacted cleverly to the neologist reduction of the basic tenets of Christianity. For him, these fundamental truths of both religions consisted of a few "statements":

a. There is one God.

b. The soul of man is immaterial.

c. The purpose of man here on earth below is to strive for a higher perfection, and with that for the possession of true happiness.

d. The soul of man is immortal.

The last statement was the most detailed:

e. God has made man for his, that is man's, true happiness. He has given him laws—that is, he has conferred upon man the power to recognize those rules with which the conduct of man must be in accordance, if his welfare is to be promoted in the best possible way. The smallest violation of these rules does not remain unchastised, or without punishment. This punishment is a necessary and natural consequence of the action, thus it is not the *vengeance* of the Creator. It is also not in proportion to the majesty of the Lawgiver, and so it cannot endure forever. It is a chastisement for the improvement of the one who has erred, and must be desired by man himself, for it is necessary and indispensable for his attainment of perfection.[66]

With this, Teller, recipient of the *Sendschreiben*, must have understood that there is no eternal punishment in hell. Consequently, the Jew, like the Christian, may hope for eternal salvation, and in view of this, he might demand tolerance already here on earth. It might have caused embarrassment to the recipient of this open letter that Friedländer did not base his claim on external arguments, for instance by appealing to the principles of natural law, but that he used arguments that the neologists, and in particular followers of apokatastasis, had developed in their struggle with Lutheran Orthodoxy. However, Teller still recognized the weaknesses of Friedländer's argumentation. Even if his statements about the religious tenets of a Christian were to meet with approval, they would not be compelling enough for inclusion in the Christian community and even less so would they make this inclusion the duty of community leaders. All that Friedländer and his friends might expect was tolerance, and Teller was prepared to grant this. That is also why no firm critique of his response was ever put forward.[67]

And yet Teller's response revealed considerable weaknesses on its own part. His formulation, and also that of most neologists, intended only a "horizontal tolerance," which even in view of the connections between one religion and another, had obvious limits.[68] His response to Friedländer hinted that, for him, a policy extending beyond toleration was only possible with a reduction of dogmas on both sides.[69] Such a formulation, however, was scarcely suitable to the establishment of tolerance when viewed against dogmatically "strict" religions, such as Orthodox Judaism or Catholicism. Therefore, it is also not surprising that in his book, which had demanded tolerance in view of the "apokatastasis of all," Leß stated concisely, "the Papacy is the direct opposite of Christianity."[70] He left open the question of whether Catholics could nevertheless be saved.

The crucial weakness of Teller's concept of tolerance and also that of most of the neologists was that they allowed for no foundation of "vertical tolerance," which would have entitled a religious group to demand for itself not only the protection of the state—or as it stood at that time, the authorities—but also to demand of it guarantees for an unforced coexistence of religions. Concerning the question of whether the renunciation of ceremonial law by enlightened Jews might clear their way to civil emancipation, he could only respond with the confused answer: "thus I must indeed leave open what a Christian state could demand from them for the attainment of this right."[71]

In the tumult over Eberhard's book, critics actually missed that he had sketched a formulation, with reference above all to Bayle, that bound together vertical and horizontal tolerance. Judgments about religious truths, he wrote, are private. They are an inalienable right, which gives "man legitimate claim to the protection of the state in the use of his own judgment. This claim is based not on the veracity of his judgments, but rather on their harmlessness with respect to the rights of other men."[72] From such a statement, it was not too far to demand that the state should grant to all religions that fulfilled their political or constitutional obligations the full rights of citizenship.

Eberhard made no attempt to connect this formulation of tolerance with those he himself had based on the teaching of apokatastasis. This endeavor would have demanded of him an acknowledgment that it was not possible to establish a comprehensive formulation of tolerance based solely on theological arguments. Only a secular formulation would be able to unite "vertical" and "horizontal tolerance." Nevertheless, it would be an injustice to him, and to the many others in the second half of the eighteenth century who revived the debate over apokatastasis, to deny that with this, they had set off on a path to tolerance.

NOTES

Barbara Picht and Jürgen Stenzel have read the manuscript of this essay with friendly patience and have made many helpful suggestions. In our conversations, Michael Brenner and Hans G. Kippenberg have given me many references to better understand the ideas presented here. I owe the initial suggestion of pursuing this topic to my dear friend Michael Meyer, and over the years I have appreciated his encouragement to develop my ideas more fully. I thank them all for their kind assistance, as well as Mark Lotito for the translation from German.

1. See Karl-Heinz Kohl, *Entzauberter Blick: Das Bild vom Guten Wilden und die Erfahrung der Zivilisation* (Berlin, 1981).
2. On this see Werner Krauss, *Zur Anthropologie des 18. Jahrhunderts: Die Frühgeschichte der Menschheit im Blickpunkt der Aufklärung*, ed. Hans

Kortum and Christa Gohrisch (Berlin, 1978), 32–47.

3. On this see Rainer Forst, *Toleranz im Konflikt: Geschichte, Gehalt und Gegenwart eines umstrittenen Begriffs* (1682; repr., Frankfurt am Main, 2003). Forst demonstrates this with the example of Montesquieu (357–58).

4. Michael A. Meyer, *The Origins of the Modern Jew: Jewish Identity and European Culture in Germany, 1749–1824* (Detroit, 1967), 11–28. See also the subsequent treatment by Jürgen Stenzel, "Idealisierung und Vorurteil: Zur Figur des 'edlen Juden' in der deutschen Literatur des 18. Jahrhunderts," in *Juden in der deutschen Literatur*, ed. Stéphane Moses and Albrecht Schöne, 114–26 (Frankfurt am Main, 1986).

5. Gotthold Ephraim Lessing, *Werke, 1743–1750*, vol. 1 of *Werke und Briefe*, ed. Jürgen Stenzel (Frankfurt am Main, 1989), 487–88. Translation by Michael A. Meyer.

6. Johann David Michaelis, "Rezension über 'Die Juden,'" in *Lessing-ein unpoetischer Dichter*, vol. 1 of *Wirkung der Literatur*, ed. Horst Steinmetz, 49–50 (Frankfurt am Main, 1969). On Michaelis, see Anna-Ruth Löwenbrück, "Johann David Michaelis und Mendelssohn: Judenfeindschaft im Zeitalter der Aufklärung," in *Moses Mendelssohn und die Kreise seiner Wirksamkeit*, ed. Michael Albrecht, Eva J. Engel, and Norbert Hinske, 315–32, vol. 19 of *Wolfenbütteler Studien zur Aufklärung* (Tübingen, 1994).

7. Johan Melchior Goeze, *Beweis, daß nicht die Verbindung der Juden, Türken und Heiden mit den Christen, nicht die daher entstehende Aufklärung durch Künste und Wissenschaften, nicht die Schiffahrt und Handlung, noch weniger Kriege und Empörungen, sondern die Missionen, die Mittel gewesen sind, und noch sind, die Erkäntnis der christlichen Lehre auf dem Erdboden auszubreiten* (Hamburg, 1782), note 7.

8. Cf. the entries "Sambatjon" and "Stämme, Zehn" in *Jüdisches Lexikon*, vol. 4/2 (Berlin, 1930).

9. On this, see Stenzel, "Idealisierung und Vorurteil," 115–16.

10. Cf. Harald Schultze, "Toleranz und Orthodoxie: Johann Melchior Goeze und seine Auseinandersetzung mit der Theologie der Aufklärung," *Neue Zeitschrift für Systematische Theologie* 4 (1962): 197–219, here 206–7.

11. Johann Joachim Spalding, *Gedanken über den Werth der Gefühle in dem Christenthum* (Leipzig, 1761), 137. For a recent treatment of Spalding's theology, see Albrecht Beutel, "Spalding und Goeze und die 'Bestimmung des Menschen': Frühe Kabalen um ein Erfolgsbuch der Aufklärungstheologie," *Zeitschrift für Theologie und Kirche* 101 (2004): 426–49.

12. Cf. Norbert Hinske, "Wolff," in *Literaturlexikon*, vol. 12, ed. Walther Killy, 404–8 (Gütersloh, 1992), 406.

13. See, with reference to Sozianism, Albrecht Beutel, *Aufklärung in Deutschland*, vol. 4 of *Die Kirche in Deutschland* (Göttingen, 2006), 215.

14. The useful overview of Gotthold Müller, "Bibliographie zur Apokatasta-

sis-Frage," in *Identität und Immanenz* (Darmstadt, 1968), has unfortunately not been brought up to date through later bibliographies. Due to
the lack of a common terminology and the complexity of the literature,
from doctrinal manuals to sectarian confessions, it is possible that I
have overlooked publications that might be relevant to this topic.

15. Jan Milič Lochman, "Apokatastasis," in *Evangelisches Kirchenlexikon*, vol.
    I (Göttingen, 1986), col. 202–3.
16. Josef Loosen, "Apokatastasis," in *Lexikon für Theologie und Kirche*, vol. I
    (Freiburg, 1957), col. 708–12, here col. 709.
17. For a good overview of the history of this idea, see Elfriede Büchsel,
    "Seligkeit der Heiden," in *Historisches Wörterbuch der Philosophie*, vol. 9
    (Basel, 1995), col. 570–74.
18. Ernst Cassirer explained: "The idea of original sin is the common ad-
    versary which united the different strains of Enlightenment philosophy
    through their struggles against it." He saw no connection, however, with
    the revival of the teaching of apokatastasis by Enlightenment thinkers.
    See Ernst Cassirer, *Die Philosophie der Aufklärung*, vol. 15 of *Gesammelte
    Werke: Hamburger Ausgabe*, ed. Claus Rosenkranz (Hamburg, 2003),
    148.
19. I follow the theoretical approach to tolerance in the extensive study of
    Rainer Forst, *Toleranz im Konflikt*.
20. Jean-Jacques Rousseau, *Schriften*, vol. I, ed. Henning Ritter (München,
    1978), 556. On this see also Forst, *Toleranz im Konflikt*, 363ff., esp. 377.
21. See particularly John Renwick, *Marmontel, Voltaire, and the Bélisaire Af-
    fair*, vol. 121 of Studies on Voltaire and the Eighteenth Century (Banbury
    Oxfordshire, 1974).
22. Jean-François de Marmontel, *Bélisaire*, Édition établie, présenté et anno-
    tée par Robert Granderoute (Paris, 1994), 175. On chapter 15, see Ren-
    wick, *Marmontel*, 157ff.
23. Marmontel, *Bélisaire*, 180–81, 187.
24. Ibid., 190.
25. Johann August Eberhard, *Neue Apologie des Sokrates*, vol. I, *Neue und
    verbesserte Auflage* (Berlin, 1776), 48.
26. Ibid., 114.
27. Ibid., 434.
28. Horst Möller, "Toleranz als 'zärtliche Mutter': Kirchen und Konfes-
    sionen im Zeitalter der Aufklärung und der religiösen Indifferenz
    (1740–1797)," in *Tausend Jahre Kirche in Berlin-Brandenburg*, ed. Gerd
    Heinrich, 325–62 (Berlin, 1999), 350.
29. Gotthold Ephraim Lessing, *Leibnitz von den ewigen Strafen*, in *Werke,
    1770–1773*, vol. 7 of *Werke und Briefe*, ed. Klaus Bohnen (Frankfurt am
    Main, 2000).
30. On this, see Klaus Bohnen in ibid., 1070–71.
31. Karl Aner, *Die Theologie der Lessingzeit* (Halle, 1929), 279. A new pre-
    sentation of the controversy is found in Johannes Schneider, *Lessings
    Stellung zur Theologie vor der Herausgabe der Wolfenbütteler Fragmente*

('s-Gravenhage, 1953), 201ff.; Alexander Altmann, *Moses Mendelssohn: A Biographical Study* (London, 1973), 553ff.; Dominique Bourel, "Die Kontroverse zwischen Lessing und Mendelssohn um die Ewigkeit der Höllenstrafen," in *Lessing und der Kreis seiner Freunde*, ed. Günter Schulz, 33–50, vol. 8 of Wolfenbütteler Studien zur Aufklärung (Heidelberg, 1985); Charlotte Coulombeau, *Le Philosophique chez Gotthold Ephraim Lessing: Individu et vérité*, vol. 105 of Wolfenbütteler Forschungen (Wiesbaden, 2005), 468ff.; Beutel, *Aufklärung in Deutschland*, 396–98. Also important are the commentaries by Helmut Göbel and Klaus Bohnen in Lessing, *Werke, 1770–1773*.

32. Cf. Johannes Schneider, *Lessings Stellung zur Theologie*, 211–12; Heyne's comment is on 211.

33. Letter of January 16, 1773, in *Briefe von und an Lessing, 1770–1776*, vol. 11.2 of *Werke und Briefe*, ed. Helmuth Kiesel with assistance of Georg Braungart, Klaus Fischer, and Ute Wahl (Frankfurt am Main, 1988), 502–3.

34. Letter of 8 April 8, 1773, in ibid., 540.

35. Ibid., 615.

36. On Bayle, see Forst, *Toleranz im Konflikt*, 315ff.

37. Lessing, *Werke, 1770–73*, 478. If I am not mistaken, Karl-Josef Kuschel interprets Lessing's position in a similar way, even if with a different emphasis, see his *Vom Streit zum Wettstreit der Religionen: Lessing und die Herausforderung des Islam*, vol. 1 of Weltreligionen und Literatur (Düsseldorf, 1998), 128ff.

38. On this, see Jürgen Stenzel in his interpretation of Lessing's fragment "Das Christentum der Vernunft" (1752–53). See Gotthold Ephraim Lessing, *Werke, 1751–1753*, vol. 2 of *Werke und Briefe*, ed. Jürgen Stenzel, 995–1002 (Frankfurt am Main, 1998). See also Wilhelm Schmidt-Biggemann's comments to § 74 and 75 in "Die Erziehung des Menschengeschlechts" (1780) and "Geschichte der Erbsünde in der Aufklärung: Philosophiegeschichtliche Mutmaßungen," in his *Theodizee und Tatsachen: Das philosophische Profil der Aufklärung* (Frankfurt am Main, 1988), 88–116, here 98.

39. Eberhard, *Neue Apologie des Socrates*, vol. 2 (Berlin, 1778), 480ff.

40. Otto Weber, *Grundlagen der Dogmatik*, vol. 2, 2nd ed. (Neukirchen-Vluyn, 1972), 504.

41. So Waldemar Oehlke, *Lessing und seine Zeit*, vol. 2 (München, 1919), 306.

42. Johan Melchior Goeze, *Beweis, daß nicht die Verbindung der Juden, Türken und Heiden mit den Christen, nicht die daher entstehende Aufklärung durch Künste und Wissenschaften, nicht die Schiffahrt und Handlung, noch weniger Kriege und Empörungen, sondern die Missionen, die Mittel gewesen sind, und noch sind, die Erkäntnis der christlichen Lehre auf dem Erdboden auszubreiten* (Hamburg, 1782), 6.

43. Joachim Whaley, *Religiöse Toleranz und sozialer Wandel in Hamburg 1525–1819*, vol. 18 of Arbeiten zur Kirchengeschichte Hamburgs (Ham-

burg, 1992), 94.

44. Gottfried Leß, *Wahrheit der Christlichen Religion*, 2nd ed. (Göttingen, 1773), preface. Four further editions of the work appeared until 1786 (cf. Johann Georg Meusel, *Lexikon der vom Jahr 1750 bis 1800 verstorbenen teutschen Schriftsteller*, vol. 8. [Leipzig, 1808], 166).

45. Ibid., 204–5.

46. Johan Melchior Goeze, *Widerlegung des Satzes: der Sturz des Ansehens Mosis, ziehet nicht nothwendig den Sturz des Christenthums nach sich* (Hamburg, 1783), 26–27; Johann Heinrich Daniel Moldenhawer, *Von der Seligkeit derer, die von Christo nichts wissen, und ihren Umständen nach nichts wissen können* (Hamburg, 1784).

47. To cite just one example, Johan Melchior Goeze, *Über die Neue Meynung von der Seligkeit der angeblich guten und redlichen Selen unter den Juden, Heiden und Türken, durch Christum, ohne daß sie an Ihn glauben* (Hamburg, 1784).

48. Thieß also specifies the theological works in which apokatastasis appears. The best contemporary overview, though it obviously does not cover the second half of the eighteenth century, is offered by Johann Heinrich Zedler, "Seligkeit der Heyden," in *Grosses vollständiges Universal Lexicon Aller Wissenschaften und Künste*, vol. 36 (N.p., 1743), 1677–82.

49. Anselm Schubert, *Das Ende der Sünde: Anthropologie und Erbsünde zwischen Reformation und Aufklärung*, vol. 84 of Forschungen zur Kirchen-und Dogmengeschichte (Göttingen, 2002), 16ff. (on this tendency in general), 220ff. (on Teller in particular).

50. Johann Georg Hamann interprets their position exactly in this sense, and in addition, he somewhat sarcastically notes that they seem to be much less concerned with the eternal salvation of the heathen than with that of free thinkers. Johann Georg Hamann, *Sämtliche Werk*, ed. Josef Nadler, vol. 3 (Wien, 1951), 119. See Büchsel, "Seligkeit der Heiden," col. 572.

51. Hans-Jürgen Schrader, "Sulamiths verheißene Wiederkehr: Hinweise zu Programm und Praxis der pietistischen Begegnung mit dem Judentum," in *Conditio Judaica: Judentum, Antisemitismus und deutschsprachige Literatur vom 18 Jahrhundert bis zum Ersten Weltkrieg*, ed. Hans Otto Horch and Horst Denkler (Tübingen, 1988), see 71–107, here 84–85.

52. Ibid., 87–88.

53. Ibid., 103.

54. Ibid., 104.

55. See Beutel, *Aufklärung in Deutschland*, 277.

56. Johann Christoph Döderlein, *Giebt uns die Bibel Hofnung zu einer künftigen allgemeinen Judenbekehrung?* (Nürnberg, 1781), 10.

57. Ibid., 11.

58. Ibid., 8.

59. Ibid., 17.

60. Goeze, *Widerlegung des Satzes*, 21–22. See the anonymous review in

Allgemeine deutsche Bibliothek 51 (1782): 78–79.

61. David Friedländer, *Sendschreiben an Seine Hochwürden, Herrn Obercon-sistorialrath und Probst Teller zu Berlin, von einigen Hausvätern jüdischer Religion*, in Friedrich Daniel Ernst Schleiermacher, *Schriften aus seiner Berliner Zeit 1796–1799*. (Kritische Gesamtausgabe, 1 Abt., vol. 2), ed. Günter Meckenstock (Berlin, 1984), 381–413. Hans Joachim Schoeps sees in Isaac de la Peyrères "Systema theologicum" (1655) a very similar proposal to a "Programm einer Wiedervereinigung der Kirchen" (Schoeps, *Philosemitismus im Barock: Religions-und geistesgeschichtliche Untersuchungen* [Tübingen, 1952], 12). However, he himself has not investigated the actual influences, and no one seems to have pursued his comments.

62. Neither the fundamental Nicolai biography of Horst Möller nor the work of Pamela E. Selwyn over Nicolai as publisher mention Friedländer. See Horst Möller, *Aufklärung in Preußen: Der Verleger, Publizist und Geschichtsschreiber Friedrich Nicolai*, vol. 15 of Einzelveröffentlichungen der Historischen Kommission zu Berlin (Berlin, 1974); Pamela E. Selwyn, *Everyday Life in the German Book Trade: Friedrich Nicolai as Bookseller and Publisher in the Age of Enlightenment 1750–1810* (University Park, Pa., 2000). Friedländer, who lived in Berlin from 1771, belonged soon after his arrival to the circle around Moses Mendelssohn (see Altmann, *Moses Mendelssohn*, 350ff.). Mendelssohn was associated with, among others, Nicolai, Eberhard, and the neologist Friedrich Germanus Lüdke, the "chief theological reviewer" (Beutel, *Aufklärung in Deutschland*, 260) of the *Allgemeine deutsche Bibliothek*. In the Handschriftenabteilung of the Staatsbibliothek zu Berlin (Nachlaß Nicolai) are found previously unnoticed letters of Friedländer to Nicolai, which indicate a personal connection between the two, though they begin in 1793.

63. Karl Wilhelm Jerusalem, Johann Joachim Spalding, Wilhelm Abraham Teller, Johann Gottfried Herder, and Josias Friedrich Christian Löffler were theologians. That Friedländer himself played a role in the intellectual life of Enlightenment Berlin is indicated in his contributions, beginning in 1786, to the "Berlinische Monatsschrift."

64. Meyer, *Origins of the Modern Jew*, 73.

65. Aside from Meyer's assertion is here to be noted Ellen Littmann, "David Friedländers Sendschreiben an Probst Teller und sein Echo," in *Zeitschrift für Geschichte der Juden in Deutschland*, vol. 6 (N.p., 1935), 92–112; Angela Nüsseler, *Dogmatik fürs Volk: Wilhelm Abraham Teller als populärer Aufklärungstheologe* (München, 1999); Friedländer, *Sendschreiben*, 389.

66. Ibid.

67. On this, see Meyer, *Origins of the Modern Jew*, 75ff.

68. On this concept and also the idea of "vertical tolerance," see Forst, *Toleranz im Konflikt*, 18–19. While "horizontal tolerance" means "the attitude or rather the virtue of persons in their conduct with one another" (17), on the other hand, "vertical tolerance is understood primarily as a

Ernst-Peter Wieckenberg

political praxis, as a form of Staatspolitik, which is concerned with the maintenance of peace, of the public order, stability, law or the constitution—and with that also always power" (17).

69. On the problem of such a reduction as a condition of tolerance, see Forst, *Toleranz im Konflikt*, 354–55, and esp. 368.

70. Leß, *Wahrheit der Christlichen Religion*, 210.

71. *Beantwortung des Sendschreibens einiger Hausväter jüdischer Religion an mich den Probst Teller* (Berlin, 1799), 23.

72. Eberhard, *Neue Apologie des Sokrates*, 121–22.

The Merchant of Venice
and the Theological Construction
of Christian Europe

Susannah Heschel

For the past hundred years, scholarship on *The Merchant of Venice* has been divided on the question of the play's attitudes toward Jews. For a considerable number of decades, scholars tended to ignore the theological motifs of the play, even as they downplayed the significance of Shylock's Jewishness and the question of the play's antisemitism. Since the publication in 1996 of James Shapiro's study *Shakespeare and the Jews,* however, studies of the play have been increasingly attentive to its Jewish and Christian elements.[1] Shapiro's book, which was less a literary analysis than a cultural study of the environment in which the play was written, demonstrated the centrality of debates over Jews within sixteenth-century England. Precisely, the absence of a formally recognized Jewish community stimulated attention to questions of Jewishness. Moreover, the prominent role of Marranos in England raised questions about the Christian nature of English nationalism, Shapiro argued.

As scholars have grown more attentive to the Christian setting of the play, its resonances with Christian theological anti-Judaism have attracted growing attention. Examining the text of *The Merchant of Venice,* Jacques Derrida proclaimed that the play "perhaps recapitulates the entire history of forgiveness, the entire history between the

Jew and the Christian" in the court's declaration "Then must the Jew be merciful."[2] Shylock, Derrida claims, "represents every Jew, the Jew in general in his *différend* with his Christian counterpart."[3] Similarly, Thomas Luxon has argued that Shakespeare "lends his astonishing imaginative powers to support some very sophisticated and elaborate versions of Protestant anti-Jewish polemic."[4]

Coming to the play from the perspective of Jewish studies, particularly from the experiences of German Jews that Michael Meyer has so thoroughly and eloquently studied, raises the question of how the play might be understood not only as an expression of Christian theological themes but also as an expression, primarily via the figure of Shylock, of Jewish attitudes toward Christianity. How does the play construct, via literature, both Christian and Jewish attitudes? What techniques of language, narrative, plot, and character are used to call our attention, even subtly, to those attitudes and to encourage us to read subversively, against the grain of commonly held interpretations? Indeed, I would like to ask how Shylock and Portia, were they to watch the play in an audience, would understand its multiple meanings—especially if they knew the history of Jewish-Christian relations that the play, as Derrida writes, recapitulates.

In narrative form, *The Merchant of Venice* staged the Christian theological problem of the presence of Judaism and transmitted the conundrum to a wide audience for centuries. Not only classical theology but also political issues of nationalism, race, and gender are expressed in the play through its interrogations of body and soul; money and blood; fathers, daughters, and patrimony; marriage and conversion; religious difference and transgendering. Readings of the play have differed widely over the centuries, and variations in productions of the play in several different cultural contexts provide clues to changes in Jewish and Christian identities and understandings of the other. As a text central to the European imagination, *The Merchant of Venice* has become a palimpsest for a wide range of exegetical and eisegetical traditions and productions. The earlier texts on which subplots of the play are based—*Il Pecorone* (mid-sixteenth century) and the *Gesta Romanorum*, a collection of texts from the late thirteenth or early fourteenth century—do not employ theological references, calling further attention to Shakespeare's addition of biblical and religious motifs that he clearly wants us to take seriously.

THE JEW IN THE CHRISTIAN REALM

The Merchant of Venice is simultaneously about the Jew of the Christian imagination and about Christianity's self-understanding about the presence of Jews and Judaism in its midst. What is the "Christianness" of Europe when Christianity's "other," the Jews, who are meant to be excluded, have a place at its center? Jeremy Cohen, in *Living Letters of the Law,* speaks of hermeneutical Jews: complex, shifting, and not entirely negative figures crafted in the interests of Christian self-definition.[5] The hermeneutical Jew is an ideological construction, a tool of Christian theology. As ideological constructs of the Christian imagination, Jesus and Shylock are probably the two most famous Jews in western civilization. The one symbolizes what a Jew might become—a Christian—and the other, what happens when the Jew remains a Jew, the bitter and usurious Shylock. Given Shakespeare's attentiveness to biblical and theological themes, it is clear why Shylock would have been perceived through the lens of Christian views of Jews and Judaism.

The presence of Jews within Christian society and the possibility of Jewish conversion to Christianity are central concerns of *The Merchant of Venice,* reflecting the disquiet of Shakespeare's era. While no recognized community of Jews existed in England during Shakespeare's lifetime, so-called New Christians had entered the country and flourished but had also attracted mistrust. The personal physician to Queen Elizabeth I, a Converso named Rodrigo Lopez, came under suspicion for attempting to poison her. He was hanged in 1594 in a public spectacle well publicized throughout the country.[6] Whereas in earlier centuries Jews could simply be expelled as a foreign body, the early modern period, with its large-scale presence of baptized Jews, faced a different problem: the Jew was now concealed within the Christian, indeed, as a Christian. Yet the converted Jew, at least in the popular imagination, was not a Christian. The transgendering that is so often at the center of Shakespeare's plots functions in the figure of Portia to call our attention to a broader question of transracial, transreligious identity: the Converso—the Jew concealed in the theological appearance of a Christian. This unstable figure, considered neither Jew nor Christian, attempted at times to be both, thus destabilizing Christian as well as Jewish identities and throwing into question the boundary between them. As a result, Shylock lent himself to a wide range of interpretations, from a *Stürmer* caricature of a Jew to a tragic figure of profound nobility.

DEPICTIONS OF SHYLOCK ON STAGE

Shylock has been portrayed over the centuries in a variety of modes— as comic fool, despised villain, or tragic hero. Those variations correlate not only to attitudes toward Jews but also to Christian self-un-

Susannah Heschel

derstanding. The play has been most fraught on the German stage, where it reached a climax of Jew-hatred in a 1943 production at Vienna's Burgtheater, by the request of Baldur von Schirach, to mark the "achievement" of a *judenrein* Vienna.[7] Shylock was played by Werner Krauss, the Nazis' leading actor, who also starred in the film *Jud Süß*. His entrance upon the stage made the audience shudder. According to the newspaper accounts:

> With a crash and a weird train of shadows, something revoltingly alien and startlingly repulsive crawled across the stage. . . . The pale pink face, surrounded by bright red hair and beard, with its unsteady, cunning little eyes; the greasy caftan with the yellow prayershawl slung round; the splay-footed, shuffling walk; the foot stamping with rage; the claw-like gestures with the hands; the voice, now bawling, now muttering—all add up to a pathological image of the East European Jewish type, expressing all its inner and outer uncleanliness, emphasizing danger through humor.[8]

The Nazis had already made good use of *The Merchant of Venice* during the first years of the Third Reich, despite difficulties with aspects of its plot. Worried about audience sympathy for Shylock and concerned that Jessica's marriage to Lorenzo violated race laws, the play was both exploited for propaganda and, in 1938, placed on a blacklist for confiscation from libraries.[9] Still, the play was produced consistently throughout the years of the Third Reich, reaching a climax in 1942–43 with seventy-two productions.[10] Strengthening the anti-Semitism of the play spurred alterations to its text. Jessica was made into Shylock's foster daughter or even an illegitimate child born of an affair between Leah and a Christian love in order to remove her Jewishness in light of Nazi racial laws prohibiting miscegenation that forbade her marriage to Lorenzo. Texts that might arouse audience sympathy for Shylock were eliminated, including, at times, his famous speech in act 3.1: "Hath not a Jew eyes?"[11] Nazi use of the play for propagandistic purposes reached its pinnacle when German radio broadcast it shortly after *Kristallnacht*, the Reich pogrom that brought about the end of viable Jewish life in Germany, on November 9–10, 1938.[12] Hitler and his propaganda minister, Joseph Goebbels, obviously knew how to manipulate master narratives, and the play was employed not to stimulate the pogrom but to calm moral qualms after it had taken place.

Depictions of Shylock over the past three hundred years have altered considerably, from the seventeenth century's subservient buffoon portrayed by Richard Burbage to Edmund Kean's terrifying, noble, and malicious figure in the eighteenth century to a tragic Shylock of the nineteenth century. Nineteenth-century historicism had cultivated a lachrymose Jewish experience, with the Jew as victim of Christian persecution, so that the ugliness of Shylock came to be seen as not his fault. The shifts are reflected in Shylock's famous speech, "Hath not a Jew eyes," which aroused belly laughs in seventeenth-century audiences, especially when it came to his line "and if you prick us, do we not bleed," with its allusion to circumcision. The speech initially reinforced rather than refuted assumptions about Jews: what is most human, according to Christian humanism, is the soul, not the body, but there is no soul in Shylock's speech, as if to demonstrate that Jews do not value the soul. The speech took on pathos only after the Enlightenment convinced audiences that Jews and Christians do indeed have the same body and that the body, not only the soul, is constitutive of the human. Yet the pathos of the speech can only be conveyed by underscoring Shylock's links to the devil; in many productions he wore a red wig, linking him to Judas.

Shylock has also been depicted in a large number of counternarratives, plays and novels that propose to retell the story from his perspective. The most significant of these is Gotthold Ephraim Lessing's *Nathan the Wise* (1779), the classic work of the German Enlightenment. Lessing wrote *Nathan the Wise* with *The Merchant of Venice* in front of him, and he intended the noble Jew Nathan to be a refutation of Shylock. Lessing had launched the quest for the historical Jesus through his publication in 1774 and 1777 of the *Anonymous Fragments* written by Hermann Samuel Reimarus. For Reimarus, Jesus was an enlightened religious teacher who had no intention of abandoning Judaism, and Reimarus argued that Christianity was the invention of Jesus' disciples after his death as an attempt to win power for themselves. Lessing's Nathan was similar to Jesus; modeled on Lessing's close friend, the Jewish philosopher Moses Mendelssohn, Nathan is a wise, kind, and generous, but deracinated, Jew whose ethnicity was nowhere depicted or performed in the play. Like Shylock, Nathan was also a widower, perhaps as reassurance to an audience nervous about Jewish men's erotic preferences.

Nathan the Wise was a huge success in Germany, quickly becoming one of the most frequently performed German plays. The play's success also altered productions of *The Merchant of Venice;* Johann Ferdinand Fleck, one of Germany's leading actors in the late eighteenth century, elevated Shylock to a figure of profound depth, idealized on par with Nathan. His portrayals were not successful among German audiences, who expected a demonic Shylock in accord with the demonic images of Jews that prevailed. Offering a philosemitic portrayal and an optimistic portrait of Jewish assimilation, *Nathan the Wise* was also a kind of amulet for German Jews, who viewed it as a promise of the goodness that lay at the heart of German culture. Indeed, Lessing's play was performed by Jews during the Third Reich as a gesture of hope, to remember what Germany might be, and it is often invoked when the evils of Nazism are remembered, as a hope for what Germany might become. Yet the specter of a philosemitic play about an enlightened Jew never erased the imagined presence of the Jew Shylock as a predatory figure of danger to Christian Europe.

What about Jewish portrayals? The first Yiddish translation of *The Merchant of Venice* was published in the United States in 1899. On the New York Yiddish stage during the twentieth century the play was extremely popular among Jewish audiences, for whom it was a chance to speak back to Christianity. The most famous Yiddish actors sought the role and portrayed a quiet Shylock, loyal to the memory of his wife and filled with love for his daughter, whose suffering at Christian hands brought him not resentment but dignity. In each of these cases, we see Shylock as the figure around which Jewish identity can be renegotiated. The implied impotence or castration of Shylock at the end of act 4 was turned in the Yiddish versions into rage against the non-Jewish world, at the same time that the Jew's dignity was asserted. In the Yiddish plays, Shylock, despite his bitterness, does not take revenge.

In 1901 Jacob Adler starred in the first Yiddish production of the play and made a big impression; he portrayed Shylock as a patriarch, a higher being, as grandeur, a triumph of long suffering, of intellect, of character, and of spiritual sufferings. Adler saw Henry Irving's portrayal of Shylock and thought it was a caricature—Irving had called Shylock a bloody-minded monster, but in order to retain the audience's sympathy for Shylock's fate, Irving modified the monster. Adler wanted to create a sympathetic Shylock who was well dressed, proud, and not cringing. Shylock's insistence on the pound of flesh was not bloodthirsty but a demand for justice. Adler also cut the script to heighten the character's prominence in the play and highlighted the drama of Shylock returning home to find Jessica gone in order to explain his transformation into a vengeful figure. In act 1, after making the contract with Antonio, Adler remains on stage alone; as the curtain falls, he raises his handkerchief and points with his staff, then twists his purple handkerchief. His face turns cunning. When he realizes Jessica is gone, he tears his garment, sighs, sinks to the ground, and sighs: "Oy, oy." In the next scene, with Tubal, he is in a fury of rage and revenge: no more dignity and self-restraint. He remains this way at the start of the trial, beginning the courtroom scene like a cornered animal and leaping at Antonio until forcibly restrained. Adler said that Shylock knew no court would uphold him, but he wanted to show that his revenge was not to take the pound of flesh but to show that his ducats have purchased it. He whets his knife sardonically. One note: Adler refused to play Shylock in English on Broadway after a tour to Philadelphia, Baltimore, Boston, and New York because his performances evoked anti-Semitic, mocking reviews in the press.[13]

How could Shylock be portrayed after the Holocaust? A 1948 Yiddish production starred the great Yiddish actor Maurice Schwartz. Some of Shakespeare's language was there "Hot nit a yid . . ." ("Hath not a Jew . . .") but the plot had some key changes. In the climactic courtroom scene, Portia's sophistries are answered by a bright young Talmudic student. Reluctantly, the judge tells Shylock to take his pound of flesh. Shylock takes his knife, raises it above Antonio, and then, Maurice Schwartz's shout reverberating through the theater, calls out: "Ikh ken nit, ikh bin a yid" ("I cannot, I am a Jew"), and he drops the knife.[14] European Christians, by contrast, had not dropped the knife, as the audience well knew.

In Israel, productions of the play in the Yishuv were quickly politicized. Supporters of the Irgun emphasized Shylock's vengeance, while those who supported the Haganah emphasized his ethical behavior as the triumph of Judaism over its enemies. For the newly emerging Hebrew culture, *The Merchant of Venice* was suspected of challenging Zionist values: why should Jews produce an anti-Semitic play? Indeed, when the play was produced by the Habima Theatre Company in 1936, it was followed by a mock trial in which Shakespeare was accused of having written an anti-Semitic play.[15] Most productions of the play in the State of Israel were undertaken by non-Jews from Europe. The noted Irish director Tyron Guthrie produced *The Merchant of Venice* in Israel in 1956, where the theme was revenge against the Diaspora mentality of Jews.[16] While the Yiddish productions stressed the suffering and pathos of Shylock at the hands of Christians, a figure who embodied two thousand years of Diasporic anguish, the Israeli productions followed the Zionist insistence on negating the Diaspora. The Jew was no longer a figure of pathos, a victim of Christian persecution.

Within the State of Israel productions of the play have tended to be critical failures for a range of reasons. The context of Christian theological nuance is foreign to Israeli audiences, and the pathos of Jewish experience is uncomfortable both for the Zionists, who repudiate Diasporic suffering, and for the leftists, who use Shylock as a political critique of Jews. In a 1994 production by Israeli director Omri Nitzan,

Shylock was presented as a Jewish terrorist. And the Israeli film *Avanti Popolo* (1988) shows a group of Egyptian soldiers captured in the Sinai Desert by Israeli troops begging for mercy by reciting a variation of Shylock's famous "Hath not a Jew" speech. Joshua Sobol's notorious play *Ghetto* (1984) presents Shylock-like Jewish council leaders in Nazi ghettos using their power against other Jews. The associations of *The Merchant of Venice* with the Holocaust seemed all too obvious.

WHAT IS CHRISTIANITY?

In interrogating the nature of the Christian, the text of the play raises the question of what constitutes the blood of Christianity, its authenticity and distinctiveness, in light of its Jewish patrimony. Can Shylock or Jessica become a true Christian? The anxiety over their conversion points to a deeper aporia of Christian theology: Is Jesus a Jew or a Christian? What marks Jesus' Christian identity—does he undergo a conversion from Jew to Christian? Not surprising, then, that Shylock's demand of Antonio's Christian flesh should arouse so much anxiety—will he circumcise the breast or the foreskin, the site that Judaizes or Christianizes? In some productions of the play, including Michael Radford's 2004 film, Shylock murmurs a Hebrew prayer as he takes up his knife, as if he were a *mohel* (ritual circumciser) about to circumcise Antonio and forcibly to Judaize him by converting him into the covenant. Similarly, Anthony Sher's 1987 Shylock on the London stage, produced by the Royal Shakespeare Company, donned a *talit* to cut his pound of flesh in order to make certain that the audience understood that the Jew, whether engaging in circumcision or ritual murder, was performing a religious act.

In Shakespeare's time, as Lynda Boose has pointed out, nation and race were used interchangeably, but the latter was used to characterize not necessarily someone of "foreign" appearance but someone of a different nationality and religion.[17] The Marranos accomplished a shift in Christian identity from an acquisition through baptism to an acquisition through a performance dependent on proper hermeneutics, as Lisa Lampert writes.[18] To be a Christian meant the ability to interpret as a Christian, and the play emphasizes that only those of proper nationality and race possess such a talent; the Catholic Spaniard and Muslim Moroccan are unable to interpret the three caskets properly and thus lose the chance not only to win Portia but to marry at all. Christianness requires both nationality and race, which together create the peculiar combination of physical beauty and moral acuity demonstrated by Bassanio's correct interpretation of the caskets. Race is marked not only by distinctive physical appearance but by a concern with incarnation, which means seeing beyond the external physical to perceive the internal spiritual. If, as Carolyn Dinshaw has argued, proper Christian exegesis is linked to erotic desire, then racialist thinking also acquires its appeal through its erotic wish to read the body and find the moral and spiritual potencies incarnate within it.[19] Bassanio, like all the suitors, must divine the true, inner meanings of the caskets to win Portia, and Portia must see through the letter of the law and find its implied meaning in order to thwart Shylock; such talents are not given to the Spanish (Catholic) or Moroccan (Muslim) suitors, nor to Shylock himself.

Jessica enacts the promise of the conversion of the Jews to Christianity, but she also demonstrates its failure; her actions spell disaster for her father, grave threat to Lorenzo, and misery for herself. Shylock pays for his conversion with his wealth and possessions, while Jessica's price is the love of her husband. As an alluring, exotic beauty who is a seduced seductress, her disconnection between outer facade and inner essence threatens a nationality based on appearance and a theology based on faith. Jessica is clear that her conversion is motivated by eroticism, not faith, reinforcing the classic aporia of Jewish conversion: in light of the Christian claim that there is no faith in the Jew, the Jew's conversion would have to be unfaithful, simply a ticket of admission into European society, as Heinrich Heine put it. Christianity becomes a stepping stone to Europe rather than coeval with it.

Jessica's seduction by Lorenzo represents a motif typical of colonialist fantasy, the seduction of the alien female, joining the play's concerns with the alien Jew living in Christian Venice and the dangers of miscegenation. The Jewess, as a figure who stands literarily between Jew and Christian precisely because of her femaleness, represents a more specific problem to the Christian seducer. As Miri Rubin argues, the host desecration accusations require a male Jewish perpetrator because only male Jews, unlike women, could be seen as fully moral agents; females are pliant and lack reason and moral faculties.[20] The conversion of a Jewish woman thus carries a different resonance reinforced by rabbinic anxiety, that a man's maleness is fragile and easily lost if, for example, he walks between two women, and a woman's Jewishness is similarly fragile and easily robbed by a seductive Gentile. Similarly, while Shakespeare's *Othello* can imagine the marriage of a black man and a white woman, Othello and Desdemona, virility and beauty, *The Merchant of Venice* can imagine only a Christian man and Jewish woman; the gender politics of race are inverted with Jewishness. A Jewess may be easily divested of her Jewishness by marriage to a Christian man, whereas the marriage of a Jew to a Christian woman renders him emasculated without losing his racial markers.

Susannah Heschel

Jessica's flight from her father's home is invariably interpreted as further evidence of Shylock's degeneracy; in most interpretations and productions of the play, Jessica herself is held blameless, a victim who flees her abusive father. Audience identification with her is taken as least problematic, given the unpleasant characters surrounding her in the play. By contrast, Jewish productions of the play signal Jessica as the villain. Her elopement is key to her father's misery and transformation into an angry, vengeful figure; in some Yiddish revisions of the play, Jessica realizes her wickedness and commits suicide. She thus gestures to Jewish audiences that she did not abandon her Judaism for another religion but rather abandoned her father for the sake of her eroticism; internally and spiritually, she remains a faithful Jew.

CHRISTIAN AS JEW

Yet a counternarrative also prevails in the play. Not only does the play recapitulate Christian attitudes toward Jews and Judaism; it also provides a searing critique of those attitudes. That counternarrative is suggested, first of all, by Shakespeare's use of cross-dressing, a common technique of his plays that is rendered all the more ironic given that only men were allowed on stage in his lifetime, so female characters were portrayed by male actors playing women who were in turn often dressed up as men. The particular use of Portia's cross-dressing in the courtroom scene, act 4.1, calls our attention to the nature of the religious arguments she is making on behalf of Christianity, which sound closer to rabbinic Judaism.

Shakespeare's magnificent rendition of the courtroom scene pits Portia, disguised as a man, speaking the logic of Talmudic casuistry disguised as Christian mercy against Shylock, whose Jewishness she pretends not to immediately recognize. "Which is the merchant here, and which the Jew?" she asks as she enters the courtroom, as if Jewishness could be concealed in Christian attire, appearance, and bearing. As Balthasar, the male jurist, she conceals, meanwhile, that she is not defending but defeating Antonio (and Venice) to become the real merchant of the play, here to gain control of the wealth and its dispersion. Shylock is the old law; she represents herself as the young dispensation. The mercy that Portia invokes—"The quality of mercy is not strain'd, It droppeth as the gentle rain from heaven"—is juxtaposed to Shylock's insistence on the literal words and legality of his bond with Antonio, and yet it is ironically Portia's literalism and legalism that triumphs over Shylock. It is her insistence on vengeance that brings about his ruin, all for the sake of protecting Christian blood; the female Christian "out-Jews" the male Jew in the rabbinic pilpul he has developed and "out-Jews" him in his capitalism, decircumcising him by forcing his baptism. Her words, evoking those of Jesus and Christianity, ironically rest on the literal-mindedness that Christians claim of Jews and also claim to have rejected and purged in their supersession of Judaism:

> This bond doth give thee here no jot of blood,
>   The words expressly are "a pound of flesh":
> Take then thy bond, take thou thy pound of flesh,
> But in the cutting it, if thou dost shed
> One drop of Christian blood, thy lands and goods
> Are (by the laws of Venice) confiscate
> Unto the state of Venice.
>   (4.1.301–8)

Portia's defeat of Shylock transpires through her employment of the methods of rabbinic pilpul and also through her cross-dressing as a man. Here, the male is Jewish, the female is Christian, and supersessionism is a form of transgendering: the Jew becomes Christian, the male becomes female—or does it? Portia as Balthasar demonstrates that just as she is disguised as a man, Christianity is ultimately nothing more than Judaism in drag.

Shakespeare is not being theologically didactic but uses irony to call the categories of Christian theology into question. Portia, the advocate of mercy, is the figure who becomes the clever, legalistic Jew—but only transvestially dressed as a man. Jesus too by analogy can only become the one who dispenses with the law if his teachings are read through a Christian lens; the Jewish reading of his teachings places him squarely within Pharisaic hermeneutical tradition. Shylock's Jewishness is signified in the play not through his faith or practice but as constructed by a Christian theological narrative that is dedicated to its eradication—and he knows it well: "You call me misbeliever, cut-throat dog, And spit upon my Jewish gaberdine," he says to Antonio (1.3.102–3). In the Christian mirror, Shylock recognizes, the Jew is not an unbeliever but far worse, a misbeliever, a misreader of the Scriptures that prefigure Christ, and a dog who, in Christian exegesis, is the figure of the Jew, who is not to receive "that which is holy" (Matthew 7:6).[21] The denigration results not in Shylock's self-contempt but in his contempt for the Christian Antonio, who knows to spit on a Jew but not how to receive the kiss of divine revelation and to suckle the breast of Torah, as do Jews. When Shylock is said to want to carve a pound of flesh from Antonio, it is from his breast, reiterating the Christian distinction between Judaism's circumcision of the foreskin and Chris-

Susannah Heschel

tianity's self-understanding as circumcision of the heart. According to that distinction, Jews do not know how to circumcise their hearts, only to stab the heart. The play enacts the Christian projective fantasy of the Jew stabbing Christ in the heart rather than sucking from his breast and wanting his blood rather than his milk.[22] "I hate him for he is a Christian," Shylock says (1.3.32), fulfilling the old Christian assumption of Jewish hatred, the justification for Christian persecution of Jews.

The presence of Jews within the Christian realm of Venice evokes an anxiety with a long heritage in Christian self-consciousness. Will the Jews be converted to Christianity, or will the Christians become Judaized? Launcelot expresses that fear when he tells his blind father, "I am a Jew if I serve the Jew any longer" (2.2.106–7). If converted, will Jews become authentic Christians, and if Judaized, will Christians lose their morals and their families? Antonio comments sarcastically, "The Hebrew will turn Christian: he grows kind" (1.3.175). The implication becomes clear: however kind Shylock may appear, he can never be a real Christian. The gnosis of the play is that its Christians are hardly kind.

Portia disposes of the threat of Shylock by invading the old, male, Jewish order and turning Shylock into a Christian and an endowing father of the newly baptized Jessica whom he had renounced as his heir. Portia forces Shylock to become the willing father by turning over his heritage to his daughter who has become what Jews should be, a Christian. Shylock becomes a father by being forced to become a Christian, metaphorically representing the effort by early Christians to force Judaism to become the willing parent of the emergent Christianity. The punitive conversion of Shylock demanded at the end of act 4 is an eradication of his very existence, taking away his livelihood, his home, his property, his ability to earn an income, and he disappears from the play. Jessica, in turn, has been the erotic Jewess who takes the family jewels when she leaves her father's home and then discovers she is isolated and unwanted as Lorenzo's new bride in act 5. Shylock's emasculation occurs in collusion between Portia, who takes his money, and Jessica, who takes "two stones, two rich and precious stones, Stol'n by my daughter" (2.8.20–21). If conversion is a kind of marriage, then Shylock's forced conversion is effeminizing; it is like a woman forced into marriage.

The impossibility of converting a Jew into a Christian throws open the question not only of Jesus' own identity but also of key doctrines of the church. Within the play, a central question is transubstantiation: If Protestants have rejected the literal transubstantiation of wine and wafer into blood and flesh, can the Jew truly be transformed into a Christian? Is it possible for Christianity to emerge from Judaism? The play raises the question of what constitutes the authentic patrimony, or bloodline, of Christianity. Can Shylock or Jessica become a true Christian? What of the Jewish blood that she will bring to the offspring of Lorenzo, a concern emphasized by Jessica's assertion that she is Shylock's daughter by blood and not by heart? The jewels and money she brings from her father's home clearly do not suffice to erase anxieties over her race; nor does her money buy her love. That is not the result of her gender but of her Jewishness, since the play makes Portia's negotiation of finances and love far more successful. Indeed, the play conflates money, blood, and faith, as Shylock's conversion is not the transubstantiation of his Judaism into Christian faith but the liquidation of his business and its transfer to Portia's Christian realm, the island of Belmont, along with his daughter, Jessica, and his bloodline. Portia, who acquires and showers wealth where she pleases, demonstrates that "money . . . is the true spirit of capitalism made flesh, the incarnation and liquefaction of flesh and blood," as Gil Anidjar has written.[23] Faith is translated into money, not for the Jew Shylock, but for the Christian Portia.

THE JEW IN THE CHRISTIAN

The difficulties in assimilating large numbers of baptized Jews into the church had become so fraught in Spain during the fifteenth century that scholars have recognized that the religious issue was infused with racial concerns: does baptism transform a Jew into a Christian, or does a Jew always remain a Jew, even when baptized? Such questions grew stronger as converted Jews—"New Christians" or, in hostile terms, "Marranos"—merged into western European society, including sixteenth-century England. Race has for too long been mistakenly understood as a modern invention and as a repudiation of religion. The presence of the Jew as Christian, the Jew within the Christian, not only became the basis for modern racial theorists to reject the possibility of Jewish assimilation, which had been the promise of the Emancipation era, but reflected a theological problem for Christian self-understanding. Had Jesus, in fact, fully transformed himself from Jew to Christian? Would his own transformation offer a legitimizing basis for the transformation of all Jews into citizens of European society? At stake was the rivalry between religion and race, both as a basis for the nation-state and as the basis for personal identity.

Yet Christianity also created its own ineradicable theological trap: the religion of mercy and forgiveness came into being through a sin that Christian culture considered unforgivable, the Jews' act of deicide. No repentance is possible, since the Jews cannot acknowledge the act of deicide without acknowledging Jesus as Christ, itself an act of conversion, not atonement. To explain the Jews' sinfulness, Christians have to define them as degenerate by nature. However, their degeneracy means they have acted not in sin but in accordance with their nature—hardly satisfying to a Christian theology of sinful deed. It is a terrible dilemma, almost comic, had not the historic punishments of the Jews for that sin been so harsh. Here too the play recapitulates the problem of forgiveness as Shylock reenacts the crucifixion scene, raising the knife above Antonio, who speaks of himself as a Christ figure, "a tainted wether of the flock, meetest for death" (4.1), a lamb of God, ready for death. As Theodor Reik pointed out, Antonio's opening lines of the play declare his sadness and weariness echo those of the gospels: "He was despised and rejected of men, a man of sorrows and acquainted with grief. . . . He hath borne our griefs and carried our sorrows." While contemporary scholars have argued that Antonio's melancholy derives from his frustrated homosexual love for Bassanio, Reik sees him as a Christ figure.[24] What Reik does not note is the position of Shylock, reenacting the Jew as the Christ-killer who enables the conversion of Jesus the Jewish messiah into Christ the redeemer of Christians. That which the Christian cannot forgive of Jews becomes the foundation of Christian faith, the moment that can never be forgotten, the Eucharist taken in memory of that conversion, an inversion of Lear's comment to Cordelia, "Forget and forgive" (4.7.84), as Henry Smith has pointed out.[25]

After all, what sort of mercy and forgiveness does the Christian court offer Shylock? As punishment for his refusal to convert his alleged vengeance into forgiveness, his property is confiscated and he is offered the alternative of death or conversion to Christianity, itself the death of his identity and spirit. Conversion comes to him as the climax of a scene of protracted verbal sadism on the part of Portia, who clearly knows in advance the trap she is setting as she presents her prosecution, always addressing him as "Jew," not "Shylock." Even when he finally agrees to accept the money instead of Antonio's flesh, Portia continues:

Soft!
The Jew shall have all justice; soft! no haste:
He shall have nothing but the penalty . . .

Therefore prepare thee to cut off the flesh.
Shed thou no blood, nor cut thou less nor more
But just a pound of flesh: if thou cut'st more

Or less than a just pound, be it but so much
As makes it light or heavy in the substance,
Or the division of the twentieth part
Of one poor scruple, nay, if the scale do turn
But in the estimation of a hair,
Thou diest and all thy goods are confiscate . . .

Why doth the Jew pause? take thy forfeiture . . .

He hath refused it in the open court:
He shall have merely justice and his bond . . .

Thou shalt have nothing but the forfeiture,
To be so taken at thy peril, Jew . . .

Tarry, Jew:
The law hath yet another hold on you.
It is enacted in the laws of Venice,
If it be proved against an alien
That by direct or indirect attempts
He seek the life of any citizen,
The party 'gainst the which he doth contrive
Shall seize one half his goods; the other half
Comes to the privy coffer of the state;
And the offender's life lies in the mercy
Of the duke only, 'gainst all other voice.
In which predicament, I say, thou stand'st;
For it appears, by manifest proceeding,
That indirectly and directly too
Thou hast contrived against the very life
Of the defendant; and thou hast incurr'd
The danger formerly by me rehearsed.
Down therefore and beg mercy of the duke . . .

Art thou contented, Jew? what dost thou say?

For the court of Venice, getting rid of Shylock (excising Judaism) was
not so simple. Converting and accepting him into Christian society
would violate the longstanding Christian wish to eradicate the Jew
from within itself. The dilemma points to the desire that can never
come to fruition without destroying the foundations of Christianity's
legitimacy as fulfilling the divine promises of the Old Testament. While
the courtroom scene on one level concerns Venetians' dislike of Jews,

on another level, it is also an intratheological Christian conundrum. Shylock, after all, is reenacting the Christian story: Jesus' sacrifice of his flesh as an act of atonement for the world.

CONCLUSION

Shakespeare confuses categories in order to call them into question, particularly Christian categories of anti-Judaism. While audiences of the play may find easy confirmation of their biases toward Jews, both the subversion of the play's pieties and the transvestial presentation of its characters suggest that Shakespeare's sophistication is mustered to undermine a theology of Christian anti-Judaism. Within the play, Christian mercy and forgiveness disguise the weapons of legalism and forced conversion. Those "Judaizations" actually occur through the machinations of Christians in their application of the law to Shylock in order to liquidate his assets and transfer his wealth to Portia's island of Belmont. Belmont exists as a ghetto of Christians who practice not the universalism that is said to characterize their religion but the kind of particularistic, ethnic exclusiveness long said to characterize Jews. Portia, the Christian, governs not by mercy but by stern and relentless law. "Which is the merchant here, and which the Jew?" indeed; which is the Christian, which the Jew? To read the play as anti-Jewish is to read it as Lorenzo reads Portia, as a "sweet lady" who drops "manna in the way of starved people" (5.1.294–5), a reading of Christian naiveté but certainly not the way Shylock experienced Portia nor how he would read the play.

The anxieties surrounding Christian theological origins, differentiation, and conversion are reflected not only in the historiographies produced in the early modern era but in the popular imagination as well. In *The Merchant of Venice,* Shylock, who appears in only five of its scenes, looms as its major character because he is a polysemic figure; as a tragic, ridiculous, threatening, and unfathomable person, he is an emblem of the complexity of the Jew in both Jewish and Christian imaginations. He symbolizes both Jew and Christian because he portrays himself as a Jew and, at the same time, mirrors the projected "jew" of the Christian imagination. The Jew as the haunt of the European Christian imagination has become a common theme in contemporary theory. Jean Francois Lyotard, for example, distinguishes between Jews and "jews," the latter referring to the imagined figures who are often evasive, fluctuating, and enigmatic.[26] For Slavoj Žižek, Jews are a "symptom" of society, representing a fantasized barrier to an ultimate apotheosis.[27] As such, the Jew is a hermeneutical device central to Christian theology, which also insists that Jews possess a unique, carnal hermeneutics considered different and inferior to the spiritual hermeneutics of Christians. In the figures of Jesus and Shylock, two specters are evoked: the Jew as redeemer, Jesus, and the Jew as curse and cursed, Shylock. The horror underlying *The Merchant of Venice* is the church's failure to have converted the Jews, but that horror is also fed by a belief that conversion will not eradicate what is repellent about Jews and will open Christian society to them. Race remains ineradicable even in the presence of the baptismal sacrament.

Shylock is not so much an anti-Christ as an anti-Jesus: Jesus is generous, but Shylock is usurious; Jesus preaches, but Shylock rages; Jesus offers his body, but Shylock demands the flesh of another. Jesus lost his life due to the unbelieving Jewish judges who tried him in their religious court according to Jewish law, while Shylock loses his existence at the hands of Christian judges bent on vengeance. Both men are religious martyrs and martyrs to their sex and gender. Neither has a wife; neither leaves a bloodline. Like the synoptic gospels, which have been read both as anti-Jewish and as Jewish texts, *The Merchant of Venice* can be read as anti-Jewish or as anti-Christian, critical of Christianity's anti-Judaism. The play accomplishes an exploration of the extraordinary, complex resonances that result from the idiosyncratic theological configurations of Christian supersessionism. Shakespeare has written a masterpiece because it resonates so strongly with western culture's master narrative of Jesus and his relationship to Judaism.

NOTES

I would like to express my gratitude for stimulating conversations about *The Merchant of Venice* with several colleagues: Timothy Baker, Lynda Boose, Lisa Lampert, Kathleen Biddick, Marilyn Reizbaum, Tom Luxon, Henry F. Smith, and Raph and Jane Bernstein.

1. James Shapiro, *Shakespeare and the Jews* (New York: Columbia University Press, 1996).
2. Jacques Derrida, "What Is a 'Relevant' Translation?" *Critical Inquiry* 27 (2001): 174–200, here 186.
3. Ibid.
4. Thomas Luxon, "A Second Daniel: The Jew and the 'True Jew' in *The Merchant of Venice*," *Early Modern Literary Studies* 4, no. 3 (1999): 1–37, here 16.
5. Jeremy Cohen, *Living Letters of the Law: Ideas of the Jew in Medieval Christianity* (Berkeley: University of California Press, 1999).
6. Dominic Green, *The Double Life of Doctor Lopez: Spies, Shakespeare, and the Plot to Poison Elizabeth I* (London: Century, 2003).

Susannah Heschel

7. The Dudleian Lecture, Harvard University, April 27, 2006; Rodney Symington, *The Nazi Appropriation of Shakespeare: Cultural Politics in the Third Reich* (Lewiston: Edwin Mellen Press, 2005), 250–51.

8. The critic's comments are recorded in Werner Krauss, *Das Schauspiel meines Lebens* (Stuttgart, 1958), 199–209; cited by John Gross, *Shylock: A Legend and Its Legacy* (New York: Simon and Schuster, 1992), 322.

9. Symington, *Nazi Appropriation*, 245.

10. Ibid., 246.

11. Ibid., 248.

12. James Shapiro, "Shakespeare and the Jews," in *The Merchant of Venice*, ed. Martin Coyle, 73–91 (New York: St. Martin's Press, 1998), 90

13. See the discussion of Jacob Adler's performances in Joel Berkowitz, *Shakespeare on the Yiddish Stage* (Iowa City: University of Iowa Press, 2002). For another analysis of Shylock by a famed actor on the Russian Yiddish stage, see Abraham Morevski, *Shylock and Shakespeare*, trans. Mirra Ginsburg (St. Louis: Fireside Books, 1967).

14. A description of that performance by Schwartz came from Martin Davis, Berkeley, California, via email to Mendele, http://www2.trincoll.edu/~mendele, vol. 3 (November 2, 1997).

15. Dror Abend-David, *Scorned My Nation: A Comparison of Translations of The Merchant of Venice into German, Hebrew, and Yiddish*, Comparative Cultures and Literatures 16, ed. Daniel Walden (New York: Peter Lang, 2003), 130.

16. Ibid., 134–37.

17. Lynda E. Boose, "'The Getting of a Lawful Race': Racial Discourse in Early Modern England and the Unrepresentable Black Woman," in *Women, "Race," and Writing in the Early Modern Period*, ed. Margo Hendricks and Patricia Parker (London: Routledge, 1994), 36.

18. Lisa Lampert, *Gender and Jewish Difference from Paul to Shakespeare* (Philadelphia: University of Pennsylvania Press, 2004), 27 and 140–41.

19. Carolyn Dinshaw, *Chaucer's Sexual Politics* (Madison: University of Wiconsin Press, 1989); cited by Lampert, *Gender and Jewish Difference*, 156.

20. Miri Rubin, *Gentile Tales: The Narrative Assault on Late Medieval Jews* (New Haven: Yale University Press, 1999).

21. For a study of medieval images of Jew as dog, see Kenneth Stow, *Jewish Dogs: An Image and Its Interpreters: Continuity in the Catholic-Jewish Encounter* (Stanford: Stanford University Press, 2006).

22. The motif of Jews stabbing Christ lies behind medieval Christian accusations of Jewish host desecration. See, e.g., the fifteenth-century English play *The Croxton Play of the Sacrament* in *Non-Cycle Plays and Fragments*, ed. Norman Davis on the basis of the edition by Osborn Waterhouse (London: Oxford University Press, 1970). For a discussion of the motif of Jewish stabbing in the Croxton play, see Sister Nichola Maltman, "Meaning and Art in the Croxton Play of the Sacrament," *English Literary History* 41, no. 2 (1974): 149–64; Lisa Lampert, "The Once and Future Jew: The Croxton Play of the Sacrament, Little Robert

of Bury, and Historical Memory," *Jewish History* 15 (2001): 235–55.

23. Gil Anidjar, "Christians and Money (The Economic Enemy)," *Ethical Perspectives: Journal of the European Ethics Network* 12, no. 4 (2005): 500.

24. Theodor Reik, "Jessica, My Child!" *American Imago* 8 (1951): 3–27.

25. Henry F. Smith, "A Footnote on Forgiveness," *Psychoanalytic Quarterly* 71 (2002): 327–29.

26. Jean Francois Lyotard, *Heidegger and "The Jews,"* trans. Andreas Michel and Mark Roberts (Minneapolis: University of Minnesota Press, 1990).

27. Slavoj Žižek, *The Sublime Object of Ideology* (New York: Verso, 1989), 125.

Toward the Popular Religion of Ashkenazic Jews

Yiddish-Hebrew Texts on Sex and Circumcision

MICHAEL STANISLAWSKI

At the end of his masterful paper "Popular Religious Beliefs and the Late Roman Historians," Arnaldo Momigliano concluded:

> Thus my inquest into popular religious beliefs in the late Roman historians ends in reporting that there were no such beliefs. In the fourth and fifth centuries there were of course plenty of beliefs which we historians of the twentieth century would gladly call popular, but the historians of the fourth and fifth centuries never treated any belief as characteristic of the masses and consequently discredited among the elite. Lectures on popular religious beliefs and the late Roman historians should be severely discouraged.[1]

These words provide a daunting backdrop to any discussion of the "popular religion" of Ashkenazic Jews in the premodern era for the simple reason that this very enterprise is plagued by basic, and possibly irresoluble, terminological and methodological obstacles—not the least of which is a reasonable and workable definition of what "popular religion" means among the Jews.

Before entering into this minefield, a bibliographic excursion might be in order.[2] One of the most curious features of the historical literature on Jewish life in central and eastern Europe in the early modern period is the relative paucity of rigorous scholarly treatments of its religious culture. Contrary to what might be expected, for example, there is not even one serious scholarly survey of rabbinic learning or halakhic history in the Germanic lands, Bohemia, Moravia, Poland, Lithuania, and Russia through the centuries, and despite the recent flurry of interest in the more flamboyant expressions of Jewish religiosity, no acceptable history of Jewish mysticism in these regions. In recent years, as a result of the broadly based resurgence of interest in religious history in general and, more specifically, of the emergence of a new generation of historians and students of Judaism who self-consciously shun the secularism and antitraditionalism of their predecessors, this problem has begun to be redressed, with impressive results. However, the gaps in our knowledge remain gaping. When we move away from what might be called the "high culture" of Ashkenazic Judaism—halakhah, homiletics, and kabbalah and, to a far lesser degree, philosophy and belles lettres—the following picture emerges. Historically, early modern Yiddish texts have been studied by two distinct and often mutually antagonistic camps: on the one hand, Yiddish (and usually Yiddishist) literary historians who sought to claim equal status and respect for Yiddish works aimed at the "folk" (as opposed to Hebrew works meant for the "elite"), and on the other, students of the "popular religion" of Judaism, frequently Reform rabbis, motivated by the desire to historicize contemporary religious reforms.[3] These scholars mined the Yiddish materials for evidence of rituals and beliefs despised by the rabbis but foisted upon them from below—customs such as *kapparot* or *tashlikh* or even the canonized version of the Kol Nidre prayer itself.[4] The former line of analysis was continued along far more sophisticated and less ideological lines in Jerusalem by scholars of Old Yiddish literature such as Khone Shmeruk and Hava Turniansky, who have produced excellent—indeed, sometimes dazzlingly erudite—studies of premodern Yiddish materials, primarily from a literary and bibliographical point of view.[5] The latter "populist" approach has most recently been revived in connection with the spread of feminist theory and women's history in Jewish Studies, as *tekhines* and other Yiddish liturgical and practical texts are analyzed to reveal a "women's religion" in early modern Ashkenazic Judaism radically different from the official, elite religion articulated by the—obviously male—rabbinate.[6]

Without in the least disparaging any of these attempts and approaches, it is crucial to note that they are based on a rather thin layer of

Michael Stanislawski

documentary evidence, compounded by truly formidable methodological quandaries. For it is no exaggeration to state that the vast majority of premodern Yiddish texts have never been subjected to any serious scholarly examination. To cite only one, though crucial, example: due to Shmeruk's efforts in particular, we finally have a reliable bibliography of the various eastern European editions of the *Tsena U-Rena*—the famous "women's gloss" of the Bible, which must rank as the most influential and certainly the most widespread text in whatever it is that might be defined as Jewish popular culture or women's religion in the Ashkenazic realm. But we still lack a comprehensive study of the *contents* of this work—what it can teach us about the spiritual and literary universe of its author and possibly its readers and thus about a vital part of the Ashkenazic *mentalité* in the early modern era.[7]

Beyond this bibliographical morass lies an analytic abyss: the basic terms of any possible analysis of the contours and parameters of a "popular culture," "popular religion," or "folk memory" in Jewish society have never been, to my knowledge, rigorously addressed. To oversimplify matters considerably, but I hope not unfairly, the model of popular or folk culture adopted—if at times unselfconsciously—by most students of the Jews has been a variation on the standard understanding of Christian popular culture in the last half-century: a model that describes a minuscule clerical and aristocratic elite with its own high culture, religion, and textual tradition poised against the great mass of the peasant population, who lived in a folklore culture unaware of and uninterested in the debates and obsessions of the elite. In this view, a popular culture has been identified and heralded for the most part as the cultural or spiritual life of the dispossessed and downtrodden, the untutored and the unorthodox, and more recently, women as opposed to men.

Quite apart from the question of whether such a two-tiered approach is appropriate to the study of Christendom, it is crucial to posit at the minimum that it is highly problematic with regard to the Jews.[8] For despite the undeniably potent differences of wealth and status among them, the Jews lacked anything resembling either a peasantry, an aristocracy, or an ecclesiastical hierarchy.[9] Thus, the gap—social, economic, intellectual, spiritual—between the clergy and the laity and between the upper and lower classes is hardly self-evident and undoubtedly substantially narrower than that in any host Christian population. Further, the innate rabbinical distaste for discussions of dogmatic or doctrinal purity resulted in a line of demarcation between heterodox and canonized practice and beliefs that was, even at first glance, extraordinarily hazy. This was immensely complicated by the inexorably difficult and constantly shifting relations between *minhag*, *nohag,* and halakhah (relations that, to say the least, have not yet been systematized by specialists in that subject). Finally, the search for a women's religion, culture, or spirituality embedded within the extant Yiddish texts is now only beginning to grapple more substantively with the fact that the vast bulk of early modern Yiddish materials was written by men and intended both "for women and for untutored men," and sometimes primarily for the latter.[10]

In sum, it seems obvious that far more work has to be done both on the basic texts themselves and on the methodological distinction between popularization and popular culture *a la juive* before we can engage in far-reaching generalizations about these texts.

The goal of this essay, then, is to contribute to this quest by examining two Yiddish translations of Hebrew edificatory works on subjects very close to the heart of any Jewish society—the meaning of sexuality and the covenant of circumcision. By examining these texts, I propose, one can establish as close as one could come to a controlled experiment: a clear way to dissect texts without falling prey to biases and preconceptions about what constitutes "folk" versus "elite" religion, except insofar as one assumes that there was a difference—deliberately left undefined—between the Hebrew- and Yiddish-reading audiences.

IGGERET HA-KODESH

Our first text is *Iggeret Ha-Kodesh* ("The Holy Letter") traditionally ascribed to the great medieval scholar and kabbalist Nachmanides but now generally believed to have been written by a kabbalist of the next generation, probably, as Gershom Scholem suggested, by Joseph ibn Gikatilla. This little book was first published in Rome in 1546 and was reprinted in Basel in 1580, in Cracow in 1594, and thereafter in virtually every major seat of Jewish printing in the early modern and modern periods—from Constantinople, Altona, Berlin, and Amsterdam to Jerusalem and New York. The edition that interests us here is the only known Yiddish translation of this work, published anonymously in Fürth in 1692.[11]

Before examining this Yiddish translation, a few words about the original: the *Iggeret Ha-Kodesh* has been regarded as an ethical gem based entirely on the kabbalah. Indeed, as other scholars have demonstrated, it marks "the first time in the history of Jewish thought [when we find] a treatise devoted to the mystical understanding of marriage," and more, it is, in general, "the first popular work in which kabbalistic teaching was applied to day-to-day life."[12] As Monford Harris put it in 1962:

'The letter is written on two levels, an exoteric and an esoteric. The exoteric furnishes the skeletal frame for the esoteric. . . . The more one studies this rather brief *Letter* the
more one is convinced that the kabbalistic secrets and hints
intimated throughout are not presented for the sake of
clarifying the meaning, etc., of marital relations. The contrary is true: marriage is discussed primarily as a vehicle
for teaching some basic secrets of the Kabbalah. This small
text was devised as a way for putting down into writing that
which one was not supposed to write down: the esoteric
kabbalistic tradition. All of the *information* about the time
of intercourse, techniques, food, etc., serves only as a frame
of reference for the esoteric doctrine.[13]

When we move to the Yiddish translation of this work, the first and
most important point to note is that the ostensible purpose of this
work is completely reversed: the esoteric core is entirely excised, leaving only the exoteric shell. What remains, then, is a fascinating sex
manual in Yiddish, aimed exclusively at men, with one exception to
which we shall return. As the frontispiece puts it, "The Holy Letter,
which was sent by the great rabbi, kabbalist, and holy man Rabbi Moses ben Nahman, to several of his friends, about how they should behave in regard to the matter of intercourse with their wives, so that
through this they will merit good and honest children who will be
righteous and pious and serve God well."[14] From the first paragraph of
the Yiddish translation to its last, every single kabbalistic reference in
the Hebrew original is absent, usually omitted entirely, though sometimes subverted by underinterpretation. Dozens of examples could be
given to establish this point, but one crucial case will suffice here. In
the second chapter of the work, on the nature of sexual intercourse,
the author of the original writes:

Behold the mystery of knowledge that I reveal to you is
the mystery of man's involvement in the mystery of wisdom, understanding, and knowledge. For the male is the
mystery of wisdom and the female is the mystery of understanding. And pure sexual intercourse is the mystery
of knowledge—this is the esoteric meaning of male and
female in the secret kabbalistic teaching. Therefore, it follows that sexual intercourse is a matter of great spiritual
import when it is done properly, and the greater mystery
is the mystery of the sexual union of the heavenly bodies
when they assume the manner of male and female.[15]

In sharp contrast, the Yiddish text reads:

> Therefore it is important for you to understand and to have others understand that sexual intercourse is called knowledge because the male is created with wisdom and the female with understanding, and the sexual union of man and woman is knowledge—that is, that man can know that this is why he was created: to increase the world in order that thereby, God will be more strongly blessed for the more people, the more purity and praise to God.[16]

But the dekabbalization of the text is not merely an act of omission but also of commission: in place of kabbalistic notions about the esoteric holiness of semen and of intercourse, we find inserted in the Yiddish text the concept of *tsnies*, sexual modesty. Where the Hebrew text teaches that a man should be in a state of holiness (*kedushah*) during sex, since the disposition of the child that results from intercourse depends entirely on the degree of holiness of the father, the Yiddish text adds:

> We will explain the following to you: the good or bad character of a person depends on the way his father behaved during intercourse with his wife—thus the child will follow, either good or bad. If he behaved with modesty [*betsnies*] he will have good children. If not, not. So you see that being faithful to God or defiling His name is entirely dependent on the condition of one's birth. Therefore, God commanded us and warned us to have intercourse with our wives in modesty, and with good thoughts—that is what being holy in sexual intercourse means.[17]

But it would be rash to conclude, as may be imagined, that the Yiddish translation betokens simply a resort to nonkabbalistic or even prekabbalistic conceptions of sex for the benefit of the nonilluminated masses. For there are quite definitely included in this tract ideas or beliefs that are not accessible to us from the normative sources on rabbinic views of sexuality. Several examples will illustrate this point:

1. Where the original contains a nonkabbalistic, normative discussion of the evils of sexual intercourse undertaken for the sake of sexual pleasure alone, and the parallel evil of masturbation, the Yiddish goes much further, admonishing the reader that when intercourse

is motivated solely by the *yetser horo* (the evil inclination)—a term that does not appear in the Hebrew original—by intoxication or by impudence (*azeskayt*), then the child born of this conception will be an *azes-ponim*, an impudent person, rejected by God. And more, that when intercourse takes place outside the bounds of marriage, as with the ignorant—"on khupe un kidushin, als vi der amarets tut"—no good child can result.[18]

2. Chapter 4 of the *Iggeret Ha-Kodesh* is a discussion of which foods should be eaten before sex, based on the premise that the nature of foods one consumes determines the nature of one's blood, which then determines the nature of one's semen, so that "coarse or unfit" food yields coarse and impure blood and then coarse and unfit semen, which then determines the "basis and structure of the embryo conceived by that union." Therefore, the Torah prohibited certain foods: "Some of them close up the heart, like fat and blood. Some, like predatory birds and beasts, make man arrogant. Some defy the ways of understanding and of wisdom, such as the hare, squirrel, the pig, and the like. Some bring about all kinds of evil and horrible diseases, such as the rodents of the earth and the sea."[19]

To this, the Yiddish adds, first, that such foods lead the Jews straight to hell; second, that children born of those who eat such foods are arrogant; and third and most revealing, that because of this "iz der akum fun muter layb ayn azes-ponim," Gentiles (or pagans, if one adopts a gentler reading) are arrogant from birth.[20]

3. Perhaps an even more glaring difference between the Hebrew original and the Yiddish translation emerges in their respective discussions of why Friday night is the best time for sexual intercourse. The original explains that on the Sabbath eve the intellectual and superior part of the soul is prominent, and thus intercourse at this time will lead to the birth of new souls appropriate to the service of the Lord.[21] The Yiddish takes an entirely different tack, affording a wonderful—and hitherto undocumented—gloss on the common kabbalistic notion of a *neshama yetera*, an additional soul granted to Jews on the Sabbath, and thus a fascinating glimpse into the religious universe of early modern Ashkenazic Judaism:

> And you should know that the word Sabbath means rest—
> not only referring to human rest but to divine rest as well.
> For the souls which all week long float from one celestial
> yeshiva to the next come together to rest in Heaven on Fri-
> day night not long before the Sabbath, to hear the teaching
> of the Messiah. Therefore, everyone who observes the Sab-
> bath is granted an additional soul, which we call the *neshome
> yeseyre*. This additional soul knows no sadness—it is divine,

all-knowing, and pure. And when, on that night, one possessed of this new, pure, divinely all-knowing soul has sexual intercourse, one without doubt brings into this world a good, strong, and understanding child.[22]

4. Finally, there are major differences between the ending of the Hebrew original and the Yiddish translation. The Hebrew ends simply by stating, "Therefore, examine the secrets incorporated into these chapters, and when you practice what I have taught you, I pledge that you will merit a righteous and saintly son who hallows God's name. May God in His mercy open our eyes to the light of His Torah, and enable us to perceive the secrets of His Torah, and bring into the world sons prepared to revere Him and serve Him, Amen."[23]

The Yiddish, we are by now not surprised, ignores the "secrets" and adds a messianic wish, or cliché—that proper sex will lead not only to pious and good sons but also to sons who will merit imminent redemption. And more interesting, the Yiddish text then continues with an addition not found in any other version of the *Iggeret Ha-Kodesh:* "Nun vayln mir biz her geshribn hobn vi zikh der mentsh mit zayner froy farhaltn zol, veln mir vayter oykh vos nutslikh shraybn vi zikh di froy in hoyz farhaltn zol [Now, since we have thus far written about how a man should behave with his wife, now we will write some useful things about how a woman should behave in the home]."[24]

Unfortunately, although the anonymous author goes on for three more pages, the result is anticlimatic: the only point, oft repeated, is that women should guard their tongues and not talk too much, that much evil flows from unnecessary chatter, and women should heed the warnings of the sages in their regard and speak only when it is necessary. Only when such behavior is internalized can one merit prompt redemption, and eternal life.[25]

ZOKHER HA-BERIT

The second text, in both chronological and logical progression, is *Zokher Ha-Berit,* a circumcision manual written by one of the most prolific and interesting popularizers of Judaism in the eighteenth century, Shlomo Zalman London, and published in both Hebrew and Yiddish in Amsterdam in 1703.[26]

Shlomo Zalman London was born in Novogrudok, Lithuania, in 1661, and between 1705 and 1735 he published and sold books in Amsterdam, London, and Frankfurt-am-Main. He is perhaps best known for his *Kohelet Shelomoh,* a bilingual combination prayer book and minhag manual that included, among many other things, a Hebrew-Yiddish dictionary called *Ḥinnukh Katan* and the Passover Haggadah with Leon de Modena's commentary *Zeli esh*. He also published a siddur with a Yiddish translation and the *Tikkunei Shabbat* of Isaac Luria, in addition to a host of other popular editions of major ethical and kabbalistic works.[27]

His first book, *Zokher Ha-Berit*, is fascinating first and foremost because of its very existence: although we know that there were circumcision manuals published before this time, this seems to be the first bilingual one, the Yiddish version of which can only be understood as aimed at instructing mohalim who did not understand Hebrew sufficiently to have access to the classic halakhic guides to the techniques of circumcision as well as its spiritual dimensions. The book is divided into two parts: the first, in Hebrew, is a concise guide to the techniques of circumcision and the ceremonies of the bris; the second is a much longer and more detailed Yiddish text.

Why London chose to issue this book he tells us very clearly, with substantial differences between the Hebrew and Yiddish statements of intent. In Hebrew he simply states that such a manual is vital, given the importance and holiness of its subject matter, and that he intended to write such a work for a long while, especially as he was a mohel himself from his youth on and realized the need for such a guide. Sensitive to possible objections to such a compilation, he explains further that he is providing a summary of the laws and ceremonies of circumcision because sometimes the women wait around before the child is brought into the synagogue on the day of his bris and the mohel has nothing to do but listen to them. Therefore, even the most experienced ritual circumciser can use this manual to review the laws and customs of circumcision during this time, to refresh his memory and make certain that he fulfills the relevant commandments properly and punctiliously.[28]

The Yiddish is quite different. He writes: "This work contains all the commandments of circumcision [*bris milah, priah umetsitsah*] and all the blessings and customs associated with them, and other useful things such as remedies and stories and case-histories, which *every ordinary mohel* can follow when he has need of them. He should behave in the manner herein prescribed. Thus will the book surely be worth its price, with its help he will merit blessings from God in the world-to-come, Amen."[29]

Interestingly, in the Hebrew prefatory materials London cites not only the Psalms, Talmud, and Midrash but the Zohar and Isaac Luria as well; thus, he learned from Luria that the essential point of circumcision depends on the intention—the *kavvanah*—of the mohel: "I found it written in the name of the Ari z"l that everything depends on the knowledge and [esoteric] intent of the mohel, who stands in the stead of the sacrificing priest: if he circumcises with proper intent, as explained below, the child will never contaminate his covenant, and will grow into a rabbi in Israel."[30] In addition, throughout the Hebrew text London cites kabbalistic works that advance esoteric interpretations of various aspects of circumcision—for example, a digression on the kabbalistic significance of *mezizah*.[31]

In the Yiddish version, every single one of these kabbalistic references is omitted. This is significant not only because it parallels and ratifies the censorial technique of our previous text but also because several decades later London himself became one of the most important popularizers of kabbalah, in Yiddish as well as in Hebrew. His *Kohelet Shelomoh*, first published in 1744, is shot through with references to both Lurianic and pre-Lurianic kabbalah, in the Yiddish as well as the Hebrew. But here, in the early years of the eighteenth century, he cannot yet allow any kabbalistic material or customs to seep through into Yiddish.

Instead, the Yiddish version of the manual provides citations and translations of the relevant halakhic material on circumcision from the Talmud, Maharil, Shulhan Arukh, and later Ashkenazic authorities and supplements these legal materials with a great deal of detail about local customs—minhagim that London himself observed or found described in various holy books. Thus, we are told that in Ashkenaz twelve small candles are lit in honor of the twelve tribes and placed near Elijah's seat during the bris;[32] that the blessing "Zeh ha-kise shel Eliyahu" ("This is the seat of Elijah") is expanded to read, "Zeh ha-kise shel Eliyahu malakh haberit she-yitgaleh be-meherah be-yamenu"[33] ("This is the seat of Elijah, the angel of circumcision, may he be revealed soon and in our days"); that a special blessing not found in the standard authorities is made for a child who has no father or mother; and that in some communities the infant is bathed before the circumcision to moisten the foreskin. He also gives several folk remedies to heal problems arising from circumcision. Thus, for example, "A mohel who God forbid wounded the member with a knife or fingernail must stop the blood from flowing and then apply the following treatment: he should take ten or eleven eggs and boil them well, peel them, remove the yolk, and burn them in one pan until they produce oil, then strain them through a linen cloth into one dish—it has been long established that this is better for a wound than regular oil."[34]

Frequently, London interrupts his presentation with little anecdotes about what went wrong with individual circumcisions and how experts dealt with these problems. He instructs his readers how to prepare to become ritual circumcisers and warns those already in the trade to stop practicing their craft if they are too old, their hands shake, or they cannot see well enough.[35]

Finally, we are led directly into the religious condition of early modern Ashkenazic Jewry in the following fascinating digression: at the end of the manual, London tells his readers that it is a commandment to end the circumcision ceremony with a joyous meal, to mark the importance of the event and the degree to which Jews are willing to serve God with their flesh and blood. However, he continues, oftentimes, and particularly in the countryside, at these post-bris celebrations people forget to obey other commandments: "eyn teyl layt un vayber un yunqs fresn un zoyfn zunder hent gevashn, zunder bentshn"—some of the men, women, and youths stuff themselves with food and drink, without washing their hands beforehand or saying grace afterward.[36] This, obviously, should not happen. Every mohel should make sure that all obey the laws, make the proper blessings, and say the proper prayers; that the circumcision be held during the day and not at night; and that during the celebration, the guests, hosts, and mohel not forget to say their daily prayers at the prescribed hours, so the celebration of any commandment does not become "eyn mitsveh haboa lidey aveyre," a commandment that leads to sin, as so often happens.[37]

It may well be argued that such stipulations are a product of their time: either that they betoken a heightened consciousness of laxity and even antinomianism in the wake of the Sabbatean debacle and the contemporary Frankist threat or, as several scholars would have us believe, that in early-eighteenth-century central Europe observance of Jewish law was already on the wane as a result of incipient modernity, leading inexorably to the appearance of Moses Mendelssohn, Reform Judaism, and ultimately to heresy.[38]

But it is far more likely and plausible to speculate that the two works we have looked at here lead us to quite a different conclusion, one not characterized by temporal or even geographic parameters, and certainly not by incipient modernism. Rather, the Yiddish *Iggeret Ha-Kodesh* and the bilingual *Zokher Ha-Berit* provide us with a brief peek into a religious universe that was a constant feature of Jewish life in the Ashkenazic realm, as elsewhere, in the late sixteenth century as much as in the early eighteenth. It can be described as a "continuous spectrum of religious culture" composed of Jews with a widely divergent range of intellectual and spiritual tools, codes, and myths, all of which were dedicated to pondering the meaning and significance of human life in general and Jewish life in particular. Instruction in these mysteries was provided, interpreted, and sometimes withheld, by a professional and semiprofessional clergy that itself embraced a wide spectrum of knowledge and access to holy script and was distinguished neither socially nor intellectually from the "laity" it served, nor by a receptivity to what later generations defined as magic or superstition. In the texts we have examined, it is apparent that the specific explication of the mysteries of life and the divine provided by the kabbalah were still, in the late seventeenth and early eighteenth centuries, deemed inappropriate for the relatively less tutored; but that too would change—for reasons as yet unclear—within a very short time. The fascinating customs and rituals revealed in these texts cannot be said to belong solely to a "folk religion" rejected by the rabbis, since there is no reason to assume that they were shunned in practice by an "elite"; yet, the putative silence of the normative sources with regard to these customs raises intriguing questions and possibilities. It may be possible to calibrate with the social status of their audience the Yiddish translations' more lively and palpable concern—compared with the Hebrew originals—with the social and political inferiority of the Jews vis-à-vis their Christian neighbors and the slightly more intense messianic longings expressed in these texts.

For now, though, what these texts point to in sum is a variegated, porous, and intriguing spectrum of Jewish religious culture in early modern Ashkenaz whose contours of region, class, and time have been obscured to us because of our collective ignorance but may be extracted and elucidated from the many dozens of works of Jewish "popular religion" that have yet to be studied.

Notes

I am indebted to Rabbi Jerry Schwartzbart, curator of rare books at the Library of the Jewish Theological Seminary of America, for his gracious help in identifying the works discussed in this essay, as well as many other Old Yiddish texts in the seminary's possession.

1. Arnaldo Momigliano, *Essays in Ancient and Modern Historiography* (Middletown, Conn., 1977), 156.
2. These comments and those that follow on the conceptualization of "popular religion" are a slightly revised version of those I made in my article "The Yiddish 'Shevet Yehudah': A Study in the 'Ashkenization' of a Spanish-Jewish Classic," in *Jewish History and Jewish Memory: Studies in Honor of Yosef Hayim Yerushalmi*, ed. Elisheva Carlebach, John Efron, et al., 134–49 (Hanover, N.H., 1998).
3. See, e.g., Yisroel Zinberg, *Di geshikhte fun der literatur bay yidn*, vol. 6 (Buenos Aires, 1961); Sh. Niger, "Di yidishe literatur un di lezerin," in *Bleter geshikhte fun der yidisher literatur* (New York, 1959), 35–107; and

Max Erik, "Bletlekh tsu der geshikhte fun der eleterer yidisher literatur un kultur," *Tsaytshrift* 1 (1926): 173–77.

4. See, e.g., Solomon Freehof, "Devotional Literature in the Vernacular," *CCAR Yearbook* 3 (1923): 375–415; and the literature cited in Herman Pollack, *Jewish Folkways in Germanic Lands, 1648–1806: Studies in Aspects of Daily Life* (Cambridge, 1981), and Joshua Trachtenberg, *Jewish Magic and Superstition: A Study in Folk Religion* (Philadelphia, 1961).

5. Khone Shmeruk, *Sifrut Yiddish: Perakim le-toledoteha* (Tel Aviv, 1978); Khone Shmeruk, *Sifrut Yiddish be-Folin* (Jerusalem, 1981); Hava Turniansky, "Ha-'bentsherl' ve-ha-zemirot beyidish," *'Alei Sefer* 10 (1982): 51–92; Hava Turniansky, *Sefer masah u-merivah 387 (1627)* (Jerusalem, 1985); Sarah Zfatman, *Ha-siporet be-yidish me-reishitah 'ad Shivhei ha-Besht, 1504–1814* (Jerusalem, 1985); Sarah Zfatman, "Mekor u-mekoriut be-'Mayse-Bikhl' ha-kadum be-yidish 'Mayse Vestindie' Prag 1665—mikreh mivhan," in *Ke-minhag Ashkenaz u-Folin, Sefer yovel le-Hone Shmeruk*, ed. Y. Bartal, H. Turniansky, and E. Mendelsohn (Jerusalem, 1993).

6. Chava Weissler, "The Traditional Piety of Ashkenazic Women," in *Jewish Spirituality from the Sixteenth-Century Revival to the Present*, ed. Arthur Green, 245–75 (New York, 1987); Chava Weissler, "The Religion of Traditional Ashkenazic Women: Some Methodological Issues," *AJS Review* 12 (1987): 73–94; Chava Weissler, "For Women and for Men Who Are Like Women," *Journal of Feminist Studies in Religion* (Fall 1989): 7–24.

7. See Shmeruk's "Di mizrekh-eyropeishe nuskhoes fun der Tsenerene," in *For Max Weinreich on His Seventieth Birthday*, 320–36 (The Hague, 1964); see the intriguing comments on this work by Julius Carlebach, "Family Structure and the Position of Jewish Women," in *Revolution and Evolution: 1848 in German-Jewish History*, ed. Werner E. Mosse et al., 156–88 (Tübingen, 1981).

8. On this enormous topic, see, inter alia, Rosalind Brooke and Christian Brooke, *Popular Religion in the Middle Ages* (New York, 1983); Jacques Le Goff, *Time, Work, and Culture in the Middle Ages* (Chicago, 1980); and perhaps most influential in America, Keith Thomas, *Religion and the Decline of Magic* (New York, 1971). For a critique of their approach, see Peter Brown, *The Cult of the Saints: Its Rise and Function in Latin Christianity* (Chicago, 1981), esp. 21–23; John Van Engen, "The Christian Middle Ages as an Historiographical Problem," *American Historical Review* 91 (1986): 519–52; and from yet another perspective, Thomas Kselman's introduction to his *Belief in History: Innovative Approaches to European and American Religion* (South Bend, Ind., 1991), and Natalie Zemon Davis, "From 'Popular Religion' to 'Religious Cultures,'" in *Reformation Europe: A Guide to Research*, ed. Stephen Ozment, 321–41 (St. Louis, 1982).

9. This despite the success of Polish Jewry in creating the Vaad Arba Arazot, the Council of the Lands, the most extensive supracommunal agency in post–Gaonic Diaspora Jewish history. Yet the Vaad was es-

sentially a lay organization without any halakhic authority. I am most indebted to my student Professor Edward Fram for his comments on this matter in an earlier discussion of this point.

10. See the revealing, if problematic, piece by Chava Weissler, "Women's Studies and Women's Prayers: Reconstructing the Religious History of Ashkenazic Women," *Jewish Social Studies* 1 (Winter 1995): 28–47.

11. The Yiddish title is *Sefer Igeres ha-koydesh* (hereafter cited as *SIH*). I used the copy in the Library of the Jewish Theological Seminary of America.

12. Seymour Cohen, introduction to his edition of *Iggeret Ha-Kodesh*, 22.

13. Monford Harris, "Marriage as Metaphysics: A Study of the '*Iggereth Hakodesh*,'" *Hebrew Union College Annual* 33 (1962): 200–205. Harris's study is the most complete and revealing analysis of this work.

14. This is the traditional title page, in Hebrew as well as in *SIH*.

15. Cohen, *Iggeret Ha-Kodesh*, 48–49.

16. *SIH*, 7.

17. Ibid., 3, cf. Cohen, *Iggeret Ha-Kodesh*, 36–38.

18. *SIH*, 10.

19. Cohen, *Iggeret Ha-Kodesh*, 94–96.

20. *SIH*, 18–19.

21. Cohen, *Iggeret Ha-Kodesh*, 70–72.

22. *SIH*, 13.

23. Cohen, *Iggeret Ha-Kodesh*, 154–55.

24. *SIH*, 29.

25. Ibid., 29–31.

26. I used the Jewish Theological Seminary's copy of the second edition of the work, published in Amsterdam in 1709–10 as *Zokher Ha-Berit* (hereafter cited as *ZHB*). For bibliographical data, see Z. Ben-Yaakov, no. 82, 154; and Steven M. Lowenstein, *Blätter für jüdische Geschichte und Litteratur* (N.p., 1904), 21.

27. On London, see *Encyclopedia Judaica*, 11:484–85.

28. *ZHB*, 3a.

29. Ibid., 9b, emphasis added.

30. Ibid., 1b.

31. Ibid., 4a–4b.

32. Ibid., 9b–10a.

33. Ibid., 10a.

34. Ibid., 12b.

35. Ibid., 13b.

36. Ibid., 16a–16b.

37. Ibid., 16b.

38. See Azriel Shochat, *'Im hilufei tekufot* (Jerusalem, 1960); and David Sorkin, *The Transformation of German Jewry, 1780–1840* (New York, 1987).

Michael Stanislawski

| 3 |

THE CONSTRUCTION OF
MODERN JEWISH HISTORY

Analyzing the Zeitgeist

Ludwig Philippson as Historian
of the Modern Era

CHRISTHARD HOFFMANN

In his seminal study *The Origins of the Modern Jew,* Michael A. Meyer
has shown how the processes of integration and acculturation of Jews
in Germany in the late eighteenth and early nineteenth centuries created the problem of Jewish self-definition in the modern world. Faced
with the dissolution of their traditional life conditions on the one hand
and the enticing promises of liberation, participation, and fraterniza-
tion of mankind on the other, how could Jews preserve a Jewish identity, how could they conciliate Jewishness and modernity? This essay
will take up these general questions by analyzing the development of
Jewish historical consciousness in the nineteenth century as represented in the work of Ludwig Philippson.

    One of the central issues in the encounter of early-nineteenth-
century German-Jewish thinkers with modernity was the relationship,
or more precisely the connectability, between the (Jewish) past and the
modern era. Out of a variety of answers to this question, three ideal
types can be distinguished:

    1. The "modernists," represented mostly by radical liberal reformers,
    identified the modern age as "Jewish," that is, as the fulfilment of
    ancient Jewish principles and promises.[1] They described Jewish

emancipation with biblical metaphors: as an exodus from Egypt or even as the beginning of the messianic age.[2] The relationship between past and present was expressed in antithetical terms originating from the Enlightenment, such as bondage versus liberation, isolation versus participation, or intolerance versus freedom of thought, which emphasized the discontinuity between the ghetto period and the present—or, rather, between the ghetto period and the anticipated future. History appeared largely as a negative foil in contrast to which progress became visible. Only the present and the future were seen as meaningful for the formation of a modern Jewish identity.

2. The "traditionalists," represented largely by neo-orthodoxy, held that Judaism stood above history, and therefore it could not be adjusted to the "spirit of the time" without losing its substance.[3] They sharply differentiated between internal and external spheres, between the unchangeable realm of the religious law on the one side and the vicissitudes of time and history on the other. Modernity and its achievements, such as emancipation, were firmly placed in the latter realm; they were part of the "material state of affairs" (*äußeres Geschick*) of the Jews, thus being of minor significance for Judaism itself.[4] The religious law, revealed at Sinai, was considered the only source of Jewish identity.

3. The "historicists" were represented mostly by moderate liberals and conservatives ("historical Judaism"). They saw Judaism as a living organism developing over time in contact with the surrounding world. The key term in the historicist view was "evolution." It expressed continuity within change and integrated a wealth of individual historical facts into a meaningful whole.[5] Making all of Jewish history the basis for Jewish identity, the historicists relativized the significance of the modern era, seeing it just as the most recent phase of an open-ended historical process. While the historicist approach allowed for a plurality of Jewish identities based on history and for a flexible response to the changes of time, it could also be seen as relativistic and without clear contours.[6] In practice, the historicist approach was therefore often found in combination with some element of essentialist attribution, defining the unchangeable core of Jewish identity either with respect to the past (as the traditionalists), or with respect to the present (as the modernists).

As the founder and long-term editor, from 1837 to 1889, of the most important Jewish newspaper in Germany, the *Allgemeine Zeitung des Judenthums (AZJ)*, as a (moderate) Reform rabbi, as a politician, scholar, and author of literary works, Ludwig Philippson was one of the most

Christhard Hoffmann

influential personalities of German Jewry in the emancipation period.[7] With his credo that the "unified essence [*einheitliche Wesenheit*]
of Judaism can only be established for certain by the totality of its
history," he firmly belonged to the historicists' camp.[8] He wanted to
be neither a "eulogist of the past" nor a "glorifier [*Verherrlicher*] of the
present."[9] In his journalism, often commenting on unfolding events,
Philippson was critical in identifying the general characteristics of his
time, thus imparting a sense of historical development to his readers.
Philippson was certainly not shy about his accomplishments. Criti-
cizing the representatives of the *Wissenschaft des Judentums* for antiquarian ivory tower learnedness detached from Jewish life, he claimed
to have done more himself for the formation and development of a
historical consciousness among Jews than all these scholars put together.[10] For Philippson, the foundation of true scholarship was Jewish life. He considered only those periods of Jewish history valuable in
which this life had developed itself into a new fullness, and only those
historical personalities and works of lasting merit that had "awakened,
nurtured, improved, and transfigured this life."[11]

Scattered as they are within his huge journalistic work, Philippson's contributions as chronicler and interpreter of the modern era
(*Neuzeit*) have never been specifically dealt with. They can only be
properly understood in the context of his general conception of history, which was shaped by the historicism and the dialectical thinking of his time. Its keys are the ideas of evolution and progress. For
Philippson, evolution is "the true law of humanity, since mankind is
a constantly growing totality . . . throughout the ages."[12] The drive of
historical development originates from the antagonism of antithetical
principles, such as the medieval principle of separation and the modern principle of participation, or the medieval principle of authority
and the modern principle of criticism. By the struggle between these
opposing principles, history gains momentum leading to the victory
of one principle over the other, or to the emergence of a new synthesis.
In Philippson's view, the ideal development proceeded along an evolutionary middle course, whereas revolutionary extremism necessarily gave rise to reactionary counteracting forces and thereby retarded
history's natural progress.[13] As was typical for the German historicist
tradition of his time, Philippson's conception of history shows a certain tension between deterministic and voluntaristic elements. On the
one hand, referring to the iron laws of history, he presents the struggle
between antagonistic principles as necessary and inevitable; on the
other hand, by juxtaposing evolution and revolution, he constructs an
ideal, organic path of development that could guide meaningful action
in the present and thus possibly influence the outcome of history.[14]

Given his universal approach to history focusing on the development of mankind from antiquity to the present, Philippson's understanding of the modern era is largely historical. Modernity is subjected to the same laws of development as the previous periods of history. Its specific character is shaped in contradistinction to the principles of the Middle Ages and can best be described with dichotomies such as participation versus separateness, equality versus inequality, criticism versus authority, constitutionalism/democracy versus absolutism, or civil society versus corporative state.[15] While Philippson certainly viewed the modern development toward participation and equality as progress compared with the Middle Ages, his assessment was rather dispassionate and did not reflect the enthusiasm of the liberation versus bondage rhetoric of the modernists. Rather it expressed scepticism about the unchecked tendency of the modern age, pointing to its totalitarian and oppressive potentiality. Writing at the time of the 1848 revolution, Philippson cautioned against the one-sidedness of the modern principle of equality that was about to level religious, spiritual, and proprietary differences:

> We can recognize here that the tendency of the modern age developing progressively in the same way as the tendency of the Middle Ages did towards division and inequality, will just as much lead to pressure and subjugation as that one. . . . The full and unrestricted tendency of the modern era would lead to a different form of oppression of society— under some organization of equality based on the power of the masses. Like in the Middle Ages, it would embody its own downfall, but in this case the decline would probably come true faster.[16]

In spite of his critical analysis, Philippson was optimistic that the modern age would escape the fate of the Middle Ages and avoid its own downfall: the progress of civilization, especially the higher cultivation of the mind (*Geistesbildung*), the mature consciousness (*Bewußtsein*), and the strongly developed sense of justice (*Rechtsgefühl*) would counterbalance the one-sided tendency of the period and prevent an extreme course of development.[17] Philippson's actions as a public figure followed consistently from this assessment of the situation; for example, he advocated social reforms in order to keep the lower classes from revolutionary activities.[18]

In Philippson's interpretation of the modern era, revolutions form the negative pole. In particular, the French Revolution is portrayed as an eruption of violence that prevented the realization of the

Christhard Hoffmann

promises of the Enlightenment and retarded the progress toward humanity that already had come a long way:

> Civilized Europe would be happier if a French Revolution had never occurred: then the redemption, the fulfilment of the big promise would have come! But that sharp terrible break, that eruption shaking the world, that sudden bold stroke tearing to pieces European society taking everything away from one in order to give it all of the sudden to the other . . . this French Revolution threw "humanity" from its sparkling throne, made it a weapon of one party, . . . stretched and crushed the evolution to death; and even if it spread many ideas faster and wider than otherwise would have happened, it did not help any of those to triumph since it filled them into the cannons and fixed them as bayonets.[19]

In the same way, the revolution of 1848, acting with impetuosity and lack of system, did not achieve its goals but had to give way to an equally passionate political reaction. The deadlock between equally extreme revolutionary and reactionary forces brought the organic development of life to a standstill. But since such a situation was unbearable in the long run, it would eventually give way to a period of compromise. With respect to his own time, Philippson was convinced that such a development would be beneficial in the end. Since the whole evolution was "nothing other than a continuous compromise between the past and the future, giving scope for the old to die in peace and for the new to prepare its birth," progress would materialize by way of compromise, toning down the extremes and making the new finding its definite form.[20]

Philippson illustrated the opposite paths of evolution and revolution by pointing to the different developments of Britain and France in modern times. Whereas the British people, regardless of social class, political orientation, or national background, stood united in their respect for the country's constitution and carried out only those changes and reforms that were in concord with the constitutional tradition, France had been split since the Revolution by terrible internal struggles and upheavals, swinging from one extreme to the other. The cause of these different outcomes, Philippson maintained, was simply that Great Britain had been shaped by a "natural historical evolution," while France had not.[21]

Looking at history in a dialectical fashion, Philippson viewed the modern era not only as opposed to the Middle Ages, but he realized that the developed principles of modernity also generated new antagonisms and countermovements. The modern tendency toward internationalization with global communication, worldwide traffic, and free trade was counteracted by the principle of nationality (*Nationalitäten-prinzip*), which demanded political independence and sovereignty for each ethnic group.[22] Other opposites were capitalism versus socialism, or materialism versus idealism.[23] In this way, by struggling between opposing forces, history proceeded indefinitely.

How did modernity shape the history of Jews and Judaism? For Philippson, Jewish history was subjected to the same tendencies and laws of development as general history. The epochal transformation from medieval to modern principles, from corporate state to civil society, from inequality to equality, had to change the legal and social status of the Jews in a fundamental way: after having lived in antiquity *as* a nation and during the Middle Ages *among* the nations, they now lived for the first time *as part of* the nations, incorporated into their civil and political life.[24]

Jewish emancipation was embodied in the enlightened principles of "true liberalism," and its realization was dependent upon the power and vitality of liberal politics. If liberalism failed, the equal status of Jews would be restricted again or even rescinded as was shown during the nineteenth century when reactionary governments, as soon as they took power, limited the rights of the Jews.[25]

Before acquiring legal equality, Jews had advanced their internal emancipation, or "self-emancipation," by actively participating in the social and cultural life of their environment and by critically reviewing and reforming their religious tradition.[26] For Philippson, it was a necessary consequence of the modern principle of participation that Judaism had to prove its worth and significance before the tribunal of a critical public, and he committed himself to that task.[27] He was convinced that the process of criticism would bring about a reformation of Judaism, purifying the law from unnecessary additions and bringing to light its true "Mosaic" essence. In the question of reform, Philippson pursued a moderate middle course between radical reformers and conservatives. As in general history, he saw the extremes as harmful to the natural progress of historical evolution and, again, he put contemporary ills, that is, the inner conflicts and factionalism of modern Jewry, down to the destructive effects of the French Revolution: in promising liberation from an age-old bondage it encouraged many Jews to give up their Judaism completely. This, in turn, led to the other extreme—the artificial revival of a Jewish Orthodoxy that had in fact long been proven outdated by the course of history: "One extreme was countered by the other in all its enormity: boundless overthrow of the law, total destruction of the historical ground, most impertinent derision of the whole historical consciousness on the one side had to be met by a rigid fettering and fossilization, a vapid perseverance and heartless obstinacy mounting to fanaticism on the side of Old Orthodoxy. . . . From this, the conflicts within Judaism and Jewry originate."[28] Philippson was also well aware of the fact that the secularizing and egalitarian tendencies of the modern age had a corrosive effect on Jewish particularity, and he tried to counter this development by promoting knowledge about the Jewish past among German Jewry.[29]

With history proceeding in a dialectical way, one extreme giving birth to the opposite one, how could progress actually come about? Did the Modern Age really represent a higher stage of human development than antiquity or the Middle Ages? Why did liberalism fail? These questions were crucial to the public debate in Germany after the abortive revolution of 1848–49, and Philippson also discussed them frequently in his *Allgemeine*. Since he had been skeptical of the desirability of a revolution from the outset, he was probably less disappointed and pessimistic than others when it actually failed.[30] In any case, he came out as a forceful defender of the idea of historical progress.[31] To be sure, Philippson too expressed his disappointment about the politically backward movement of the restoration years, in particular with respect to Jewish emancipation.[32] Time and again, he noted the intricacy of the present situation, the "true chaos of phenomena and movements," the "confused muddle of forwards and backwards."[33] Living on the "ship of the nineteenth century" meant struggle and suffering in rough weather, with no view of the sought-after harbor.[34] At the same time, Philippson insisted on viewing current events in historical perspective: "The moment puzzles, time illuminates."[35] Contrasting the present state of Jewish affairs with that a half-century earlier, he confirmed tremendous changes and transformations for the better.[36] The achievements of the modern era, such as the abolition of serfdom and slavery, of absolutism and censorship, and the initiation of religious freedom and equal rights, were beyond recall and constituted a solid foundation for the future.[37] In a series of public lectures on "the results in world-history," delivered in Magdeburg at the end of 1860, Philippson substantiated this optimistic conception of history.[38] Even in the 1880s, when the pogroms in Russia and the emergence of modern antisemitism indicated the return of the Middle Ages in the nineteenth century, he did not abandon his belief in progress.[39] The evolution of mankind toward humanity, he reassured his readers, did not proceed in a straight line, but often followed a zigzag between opposite extremes.[40] Temporary retrogressions would only reinforce the need for reforms thus strengthening progress in the end. A total downfall of civilization, comparable to the victory of the barbarians over Rome in late antiquity, was inconceivable in the present. Even if individual countries might betray the principles of humanity, mankind as a whole could not.[41]

For Philippson, the aim of historical evolution embodied the materialization of those social principles that had been revealed in Mosaism and that were preserved and spread by Judaism throughout history.[42] Assessing the modern era by this standard, he was able to recognize the work of Providence and the progress of mankind. Accordingly, he reminded his readers that the events of the day should not be judged according to the one-sided standpoint of whether or not they were beneficial for the civic emancipation of the Jews but rather by the yardstick of the "great social principles of Mosaism," which included emancipation.[43] As a Mosaic principle, the idea of emancipation was seen as universal, not limited to Jewish history but extending over the whole world. When, in May 1865, the victory of the Northern states in the American Civil War became evident, Philippson wrote an editorial under the headline "The Two Greatest Events of Our Century."[44] In it, he argued that the abolition of serfdom in Russia and the end of slavery in the United States were the two most important single events of the nineteenth century. They should not only be seen as "victory of personal freedom and human dignity" but also as "victory of the Mosaic over the pagan principle." Philippson went on: "Yes, it is the Mosaic principle, that has come to final victory in both events. Drawn from a country where the whole people had become serfs, Mosaism did not tolerate serfdom on its own soil. . . . Mosaism is the only religion which has proclaimed and executed this principle as a religious one. More than three millennia have passed by since then, but it grew stronger and stronger over time and it guarantees by its successes that it will rule all over the world some day."

In another example of the same argument, and despite his strong reservations against the French Revolution, Philippson praised the French National Assembly for enacting in 1789 the "Mosaic principle" of equality before the law, thus "laying the foundation stone of our present-day status in social and civic life."[45] He even quoted appreciatively a non-Jewish French author who claimed that the Jews viewed the French Revolution as "predisposed in Hebraism," as an "unconscious execution of Isaiah's will," and who considered the belief in progress of mankind a "Jewish idea."[46] Also other political reforms of the day, such as the introduction of freedom of trade or the abolition of the secular power of the clergy, were welcomed by Philippson as inspired by "Mosaic principles."[47] He thus identified "the social and political principles and doctrines of Judaism with those of mod-

Christhard Hoffmann

ern liberalism"—despite his critical reservations, in particular cases, against liberalism's secularist politics that he regarded as restrictive of the freedom of religion.[48] In Philippson's view, which at this point reflected largely the modernist position, the materialization of liberal principles was tantamount to the mission of Judaism. Jews could feel at home in the country of modernity.

In studying the encounter of Judaism with modernity, one of the crucial questions is that of perception: What did Jews actually think modernity was? How did they relate it to Jewish religious tradition and history, thereby constructing new forms of Jewish identity? The rigid normative views of both modernists and traditionalists—both those essentializing modernity and relativizing the past and those essentializing tradition and relativizing the present—did not, in the long run, allow for a flexible and differentiated response to the changes and challenges of the modern age. Understanding these changes as part of a universal historical process (evolution), however, made it possible to mediate between tradition and renewal and to define Jewish identity historically, that is, as dependent on context and open to change.

The historicist approach did not only relate to the past. The present day was also to be understood historically in order to give orientation and enable meaningful action in contemporary society. This function of historical consciousness is clearly evident in the writings of Ludwig Philippson. Historicizing the modern era inevitably meant to relativize its significance and to critically reassess its achievements. By integrating modernity into the stream of history, Philippson helped to overcome the one-sidedness of both modernists and antimodernists and presented a more colorful, contradictory, and realistic image of the contemporary period. But Philippson was not just an observer. He did not record the changes of time as if he had no share in it. His perception and interpretation of the modern era were shaped (and limited) by his religious worldview, which equated the essence of Judaism with the general social and political principles of liberalism and sustained his optimistic belief in progress and humanity.

NOTES

1. See Michael A. Meyer, "Modernity as a Crisis for the Jews," *Modern Judaism* 9 (1989): 151–64, here 160–61.
2. See, e.g., Gotthold Salomon, *Israels Erlösung aus Druck und Knechtschaft, oder auf welchem Wege können wir zu einer würdigeren Stellung in der bürgerlichen Gesellschaft gelangen? Predigt am Peßach-Feste* (Hamburg: Hartwig Müller, 1829); [Moritz Samuel] Freystadt, "Der Messias," *Sulamith*

8 (1838): 224–26.

3. See, e.g., Samson Raphael Hirsch, "Der Jude und seine Zeit," *Jeschurun* 1 (1854–55): 14–25; Abraham Levi, "Weltgeschichte-Judentum [poem]," *Jeschurun* 10 (1864–65): 234–36.

4. Ben Usiel [i.e., Samson Raphael Hirsch], *Neunzehn Briefe über Judenthum* (Altona: Hammerich, 1836), 83; English translation in Rabbi Samson Raphael Hirsch, *The Nineteen Letters on Judaism*, prepared by Jacob Breuer (Jerusalem: Feldheim, 1969), 112.

5. On the history and use of the term *evolution*, see Wolfgang Wieland, "Entwicklung," in *Geschichtliche Grundbegriffe. Historisches Lexikon zur politisch-sozialen Sprache in Deutschland*, vol. 2, ed. Otto Brunner, Werner Conze, and Reinhart Koselleck, 199–228 (Stuttgart: Klett-Cotta, 1975), 201–2.

6. On the later criticism of Jewish historicism by German-Jewish thinkers, see David N. Myers, *Resisting History: Historicism and Its Discontents in German-Jewish Thought* (Princeton: Princeton University Press, 2003).

7. On Philippson, see Meyer Kayserling, *Ludwig Philippson: Eine Biographie* (Leipzig: Mendelssohn, 1898); Johanna Philippson, "Ludwig Philippson und die Allgemeine Zeitung des Judentums," in *Das Judentum in der Deutschen Umwelt, 1800–1850. Studien zur Frühgeschichte der Emanzipation*, ed. Hans Liebeschütz and Arnold Paucker, 243–91 (Tübingen: Mohr, 1977).

8. Ludwig Philippson, "Vorlesungen über Geschichte, Inhalt, Stellung und Beruf des Judenthums," *AZJ* 11 (1847): 1–4 and 17–20, here 3.

9. Ludwig Philippson, "Eine schöne Erscheinung aus der neuern Zeit," *AZJ* 36 (1872): 119–22, here 119.

10. Ludwig Philippson, "Wissenschaft und Leben," *AZJ* 20 (1856): 619–20.

11. Ibid.

12. Ludwig Philippson, *Die Religion der Gesellschaft und die Entwickelung der Menschheit zu ihr* (Leipzig: Baumgärtner's Buchhandlung, 1848).

13. Ludwig Philippson, "Ein Blick auf die Weltlage," *AZJ* 29 (1865): 373–77, here 376–77.

14. See Reinhart Koselleck, "Geschichte, Historie," in *Geschichtliche Grundbegriffe*, 2:647–717.

15. See, e.g., Ludwig Philippson, "Unsre Zeit," *AZJ* 12 (1848): 493–95; Ludwig Philippson, "Das neunzehnte Jahrhundert," *AZJ* 40 (1876): 671–73; Ludwig Philippson, "Die Wandlungen in der neueren Zeit und im Judenthume," *AZJ* 39 (1875): 115–18.

16. Philippson, "Unsre Zeit," 494.

17. Ibid., 495.

18. On Philippson's social thought, see Uriel Tal, "German-Jewish Social Thought in the Mid-Nineteenth Century," in *Revolution and Evolution: 1848 in German-Jewish History*, ed. Werner E. Mosse, Arnold Paucker, and Reinhard Rürup, 299–328 (Tübingen: Mohr, 1981); and the comment by Michael A. Meyer in Mosse, Paucker, and Rürup, *Revolution*

and Evolution, 329–35.
19. Ludwig Philippson, "Das vorige und gegenwärtige Jahrhundert," *AZJ* 17 (1853): 367–68, 379–81, 405, and 446–47, here 380–81.
20. Ludwig Philippson, "Ein Blick auf die Gegenwart," *AZJ* 29 (1865): 373–77, here 377.
21. Ludwig Philippson, "Politische Briefe," *AZJ* 28 (1864): 171–73, 187–90, and 203–6, here 204–5. See also Ludwig Philippson, "Einige Blicke auf die Weltlage," *AZJ* 25 (1861): 45–47, 59–61, and 79–80, here 79–80.
22. Ludwig Philippson, "Ein Brief über die Politik in der Gegenwart," *AZJ* 30 (1866): 127–30, 143–46, 160–62, and 241–43, here 128–29.
23. See, e.g., Ludwig Philippson, "Der Classenkampf in Deutschland," *AZJ* 42 (1878): 369–71, 385–87, 401–3, and 417–20; Ludwig Philippson "Ist die Tendenz unsrer Zeit wirklich eine materialistische?" *AZJ* 24 (1860): 1–3.
24. Philippson, "Vorlesungen," 19.
25. Philippson, "Ein Brief über die Politik der Gegenwart," 241–42.
26. Ludwig Philippson, "Das Judenthum und die Emanzipation," *AZJ* 14 (1850): 29–31, here 30.
27. See, e.g., Philippson, "Vorlesungen," 1–2.
28. Ludwig Philippson, "Das vorige und das gegenwärtige Jahrhundert," *AZJ* 17 (1853): 447.
29. See, e.g., Philippson, "Wissenschaft und Leben," 619–20. See Nils Roemer, *Jewish Scholarship and Culture in Nineteenth-Century Germany: Between History and Faith* (Madison: University of Wisconsin Press, 2005).
30. See, e.g., Philippson, *Religion der Gesellschaft,* 168.
31. See, e.g., Ludwig Philippson, "Der Fortschritt," *AZJ* 17 (1853): 253–54; Ludwig Philippson, "Die fortschreitende Entwickelung," *AZJ* 22 (1858): 57–60; Ludwig Philippson, "Die fortschreitende Entwickelung," *AZJ* 48 (1884): 49–52, 65–67, 81–83, 97–99, 129–31, 145–47, and 161–63.
32. Ludwig Philippson, "Kurzer Rückblick auf 1850 und 1800," *AZJ* 15 (1851): 13–14, here 13.
33. Ludwig Philippson, "Von der Nothwendigkeit des Judenthums," *AZJ* 22 (1858): 627–30, here 628; Ludwig Philippson, "Unser Jahrhundert," *AZJ* 34 (1870): 717–21, here 721.
34. Philippson, "Das neunzehnte Jahrhundert," 673.
35. Ludwig Philippson, "Wie hat der religiöse Sinn die Weltbegebenheiten zu beurteilen?," *AZJ* 15 (1851): 25–26, here 26.
36. Philippson, "Kurzer Rückblick auf 1850 und 1800," 14.
37. Ludwig Philippson, "Eine Zeitbetrachtung," *AZJ* 42 (1878): 193–94, here 194.
38. Ludwig Philippson, *Ueber die Resultate in der Weltgeschichte* (Leipzig: Baumgärtner, 1860).
39. Ludwig Philippson, "Das Mittelalter im neunzehnten Jahrhundert," *AZJ* 47 (1883): 611–14. A close reading of Philippson's articles does

not support Roemer's statement (*Jewish Scholarship*, 92) that "the *Allge-meine* . . . maintained that anti-Semitism and the decline of religiosity had wrecked the promises offered by the modern era."

40. Ludwig Philippson, "Die Humanität," *AZJ* 48 (1884): 1–2.
41. Philippson, "Die fortschreitende Entwickelung," 163.
42. Ludwig Philippson, "Einige sociale Fragen der Gegenwart, vom Mosa-ismus entschieden," *AZJ* 26 (1862): 515–17; Ludwig Philippson, "Politi-sche Fragen vor dem Forum des mosaischen Rechtes," *AZJ* 26 (1862): 621–23, here 621.
43. Philippson, "Einige Blicke auf die Weltlage," 45–46, 59–61, 79–80, here 45.
44. Ludwig Philippson, "Die beiden größten Ereignisse unseres Jahrhun-derts," *AZJ* 29 (1865): 283–85.
45. Ludwig Philippson, "Das Centenarium von 1789," *AZJ* 53 (1889): 49–50, here 50
46. Ludwig Philippson, "Das Judenthum und 1789," *AZJ* 53 (1889): 494–96.
47. Ludwig Philippson, "Staat und Religion, die religiöse Gesellschaft," *AZJ* 53 (1889); Ludwig Philippson, *Weltbewegende Fragen in Politik und Religion; Erster Theil, Politik* (Leipzig: Baumgärtner, 1868), 105; Philipp-son, "Einige Blicke auf die Weltlage," 59–61.
48. Ludwig Philippson, "Der Liberalismus und das Judenthum," *AZJ* 36 (1872): 441–43, 463–66, and 501–4, here 441.

German Historians and the Jews

Peter Pulzer

One of the main concerns of German-Jewish historiography in our times has been the encounter of the Jews of central Europe with modernity. It is difficult to think of any living scholar who has made a more notable contribution to our understanding of it than Michael Meyer. One need only mention his calling card to the profession, *The Origins of the Modern Jew*, and the later *Response to Modernity* and *Jewish Identity in the Modern World* to appreciate the effect he has had on both sides of the Atlantic. From the mid-eighteenth century onward Jews could not avoid facing the challenges posed by modernity, whether this took the form of the Enlightenment, revolution, Romanticism, or nationalism. They responded in a wide variety of ways, ranging from ultra-Reform to neo-orthodoxy; to all of these Meyer has done ample justice. There is, however, a reciprocal aspect to this face-to-face relationship, namely, the encounter of modernity with the Jews. This too was far from uniform. For many luminaries of the Enlightenment, Jews were a relic of the past, backward and tradition-bound in their beliefs and their occupational structure.[1] As such, they were an anomaly in the modern world, to be either rejected or forcibly assimilated into the modern European world.

To some Romantic nationalists who, however strongly they might be attached to the legacy of the past, also constituted a form of modernity, Jews were the enemy within, a "state within the state," alien and unassimilable. But there were also those in various German states, as well as Austria, France, and the Netherlands, who saw in the defects of the Jews a reflection of the defects of the societies in which they lived. For figures as different as Christian Wilhelm Dohm and Wilhelm von Humboldt the reform of the Jews, their emancipation from their misery and superstitions, was contingent on the general reform of the states and societies in which they lived. However patronizing these attitudes might seem to the observer in the twenty-first century, what distinguished them from the competing prescriptions of their time was that they took the Jews of their time seriously. As these advocates saw it, Jews had survived and had come to stay. The best thing that could happen to them and to those they lived among was that they become full citizens. This recognition had a further consequence. If the Jews of the Christian era were merely an anomaly and an anachronism, then the history of postbiblical Jewry would be of no interest. If, however, postbiblical Jewry retained a collective legitimacy, that would put its history in a different light.

An early indication of this revised view came from an unexpected quarter. On February 27, 1792, Johann Kaspar Schiller wrote to his son Friedrich, then a professor of history at Jena, "As far as I know we have no complete or coherent history of the Jewish people since its dispersion throughout the world. It seems to me that this would be an important as well as worthy topic to occupy a scholar, who would, however, need learned Jews by his side to supply him with materials. A skillful working out of this would incidentally be of great interest to Christianity."[2] There are both modern and archaic elements in the elder Schiller's advice. On the one hand he assumes that the postbiblical history of the Jews has intrinsic value and that it could be written only by Jewish and Christian scholars in collaboration. On the other he also assumes the existence of a separate Jewish people that, while living among the Christian peoples of Europe, does not form part of them. The younger Schiller had in fact anticipated his father's suggestion, but his interest was restricted to Moses the Egyptian rather than Moses of Dessau. In his lecture "Moses' Mission," delivered in 1790, he acknowledged the contribution of the Jewish religion not only to the doctrine of monotheism but to the Enlightenment of his own time. The Jewish past, in other words, was relevant to the present: "The nation of the Hebrews must appear as an important, universally historical people and everything that is bad that is customarily said about this people, all attempts by witty minds to diminish it will not stop us from treating it justly. . . . We must value them as an unclean and common receptacle, but in which something very precious was preserved; we must honour them for being the conduit, however unclean it may have been, that providence chose to deliver to us the noblest of all properties, the truth." He nevertheless declared that this Jewish mission was now over; the Diaspora marked the exit of the Jews from history.[3]

Both the elder and the younger Schillers' preoccupation with Jewish history occurred at a time when, first in Germany and then in France, the question arose how Jews could reenter history. If either Jews or gentiles were to concern themselves with the future of the Jews, in particular with a future that would put an end to their centuries-long exclusion, then their history would once more have to be taken seriously. Two hundred years later this future, too, has become the past. In the aftermath of the *Shoah* Hannah Arendt concluded that the task of investigating the "altogether unique phenomenon [of] the German-speaking Jews and their history . . . can be attacked only now, after the history of the German Jews has come an end."[4] In the half-century that has elapsed since she passed this judgment, the revival of Jewish life in Germany renders Arendt's premise in need of revision. German-Jewish historiography has certainly flourished since 1945, whether in journals, monographs, or collective works. The fact that the German version of the four-volume *German-Jewish History in Modern Times*, edited by Meyer, was adopted by a major book club and is now available in paperback shows that interest in this subject, and above all the assumption that German history without Jews is incomplete, has spread beyond professional specialists into at least a part of the general reading public in Germany and elsewhere. Yet there is a curious uncertainty about the exact status of the subject of our inquiries. In a ceremony in Bonn in 1997, our collective work (the four-volume history mentioned earlier) was presented under the title "Jewish History in Germany—Germany in Jewish History." In the *Encyclopaedia of German History*, published by Oldenbourg, however, Shulamit Volkov's volume is titled *Die Juden in Deutschland, 1780–1918*, while that by Moshe Zimmermann is titled *Die deutschen Juden, 1914–1945*. Even within one and the same book we come across contradictory categorizations. The volume edited by Dirk Blasius and Dan Diner bears the subtitle "Leben und Selbstverständnis der Juden in Deutschland," while the chapter by Rainer Walz is titled "Lage und Selbstverständnis der deutschen Juden im 16 Jahrhundert." What is going on here? Is there a German-Jewish history? A Jewish history in Germany? A history of the Jews of Germany? A history of German Jews? A Germany in Jewish history?

Up to the middle of the eighteenth century the question would not have been worth asking. We know a good deal about the history of Jews in Germany over the millennium-and-a-half from Roman times to the Enlightenment, even if there is some uncertainty over how continuous this Jewish presence was. We know about some of the eminent Jews of medieval Germany, like Charlemagne's ambassador Isaac of Aachen and the learned lawyer Joseph ben Gershon (Yosel of Rosheim), but the eminence of these elite figures, who feature so proudly in Jewish accounts of the period, merely emphasizes how exceptional they were. There is also evidence for contact and interaction lower on the social scale. The periodic prohibitions by ecclesiastical and lay authorities of marriages between Christians and Jews or of the employment of Christians by Jews suggest that these practices were quite common. One does not have to forbid actions unless they occur. The same applies to the Jewish anathemata against converts to Christianity and the decrees by Duke Frederick II of Austria against the ill-treatment of Jews. So too after the Reformation and Counter-Reformation, even after the virtual ghettoization of Jewish populations, it is difficult to imagine the history of the German states without their Jews. This applies to the so-called court Jews—bankers, tax collectors, mintmasters, and military furnishers—as well as to the grain merchants, cattle dealers, peddlers or the underworld of jugglers, mountebanks, beggars, and thieves. Some court Jews played a crucial role in European history, like Behrend Lehmann, without whose millions Augustus the Strong of Saxony could not have acquired the Polish crown. Others exemplified what a dangerous game theirs was. The Brandenburg mintmaster Lipman ben Juda and the court factor Joseph Süß Oppenheimer of Württemberg became legendary in a different way. Falling out of favor after the deaths of their patrons, both suffered gruesome public executions. They became cult figures for engravers and ballad singers, but this was not the same as featuring in a systematic history of German Jews. That did not as yet exist.

Nor were these court Jews the antecedents of the later assimilated Jews of western and central Europe. While some of them continued to observe their religion in a traditional way, others acquired the style and culture of their employers. They abandoned traditional clothing, shaved off their beards, and had their portraits painted. They could write and converse in perfect literary German. Some of them converted to Christianity; a few acquired titles of nobility. Their aim was to distinguish themselves from the mass of the Jewish population, not to act as a role model for them. Nevertheless, the emergence of this stratum, as well as a small number of educated bourgeois, means that we can now pose our central questions: When did the Jews of Germany become German Jews, or at least when did they want to do so?

And when, if at all, were gentile Germans, prepared to reciprocate?

The first stirrings of a movement for Jewish integration occurred at a time when there was not yet a fully developed German national consciousness. For many enlightened gentile Germans the solution lay in a cosmopolitan ethical humanism, as with Gotthold Ephraim Lessing, whose Nathan the Wise wants to transcend his and the Templar's religion so as to become "ein Mensch." And Wilhelm von Humboldt's prescription for Jews to become Christians is another form of universalistic redemption. It was Moses Mendelssohn who first hinted at the concept of the Jew as German, when he reprimanded his antagonist Johann David Michaelis for contrasting Jews with Germans rather than with Christians.[5] When a German national consciousness did emerge, during and after the Napoleonic wars, this development was not favorable to Jewish aspirations. Inspired by Romanticism, this reaction against the Enlightenment rested on the doctrine of the Christian state, thereby reemphasizing the distance between Christians and Jews. Gone were the days when the leading maskilim met on equal footing with Lessing, Johann Caspar Lavater, and Friedrich Nicolai, or when Salomon Maimon and Lazarus Bendavid were welcome contributors to Schiller's periodical Die Horen. Following the temper of the times, Jewish advocates of civil equality now moved from the appeals to natural law that had prevailed during the Enlightenment to a claim of membership in the German nation. No one expressed this more clearly than Gabriel Riesser, the father of the emancipation movement: "We are not immigrants, we are native-born [he wrote in 1833 in a submission to the legislators of Germany], and because that is what we are, we have no claim on any other homeland; we are either Germans or we are homeless. . . . We want to belong to the German fatherland; we shall belong to it throughout."[6]

One of the consequences of the turn to Romanticism was a greater interest in the past, in particular the national past. But Jews entered the German national past only slowly, and how they did this often reflected the political predilections of each particular author. The initiative came from the Jewish side in the creation of the Association, later the Academy, for the Scholarship of Judaism in 1819 and in the comprehensive histories by Isaac Jost, Abraham Geiger, and Heinrich Graetz.[7] Significantly, these works were written in German, the language of the Jewish Enlightenment, by authors who held no positions at German universities. They were aimed at a well-defined and limited audience; theirs were books by Jews about Jews for Jews, which was one of the reasons that they did not initially find a wider echo.

Christian scholars who took postbiblical Judaism seriously tended to have a liberal political agenda. The clearest example of this was to be found in *The History of the Jews*, by the dean of St. Paul's Cathedral in England, Henry Hart Milman, first published in 1829. The third edition of 1863, titled *The History of the Jews from the Earliest Period down to Modern Times*, was subsequently reissued in numerous abridged and popular editions until well into the twentieth century. To "work on the hereditary religious pride of the Jews," Milman argued that Christianity "must put off the hostile and repulsive aspect which it has too long worn; it must show itself as the faith of reason, of universal peace and good-will towards men."[8] To demonstrate how deserving the Jews of his day were of this reformed attitude, he concluded, "the History of the Jews will be fitly closed by a brief and rapid view of the services (the intellectual services, exclusive of those connected with the industry and commerce of the world) rendered to mankind by this remarkable race during the ages which they have passed through, . . . services either direct and manifest, or through remoter influences more difficult to trace in their effects on the knowledge, civilisation and humanity of the world."[9]

Two German scholars who followed the elder Schiller's advice in consulting Jewish colleagues were the Tübingen theologian August Friedrich Gfrörer and the legal historian Johann Ernst Stobbe. Like Milman, they had a clear political agenda. Gfrörer supported Jewish emancipation and called for a reformation of attitudes toward the Jews of his day: "One cannot examine the character of the Jewish people without a glance at its present-day condition and what else beside blame and accusation against our own cruelty. Let us cease treating the Jews as white negroes, then they will no longer hate us as tyrants or deceive us as fools. . . . This must change: we want to treat them as fellow-citizens, they must do the same!"[10] He also found praise for the mildly liberal 1818 law on Jews in Württemberg, concluding optimistically that "a more intimate contact between Jews and Christians, which the law must bring about, would end the senseless hatred of each against the other."[11] Thirty years later Stobbe, unlike his predecessor and indeed unlike Jost and Graetz, concentrated on the Jews of Germany in the Middle Ages, significantly referring to them as "German Jews" as often as "Jews in Germany."[12] He saw his mission as didactic in two ways, first since "works on the history of the Jews are so little known in non-Jewish circles that even the educated . . . have an incomplete acquaintance with the history of this people in Germany."[13]

Also, his account of the legal disabilities under which Jews lived is what one would expect of a nineteenth-century liberal: "It has been left to our century to grant them a home and the equal protection of the laws. It will be only a short while [he was writing in 1866, three years before the enactment of complete civil equality by the Reichstag of the North German Confederation] before the equality of civil and civic rights will not be subject to manifold restrictions even for Jews, but will become true." He did warn, however, that "much was still lacking" in the full realization of emancipation.[14]

Many other accounts of the place and role of Jews in German history were unfavorable and designed to further the antisemitic agenda that was increasingly part of the postunification nationalist consensus. The prime, but not the only, example of this trend was Heinrich von Treitschke. He saw the attempt by Jews to enter civil and intellectual society on an equal footing as destructive of German culture, and he evoked the threat of a "German-Jewish hybrid culture." Yet his demand that the Jews "should become Germans and feel themselves simply and straightforwardly German" was unconvincing; if half the faults he attributed to Jews were genuine, they would not manage the metamorphosis in a hundred years.[15]

These contradictory trends point to a familiar and unresolved question. Gershom Scholem formulated it by questioning whether there had ever been a German-Jewish symbiosis or even a German-Jewish dialogue. The concept of such a dialogue is surely misleading, for it assumes what it is meant to demonstrate, namely, that Germans and Jews were recognizably separate categories. It is precisely this separateness that many German Jews of the imperial and Weimar periods, from Hermann Cohen downward, would have denied. What could occur, and to a limited extent did occur, was a Jewish-Christian dialogue, though it was at times an uncomprehending and bad-tempered one. The best example for the years before 1914 was the one in which the church historian and liberal Protestant Adolf von Harnack and the young Leo Baeck were the protagonists.[16] Harnack's *Das Wesen des Christentums*, which was a worldwide bestseller for over three decades, was designed to establish the radicalism of the historical Jesus. While much of his quarrel was with Catholicism rather than Judaism, he caused much offense among Liberal Jews precisely because of his own liberal starting-point, for his argument, for all his innovative apparatus, was bound to lead to familiar conclusions about the aridity of the Jewish religion at the time of Jesus and its anachronism thereafter. It was precisely this point that Baeck disputed, in what began as a journal article, then appeared in book form in 1905 as *Das Wesen des Judentums* and developed into his life's work, pointing to the intimate links between Jesus and rabbinical Judaism.

Yet Harnack and Baeck were like ships in the night, passing each other unseen. In this respect Harnack's liberal Protestantism differed from that of his mid-century predecessors whom we noted earlier.

While his dismissal of modern Judaism could be exploited by anti-semites inside and outside the Protestant Church, he himself must be acquitted of any such intention. But unlike Gfrörer or Stobbe, he was profoundly uninterested in what his Jewish contemporaries thought. His copy of *Das Wesen des Judentums* remained uncut in his library.[17] Harnack's influence remained strong, representing as it did a variant on the dominant opinion of the time. It echoed the reason that the leading Orientalist Julius Wellhausen had given some years earlier for ignoring the postbiblical period. With its decision "to preserve itself according to the letter," Wellhausen argued, "Judaism closed itself off. The voluminous Jewish literature of the Middle Ages cannot really be regarded as a product with genuine roots."[18]

Though Liberal Judaism and liberal Protestantism would never converge, their relationship could take forms other than the Harnack-Baeck encounter, as in the various efforts to establish chairs in Jewish subjects at German universities. In the emancipatory atmosphere of 1848, the first proposal by Leopold Zunz to seek a chair of Jewish history and literature at Berlin that would symbolize the new equality of all faiths foundered, not least on the opposition of Leopold von Ranke.[19] Later attempts from the liberal Protestant side also had a political intent. In response to the ritual murder affair in Konitz in 1900, the theologian Hermann Strack proposed the creation of a chair of Jewish literature, religion, and history, given "the ignorance of the educated classes and above all the clergy concerning Jewish problems."[20] The most serious attempt in this direction came in the proposal by Martin Rade in 1912 to create a faculty of Jewish theology at the newly founded University of Frankfurt. This was partly in recognition of the role of Jewish philanthropy in its establishment, partly because of his own interest in the deconfessionalization of modern culture, but above all because he respected the *Wissenschaft des Judentums* as speaking for the "living religion . . . of 600,000 German citizens" and hoped to end the habit of "viewing and treating the Jews as an alien people."[21] This too came to nothing, as did the further initiative in 1915 of Max Löhr for a chair specifically for the *Wissenschaft des Judentums* to be devoted to "the whole post-biblical, including mediaeval Judaism" so as to bring about "an enlightening understanding of the unique historical appearance of Jewry."[22]

That all these initiatives failed is significant, but so is the fact that they were made at all. What their proponents shared was the assumption that the meaningful history of the Jews had not come to an end with the fall of Jerusalem, that Jewish thought and beliefs had continued to develop in the Diaspora, and that with the coming of civic equality the time had come to integrate Jewish scholarship into the academic mainstream. Put differently, they accepted the existence and indeed the future of the German Jew—a standpoint that could not be in greater contrast with that of Harnack, for whom Christianity represented "a liberation from historical Judaism and its outdated religious laws."[23]

There was some further progress in Jewish-Christian rapprochement during the Weimar period, though this was counteracted by the growing ideological polarization of the time.[24] Academic positions in Jewish studies were established in a number of universities, though these were in the main devoted to ancient Judaism. Exceptionally, Martin Buber lectured at Frankfurt and Adolf Kober at Cologne on postbiblical Jewry. There was only one tenured position in this discipline held by a Jew, Lazar Gulkowitsch, who was appointed to a chair at Leipzig in 1932. Literary collaboration also improved. The Protestant reference work *Die Religion in Geschichte und Gegenwart* contained articles by Ismar Elbogen, Leo Baeck, and other representatives of the *Wissenschaft des Judentums*. The fourth edition of the Catholic encyclopedia *Der Große Herder*, part of which was published after the Nazi assumption of power, contained numerous bibliographical references to works by Jewish authors. In return, special issues of Martin Buber's periodical *Der Jude* and the *C.-V.-Zeitung* contained contributions by Christian as well as Jewish authorities. Indifference toward the Jewish component of Germany's cultural heritage was not, however, restricted to gentiles. On March 27, 1942, Victor Klemperer, the son of a rabbi, a convert to Protestantism and married to a Christian wife, confided to his diary that only through reading Elbogen's history of the Jews in Germany had he become aware of the extent of nineteenth-century antisemitism: "Of all of this I knew little; nothing, perhaps did not want to know anything about it. Nevertheless: I *think* German, I *am* German—I did not give it to myself, I cannot tear it from myself."[25]

Since 1945 there has been a surge in German-Jewish historiography for which the Leo Baeck Institute deserves much credit, though aspects of this trend are problematic. For instance, while the proliferation of chairs in Jewish history at German universities ensures that the subject is no longer ignored, this does not guarantee its integration into the general historical discourse. Postwar German historians have not found it easy to see "German Jews as Jews and German Jews as Germans [as] two sides of a coin," in Michael Meyer's formulation.[26] While Golo Mann recognized in 1958 that what Germans thought about Jews revealed much about the condition of Germany, he had very little to say about Germany's Jews.[27] Even a fairly recent standard work, Thomas Nipperdey's three-volume history of the nineteenth century, treats Jews in separate sections devoted to religious minorities. It is only with Hans-Ulrich Wehler's *Social History of Germany* and Heinrich August Winkler's account of the modern period that Jews appear fully in the dramatis personae. The same applies to some of the excellent local studies and accounts of associational life that have appeared in the last ten years or so.

The story of the integration of Jews into the German historical narrative is one of two steps forward, one step back. There was the Enlightenment phase, with its message of common humanity but lack of sympathy with historically determined Jewish peculiarity. There was the revolutionary phase, in which Jews were to be the beneficiaries of the Rights of Man, but which came to an end with the defeat of the endeavors of 1848 – 49. There were the efforts of individual liberal Protestants to reprieve the Jews of their day from the patronizing dismissal of their significance and dignity through a serious and scholarly study of the life and thought of postbiblical Jewry. These approaches were at all times contested, and many contemporaries thought that the experience of the Third Reich meant that all that had gone before had been in vain. The conscientious historian has to see the German Jew as a moving target. Nobody has pointed this out better than Meyer, stressing that "as Jewish integration proceeds during the nineteenth century . . . in most instances the Jew as Jew gives way more and more to the Jew as German. The composition of the image is altered as German elements merge with or displace Jewish ones."[28]

As a warning against all generalizations, whether those of unilinear progress or of foreseeable disaster, let us end by considering an obscure episode involving the German-Jewish historian Raphael Straus, who was commissioned by the Union of Bavarian Jewish Communities to compile a documentary compendium on the history of the Jews of Bavaria. In recommending his admission to the archives the director, Dr. Otto Riedner, stated fully in the spirit of Johann Kaspar Schiller: "His intention is to be warmly welcomed. Preparatory work of this kind is essential for any account of the history of the Jews in Bavaria. It will at the same time be of value for Bavarian and German history."[29] The date of the recommendation is March 24, 1933. What can we conclude from this little correspondence? That we can all have a go at forecasting the future: the real challenge consists in being able to prophesy the past accurately.

NOTES

1. E.g., Immanuel Kant, *Religion within the Limits of Reason Alone*, trans. and ed. Theodore M. Greene and Hoyt H. Hudson (New York: Hudson, 1960), 116 – 21; Georg Friedrich Wilhelm Hegel, "The Spirit of

Christanity and Its Fate," *Early Theological Writings*, trans. T. M. Knox (Chicago: University of Chicago Press, 1948), 177–205; François Marie Arouet de Voltaire, *Essai sur les Moeurs et l'Esprit des Nations et sur les pricipaux Faits de l'Histoire depuis Charlemagne jusqu'au Louis XIII* (Geneva, 1756; Paris: P and F Didot, 1802). See also Jacob Katz, *From Prejudice to Destruction: Anti-Semitism 1700–1933* (Cambridge: Harvard University Press, 1980), 34–47; and Arthur Hertzberg, *The French Enlightenment and the Jews* (New York: Columbia University Press, 1968), 268–313.

2. Norbert Oellers, "Goethe und Schiller in ihrem Verhältnis zum Judentum" in *Conditio Judaica: Judentum, Antisemitismus und deutschsprachige Lteratur vom 18. Jahrhundert bis zum ersten Weltkrieg*, ed. Hans Otto Horch and Horst Denkler (Erster Teil Tübingen: Niemeyer, 1988), 109.

3. Friedrich Schiller, "Die Sendung Moses'," *Historische Schriften* (Nationalausgabe XVII), vol. 1 (Weimar: Insel, 1970), 377–78.

4. Hannah Arendt, *Rahel Varnhagen: The Life of a Jewess* (London: East and West Library, 1957), xiii.

5. Moses Mendelssohn, "Anmerkungen zu des Ritter Michaelis Beurtheilung des ersten Theils von Dohm, Über die bürgerliche Verbesserung der Juden," *Gesammelte Schriften*, vol. 3 (Leipzig: Brockhaus 1843–45), 367.

6. Gabriel Riesser, "Vertheidigung der bürgerlichen Gleichstellung der Juden gegen die Einwürfe des Herrn H. E. G. Paulus. Den gesetzgebenden Versammlungen Deutschlands gewidmet," *Gesammelte Schriften*, vol. 2 (Frankfurt am Main: Riesser-Stiftung, 1867–68), 133, 183–84.

7. Isaac M. Jost, *Geschichte de Israeliten seit der Zeit der Maccabäer bis auf unsere Tage*, 10 vols. (Berlin: Schlesinger, 1820–47); Abraham Geiger, *Das Judentum und seine Geschichte von der Zerstörung des zweiten Tempels bis zum Ende des zwölften Jahrhundert* (Breslau: Schletter, 1865–71); Heinrich Graetz, *Geschichte der Juden von den ältesten Zeiten bis auf die Gegenwart*, 11 vols. (Leipzig: Leiner 1853–75).

8. Henry Hart Milman, *The History of Jews from the Earliest Period down to Modern Times*, 3rd ed. (London: John Murray, 1863), 3:424–25.

9. Ibid., 426.

10. August Friedrich Gfrörer, *Geschichte des Urchristentums* (Stuttgart: E. Schweizerbart, 1838, Erste Abtheilung), xxvii.

11. Ibid., 206.

12. Otto Stobbe, *Die Juden in Deutschland während des Mittelalters in politischer, socialer und rechtlicher Beziehung* (Braunschweig 1866): "deutsche Juden," v, 8; "Juden in Deutschland," vii, 193.

13. Ibid., vii.

14. Ibid., 193, viii.

15. Heinrich von Treitschke, "Unsere Aussichten" *Preußische Jahrbücher*, September 15, 1879, 573.

16. Adolf von Harnack, *Das Wesen des Christentums. Sechszehn Vorlesungen*

vor Studierenden aller Facultäten im Wintersemester 1899/1900 an der Universität Berlin (Leipzig: J. C. Hinrich, 1900); Leo Baeck, *Das Wesen des Judentums* (Berlin: Nathansen and Lamm, 1905).

17. Christian Wiese, "Ein unerhörtes Gesprächsangebot: Leo Baeck, die Wissenschaft des Judentums und das Judentumsbild des liberalen Protestantismus," in *Leo Baeck 1873–1956. Aus dem Stamme von Rabbinern,* ed. Georg Heuberger and Fritz Backhaus (Frankfurt am Main: Jüdischer Verlag, 2001), 168n33.

18. Julius Wellhausen, *Israelitische und Jüdische Geschichte* (Berlin: Georg Reimer, 1894), 342.

19. Hans Liebeschütz, *Das Judentum im deutschen Geschichtsbild von Hegel bis Max Weber* (Tübingen: J. C. B. Mohr, 1967), 64–66.

20. Günter Brakelmann, Martin Greschat, and Werner Jochmann, *Protestantismus und Politik. Werk und Wirkung Adolf Stoeckers* (Hamburg: Christians, 1982), 234n212.

21. Christian Wiese, *Wissenschaft des Judentums und protestantische Theologie im wilhelminischen Deutschland: Ein Schrei ins Leere?* (Tübingen: J. C. B. Mohr, 1999), 335–40.

22. Ibid., 346–55.

23. Harnack, *Das Wesen des Christentums,* 108.

24. For an overview, see Henry P. Wassermann, *False Start: Jewish Studies at German Universities during the Weimar Republic* (Amherst, N.Y.: Humanity Books, 2003).

25. Victor Klemperer, *Ich will Zeugnis ablegen bis zum Letzten. Tagebücher 1933–1945,* vol. 2 (Berlin: Aufbau Verlag, 1995), 56.

26. Michael A. Meyer, "Jews as Jews versus Jews as Germans: Two Historical Perspectives," intro. to *Leo Baeck Institute Year Book XXXVI* (1991), xvii. Reprinted in Michael A. Meyer, *Judaism within Modernity: Essays on Jewish History and Religion* (Detroit: Wayne State University Press, 2001), 76–86.

27. Golo Mann, *Deutsche Geschichte des 19. und 20. Jahrhunderts* (Frankfurt am Main: S. Fischer, 1958), 466–68, 470–71.

28. Meyer, "Jews as Jews," xxii.

29. Christian Wiese, "Zwiespalt und Verantwortung der Nähe," *Kalonymos,* 7. Jg., Heft 3–4, 5.

10

The "Return of the Jews to History"

*Considerations about
an Ideological Concept*

EVYATAR FRIESEL

Considering the central place that historical awareness has in modern Jewish thought, it is no wonder that reflections about the place of the Jews in history provide an important theme for Jewish intellectual discourse. The topic looms large in the work of Michael Meyer, and in the thirty years I have been privileged by Michael's friendship the theme has frequently come up in our conversations.[1]

As a concept, the return of the Jews to history represented one of the answers—a Jewish one—to questions about the status of the Jewish *ethnie* in modern Europe. Supposedly, the Jews had left history at some point in the remote past, but were returning to history in modern times. From a contemporary perspective, that formulation presents a riddle: like several other intellectual notions in Jewish life of the first half of twentieth century, the idea of such a return has lost much (if not all) of its significance. A symposium held in Jerusalem on the theme in 1997 was emblematic. The resulting volume brought about thirty worthy contributions of outstanding Israeli scholars dealing with different historical periods and perspectives, but the only essay that focused directly on the theme was S. N. Eisenstadt's introduction; otherwise the subject remained largely unaddressed, at least in the sense of where the issue stood two generations earlier.[2] Apparently, Jewish intellectual interests have turned to other directions.

Looking back, what was the general ideological background of such a "return to history"? And if views have changed, what understanding about the historical situation of the Jews has established itself in our days?

Before its so-called emancipation, Jewish society lived in a framework where present life was rigorously prescribed by religious obligations inherited from the past, with past and present bound to a messianic vision of the future. The inroads of modernization, which rocked centuries-old patterns of relation between the Jews and the peoples in whose midst they lived, also posed before Jewish society new questions about the characteristics of its group identity. In an evolving reality where Jews gradually became citizens of European states, the self-centered Jewish historical vision of old was inevitably due to collapse.

What exacerbated the situation was that early modern reflections about the place of the Jewish people in history arose from among thinkers of the general milieu—indeed, much of the intellectual impetus relating to the theme originated from non-Jews. The European Enlightenment produced a long and distinguished line of new secular or semisecular considerations about the historical condition of the Jews—a long and distinguished line, perhaps, but from a Jewish point of view hardly a soothing one. Arnold Toynbee's twentieth-century pronouncement that the Jews were a historical fossil, which became the object of angry retorts (to my best knowledge, *all* of them produced by Jews), was rooted in related views of European thinkers since the late eighteenth century.

The stock phrase "the return to history" of the Jews was mainly of Zionist coinage. Although embedded in a broadening study of Jewish history according to methods that Jewish intellectuals absorbed from European higher learning, the formulation reflected Zionist confrontation with those (Jews as well as non-Jews) who denied or limited a specific Jewish presence in modern social and political life. The conceptualization of the Jewish presence in history involved, then, two uneasily related parts: first came the gentile formulation about the exit of the Jews; much later came the Zionist idea of their return. Up to a point, a "return to history" implicitly accepted the claim (of a highly doubtful ideological pedigree) of a former "exit." However, the Zionist assertion about the return was only indirectly related to the original intention of the concept. The Zionist emphasis was on the present; as a well-defined people the Jews should become full and active participants in modern life in all its expressions, including within the framework of an independent state. The connection to the Jewish past fulfilled for the Zionists an ideological function, albeit an essential one: history was the justification for the establishment of the renewed political entity of the Jews in *Eretz Israel,* the Land of Israel.

Even when Jews and non-Jews arrived at diverging views about the historical conundrum of the Jews, the terms of intellectual reference on both sides were broadly related, since both sides employed similar tools of historical analysis and interpretation. However, this very approach, according to which the Jews were considered in terms of belonging or not belonging to history collapsed in recent times, because of developments that reflected intellectual trends in western academic circles regarding history as a humanistic discipline.

The historical calling was subjected in recent decades to a spirited assault from different quarters of the academy: from the social sciences, economics, the behavioral sciences, and especially from philosophy. The very sense of history as an academic discipline was questioned. Methods of historical work were critically analyzed, dissected, deconstructed. What happened is apt to cause uneasy reflections about modern ways of humanistic thought and work. The critique against history as a scientific discipline moved between the self-proclaimed walls of constructionism, deconstructionism, and reconstructionism, one learned scholar feeding his learned comments on the comments of the learned scholar before or beside her, and ultimately reaching the conclusion that the past and the historical description of the past are different things.

The critics declared that the past was unreachable and that the very formulation of attaining a "reality" of days gone through its textual description was an illusion, one that, so the implication, no truly reflective person should be caught at. Every description of the past, it was stressed, is but an artificial creation, a genre of literature, sometimes good, sometimes less so, but basically a literary construction. The hallowed reliance of historians on documentary evidence was compared to the imaginary clothes of the emperor in Hans Christian Andersen's fairy tale.

In fact, the main guns of the critique were directed less toward historical science in general than against the most ambitious branch of the discipline, historicism. Historicism not only laid claim to the elucidation of supposed laws regarding the development of human societies but dangled also before all those interested the daunting possibility that the right elucidation and interpretation of the past, and of the nexus between this explained past and the present, established the possibility to foresee and even to plan (at least in a general way) the developments of the future. Such a positivist frame of mind was built on the convictions of the Enlightenment and its main pillars, such as rationalism, the belief in progress, and the trust in the positive nature of mankind. However, the miseries of the two world wars in the first half of the twentieth century worked havoc on such certainties and caused an understandable intellectual wariness, not to say demoralization, among western thinking persons. The confidence that history may provide a key to the foreknowledge of human social evolution was one of the many creeds that collapsed in the intellectual reassessment that began already in the wake of the havoc brought by World War I and imposed itself with additional cogency after World War II, at least in the western noncommunist world.

THE CASE OF THE JEWS

In the large framework of these academic debates the issue of the return of the Jews to history occupied, obviously, only a very small corner—small but significant for those who were engaged in the intellectually uphill task of trying to formulate a comprehensive view about the present-day condition and prospects of the Jewish people. According to the opinion that the past cannot be presented as a cognitive reality since it is only an exercise in literary creativity, the idea of a return of the Jews to history appeared as little more than an ideological lucubration. If so, what to do about the fact that in the Jewish case the historical connection was related to far-reaching practical consequences, as an indispensable ideological component of an ultimately successful political movement, Zionism? Here, a perceived past was the basis for present collective action. Furthermore, it was an approach that enjoyed international endorsement; as the 1922 preamble of the League of Nations–sponsored British mandate for Palestine stated, "recognition has thereby been given to the historical connection of the Jewish people with Palestine and to the grounds for reconstituting their national home in that country."

One answer was that the Jews had never left history and in their particular way had participated, over the centuries, in the historical development of the societies in whose midst they lived—a pattern that was repeating itself in the changing conditions of modern times. In its most comprehensive way, that approach was elaborated in the early twentieth century by the Jewish historian Simon Dubnow. Another response stated, along classical Zionist logic, that with the creation of Israel the Jews had returned to history and were now a people as normal as any other.

A majority of the participants at the 1997 symposium mentioned earlier tended to the first possibility, although most were closer to a

Zionist view of modern Jewish life. Apparently the general collapse of the historicist approach has dimmed also in Jewish quarters the idea of a "return to history" bound to some idealistic meta-historical scheme. It seems that by the end of the twentieth century diverse Jewish ideological orientations have met in a pragmatic view about the contemporary situation of the Jewish *ethnie*. It was accepted that a part of the Jews lived in a Jewish state, a part in the Diaspora (the question if this meant "exile" or "dispersion" lost relevancy), and the old principle of *Klal Israel* (of which "Jewish peoplehood" is a most appropriate translation) retained much of its classical significance.

NEO-HISTORICISM AND THE JEWS

Thus we may summarize the Jewish perspective. From a non-Jewish angle, however, the issue of the historical ways of the Jews—especially in the vital Israeli community, has for many remained an issue still open. In terms of historical analysis, in recent years a worrying dichotomy has developed between major Jewish and major non-Jewish approaches, foremost regarding the State of Israel, although the diverging opinions also reflect on the Jews in general. One might believe that a supposedly objective stance would recognize the Zionist enterprise in Palestine as one of the most original human developments of modern times. The successful creation of a new Jewish society built on and by immigrants arriving from all over the world, rooted in very diverse cultural and political traditions, has no parallel in modern human experience. In a land with few natural resources and surrounded by enemies, the new Israelis created a democratic society with a quality of life, a level of education and an economic structure comparable to mid-echelon European countries. The State of Israel demonstrates the vitality of the Jews as a group and its tenacious attachment to the land of its origins, Eretz Israel. Israel represents an astonishing adaptation of the Jews to modernity in terms of Jewish collective existence, including a political framework.

Against that view, however, an opposite one emerged in recent decades, shared by Muslims all over the world. For Muslims the creation of Israel is a wrong against the Arab nations, perpetuated in a land that supposedly did not belong to the Jews and to the detriment of a defenseless local native population—a wrong, then, whose correction (or even punishment) justifies far-reaching means. True, a measure of understanding has been reached between Israel and some of its Arab neighbors. Diplomatic relations have been established with Jordan and Egypt, and limited political contacts exist also with other Muslim countries. Hopefully, similar arrangements will be reached with the Palestinian Authority, which aspires to create a Palestinian state. Nevertheless, at this time the confrontation continues mostly unabated.

In spite of its bitterness, the conflict between Israel and the Arab nations is basically a political one about legitimate ownership of the land. The ideological reverberations of that struggle appear, at least so far, as a result rather than a cause of the struggle. If so, a political solution might point a way out of the conundrum, an opinion that is shared by more reflective persons of both sides. As the saying goes, the devil is in the details, but at least there is a common broad strategic view about the problem.

In comparison, between the Christian West and the Jews there were in the past, including the fairly recent one, deep-rooted tensions of a basically religious and later ideological character that caused more than one catastrophe for European Jewry. It is argued that in our days those strains have been put to rest. Have they? The religious and ideological differences between the Christian West and the Jews may have reached a laudable low point—but has an alternative and more positive view about the Jewish condition established itself in western understanding? If not, then in moments of stress the differences of old, deeply rooted and basically ideological in character, are apt to flame up again. From a Jewish perspective, that matter is a vital one: in the developing tensions between the West and Islam, it is on the western side that contemporary Jewry, however defined and organized, wants and needs to find place, recognition, and support.

Have those differences of old really disappeared? Comments about the wisdom or lack of wisdom in creating a Jewish state in Palestine are not uncommon in the European press and public opinion. Well-intentioned people in western countries, many of them with academic credentials, dwell in sober and measured words on the amount of injustice that Israel has caused the Palestinians, the unsettling factor that a Jewish state represents in a Muslim Middle East, the dangers that the Israeli-Arab confrontation may represent to world peace. Who knows, it is mused, if the creation of a Jewish state was not a mistake. The sober and measured words do not extend to whatever hardships the Jews may have experienced in over half a century of conflict in Palestine. And hanging unformulated in the air is the corollary to all this: if an error was committed, in a rational world it is desirable to correct mistakes, is it not? Now, if the observation is made that this whole train of thought, from the first sentence onward, is contaminated (in many cases unconsciously) by a contemporary strain of Jew-hatred, that such a logic is sowing the ideological justification for a new Holocaust, the reaction is (mostly) wide-eyed astonishment. Historicism may be discredited as an intellectual tool, but Israel still remains the object of historicist-like pronouncements. Opponents of Jewish statehood in the Muslim world and doubters in the Christian West indulge, in spite of their differences, in plans regarding "what to do" about the Jewish state. Such a frame of mind and expression is apparently unique in contemporary political thought and unheard of even regarding present-day states that in international political opinion are classified as "failed." At the end of the day, broad sectors of general society seem still fixed to the terms of reference regarding the Jews established by the European Enlightenment in the late eighteenth century: if and how the Jews belong to history. Now, the true implication of the question has become clearer. It is not "in history" that the presence of the Jews is questioned but in actual, present-day life.

The renaissance of the Jewish community in the historical Land of Israel has proved immensely fruitful in the Jewish sense, both in Israel and in the Jewish Diaspora. And yet, in terms of the relationship between Jews and non-Jews, all this has insufficient positive reverberations. The Jews seem unable to find an undisputed place among the peoples of the earth. They were an irritant in nineteenth- and twentieth-century Europe. As represented by the most vital public creation of modern Jewry, Israel, they are an irritant in the twentieth- and twentieth-first-century Middle East. According to the Zionist prognosis, a Jewish state should bring about the so-called normalization of the Jews and put an end to the "Jewish problem." Obviously, neither happened, at least not regarding Israel. The creation of Israel, it turns out, may express the ultimate modernization of the Jews, but it did not make the Jewish condition any easier: Jewish statehood has become a focus of tension between Jews and non-Jews as severe and as dangerous as antisemitism of old.

An alternative view of the Jewish reality in present times has to be offered, one that is persuasive also from a general, non-Jewish perspective. True, against deep-rooted prejudice rational argument is mostly powerless. But there are sectors in general public opinion that honestly and without bias inquire about the present situation of the Jews, their achievements and their problems. Their inquiries deserve elucidation.

This is not an easy task. The chronicle of Jewish life in the seven or eight decades from the late nineteenth century to the middle of the twentieth century is a chaotic mixing of outward and inwardly pulling tendencies, where each decade produced new sociological shades, where the burden of migration added a potent element of existential unsettledness and the darkening clouds of antisemitism a vital threat. A historical perspective, from the still relatively short distance of our era, suggests that this period was the most turbulent time in Jewish history since the upheavals at the end of the Second Temple period two thousand years ago.

In such a situation, how did it happen that the Jews were able to create an independent state, and more, in a place where only a few Jews lived at the beginning of the modern age? Certainly, it was not because Zionism brought the Jews "back to history." The Jewish people never left history in the sense that European historians and philosophers suggested from the Enlightenment onward. On the contrary, a convincing reason for modern Jewish achievement is that Jewish society was very much a part of current life and well endowed with the social means to benefit from the developments of the last two centuries.

It is not the case, as has been claimed by both gentiles and Jews, that after the Holocaust the peoples of the world, supposedly moved by remorse, decided to compensate the Jews with a state. Such a line of reasoning is simplistic, to say the least. Instead, Jewish statehood was established *in spite* of the destruction of European Jewry. The Zionists were able to establish and to defend a state at the hour of utmost prostration of the Jewish people, which seems to strengthen the view that the Jews were well prepared, in spite of all obstacles, for the opportunities of the modern age.

The destruction of European Jewry in the mid-twentieth century beclouds the fact that Jewish social, economic, and cultural integration in the Western world had extremely successful aspects. Indeed, a major cause for the flare-up of antisemitism in the nineteenth and the twentieth centuries was the social and economic achievements of the Jews. Regarding the Zionist movement, the suggestion is here offered that Zionism did well in the first place because it was part and parcel of upward-directed Jewish society.

This, of course, is by far not the whole reason. There were also other ideological tendencies in modernizing Jewry, and in principle they all benefited from the positive trends in Jewish life. The evolving Jewish society was not a monolithic ideological bloc, quite the contrary. Few ages in the long history of the Jews produced such an array of diverse and clashing internal positions, each with its own social and ideological program, most of them either opposed to or untouched by the Zionist analysis of the Jewish condition, and especially by the political consequences envisaged. There were the so-called (by the Zionists) assimilationists, who sought to integrate along the paths opened by the modernization of western society in their respective general societies in Europe or in the Americas. Or the members of the powerful Jewish labor movement that developed in eastern Europe, who defended their own prognosis about the future of the Jews. Or the orthodox and ultra-orthodox represented by Agudas Yisroel and by groups ideologically close to that party, suspicious about secularization in general and particularly about a secular interpretation of the Jewish future. And last, Zionism had only a limited appeal for the Jewries in Muslim countries, living in sociological conditions very different from those of European Jewry. Once the Zionist political hopes were realized and Israel established, most of those diverse sectors in Jewry closed ranks around the Jewish state and participated in its development, each sector according to its own lights, from pale sympathy to financial and political support to outright aliyah. This, however, was the end of the story, not its beginning and not even its middle.

Among those diverging tendencies, Zionism represented, then, a path of its own, embodying a peculiar mix of historical values and modern ideologies. Political Zionism expressed a certain moment in Jewish modernization, especially in eastern European Jewry, where a background of religious ties and community bonds combined with a degree of openness to the patterns of political thought and the models of public action current in general European society. Zionism amalgamated major deep-rooted spiritual components of Jewish self-awareness, such as *ahavat tsion,* the love for Zion, and *shivat tsion,* the hope for the Return, with ideological and political European ideas such as nationalism and statehood. In the complex interplay of Jewish and general influences that met in Zionism and created inside the movement competing trends and subtrends, there were two factors that remained stable: the attachment to the Land of Israel and the hope of the Return. The rest were ideological constructions: Zionism was explained according to the views of each of its factions, in terms of need, of right, of hope.

Understandably, such an explanation is difficult to digest intellectually for those educated in the accepted categories of western political and historical thought. Nevertheless, experience with historical work in the posthistoricist age should convince us that open-mindedness regarding the sagas of different societies makes us in the end wiser. The history of any society has particular and peculiar traits, the history of the Jews apparently even more so. And regarding Zionism, not only the internal strength of the idea but even more so the relative broadness of its appeal gave it what may be called "historical legitimacy." In its diverse shadings, the Jews' connection to the Land of Israel and the dream of the Return had a measure of significance even for certain sectors of the Christian world and, much more so, for a wide range of Jews: from the religiously orthodox to the highly acculturated, from Jews in Christian lands to Jews in the Muslim countries.

In this context, a personal note: I arrived in Israel in October 1953, on the ship *Negba*, a member of a Zionist-socialist youth movement in Brazil and soon a *haver* (fellow) of a kibbutz in the Negev region. We disembarked from the ship from one gangway, while through a parallel exit left a party of *olim* (immigrants) from Morocco. On the quayside the Moroccan Jews fell on their knees, kissed the soil of the Holy Land, and said the *shehehiyanu* prayer: "Blessed be Thou Lord, who brought us to this day." We, the Zionist-socialist revolutionaries, looked on, quietly astonished. A world of ideological concept and social experience separated our two groups, each one originating from far-away lands. And nevertheless, there we stood at that quay, all of us brought there by the same idea.

In summation, we see that the changes that Zionism produced in the contemporary Jewish condition were built on elements of Jewish identity, with deep historical roots that amalgamated with the demands and possibilities of the modern Western world. The result, renewed Jewish statehood, is a natural development, albeit with very specific traits. From a general Jewish perspective, it is a situation not unknown from the Jewish past: a part of the Jews dwells as citizens of different nations, while another part lives as citizens of a Jewish state.

A major task of modern Jewish historiography, therefore, is to create a conceptual bridge with general society that contributes to a common understanding about the present situation of the Jews, unencumbered by historicist premises and presumptions. Such an understanding may finally bring about the acceptance of the Jews as they are, and not as they should be.

NOTES

1. See the six articles under the title "Reflections on Jewish Historiography" in the collected essays of Michael A. Meyer, *Judaism within Modernity: Essays on Jewish History and Religion* (Detroit: Wayne State University Press, 2001).
2. S. N. Eisenstadt and Moshe Lissak, *Zionism and the Return to History: A Reappraisal* [in Hebrew] (Jerusalem: Yad Ben-Zvi Press, 1999).

Evyatar Friesel

Simon Rawidowicz on the Arab Question

A Prescient Gaze into
the "New History"

DAVID N. MYERS

Few contemporary historians of modern Jewry have had as deep and enduring an impact as Michael Meyer. From the appearance of his first book, *The Origins of the Modern Jew,* some forty years ago (1967), Professor Meyer has had a major hand in shaping the categories and analytical framework by which we measure the modern Jewish experience. *Origins* laid out in characteristically meticulous and elegant fashion the core ideals and tensions that shaped German Jews at the crossroads between the Enlightenment and Romanticist eras. Comparable in significance to Jacob Katz's *Out of the Ghetto* and George Mosse's *German Jews beyond Judaism,* Meyer's text made a compelling argument that German Jews, in their confrontation with the new philosophical ideas (including modern notions of historical causality) of the *Aufklärung,* modeled the broader encounter of Jews with modernity itself. Though scholars have since attempted to move beyond the perceived Germano-centrism of this perspective, it is owing to the manifold scholarly virtues of Michael Meyer that German Jewry received as vivid, textured, and consequential a portrait as it did.

One of the qualities that distinguishes Meyer over the course of some four decades of scholarly labor is his ability to synthesize large bodies of historical material into clear, but not reductionist, lines. This skill is evident already in *Origins,* in which each chapter ranges widely across a rich array of sources and personalities without losing sight of the narrative thread. It is perhaps even more obviously present in Meyer's second book, the encyclopedic *Response to Modernity* (1988), which exhaustively chronicles the life history of the Reform movement from its German origins to its American fulfillment. Moreover, Meyer's work as editor (along with Michael Brenner) of the four-volume *German-Jewish History in Modern Times* (1996–98) attests to his boldness in conceiving a sweeping and polychromatic analysis of German Jews. And yet it may well be that the most synthetic piece of work he ever wrote was his brief but classic essay from 1975, "Where Does the Modern Period of Jewish History Begin?" Here Meyer drew on his superb grasp of competing ideological and generational currents in modern Jewish historiography to summarize and critique existing schemes of periodization of the Jewish past.[1] He was especially attentive, good historian that he is, to the difficulties of producing a single temporal framework for such a geographically and cultural expansive entity as the Jews.

That said, we would be reducing Michael Meyer to a one-dimensional portrait as an antiquarian scholar if we simply noted his commitment to excavating the past. As an entire generation of graduate students in modern Jewish history knows well, he is an exceptionally generous and incisive reader of research in progress. I recall with great fondness and deep gratitude that every piece of my work that I sent to Michael, including an unwieldy dissertation, was significantly improved by his suggestions, large and small; conversely, work that I neglected to send him suffered. What makes his thorough and famously rapid reading of the work of so many of my generation so impressive is that he was not formally our *Doktorvater.* Without any official institutional obligation, Michael Meyer contributed and continues to contribute to the formation and growth of junior scholars for the best of reasons: a genuine and deep-seated sense of collegiality.

There is a related quality of Professor Meyer's that merits our attention, and conclusively undermines the image of a cloistered scholar frozen in the past, namely, his deep engagement with questions of contemporary Jewish identity (to wit, his books *Jewish Identity in the Modern World* [1990] and *Judaism within Modernity* [2001]), as well as his profound commitments to the Reform movement, Zionism, and the State of Israel. It is precisely Meyer's willingness to allow the past to inform our choices in the present that brings us to the subject of this essay: Simon Rawidowicz (1896–1957). With characteristic insight, Michael Meyer introduced a collection of writings written by this seminal, though underappreciated, Jewish thinker on the occa-

David N. Myers

sion of the fortieth anniversary of his death. In the introduction, he noted that Rawidowicz attracted few followers to his vision of a dual-centered Jewish nationalism whose cultural capitals were located not in the Diaspora *or* the Land of Israel, but rather in *both*. It was not merely this iconoclastic vision that consigned him to obscurity; it was also the fact, Meyer noted, that Rawidowicz insisted on Hebrew as his primary written language while living his entire life in the Diaspora.

And yet Meyer was able to see the intuitive genius of Rawidowicz through the ideological and linguistic haze. In particular, it was Rawidowicz's insistence on a genuine partnership between Diaspora and the Land of Israel—a *shutafut* according to his recurring Hebrew phrase—that caught Meyer's attention. This idea reflected an undeniable demographic reality, namely, that the Diaspora contained a critical mass of Jews (the overwhelming majority of the global Jewish population when Rawidowicz was active, and about half today), and was not likely to disappear. Meyer observed that the concern for a mutually respectful partnership that was a hallmark of Rawidowicz's thought "has become common coin of the seemingly endless dialogues that have taken places between the two 'sides.'"[2] He went on to point to other aspects of Rawidowicz's thought that, while relatively marginal in his day, had assumed new significance in the present: for example, Rawidowicz's invocation of the language of Jewish continuity, as well as his insistence that the Jewish people, though dispersed in different locales, was an indivisible unity. Even more provocatively, Meyer observed that Rawidowicz's gnawing concerns about Zionism—its desire for hegemony in the Jewish world vis-à-vis the Diaspora, set against its drive to establish a "normal" political state—had not been allayed a half-century after the State of Israel was created.

Michael Meyer's appreciation for Rawidowicz's prescience did not—indeed could not—take note of one unknown feature of his thought. In the course of writing the nine-hundred-page book that encapsulated his distinctive philosophy and ideology, *Bavel vi-Yerushalayim* (1957), Rawidowicz authored a thirty-three-page chapter that was planned as an appendix but never saw the light of day.[3] The chapter, titled "Between Jew and Arab," dealt with an issue that Rawidowicz had vowed never to speak about in public but evidently felt compelled to address at the time: the relationship of Zionism and the State of Israel to the Arab population of historic Palestine. It remains something of a literary mystery why this chapter was not included in the published version of *Bavel vi-Yerushalayim*. What is known is that sometime between 1955 and 1957, a decision was made not to include the chapter, already in galleys, in the published version of the book. The reason for this exclusion is not known, though one can certainly understand why

Rawidowicz or his printer, one Jacob Fink in Paris, might have chosen to withhold such a potentially explosive chapter from publication.

The chapter rested on the claim that the age-old debates over the status and location of the Jews, comprising what is known as the Jewish question, must now give way to questions about the desired status and location of Palestinian Arabs. This is not to say that Rawidowicz was motivated by a deep sense of identification with the Arabs of Palestine. Nor did he believe that the creation of the State of Israel had conclusively resolved all lingering issues of *Jewish* identity (e.g., by "proving" the superfluity of the Diaspora). On the contrary, the seminal events of 1948 raised, for Rawidowicz, the troubling specter that political sovereignty might require an unwelcome descent into the abyss of immorality of the gentile nations.

In reflecting on this fundamental question of power, Rawidowicz came to believe that the Arab question—the status of Arabs in Israel and refugees outside of it—was, in fact, a Jewish question, one that posed a formidable challenge to the political sagacity and ethical norms of Israel (as Rawidowicz preferred to refer to the Jewish people, refusing to surrender that name to the newly created state).[4] The fact that he spoke so bluntly and sharply about this challenge may be surprising, though there were others Jewish thinkers in Israel and beyond—Hannah Arendt, Hans Kohn, and Yeshayahu Leibowitz come to mind—who voiced similar concerns about the relation between power and morality in this period. What makes Rawidowicz's chapter especially bracing is the counsel he offered in "Between Jew and Arab." For the State of Israel's own sake, he argued, it was an urgent task not only to end all forms of discrimination against Arab residents within its borders but to consider *the repatriation of Arab refugees* outside of them.

Written in the first half of the 1950s, Rawidowicz's chapter reminds us that it was not the so-called New Historians in Israel during the late 1980s and 1990s who first brought to public attention the status of Palestinian Arabs in Israel and the fate of the refugees. There can be little doubt that this cadre of scholars who came to public prominence over the past two decades, figures such as Benny Morris, Ilan Pappé, Tom Segev, and Avi Shlaim, introduced a new critical spirit into the historiography of 1948.[5] Drawing on a large trove of newly available archival material, this cohort quite consciously sought to undermine a number of key tenets of Israeli collective memory. These included the belief that (1) the British decisively favored the Arab side in the terminal stages of its Mandate over Palestine; (2) the Jewish/Israeli side was at a distinct military disadvantage versus the Arab side when hostilities broke out in late fall 1947 through 1948; (3)

the Jewish/Israeli side was in constant search of peaceful options to resolve the conflict; and (4) the hundreds of thousands of Arabs who took flight from Palestine/Israel in 1948 did so largely of their own accord.[6] This last claim generated the most controversy, with debate raging over whether the flight of Palestinian refugees was driven by Jewish expulsions or the fear of them or by the calls of Arab leaders abroad to take temporary leave of Palestine before returning in the wake of a victorious Arab army.[7]

Unlike the New Historians, Simon Rawidowicz did not engage in serious archival research into the various aspects of the War of 1948. But his chapter "Between Jew and Arab" did rest on an assumption that seemed to stand at odds with Israeli popular memory up to the time of the New Historians, namely, that the Jewish/Israeli side bore a measure of responsibility for the Arab refugee problem and should take steps to acknowledge and act on that responsibility.[8] In fact, his chapter bristles with prophetic indignation at what he perceived to be a lapse in Jewish ethical and political judgment in treatment of Arabs in the midst of and after the War of Independence.

The aim of this essay is to shed light on Rawidowicz's unique perspective on this exceptionally sensitive issue. Notwithstanding the fact that his chapter was not included in *Bavel vi-Yerushalayim* and thus dwelt in obscurity for a half-century, it contains the kind of prescience that few in Rawidowicz's day recognized, though which Michael Meyer, with his keen historical sensors, aptly saw as characteristic of him. Before turning to Rawidowicz and his chapter, though, we must first recall a number of voices that pierced the veil of silence in which the Arab question was often cloaked in Jewish circles in Israel and the Diaspora.

The controversy generated by the New Historians in Israel derived, to a great extent, from their self-conscious attempt to "de-idealize Zionist history" through a mix of "an interdisciplinary approach, healthy skepticism, and a thorough understanding of the other side's historical narrative."[9] And yet, the assertion of a historiographical revolution—in this case, coming as much from their opponents as from the New Historians themselves—is often somewhat exaggerated. While some of the New Historians trumpeted bold methodological or evidentiary breakthroughs, others acknowledged that they were not the first to happen onto controversial conclusions. For example, both Avi Shlaim and Benny Morris point to the 1959 work of the Iraqi-born Israeli political scientist Rony Gabbay, *A Political Study of the Arab-Jewish Conflict: The Arab Refugee Problem,* as an adumbration of the New Historians' work on the Palestinian refugee question. While acknowledging Gabbay's limited archival pool, Morris nonetheless lauded his book as "a remarkable achievement."[10] Gabbay had no access to the rich trove of archival materials (e.g., Haganah, IDF) that Morris used in his 1988 book *The Birth of the Palestinian Refugee Problem*. Rather, he relied on an extensive network of interviews with Middle Eastern and European officials, UN and government documents, and newspapers to trace the origin, unfolding, and scope of the Arab refugee problem. He sought to strike a judicious balance in producing a careful, stage-by-stage account of the refugee problem that took stock of both Arab and Jewish sides. Ultimately, Gabbay placed a good deal more responsibility for the initiation of hostilities—and the creation of the refugee problem—on the Arab than on the Jewish side. And yet, he did notice a shift in Israeli attitudes and behavior toward Arab residents of Palestine in the late spring and summer of 1948. In addition to "the great use by the Jews of psychological warfare," there were also cases, he noted, in which "reluctant Arabs were forced to flee into Arab country [*sic*]."[11] Gabbay added that following the evacuation of Arab villages, "looting and pillaging of Arab properties, and the commandeering of goats, sheep, and mules by the Israelis were not uncommon features."[12]

Gabbay's assertion that both psychological pressure and forced expulsions by the Jewish side contributed to the Palestinian refugee problem directly challenges David Ben-Gurion's oft-expressed view that "the State of Israel expelled nobody and will never do it."[13] It appears that by the time Gabbay published his dissertation in 1959, Israeli public memory had consolidated around Ben-Gurion's view of the events. But that process of consolidation took a number of years following the events themselves. One of the most detailed analyses of this process is Anita Shapira's comprehensive study of the reception of "Hirbet Hizah," the long story published in 1949 by the author S. Yizhar. Yizhar's extraordinary story revealed the moral qualms of the narrator, an Israeli soldier, who watched with a mix of powerlessness and dismay as his comrades expelled Arab women, children, and the elderly from their village in the late stages of the War of Independence.[14] Throughout the story, the narrator struggles to justify the actions of his comrades, at one point asking: "Do we really have to expel them? What can they do to us? What evil can they cause? What's the purpose?"[15]

Shapira traces in considerable detail the waves of public attention and controversy stirred up by Yizhar's story, beginning with one in the immediate aftermath of its publication. She notes that critics from 1949 to 1951 largely concurred on the literary merit of Yizhar's work, a landmark of Hebrew fiction in his generation. But they dif-

David N. Myers

fered widely on the lessons of "Hirbet Hizah." While one critic declared, not surprisingly, that the story abetted the enemies of Israel, others believed that Yizhar represented a voice of conscience that was often drowned out in the quest for military victory and political sovereignty.[16] One reader who admired Yizhar's courage lamented the fact that "the tortured victim of yesterday turns into the torturer the moment he picks up the whip, and the exile of yesterday now banishes others. Overnight, those who suffered injustice over centuries become themselves its perpetrators."[17] Here the assumption of power entailed not only an erasure of the Jewish past but also, this critic implied, a serious erosion of the ethical consciousness borne of the Jews' long historical experience.

Interestingly, while there were competing opinions about the virtue of publicizing the act of expulsion described in "Hirbet Hizah," the debate seemed not to focus on whether expulsions did or did not take place. Many assumed that they did and proceeded either to justify or condemn them. Shapira notes that Israeli intellectuals "apparently did not hesitate to openly address the expulsion issue" in this period. And they were not alone. Israeli political activists, especially those associated with the Communist Party (MaKI) or the Marxist-inspired Zionist Mapam, expressed clear knowledge of and condemnation for acts of expulsion. In early May 1948, Mapam's resident expert on Arab affairs, Aharon Cohen, declared that "a deliberate eviction (of the Arabs) is taking place. Others may rejoice—I, as a socialist, am ashamed and afraid."[18] A month later, Mapam's political committee announced its opposition to "the objective of expelling the Arabs from the areas of the emergent Jewish state."[19] Subsequently, debate ensued within the party over the question of whether the expelled Arab refugees should be permitted to return to their homes in Israel.

The interrelated questions of expulsion and return were not restricted to party deliberations behind closed doors. *Al ha-mishmar*, the Mapam-affiliated paper, carried articles from party leaders discussing them, especially after the Israel Defense Force actions in Ramla and Lydda in which some scores of thousands of Arabs—estimates range between forty and seventy thousand—were expelled from their homes.[20] For example, Meir Ya'ari, in a published version of a speech from July 30, 1948, recalled the view of some comrades who said, "We did not expel them [the Arabs]. They left of their own accord." He countered that while "it is true that hundreds of thousands fled, they did not always do so of their own accord."[21] The next day, Alexander Pereg wrote a lengthy article in the paper that challenged the impression that the expelled refugees constituted a grave danger to the state: "The vast majority of the villages did not collaborate with the invaders [i.e., the invading Arab armies], and we should accept these residents back into our State as citizens with full rights."[22]

It would, of course, be a vast overstatement to claim that these views were universally shared across the political spectrum. In fact, they occupied a clearly identifiable but unmistakably small place in Israeli public opinion of the time. To wit, although Yitzhak Rabin recalled that David Ben-Gurion himself seemed to authorize the expulsion of Arab residents of Ramle and Lydda, Ben-Gurion and many of his colleagues in the dominant Labor Zionist party, Mapai, held to the line that Arabs left Palestine in 1948 of their own volition or because they were encouraged to do so by local or neighboring Arab leaders.[23] Consequently, one finds few mentions of expulsion in the pages of the Mapai-affiliated paper, Davar.[24]

But that is not to say that Mapam or Al ha-mishmar were the only sources attesting to Israeli awareness of acts of expulsion. Others included MaKI and its organs Kol ha-'am and Al-Ittihad, Ha-'olam ha-zeh, edited by Uri Avnery, and the less well known Ner. This last publication was the fortnightly journal of the Ihud Association, which was the latest incarnation of the Jewish peace camp whose roots lay in Brit Shalom (founded in 1925). The establishment of the State of Israel in 1948 had dashed the long-held hopes of this circle for a binational polity in which Jews and Arabs share power. Nevertheless, both Ihud and Ner continued to be animated by a Jewishly grounded moral commitment to improve relations between Jews and Arabs. Moreover, from its opening issue in February 1950, the journal was replete with reports of expulsion, displacement, and discrimination against Arabs, many of which were sprinkled with appeals to Jewish conscience and references to classical Jewish sources. Ner's editor, Rabbi Binyamin (Yehoshua Radler-Feldmann), used the journal—and a variety of pseudonyms—to challenge Israeli society to assume responsibility for the expulsions of Arab residents and to accept their right to return to Israel.[25] In this respect, as well as in the traditionalist Hebrew idiom in which he wrote, Rabbi Binyamin recalls his fellow eastern European Jew Simon Rawidowicz though the two men appear not to have been in touch at all in this period. Meanwhile, some of Rabbi Binyamin's old colleagues from the Brit Shalom days, most notably the Hebrew University philosopher Shmuel Hugo Bergmann, felt that the winds of history had swept past the Ihud/Ner crowd—indeed, that it no longer had the moral right or obligation to criticize a society of which its members were part.[26] Still, the journal stuck to its guns up to the mid-1950s, maintaining focus on the refugee question and entertaining a variety of proposals on how to resolve it (e.g., through either a partial or full right of return) in a relative public vacuum.

To be sure, there were periodic, and at times quite passionate, debates in Israeli Jewish society regarding the status of Arab residents who remained within the boundaries of the new state. One such debate arose in the midst of and after Knesset deliberations over the Nationality Law (passed on April 1, 1952), which established a different and more difficult path toward citizenship for Arabs (as against Jews, who received automatic Israeli nationality under the Law of Return).[27] There were also intense, if episodic, discussions in Israel over the morality of force, especially after the Qibya (1953) and Kafr Kasem (1956) events in which scores of Arab civilians were killed by the Israeli army in the midst of its campaign to combat violent infiltrators across Israel's borders.[28]

And yet, public debate over expulsions undertaken by Jewish-Israeli forces in 1948 seemed to wane by the time of the Nationality Law and the Qibya episode in 1952–53. Indeed, Anita Shapira notes in her essay on the reception of "Hirbet Hizah" that "the expulsion, which at the beginning of the 1950s had been acknowledged as an obvious fact of the war, was now transformed into a virtual 'state secret'—of course, with many 'confidants.'"[29]

In explaining this process, Shapira suggests that "the suppression of the expulsion's memory" resembled to some extent another therapeutic forgetting: the suppression of memory by Holocaust survivors. In fact, there may be more than a mere resemblance. According to Shapira, this suppression resulted from a variety of factors: the absence of contact with and knowledge about one-time Arab neighbors, the continuing enmity of the surrounding Arab world toward the State of Israel, and the addition of hundreds of thousands of new immigrants to the State of Israel (doubling its population within three years) who did not share a common memory with those who had passed through the war.[30] But to these factors we might add another causal explanation drawn from the admittedly speculative domain of collective psychology. That is to say, the tale of Arab dispossession, or at least the pieces of a tale that were visible in public discussions mentioned earlier and elsewhere, were dislodged in Israeli public memory by a much larger tale of dispossession: that of the Jews themselves during the Holocaust. Certainly, in chronological terms, the transformation of the memory of expulsions from "obvious fact" to "state secret" coincides with the major efforts at institutionalizing the place of the memory of the Holocaust in Israel. The bill to create Yad Vashem and Israel's Martyrs' and Heroes' Remembrance Authority passed the Knesset on May 18, 1953. This legislative act reflected not only a significant attempt to memorialize the Holocaust in Israel but also, as Tom Segev has argued, a broader endeavor to mold popular consciousness of the State of Israel as the custodian of the Jewish people—and consequently, as the repository of public memory of the Holocaust, as well as the clear antithesis to Diaspora passivity.[31] Although it is difficult to prove a direct causal link, it remains a striking—and thoroughly understandable—feature of the evolving Israeli-Jewish public consciousness that attention to the plight of Arab refugees and the memory of expulsions by Jews diminished as attention to the plight of Jewish refugees (mainly, but not exclusively from Europe) and the memory of the extermination of Jews increased.

Against the backdrop of the tectonic shifts of memory hinted at here, we turn at last to the intriguing legacy of Simon Rawidowicz. Rawidowicz led a peripatetic career as scholar and ideologue that carried him from his native Lithuania to Germany, England, and finally the United States. Toward the end of his life, in 1951, he realized a lifelong dream by being appointed to the faculty of Brandeis University, precisely the kind of Jewish institution of higher learning that he once dreamt of as a latter day Sura or Pumbedita.[32] It was in his Brandeis years that Rawidowicz began to pull together the strands of his distinctive philosophy of Jewish life into the two volume *Bavel vi-Yerushalayim;* it was also in this period, between 1951 and 1955, that he wrote "Between Jew and Arab," intended, as we noted at the outset, for inclusion in *Bavel vi-Yerushalayim* but withheld from the final version.

Both geographically and politically, Rawidowicz was at a remove from the public debate that ensued in the State of Israel regarding the treatment of Arabs during and after the war. And yet, he was remarkably well informed about Israel's political, cultural, and literary scene, due in no small part to the regular newspaper clippings sent to him from Tel Aviv by his brother, Avraham Ravid. Moreover, he was deeply consumed by the consequences, political and moral, of the Jews' assumption of sovereignty for Jewish history and the history of Palestine. This prompted him, at the outset of "Between Jew and Arab," to break his long-standing vow not to discuss the Arab question in public. The result was one of the most trenchant and gripping accounts of that question by a Jew, in Israel or outside.

According to Rawidowicz, the conflict between Jews and Arabs after 1948, "is no longer about 'two people holding on to a garment,' both of whom claim to the master watching over them that the garment is all theirs. Rather, one has grabbed hold of it, dominates, and leads, while the other is led. The first rules as a decisive majority, as a nation-state. The other is dominated as a minority. And domination is in the hands of Israel [i.e., the Jewish people]."[33]

David N. Myers

While Rawidowicz placed the blame for initiating the hostilities of 1948 on the Arab side, he nonetheless noticed a dramatic reversal of fortune, in which the Jews became a national majority and the Arabs a national minority. This, to his mind, reflected the new burden of sovereignty and the attendant demand for a clear ethics of power. "Arabs," Rawidowicz wrote, "dwell in the State of Israel by right, not sufferance—just like any minority in the world, including the Jewish minority which dwells where it dwells by right, not sufferance" (3). There are a number of features of this sentence worthy of our attention. First, Rawidowicz was expressing support for the right of Arabs to live in freedom and equality on their land as a matter of principle, consistent with the recently approved Universal Declaration of Human Rights of 1948, which he alludes to in his text (4).[34] Second, he was using a formulation "by right, not sufferance" that should have resonated in the ears of Jews, having been invoked by a young Winston Churchill in 1922 in a British government document that discussed the Jewish presence in Palestine.[35] And third, he was constantly mindful, given his own unyielding commitment to a vibrant Jewish presence in the Diaspora, of the possible linkage between the State of Israel's treatment of its Arab minority and the treatment of Jews by host countries the world over.

For this combination of reasons, Rawidowicz watched the early steps of the Knesset, Israel's Parliament, with alarm. He did *not* consider the Law of Return (1950), which accorded Jewish immigrants a nearly automatic path to citizenship, as especially dangerous. However, the 1952 Nationality Law was another story. In order to qualify for Israeli citizenship, non-Jews (the overwhelming majority of whom were Arabs) had to satisfy a number of conditions, the most important of which were that (a) they be registered with the state by the time of the enactment of this law (July 14, 1952) and (b) they were to have been continually present in the state from 1948 until the enactment of the law. The law excluded those who left the boundaries of what would become the State of Israel during the hostilities, including both refugees who remained permanently outside of the State of Israel and those who subsequently returned to their homes or to another place in Israel. Rawidowicz felt that those thousands of Arabs who had left and returned (including the vast majority of the so-called infiltrators [*mistanenim*] who had no violent intentions), or those who had not yet registered with the state, were unfairly precluded from citizenship in the state of their residence.[36] "Neither the ingathering of the exiles nor the security needs of the State," he declared, "require these discriminatory clauses." After all, "discrimination is discrimination, even when it serves the security needs of a state" (4).

It was a mix of ethical and pragmatic political considerations that prompted Rawidowicz's intervention. On one hand, he wrote that "morality itself protests against these discriminatory clauses" (4). On the other hand, he was concerned, as we have seen, that Jews would replicate some of the discriminatory laws that had been inflicted upon them in the Diaspora. This would not only increase the enmity of the gentile world toward the new State of Israel; it could also pose new risks to the well-being of Jewish communities outside of Israel.

In light of these concerns, Rawidowicz was disturbed that Jews were not more vocal in protest. He was especially irate that the Jewish press in the Diaspora, with a measure of critical distance from the events unfolding, did not raise its voice but instead chose the path of silence. If only Diaspora journalists had "protested as they should have, they would have earned a reward for their protest, as would have the State of Israel itself" (5). By contrast, Rawidowicz observed with admiration those in Israel who voice their criticism "even if they are not many in number, even if their voices do not always carry like a trumpet" (6).

Indeed, this circle was powerless to prevent further discriminatory acts. On the heels of the Nationality Law came, in March 1953, the Land Acquisition Law by which the Knesset authorized the state to claim for its use property that (a) was currently "not in the possession of its owners" and (b) was required for "purposes of essential development, settlement, or security."[37] The wide latitude of these clauses, especially the second, effectively denied the property claims of those Arab residents who had left their homes during the war-time hostilities but resettled elsewhere in Israel—a group known by the deadly bureaucratic oxymoron "present absentees" (nokhehim nifkadim). While present in the State of Israel as legal residents and, ultimately, citizens, the "absentees" were prevented from reclaiming, or even visiting, their homes.[38]

Rawidowicz knew that this curious discriminatory status of the "present absentees" was justified as a function of Israel's security concerns. But he refused to accept it. Shifting the focus from the legal regulations of the State of Israel to the legal ethics of the Bible, he declared that "it is forbidden for the Jewish people to adopt the laws of the Gentiles and expropriate the property of an enemy or combatant who was vanquished on the battlefield."[39] Moreover, "it is not advisable for a weak and poor people, weak and poor even with the crown of statehood on its head, to pillage and plunder" (7).[40] The state's haughtiness, he feared, would only strengthen the hand of Israel's enemies,

Rawidowicz found few allies among his compatriots in the Diaspora, whose press, he felt, assumed an unprincipled posture of si-

David N. Myers

lent consent vis-à-vis the government's treatment of Arabs. More admirable in this regard was the press in Israel, which was willing to open its pages to voices "that are bitter over the discrimination against Arabs." And these voices provided a window to some restrained optimism on Rawidowicz's part. "There will arise among the Jews," he predicted, "those who will protest and struggle to eradicate the evil in their midst." Ultimately, he hoped that these voices of conscience in Israel would be able to "rectify any wrong within its borders, either by choice or coercion" (7).

Rawidowicz proved far less sanguine about another matter that, in his view, stood at the heart of the enmity between Jew and Arab: "the denial of repatriation that was imposed upon the Arabs who left Palestine—or took flight from it—with the outbreak of war between the State of Israel and the Arab countries, or more accurately, with the attack of the Arab countries" (7). The brashness of this formulation almost takes the breath away. Here, after all, was a Jew who regarded himself as a proud and loyal member of his people. Not only had he never manifested interest in the fate of Palestinian Arabs prior to this point. Despite his concerns about Zionism's impulse to negate the Diaspora, he shared the goal of Jews' reclaiming the Land of Israel and reviving Hebrew culture there. To call, then, for the repatriation of hundreds of thousands of Palestinian Arabs in the early 1950s was an extraordinary act, one that placed Rawidowicz among a very small number of Jews.[41]

For Rawidowicz, the fateful "decree of the refugees" (*gezerat ha-pelitim*), as he called it, was one of the most important political and moral issues facing the State of Israel and world Jewry.[42] Indeed, "the question of these refugees," he argued, "is not an Arab question: it is a *Jewish question*, a question that 1948 placed upon the Jewish people" (28).

Limitations of space prevent a full unpacking of Rawidowicz's chapter. But it is important to give a flavor here of the blend of perspectives—that of the admonishing prophet and the hard-core realist, the compassionate universalist and the proudly parochial nationalist—that gives force to his extraordinary text. We should also mention in this context that Rawidowicz was himself uprooted, along with his family, from their Polish-Lithuanian hometown of Grayevo by the outbreak of World War I; this experience may well have played a role in his sensitivity to the plight of those displaced by the hostilities of 1948.

In any event, Rawidowicz did not dwell at great length on the causes of the flight of Arab refugees:

It matters little whether they left because their Arab brothers and British friends incited them to do so by promising them a quick return to a Palestine in which there would be no State of Israel, or whether they fled out of fear of the Jews (and the Deir Yassin massacre, for example, certainly could have frightened the Arabs of this country), or out of the chaos of war which uproots people from their place of residence and sweeps them beyond the borders, or out of political naïveté and "technical" ignorance (it is told that a night rain storm once drove the Arabs from their homes in Safed, and they believed that it was a "secret weapon" of the Jews that triggered the storm). (7–8)

From this last sentence, it is obvious that Rawidowicz was not smitten with the "Arab-Oriental romanticism" of some fellow Jews; nor did he count himself among "those who bestow glory on the Arabs either in the past or the present" (31). His motivation in addressing the question of the refugees was almost entirely to advance the welfare and good name of his fellow Jews. But here too, as in the case of the earlier discussion of Israeli Arabs, his analysis followed the intersecting paths of practical politics and ethical propriety.

Thus, Rawidowicz reiterated his concern that the mistreatment of Arabs—in this instance, avoidance of the refugee problem—would have a negative effect on the State of Israel. Not only would it fortify the resolve of neighboring Arab countries in "refus(ing) to come to terms with the existence of the State of Israel" (10); it would also encourage them to continue their economic boycott of Israel. Rawidowicz advanced yet another, and rather novel, economic argument in discussing the plight of the refugees, one that presaged claims that have been made in more recent debates on the place of immigrants in the West. That is, he insisted that the State of Israel's economy would benefit greatly from the refugees' return: "The rates of food and agricultural production would be much improved if the Arabs were able to return and perform their work." On the whole, the returning refugees could serve as a vital tool "in improving political relations between Jews and Arabs in the world, but also in strengthening the economic position of the State of Israel" (10).

At almost every turn, Rawidowicz invoked the principle that harm done to the refugees could be turned back upon the Jews. That harm would not only result from the ongoing hostility of the Arab and Muslim worlds; it would also issue from the West, though not in the most obvious of ways. Rawidowicz was aware that in the wake of the Holocaust, the Western world, burdened by its own guilt, "hesitated to

David N. Myers

come . . . and preach to us about morality" (11). In fact, that world—the very world "that accepted Hitler and his ilk"—"now understands the State of Israel when it locks its gates to the refugees."

Rawidowicz sensed grave danger in this "understanding," as he made clear from the following biblical allusion: "Jacob [i.e., the Jews] was 'not understandable' to Esau [i.e., the gentiles] during his whole life. In this very 'lack of understanding' lurks one of the sources of Esau's hatred for Jacob. When Esau does not comprehend the language of Jacob, 'have no fear, Jacob my servant' [Jeremiah 46:28]. When Esau begins to comprehend the language of Jacob, woe unto Jacob. . . . I fear that from 1948 onward, Esau has been defiling Jacob through this 'understanding'—the two have become alike. The twins are no longer struggling with one another. They have begun to understand one another" (12).

The fact that Jacob and Esau—the State of Israel and the nations of the world—now "understood" each other meant they had come to inhabit the same immoral universe. In haunting biblical language, Rawidowicz lamented this descent of the Jewish state "into the valley of the shadow of death" (Psalm 23:4) (9). From the time of the Hasmonean kingdom until the present, he added, "there was not a single solid complaint in the arsenal of the haters of Israel" (12). But 1948 signaled a dramatic change. The Jews not only assumed political power but also the ethical norms of the surrounding world. This was an occasion for antisemites to celebrate. But even more worrisome was that "intellectuals and historical scholars" who were not antisemites were now beginning to sense that the Jews had lost their age-old moral compass, itself the source of their uniqueness in the world (13).

Rawidowicz's concern here was an extension of his lengthy discussion and critique of 1948 in *Bavel vi-Yerushalayim*, comprising nearly four hundred pages and the entirety of part 2. The return of the Jews to sovereignty after two millennia, greeted with joy and even messianic anticipation by many Jews, was the cause of sober reflection for him. He feared that the dizzying triumphalism of the day would only embolden those Zionists who were intent on "negating the Diaspora." It would also enshrine political power, rather than cultural vitality, as the defining feature of the Jewish nation. In the process, the Jews' finely tuned moral antennae would be dulled.

This critique of Jewish power made Rawidowicz vulnerable to the charge of being a pie-in-the-sky utopian, and he was well aware of it. He countered by challenging the "imagined realism" of those who refused to consider the return of the refugees. Hurling back the charge against his putative accusers, he observed, "But in fact what is 'utopian' is the total avoidance of the question of the refugees, delaying its resolution from year to year. It is dangerous to transfer the resolution to the U.N. or to the Arabs. There is no other way than the elimination (of this problem)—and by Jews themselves" (30–31).

Despite the fact that Rawidowicz had once taken on the literary persona of "Ish Boded"—Lonely Man—he did not revel in being a solitary voice on the plight of the refugees. He was bitterly disappointed that the leaders of the Zionist movement and the State of Israel had neglected their erstwhile ethical imperative as Jews. "If one had said to David Ben-Gurion, Chaim Weizmann, Yitzhak Ben-Zvi, and their friends before 1948," he surmised, "that they were soon to stand as the leaders of a State of Israel that did not permit Arab refugees—men, women, and children—to return to their possessions, and *uprooted* them from their roots and rendered them homeless—would they not see in this claim a contemptible libel of the haters of Israel and Zion who aimed to desecrate the name of Israel and besmirch Zionism in the world?" (24). Zionists of all ideological stripes had promised to pursue a peaceful path with the Arabs of Palestine, but Rawidowicz was especially dismayed by the failure of the Labor Zionists to act on their rhetoric. In fact, he noticed a wide gap between "the lovely declarations . . . about peaceful co-existence" and their actual behavior.

Although Rawidowicz repeatedly refers here, as in *Bavel vi-Yerushalayim*, to 1948 as a caesura, he also intimates that the gap between word and deed may well extend back before 1948. In a lengthy footnote, he singled out the legendary "prophet of the religion of labor," Labor Zionist leader A. D. Gordon (1856–1922), and wondered how deep and sincere his commitment to equitable relations with Arabs in Palestine ran (25). Did Gordon actually believe his own rhetoric that the Jewish side could act according to "humane and cosmic ideals" in its dealings with the Arabs? How would he have responded to the specter of hundreds of thousands of displaced Arab refugees or to the fact that Jews lived in "expropriated and conquered homes?" Indeed, would Gordon have "blurted out like his friends and disciples at Degania, Nahalal, and elsewhere that 'we have no stain on our hands, we are righteous and have not sinned?'" (25). It was precisely this sense of self-virtue, especially among those socialist Zionists committed in name to equality, that most agitated Rawidowicz.

His doubts about the sincerity of this strand of Zionist rhetoric did not carry over to one prominent Labor Zionist of the 1948 generation, S. Yizhar, whom Rawidowicz admired deeply. Yizhar was, to his mind, "the one writer who salvaged the honor of our Hebrew literature in the State of Israel when he protested in his stories ('Hirbet Hiz'ah' and 'Ha-shavui') the injustice done to the Arabs" (17). Rawidowicz quoted extensively from a discussion Yizhar conducted with Zionist youth after the War in which he contrasted the earlier rhetoric of coexistence with the Arabs to the later practices of exclusion of discrimination. Once upon a time, Yizhar noted, we used to speak of "ourselves and our neighbors" in benign terms, alluding to the title of Ben-Gurion's collected essays on the Arab question. But now, the Arabs are referred to as "not trustworthy," a "fifth column," and "hav[ing] no place in this country."[43] This abrupt reversal of rhetoric, Yizhar insisted, was a "breach of faith" by Zionist leaders, political parties, and, above all, educators once loyal to humanist values. For Rawidowicz too, 1948 indeed marked a bold new turning point in many regards. Nevertheless, the troubling rhetoric and action that he observed were not creations ex nihilo. They were the logical culmination of the dominant, though not sole, Zionist path, one that combined disregard for the Diaspora with disregard for the non-Jewish residents of Palestine/Israel—and that was aptly summarized by one unabashed advocate as "cruel Zionism."[44]

The inescapable conclusion toward which Rawidowicz's chapter, "Between Jew and Arab," moved was that the State of Israel must take decisive and painful steps to redress the refugee question. To his mind, it should have done so already in the aftermath of the 1949 armistice agreements into which Israel entered with its Arab neighbors. Failing that, it should now boldly proceed to "open the gates of the State to Arab refugees after the Arab countries have arrived at a peace treaty with it—excluding those Arabs who endanger the security of the State" (28). In fact, the question of sequence—whether to repatriate the refugees before or after a peace treaty—was the subject of intense debate in the midst of the armistice agreements. The Arab side insisted that any discussion of a peace agreement must follow an agreement by Israel to accept the return of at least some of the refugees. Meanwhile, the Israeli side, principally Foreign Minister Moshe Sharett, was prepared to discuss, if only for tactical reasons, some form of return of Arab refugees, but only as part of a comprehensive peace plan.[45]

The idea of repatriation, either before or after a peace agreement, did not last long on the agenda of Israeli diplomacy. No politician of the ruling Mapai party would have accepted Rawidowicz's argument that "five or six hundred refugees from the State of Israel outside of its borders are much more dangerous to the State than five or six hundred thousand additional Arab citizens within its borders" (29). And few resonated to his claim that the fate of Jewish morality hinged on the resolution of the Arab question, even when Rawidowicz emphasized: "It is not for their honor that I am anxious; it is for *our honor*. I am concerned for *our soul*, for the cleansing of the garment of Israel"

(31). Notwithstanding this expression of self-interest, one could readily imagine Israeli political and military leaders dismissing this kind of talk, insisting that they did not have the luxury of caring for the Jewish soul when the Jewish body was faced with daily challenges to its physical well-being.

As we have seen, there was in the years immediately after the 1948 war some discussion of a complex of sensitive issues relating to the Arab question: statutory discrimination, expulsions, and even the prospect of return. And there were a number of Israeli intellectuals in this period who persisted beyond the immediate postwar period in expressing concern over the relationship between Jewish power and morality (e.g., Martin Buber, Ernst Simon, Rabbi Binyamin, Yeshayahu Leibowitz).[46] Nonetheless, the harsh economic and social realities of sustaining a fledgling state filled to the brim with new immigrants— alongside the ongoing enmity of Israel's neighbors and, we speculated earlier, the entry of Holocaust in Israeli collective consciousness—virtually assured that Rawidowicz's chapter would find a very limited receptive audience.

Of course, this chapter found no audience at all, for "Between Jew and Arab" was never published. As we noted at the outset, someone, most likely Rawidowicz or his printer in Paris, Jacob Fink, decided to exclude it from the final version of *Bavel vi-Yerushalayim*. Perhaps Rawidowicz, after pouring so much of his passion into the chapter, had achieved the emotional catharsis he needed. Perhaps he feared that the chapter would altogether undo any positive reception that *Bavel vi-Yerushalayim* might otherwise have received. Perhaps he simply did not want to face the wrath of his fellow Jews. Or perhaps the lingering hostility between Israel and her Arab neighbors, as well as the persistent fear of a "second round" of war, modified his view of Jewish responsibility for the Arab question.

Whatever the case may be, the chapter stands out for its prescience fifty years later. In fact, prescience was a distinguishing feature of Rawidowicz's thought, as Michael Meyer reminds us in recalling his insistence on a meaningful partnership between Israel and the Diaspora. To be sure, there is in Rawidowicz's thought a certain air of the unreal at times—as in his unceasing belief in a vibrant Hebrew culture in the Diaspora. In the case we have discussed here, was it really practicable to repatriate hundreds of thousands of Palestinian refugees in the 1950s? Did he really understand the logistics, not to mention the politics and symbolism, involved in such an act? Could he not have predicted how difficult it would be then, not to mention now?

David N. Myers

But before dismissing Rawidowicz as starry-eyed academic, cloistered in the comfortable if distant environs of Waltham, we should recall that the question of the refugees has, in fact, not disappeared. It emerged as a significant bone of contention in the late stages of the Oslo peace process in 2000–2001, revealing a deep—and, at least from one side, previously unacknowledged—divide in self-perception between Israeli and Palestinian camps. Likewise, Rawidowicz's concern about discrimination against Arabs within the boundaries of Israel has been periodically echoed by various public officials and government ministers, most recently by the government-sponsored Orr Commission of 2003 that investigated the deaths of thirteen Arab citizens in November 2000.

More globally, Simon Rawidowicz's reflections on the modern Jewish experiment with political power have had their own interesting reiterations of late, and not just by those well known for their opposition to Zionism. Writing some three years after the outbreak of the Second Intifada in 2003, Avraham Burg, the former speaker of the Knesset, wrote: "The Zionist revolution has always rested on two pillars: a just path and an ethical leadership. Neither of these is operative any longer. The Israeli nation today rests on a scaffolding of corruption, and on foundations of oppression and injustice. As such, the end of the Zionist enterprise is already on our doorstep."[47]

This harsh epitaph, emanating from a respected Israeli political leader, resonates with Simon Rawidowicz's powerful admonition from a half-century earlier. Whereas Burg was driven to despair by those he called the "corrupt lawbreakers" who settled the West Bank and Gaza after 1967, Rawidowicz was unnerved by the indifference of Jews to the flight of Palestinian Arabs in 1948. Neither Burg nor Rawidowicz drew comfort or joy from what they saw as the precipitous decline in ethical behavior among Jews in their respective day. Nor, for that matter, did their criticism win them wide acclaim from fellow Jews. Many would see them as naïve, even dangerously so, about the harsh world of modern politics. But one could also see them as beacons of conscience who, while swimming against the current, held to the belief that the success or failure of Zionism hinged on its successful negotiation of the newfound power of sovereignty, as well as on its attitude and behavior toward its non-Jewish neighbors. In this, as in so many other matters, Simon Rawidowicz exhibited uncommon wisdom and clairvoyance, rare qualities that we would do well to acknowledge fifty years after his death.

This article emerges out of a forthcoming book, *Israel, Jewish Power, and the Arab Question*, which analyzes (and translates into English) a chapter written by the distinguished Jewish thinker Simon Rawidowicz. Titled "Ben 'ever le-'arav," the chapter was intended for, but never published in, Rawidowicz's two-volume work *Bavel vi-Yerushalayim* (London: Ararat, 1957). I would like to express my deep gratitude to Professor Benjamin Ravid for his many kindnesses and assistance in enabling my study of his father, including his providing me with a copy of the text in question. I would also like to thank my teacher and colleague Arnold J. Band, who joined me in translating the chapter, which is here rendered into English as "Between Jew and Arab." (Page numbers in parentheses throughout the text refer to the Hebrew original.) I would also like to thank Arnie Band, Derek Penslar, and Nomi Stolzenberg for their helpful readings of this paper, as well as Hillel Eyal for his excellent research assistance.

1. Michael A. Meyer, "Where Does the Modern Period of Jewish History Begin?" *Judaism* (Summer 1975): 329–38.
2. See Meyer's foreword to the reissued volume of Rawidowicz's writing, *State of Israel, Diaspora, and Jewish Continuity,* ed. Benjamin C. I. Ravid (Hanover, N.H.: University Press of New England, 1998), 6.
3. Among the few to have read and commented on the chapter are Ravid, *State of Israel,* 43–44; Avraham Greenbaum, "Rawidowicz at Brandeis University (A Memoir)," *A History of the Ararat Publishing Society* (Jerusalem: Rubin Mass, 1998), 50; and Noam F. Pianko, "Diaspora Jewish Nationalism and Identity in America, 1914–1967" (PhD diss., Yale University, 2004), 193–95.
4. Indeed, this became the topic of a well-known exchange of letters Rawidowicz had with David Ben-Gurion in 1954, excerpted in Ravid, *State of Israel,* 194–204. The full exchange can be seen in Simon Rawidowicz, *Bavel vi-Yerushalayim* (London: Ararat, 1957), 2:872–909.
5. Among the significant titles are Benny Morris, *The Birth of the Palestinian Refugee Problem Revisited* (Cambridge: Cambridge University Press, 2004); Ilan Pappé, *Britain and the Arab-Israeli Conflict, 1948–51* (London: Basingstoke, 1988); Avi Shlaim, *Collusion across the Jordan: King Abdullah, the Zionist Movement, and the Partition of Palestine* (Oxford: Clarendon, 1988); and Tom Segev, *1949: The First Israelis* (New York: Free Press, 1986). This new Israeli research has generated its own scholarly scrutiny. See, e.g., the largely sympathetic treatment of Laurence J. Silberstein, *The Postzionism Debates: Knowledge and Power in Israeli Culture* (New York: Routledge, 1999); or the highly critical account of Efraim Karsh, *Fabricating Israeli History: The New Historians* (New York: Frank Cass, 1997). We should be careful to note, as have several of those mentioned earlier, that it was not they who uncovered the refugee problem. Earlier Palestinian historians, while relying on fragmentary sources, nonetheless wrote extensively about the refugees, most signifi-

cantly, 'Arif al-'Arif, author of a six-volume history of 1948 titled *Al-Na-kba* (The catastrophe) that was published from 1956 to 1960. For a brief discussion of Palestinian literature on the subject, see the preface to *All That Remains: The Palestinian Villages Occupied and Depopulated by Israel in 1948* (Washington, D.C.: Institute for Palestine Studies, 1992), xv–xvi.

6. See the enumeration of the key issues at stake in Benny Morris, "The New Historiography: Israel and Its Past," in *1948 and After: Israel and the Palestinians*, 1–34 (Oxford: Clarendon, 1990); and Avi Shlaim, "The Debate about 1948," *International Journal of Middle Eastern Studies* 27 (1995): 287–304.

7. Inflamed passions arose among politicians who, in the early years of this century, began to call into question the way in which Israeli historical textbooks had been rewritten in the latter half of the 1990s (e.g., to account for some of the conclusions of the New Historians). Former Education Minister Limor Livnat, in particular, took a strong stand against revised textbooks, including those that made reference to Jewish acts of expulsion, arguing that "no nation studies its history from the point of view of its enemy or the point of view of the United Nations." Her letter in *Ma'ariv* from March 7, 2001, is quoted in Majid al-Haj, "National Ethos, Multicultural Education, and the New History Textbooks in Israel," *Curriculum Inquiry* 35, no. 1 (2005): 55. Interestingly, even Israeli scholars who are critical of the New Historians no longer claim that the flight of Palestinian Arabs was exclusively the result of instructions from neighboring Arab countries. See, e.g., Yoav Gelber's discussion of expulsions in Ramle/Lod and during Operation Hiram in his *Komemiyut ve-Nakba: Yisra'el, ha-falestinim umedinot 'Arav, 1948* (Or Yehuda: Devir, 2004), 246–47 and 350–51. Indeed, Derek Penslar observes: "Twenty years after the appearance of the first fruits of the new history, many of its arguments have been accepted into the Israeli historiographical mainstream. It is now conventional wisdom that, as Benny Morris argued back in 1987, substantial numbers of Palestinians were expelled fom their homes in 1948, and the Arab states' military capabilities were far less, and those of the Zionists far greater, than raw numbers would suggest." See Derek J. Penslar, *Israel in History: The Jewish State in Comparative Perspective* (New York: Routledge, 2007), 44–45. For a more traditional account that focuses exclusively on the claim that Palestinian Arabs were encouraged by Arab leaders to take flight, see Shabtai Tevet's rebuttal of Benny Morris, "Charging Israel with Original Sin," *Commentary* (September 1989): 24–33.

8. On the question of Israeli responsibility, see Ian Lustick's interesting chapter "Negotiating Truth: The Holocaust, *Lehavdil*, and al-Nakba," in *Exile and Return: Predicaments of Palestinians and Jews*, ed. Ann M. Lesch and Ian S. Lustick, 106–32 (Philadelphia: University of Pennsylvania Press, 2005).

9. Ilan Pappé, "Critique and Agenda: The Post-Zionist Scholars in Israel,"

History and Memory 7, no. 1 (1995): 82, 85.

10. See Morris, "New Historiography," 16–17; as well as Shlaim, "Debate about 1948," 289.

11. Rony Gabbay, *A Political Study of the Arab-Jewish Conflict: The Arab Refugee Problem* (Geneva: E. Droz, 1959), 109–10.

12. Ibid., 110n158.

13. This was Ben-Gurion's statement to Claude de Boisanger, the Frenchman who chaired the UN's Palestine Conciliation Commission on April 7, 1949. Qtd. in Morris, *Birth of the Palestinian Refugee Problem*, 260. More than a decade and a half later, Ben-Gurion repeated the claim that "the Arab refugees fled of their own free will" in a conversation in 1966 with Israeli Arab member of Knesset Tewfik Toubi. See the transcript of their conversation in Zaki Shalom, "Ben-Gurion and Tewfik Toubi Finally Meet, October 28, 1966," *Israel Studies* 8, no. 2 (2003): 57. However, Morris recalls that various scholars, including Ben-Gurion's own biographer Michael Bar-Zohar, asserted that it was Ben-Gurion himself who issued an expulsion order for Ramle and Lydda (Lod). See Morris, "New Historiography," 4.

14. S. Yizhar, "Hirbet Hizah," in *Shiv'ah Sipurim*, 37–88. See also Anita Shapira, "Between Remembrance and Forgetting," *Jewish Social Studies* 7, no. 1 (2000): 3.

15. Yizhar, "Hirbet Hizah," 74.

16. Shapira, "Between Remembrance and Forgetting," 23.

17. M. Roshuld's article in *Be-terem* (12–13 [November–December 1949]: 75) is quoted in ibid., 13.

18. Cohen's memorandum of May 6, 1948, is quoted in Benny Morris, "Mapai, Mapam, and the Arab Problem in 1948," in Morris, *1948 and After*, 46. See also Joel Beinin, *Was the Red Flag Flying There? Marxist Politics and the Arab-Israeli Conflict in Egypt and Israel, 1948–1965* (Berkeley: University of California Press, 1990), 33.

19. Qtd. in Morris, "Mapai, Mapam, and the Arab Problem," 52.

20. Morris, *Birth of the Palestinian Refugee Problem*, 423–36.

21. Meir Ya'ari, "Ki tetsu le-milhamah," *Al ha-mishmar*, July 30, 1948.

22. Alexander Pereg, "Medinat Yisrael veha-kefar ha-'aravi," *Al ha-mishmar*, August 1, 1948.

23. The claim that Ben-Gurion ordered the expulsion of Arabs from Ramle and Lydda emerges out of the testimony by Yitzhak Rabin to Michael Bar-Zohar, author of a three-volume biography of Ben-Gurion. Benny Morris describes the encounter as follows: "Someone, possibly (Yitzhak) Allon, after hearing of the outbreak in Lydda, proposed expelling the inhabitants of the two towns (Lydda and Ramle). Ben-Gurion said nothing, and no decision was taken. Then Ben-Gurion, Allon and Rabin stepped outside for a cigarette. Allon reportedly asked: 'What shall we do with the Arabs?' Ben-Gurion responded with a dismissive, energetic gesture with his hand and said: 'Expel them [*garesh otam*].'" What remains unclear to scholars is whether Ben-Gurion actually uttered the

words or Allon and Rabin understood his hand gesture to mean that. See Morris's discussion in *The Birth of the Palestinian Refugee Problem*, 429, 454n88.

24. It was also rather common, on the right end of the Zionist spectrum, to resist the claim of Jewish expulsions by insisting that the exodus was the result of orders issuing from the Arab world. Instructive in this regard is the work of the American historian Joseph B. Schechtman, who authored a biography of Vladimir Zev Jabotinsky and was closely aligned with the Revisionist Zionist movement. Schechtman's 1952 book, *The Arab Refugee Problem*, posits that the "mass flight of the Palestinian Arabs is a phenomenon for which no single explanation suffices." While placing the onus of responsibility on Arab leaders (those of the Arab Higher Committee and later leaders of neighboring countries), he does not include among his explanations expulsions by Jewish forces, with the exception of Deir Yassin, which he calls the "unfortunate single incident of the war." See Joseph B. Schechtman, *The Arab Refugee Problem* (New York: Philosophical Library, 1952), 4, 11.

25. See, e.g., his articles in *Ner* 2, nos. 1–2 (1950): 3–4; and 2, nos. 3–4 (1950): 3–6, 13. By 1952 Rabbi Binyamin had modified his call for a return of Arab refugees without preconditions to a partial return based on a mix of realism and idealism. Cf. *Ner* 3, nos. 5–6 (1951–52): 2–3.

26. See Shmuel Hugo Bergmann, "Sefekot," *Ner* 1, no. 4 (1950): 3–4. "It is true that there are many sins that lie at the foot of the foundation of our state. But these sins—we must see and assess them in light of our history since 1933. If there was a sin in the expulsion of Arabs from certain places, and in our malevolent attitude toward them, then we all took part in that sin, in that malevolent attitude. We must not place ourselves above responsibility for this, as if we were better than others."

27. See, e.g., "Vikuah so'er 'al hok ha-'ezrahut" [Stormy debate on the nationality law], *Ha-arets*, March 27, 1952, or the report several days after the law was implemented, "Shevitat maha'a kelalit shel ha-ukhlusyah ha-'aravit neged hok ha-'ezrahut ha-giz'ani" [General protest strike of the Arab population against the racist citizenship law], *Kol ha-'am*, July 15, 1952. For a fundamental legal discussion of the law, see David Kretzmer, *The Legal Status of the Arabs in Israel* (Boulder, Colo.: Westview Press, 1990), 35–48. More recently, Shira Robinson has offered a probing analysis of the extension of citizenship to Arabs in Israel, regarding this act as much as a means of regulation and *exclusion* (i.e., of former residents of Palestine) as of *inclusion*. See Shira Nomi Robinson, "Occupied Citizens in a Liberal State: Palestinians Under Military Rule and the Colonial Formation of Israeli Society, 1948–1966" (PhD diss., Stanford University, 2005).

28. Benny Morris has chronicled the public debate over Qibiya, noting that the mainstream press accepted Ben-Gurion's fallacious account that the IDF was not responsible for the episode while a smaller number (*Ha-arets*, *'Al ha-mishmar*, and *Kol ha-'am*) rejected his claims. See "Ha-

'itonut ha-yisre'elit be-farashat Qibiya," in his *Tikun ta'ut: Yehudim ve-'aravim be-erets-Yisra'el, 1936–1956* (Tel Aviv, 2000), 175–97.

29. Shapira, "Between Remembrance and Forgetting," 25.

30. Ibid., 26. To these explanations, we must add the concerted efforts of Israeli politicians, government officials, and researchers to count and categorize the refugees and then to rebut their claims to return to their homes. See the study of this effort during the years 1948–52 by Haya Bombaji-Sasportas, "Kolo shel mi nishma/kolo shel mi mushtak: havnayat ha-siah 'al 'be'ayat ha-pelitim ha-falastinim' ba-mimsad ha-Yisre'eli" (master's thesis, Ben-Gurion University, 2000).

31. Tom Segev, *The Seventh Million: The Israelis and the Holocaust* (New York: Hill and Wang, 1993), esp. 421–45.

32. See the comments of Rawidowicz's alter-ego, Ish Boded, "Shivre devarim," *Metsudah* 5–6 (1948): 560.

33. The reference to the struggle over the garment is to Baba Metzia 1:1. Also, Rawidowicz always used the term "Israel" in the sense of "Klal Yisrael," and never to mean the State of Israel.

34. The declaration expressly mentions in article 15 that "everyone has the right to a nationality" and that "no one shall be arbitrarily deprived of his nationality nor denied the right to change his nationality." See www.un.org/Overview/rights.html.

35. As British secretary of state for the colonies, Churchill actually sought to dilute somewhat Zionist expectations over the Balfour Declaration of 1917. The resulting White Paper of 1922 expressly declared that His Majesty's government's aim is *not* to make Palestine "as Jewish as England is English." At the same time, Churchill did want to clarify that "it is essential that it [the Jewish people] know that it is in Palestine as of right and not on the sufferance." See www.yale.edu/lawweb/avalon/mideast/brwh1922.html.

36. Rawidowicz estimates the number of those excluded by this law at 15,000 out of some 180,000 Arabs in Israel in 1953.

37. Israel Land Acquisition (Validation of Acts and Compensation) Law, 5713-1953.

38. This group has generated a good deal of scholarly attention, but among the most interesting accounts is the series of interviews conducted by the Israeli author David Grossman in *Sleeping on a Wire: Conversations with Palestinians in Israel* (New York: Farrar, Straus and Giroux, 1993).

39. The accusation of expropriation recalls the case of the ancient Ahab, king of Samaria, who expropriated the land of Naboth, his neighbor, and then put him to death (1 Kings 21). This series of actions enraged God, who enjoined Elijah to confront Ahab and ask, "Have you murdered and also taken possession?" (1 Kings 21:19).

40. Rawidowicz's phrase "a weak and poor people" (am halash ve-dal) recalls a similar phrase in Zephaniah 3:12 ("an afflicted and weak people"—am ani ve-dal). Also, the phrase "pillage and plunder" appears in a number of places in the prophetic writings (e.g., Isaiah 10:6, Ezekiel 38:12).

41. Naturally, the call would be much more commonly sounded among the Arab refugees themselves, as well as among their supporters in the Arab and Muslim worlds, especially in the midst of negotiations with Israel (from the armistice talks in 1949 to the Oslo peace process of the 1990s).

42. The term *gezerah* reflects both the richness and the traditional bent of Rawidowicz's Hebrew. The term can be translated variously as "plight," "decree" (especially an *evil* decree), or "catastrophe" (as in *gezerot ta"h ve-ta"t*, referring to the Chmielnicki massacres of 1648–49). Rawidowicz's usage contains elements of all three of these English words.

43. "Between Jew and Arab," 18. Yizhar's conversation is found in *Divre siah: hartsa'ot ve-diyune haverim* (Tel Aviv: Mifleget po'ale Eretz Yisra'el, 1951), 2:52–53.

44. The term is the title of a small pamphlet by the Hebrew writer and collector Avraham Sharon (né Schwadron), *Torat ha-Tsiyonut ha-akhzarit* (Tel Aviv: Sifriyat De'ot, 1943–44). Rawidowicz found Sharon's views distasteful in two regards: first, in his advocacy for a Zionism that severed its connections to the Diaspora and, second, in his advocacy of the "transfer" of Arabs from Israel.

45. For a discussion of the various proposals considered by Israel and often advanced by Sharett—e.g., the "Gaza plan" and the "100,000 offer"— see Morris, *Birth of the Palestinian Refugee Problem*, 549–80.

46. Perhaps most interesting in this regard is Yeshayahu Leibowitz, who in an essay written shortly after Qibiya excoriated those who had placed the veil of divine sanctity upon the State of Israel: "If the nation and its welfare and the country and its security are holy . . . then Kibiyeh [sic] is possible and permissible." At the same time, Leibowitz, in contrast to Rawidowicz, Buber, or Simon, was altogether skeptical that there was a *Jewish* morality to speak of, arguing that "morality does not admit a modifying attribute and cannot be 'Jewish' or 'not Jewish.'" Leibowitz's essay, originally published in the Israeli journal *Be-terem*, was included as "After Kibiyeh," in his English collection *Judaism, Human Values, and the Jewish State* (Cambridge: Harvard University Press, 1992), 189–90. See also the discussion by Ehud Luz, "'Jewish Ethics' as an Argument in the Public Debate over the Israeli Reaction to Palestinian Terror," *Israel Studies* 7 (2002): 134–56.

47. Avraham Burg, "The End of Zionism," *Guardian*, September 15, 2003. This essay was completed before the appearance of Burg's book *Le-natseah et Hitler* (Tel Aviv: Yedi'ot aharonot, 2007) and his controversial interview with Ari Shavit in *Ha-arets* on June 6, 2007. In the book and interview, Burg went a good deal further than he had earlier, questioning the wisdom of Zionism and of Israel as a Jewish state.

Jewish Religion and Capitalism

Avraham Barkai

Seitdem geht Israel wie die Sonne über Europa, wo es hinkommt,
sprießt neues Leben empor, von wo es wegzieht, da modert alles, was
bisher geblüht hat.
  [Israel passes over Europe like the sun: at its coming new life bursts
forth; at its going all life falls into decay.]
  —Werner Sombart, *Die Juden und das Wirtschaftsleben*

The chapter epigraph is a statement in the introduction to Werner
Sombart's famous book on the Jews and the economy. It appeared in
1911, to refute, as its author explicitly declared, Max Weber's theses on
the role of Protestant Puritanism in the rise of modern capitalism.[1] "A
careful examination of Weber's argumentation convinced me," Sombart writes, "that all those parts of the Puritan dogma which appeared
to me to be of real significance for the development of the capitalist
spirit were borrowed from the concepts of the Jewish religion."[2] We
will return to the respective treatment of the religious sources of the
Jews' economic behavior by both authors but first shed a cursory look
on the tradition of identifying "the Jews" per se as capitalists.

Even before these learned scholars tried to prove the immanent
"capitalist" character of the Jews, earlier socialist or anarchist writers
had taken up the Middle Age stereotype of the Jewish usurers and
accused them of being the founders and leaders of the international
haute finance. Raised in the tradition of Christian anti-Judaistic theology and popular prejudice, they sought, quasi in the footsteps of Jesus

Christ, to drive the Jewish moneylenders from the temples of modern society. The French utopian socialist Charles Fourier opposed the emancipation of the Jews as premature because, following their religion, they separated themselves from and financially exploited their Christian neighbors. "After no more than a century they will organize their clique in every town, associate only among themselves and . . . finally purloin every trade profession from the French citizens."[3] Fourier's disciple Alphonse Toussenel continued the trend to its extreme. Fourier's polemic chastised the Orthodox Jewish petty traders and moneylenders in the contested German-French province of Alsace. Toussenel attacked the assimilated bourgeois Jews of Paris, identifying them with the abhorred "financial feudalism."[4] Though he admitted that there were also non-Jewish financiers around, he explained this generalization by the "popular linguistic interchange of Jew, banker, haggler." His personal contribution consisted, however, in his attempt to base the traditional anti-Jewish stereotype and the evils of financial feudalism on the Old Testament: "Whoever reads the Bible . . . must find written in the Jewish prayer books that the exploitation of the globe was granted by God to the servants of his law."[5]

Karl Marx adopted the same "popular linguistic interchange" in his famous essay "On the Jewish Question," which appeared at about the same time. Much ink has been spilled about the question whether this work proves that Marx was an antisemite. Be that as it may, the tractate was a philosophical treatise in the discourse of the young disciples of Hegel in which Marx advocated granting the Jews full political emancipation. His discussion with Bruno Bauer is complex and its importance today marginal. But his generalizing identification of the Jews with capitalism was of long lasting influence on the way in which Socialist parties dealt with the "Jewish problems." Eventually the best remembered passages of the essay were to become standard ammunition in the repertoire of antisemitic invective:

> Suchen wir das Geheimnis des Juden nicht in seiner Religion, sondern suchen wir das Geheimnis der Religion im wirklichen Juden. Welches ist der weltliche Grund des Judentums? Das praktische Bedürfnis, der *Eigennutz*. Welches ist der weltliche Kultus des Juden? Der *Schacher*. Welches ist sein weltlicher Gott? Das Geld. . . . Das Geld ist der eifrige Gott Israels, vor welchem kein anderer Gott bestehen darf. . . . Der Gott der Juden hat sich verweltlicht, er ist zum Weltgott geworden. . . . Die *gesellschaftliche* Emanzipation des Juden ist die *Emanzipation der Gesellschaft vom Judentum.*

[Let us look for the secret of the Jew not in his religion but rather for the secret of the religion in the actual Jew. What is the secular basis of Judaism? *Practical* need, *self-interest*. What is the worldly cult of the Jew? *Bargaining*. What is his worldly god? *Money*. . . . Money is the jealous god of Israel before whom no other god may exist. . . The god of the world has become secularized and has become the god of the world. . . . The social emancipation of the Jew is the emancipation of the society from Judaism.][6]

The stereotypes of "the Jews" as rich financiers personifying the capitalist system persisted inside the Socialist parties during most of the nineteenth century and did not entirely disappear in the twentieth. Socialist leaders who raged against the "capitalistic Jews" were not necessarily antisemites, but they felt that a grain of antisemitism may serve their cause. Thus, for example, August Bebel (1840–1913) claimed while addressing the fourth convention of the German Social Democratic Party in 1893: "The Christians, who have forced the Jews into commerce during one and a half millenia, have to blame themselves if the Jews are such bustling tradesmen." Nevertheless he declared that antisemitism would in the end "only serve the Social Democrats, . . . when those social strata who still belong to the politically most sluggish and mentally lazy [people] . . . will realize that capitalist Jewry is only a part of the capitalist society; that what matters is not the liberation from Judaism, but that from capitalism, with which capitalist Jewry stands and falls."[7]

The Austrian Social Democrats, confronted with the most extreme antisemitic movement of the time, and uncomfortably counting some prominent men of Jewish descent at the helm of their party, were even more outspoken. In 1891 their founder and chairman Victor Adler obstructed a clear-cut resolution against antisemitism at the convention of the Second Internationale in Brussels. Justifying this action six years later, he declared that "the Jewish question had been greatly exaggerated. . . . To be afraid of antisemitism is as ridiculous as to be afraid of the Jews themselves. . . . The special feature of the Jewish problem as it manifests itself in Vienna is that the capitalist bourgeoisie has a Jewish complexion. It is sad that the Jews have to bear that burden. But I and others have grown tired of always finding Jews in our soup."[8] The old Friedrich Engels warned the leaders of the Austrian Social-Democrats against the dangers of this identification in an open letter from London in April 1889. He described the suffering of Jewish workers in England, "who are the most exploited and miserable of all workers," and analyzed antisemitism at great length as "the reaction against capitalism on the part of backward, medieval strata in modern society . . . in the guise of imaginary socialism. . . . And after all this they demand that we adopt antisemitic policies in order to combat capitalism? . . . You should ponder carefully on whether anti-semitism will not inflict on you a disaster far greater than any possible benefit it can bring you."[9]

To return to the main topic of this essay: the negative attitude toward trade, generally and specifically toward Jewish trade, as an "un-productive" economic activity was inherited from the Physiocrats of the eighteenth century.[10] Since then this attitude had become not only one of the antisemitic stereotypes that outlived preindustrial society, but was also internalized by some Jewish circles. In nineteenth-cen-tury Germany, Jewish charitable organizations not only proclaimed the necessity but also practically tried, with little success, to reverse the abnormal vocational structure of the Jews by training them in agricul-ture and the crafts.[11] Well-meaning non-Jews regarded the economic "normalization"—or in their language, the "civil improvement"—of the Jews as a condition for their legal emancipation.[12] We do not know how many Jewish youngsters attended these training courses, but for a time they seem to have involved quite a number of orphans and chil-dren of needy families. What we know for sure is that the long-term influence of all these well-meant endeavors was negligible. Not many wealthy Jews thought of applying the efforts of "normalization" to the education of their own children, convincing them to leave the flourish-ing businesses of their parents to become farmers or artisans. To the very end of the existence of German Jewry most of its members pre-ferred to take advantage of the market economy in commerce and fi-nance, rather than joining the ranks of the rural or urban proletariat.[13]

The negative image of the Jewish merchants and petty trades-men, moneylenders and currency changers, was deeply embedded in the popular prejudices of Christian Europe. Worried by the accusa-tions that Jewish religious law permitted fraudulent business deals with non-Jews, rabbis and learned scholars sought for ways to disprove them. One old anti-Jewish argument concerned the hallowed Kol Ni-dre prayer on the eve of Yom Kippur. Without going into the details of internal Jewish debates since its introduction into Jewish ritual in the ninth century, they certainly prove the uneasiness caused by its inter-pretation by the non-Jews. An unsophisticated reading of the prayer's text could indeed arouse suspicions. Sung by the ḥazan at the start of the service in its age-old solemn melody it could be conceived as a legal absolution of all attending Jews from their prior and also future commitments. Not only religious reformers but even Samson Raphael Hirsch, who later became the leading figure of the separatist neo-orthodoxy in Germany, removed the prayer from the liturgy of his community in Oldenburg in 1839. Five years later its replacement was unanimously recommended in by the first assembly of German rabbis in Brunswick in June 1844.[14]

Neither Sombart nor Max Weber was entirely free from the traditional prejudice toward commerce and finance, but their attitudes toward modern capitalism differed in many ways. In Sombart's opinion capitalism started already in the late Middle Ages, as a result of the separation of economic activities from self-consumption, to become a means of earning money at a profit. In 1902 Sombart had set the "birth-hour" of capitalism with the sack of Constantinople in 1204. There it rose like a deus ex machina as "commerce-capitalism" from the loot of Byzantine treasures.[15] Nine years later Sombart transferred not only the birth date of capitalism from 1204 to 1492 but also its birthplace from Asia Minor to the Netherlands, France, and England. This time the "start-off" resulted from the expulsion of the Jews from the Iberian Peninsula. Sombart "generously" granted the Jews the decisive role in the rise of capitalism and their migratory movements the role of its expansion. The double-edged ambivalence of this "generosity" evolved not long after, when his critical attitude toward the capitalist system came to the fore.

Between the publication of Sombart's books quoted earlier, Max Weber published his fundamental study on the rise of capitalism. Weber defined capitalism much more positively than Sombart, as the industrial organization of the economy, based on free labor. He explicitly turned against the negative evaluation that saw the main characteristic of capitalism in the uncurbed *appetitus divitiarum infinitus*, that is, the unlimited craving for enrichment.[16] Weber also fixed no exact date for the birth of capitalism, stressing the different stages of the process in different countries. Without neglecting former economic systems that showed early capitalist symptoms, Weber confined his main study to modern, western European capitalism, not distinctively observable before the sixteenth or seventeenth century. His historical periodization follows essentially that of Karl Marx, but in contrast to Marx's materialist determinism Weber accorded a decisive, though not exclusive, role to the changes in ideological and religious norms of the times. More specifically, he underlined the influence of the Reformation, especially of Puritanism, based on the teachings of John Calvin (1509–64), for the development of capitalism.

Sombart, as quoted earlier, wrote his work on the Jews in the economy explicitly as a refutation of Weber's main theses. Over seventy pages of Sombart's book were accordingly devoted to a detailed description of the religious laws and directives prescribing the Jews'

Avraham Barkai

economic dealings and behavior, at the level of its author's knowledge—or that of his assistants, who were probably Jewish. But alas,
despite this demonstrated erudition the main argument of the book,
quasi qualifying the Jews to become the precursors and founders of
capitalism, was not based on their religious norms but on their racial
characteristics, which were said to be reflected in their religion. The
"alle anderen Einflüsse weit übergipfelnde Bedeutung der Juden für
das moderne Wirtschaftsleben" (importance of the Jews to modern
economic life, which is much more significant than any other contribution) he ascribed to "der [historisch zufälligen] Tatsache, . . . daß ein
ganz besonders geartetes Volk–ein Wüstenvolk und ein Wandervolk–
unter wesensverschiedene Völker–naßkalte, schwerblütige, boden-
ständige Völker–verschlagen worden ist. . . . Wären sie alle im Orient
geblieben, . . . wäre (es) niemals zu dem Knalleffekt der menschlichen
Kultur: dem modernen Kapitalismus gekommen" (a very peculiar people—a desert people and a nomadic people—was dispersed among
peoples of a different nature: wet and cold peoples, of heavy blood, and
tied to their soil. . . . Would [the Jews] have remained in the Orient, . . .
the big bang of human culture, modern capitalism, would never have
occurred).[17]

The unmistakable racist undertones of this statement call for a
few remarks on Sombart's ideological development and political affiliations in the years to come. As a member of the Historical School
his attitude toward economic liberalism was, to say the least, skeptical
from the start. Already in 1903 he had advocated increased intervention of "statesmanship techniques" in the economy, which would lead
to what he then defined as "social capitalism."[18] An increasing preference for what he defined as a modern economic *Kameralismus* is evident from Sombart's later publications.[19] Later he became one of the
venerated teachers of the ultranationalist Young Conservatives who
gathered in the 1920s around the influential journal *Die Tat*. Finally,
in 1934 he published a book that hailed the Nazi regime as the bearer
of German socialism that had arrived to replace the perhaps necessary but basically immoral system of capitalism that had hampered
Germany's social and national development.[20]

Max Weber's study on ancient Judaism was published posthumously in 1920.[21] Weber refrained from presenting his work as an
answer to Sombart's opus and accorded him no detailed discussion
in the text. The book is the third part of his research on the relation
between economic development and religions. He intended to include
all major religious beliefs and confessions of the world but did not
complete the work before his death, at the age of fifty-six, in 1920.
Unlike Sombart's volume on the Jews, Weber's study is an achieve-

ment of profound scientific research. Weber did not claim that his narrative on the ancient kingdoms of Israel and Judea was based on primary sources. They were written in languages that he—like Sombart—could not read. But his work shows a broad knowledge and understanding of the secondary literature extant at his time. Leaning strongly and approvingly on the path breaking studies of German historians and biblical scholars like Julius Wellhausen (1844–1918) or Eduard Meyer (1855–1930), Weber explicitly disclaimed presenting "'new' facts and conceptions. . . . New to some extent is only the way to explore these matters in the light of some sociological questions."[22]

On the basis of these works, internationally regarded to be leading in their fields in their own time and later, Weber developed his conception of the pariah character of the Jewish people. A detailed description of the way in which Weber analyzed the religious and moral norms of the Jews from antiquity to the period of the Talmud would exceed the limits of this essay. The essence of the work is the conclusion that the Jews separated themselves voluntarily from their environmental societies, motivated by their religious norms and inhibitions, before they were compelled to do so by external pressures. As the work remained unfinished, Weber could not follow up his narrative of the Jews and their economic standing to the times of their dispersion in the Diaspora. Nevertheless he evidently deemed his finding sufficient to prove what he called the pariah character of the Jews, a term borrowed from the Indian caste system: "ein Pariavolk . . . ein rituell, formell oder faktisch von der sozialen Umwelt geschiedenes Gastvolk. Alle wesentlichen Züge seines Verhaltens zur Umwelt, vor allem seine längst vor der Zwangsinternierung bestehende freiwillige Ghettoexistenz und die Art des Dualismus von Binnen-und Außenmoral lassen sich daraus ableiten" (a pariah people . . . a people separated from their social surroundings ritually, formally, or factually. All significant traits of its behavior toward its surroundings—in particular its ghetto existence, which existed voluntarily long before the first ghettoization, and the dualism of an internal versus an external morality—can be derived from this fact). On this characterization Weber based his conception of the Jewish pariah capitalism.[23]

Weber's description of the Jews' place in economic developments through the ages proves his ambiguous attitude toward their preference for commerce, and toward commerce in general, which he shared with many of his contemporaries. This was probably the reason for his denying any positive relation between Jewish religion and capitalism. Among the Jews,

Niemals konnte . . . ökonomischer Erwerb eine Stätte re-

ligiöser "Bewährung" werden. . . . Das Gebiet der Bewährung der Frömmigkeit liegt beim Juden auf einem durchaus
anderem Gebiet als dem einer rationalen Bewältigung der
"Welt," insbesondere der Wirtschaft. . . . Jedenfalls haben
jene orientalischen, südeuropäischen und osteuropäischen
Gebiete, in denen sie am längsten und meisten heimisch
waren, weder in der Antike noch im Mittelalter noch in der
Neuzeit die dem Kapitalismus *spezifischen* Züge entwickelt.
Ihr wirklicher Anteil an der Entwicklung des Okzident be-
ruhte höchst wesentlich auf dem *Gastvolk* charakter, den
die selbstgewollte Absonderung ihnen aufprägte.

[Economic livelihood could never become a place of religious "trial." . . . Religious trial is shown among the Jews
in quite different realms. . . . The oriental, the southern European, and the eastern European regions, in which Jews
lived most of the time and in which they felt most at home,
never developed the traits characteristic of capitalism, neither in antiquity nor in the Middle Ages nor in modern
times. Their real contribution to the development of the
western world was based at most on their character as a
guest people, caused by their voluntary separation.][24]

Weber did not mention Sombart in the context of this quotation, but he must have been aware of its contrast to Sombart's theses.
The tenor of his description and the terms he chose to describe and
characterize the economic function of the Jews do not exactly make
him a philosemite. But even historians and scholars of religion who
disagreed with Weber's conclusions never missed paying respect to
his scholarly integrity and his meticulous research. Sombart's concoction was, on the contrary, severely criticized.[25] Sombart, as we have
seen, repeatedly changed his ideological attitude toward capitalism,
but when he wrote his book on the Jews in the economy it had already
turned to being rather negative. Those Jewish publicists, who admired
him, either for according the Jews a prominent role in the economic
achievements of modern Europe, or later for his "benevolent" praise
of the aspirations of Zionism, missed his point.[26] For the Sombart
of these years nominating the Jews as the creators of capitalism did
not mean to give a compliment to the Jews. And he was certainly not
the only antisemite who welcomed Zionism as a means to "free" Germany from its Jewish citizens.

This essay does not intend to pass judgment as to whether Sombart or Weber was right with regard to our topic. However, a short
historical survey of the relation between the economic pursuits of the

Jews in Germany and the economic development of the country may be appropriate; the German official statistics were used by Sombart to prove his theory and are still the largest and most complete quantitative evidence of the interaction of Jewish economic history and the rise of capitalism. But we should be aware of the pitfalls of generalization. The effects of capitalism on the Jews were not the same everywhere. In the regions of their dense settlement in eastern Europe, for instance, most of them were hit hard by the belated capitalist development. The fate of the German Jews under capitalism can probably be regarded as paradigmatic at best for early industrialized countries with a relatively small Jewish population like England, France, or the United States.

No one would claim that the Jews played a primary role in the technical process of Europe's industrialization. Jews took no part in the technical innovations in agriculture that created the masses of free labor before the Industrial Revolution in England or in the later process of its industrialization. In countries where the process of industrialization was delayed, Jewish bankers did finance innovations in some specific branches, like the development of the railways, especially in eastern Europe and the Balkans.[27] But granting these small numbers of Jewish financiers the decisive role in the industrialization of these countries would be more than their due. Their influence was important but only in an economically and geographically limited area. With regard to Germany I concluded years ago, based on extant and my own research, that "in some small and restricted areas . . . Jewish entrepreneurial initiative was certainly beneficial. . . . In some branches their part was proportionally higher than in others. But in the general framework of the whole country's economic development this could, . . . carry only little weight. Had there been no Jews [at all], the course of German industrialization would hardly have been different."[28]

But the Jews were, of course, influenced by industrialization and the social transformations of their environment in a way that was different from their gentile neighbors. Different enough, indeed, to speak of their group-specific "fate" during and after the rise of capitalism. This because, as Simon Kuznets has convincingly shown, every distinctive small minority shows different traits not only in their ethnic, cultural, or religious characteristics but also in their vocational and social structure and economic behavior.[29] As far as these differences were, in the case of the Jews, the result of persecutions or discrimination in precapitalist societies because of their beliefs and rites, one may relate them to their religion, or rather the prevailing prejudice against it, even after a great part of modern Jews were quite alienated from it.

It is, however, more important to ask whether these specific vocational and economic traits were helpful for the adjustment of the Jews to the capitalist development in their respective countries. In the case of the German Jews, the answer is evidently affirmative. Not only the small elite of rich bankers and merchants but also many of the less prosperous Jews had been able to improve their economic situation already in the early nineteenth century, before the start of Germany's industrialization. The rapid increase of the population and the expanding market economy found them prepared to make use of their training and expertise in the commercial branches of those consumer goods in which most of the gainfully employed Jews were concentrated. The result was a remarkable increase in their average incomes and their properties, in absolute terms as well as relatively, that is, compared with the general population. Around 1800 one quarter of all German Jews were still defined as "vagrants" and "beggar Jews," lacking settlement rights and living at a very low level of subsistence. At mid-century, shortly before the country's industrial "take-off," some 70 percent of all Jewish families were already on the tax rolls, though most of them in the lowest income brackets. At the foundation of the German *Reich* in 1871, over 60 percent of them belonged to the better-situated middle class, and quite a few had gained considerable properties.[30] The same applies even more to the nearly quarter million Jews who emigrated between 1820 and the end of the century from German-speaking countries to America. The unavoidable conclusion is that although the Jews in the countries of early modern capitalism were not its founders, they certainly were among its beneficiaries. Was this because they were the collective bearers of gifts and capacities that enabled them to adjust, better than the non-Jews in their environment, to the structural economic changes of industrialization and the expanding market? And if so, to what extent were these capabilities engrained by the teachings, the norms, and the values of their religion?

The answer to the first question is that the Jews had no need to change their economic profile and pursuits in order to adjust to the new market conditions. They could easily benefit from them by continuing in their traditional vocations and industries on a higher level. In this process moneylenders became bankers, and shopkeepers the owners of larger outlets of consumer goods, of big department and chain stores. Former itinerant peddlers installed themselves in shops or as commercial travelers. The indeed remarkable improvement of their economic stature resulted from the expansion and diversification of commerce, while a relatively small number of Jewish entrepreneurs ventured into industrial production. The only noticeable change in the German Jews' vocational structure was their increased part in the professions, but also here most of them preferred self-employment as independent lawyers or medical practitioners.[31] This means that the Jews were well prepared to use the new opportunities the expanding capitalism opened up for the commercial and financial functions in which they had for generations gained experience. At that stage they certainly were in an advantageous position compared with the mass of new non-Jewish competitors and made the best of it.

But on the other hand the Jewish middle class in Germany demonstrated an astonishing lack of flexibility when the further development of the once established capitalist economy asked for vocational readjustment. Close to 50 percent of all gainfully employed Jews worked in commerce in 1925, mainly in its "traditionally Jewish" branches, like clothing and household goods, and close to two-thirds of them were self-employed. None of the decades-long preached "productivization" or "normalization" of the Jewish vocational structure occurred when self-employment ceased to be an advantage and the incomes of the owners of small and medium stores and workshops declined. Their majority strenuously held on to their small- or medium-sized family businesses in the overfilled branches of consumer goods retail outlets despite the growing and aggressive competition by gentile newcomers and the quickly expanding department and chain stores. A considerable number of self-employed German Jews were seized by the severe crisis of the "old middle-class" at the end of the nineteenth century that reached catastrophic dimensions after World War I.

A convincing explanation for this lack of flexibility and adjustment at a time when the political emancipation of the Jews had removed the legal barriers to their choice of settlement and vocations is still lacking. We also have no explanation for the amazingly constant resemblance, historically and to date, of their economic pursuits and vocational specialization in far-apart countries at very different stages of industrial and capitalist development. Can we possibly explain them, in the wake of Max Weber's theories, by the heritage of engrained religious traditions and values still being effective in secularized times, when most Jews no longer obey their religious law and are ignorant of its teachings? With regard to their importance in the life of the Jews in any of their settlement countries before modernity, Weber's arguments seem quite plausible. It may also be true that the Jews' observance of strict dietary and Sabbath religious laws estranged them from their neighbors, who were offended by what appeared as Jewish arrogance. But his socioreligious analysis that accorded the religion of the Jews the dominant, if not the only, determinant of their economic behavior, and by this their "pariah" character, remains questionable. It ignores historical developments and constraints and does not explain

Avraham Barkul

how the Jews attained their most striking economic achievements after most of them had already shed the rituals and behavioral rules of their religion. If according to Marx the *Sein* (being) determines the *Bewusstsein* (mind), the Jews seem to have held on to their group-specific material *Sein* long after an intense and long process of acculturation had adjusted their *Bewusstsein*—or in Marxian terms their "ideological superstructure"—to the values and norms of their environment.

Notes

1. Max Weber, *The Protestant Ethic and the Spirit of Capitalism*, trans. Talcott Parsons (New York, 1958). The German original appeared first in 1904–5 in the *Archiv für Sozialwissenschaft und Sozialpolitik;* a revised but uncompleted version in 1920 in Weber's *Gesammelte Aufsätze zur Religionsphilosophie.*

2. Werner Sombart, *Die Juden und das Wirtschaftsleben* (Leipzig, 1911), v.

3. *Publication des manuscripts de Charles Fourier*, vol. 3, (Paris, 1853–56), 36.

4. Alphonse Toussenel, *Les Juifs rois de l'époque, Histoire de la féodalité financière* (Paris, 1845). For a detailed study see Edmund Silberner, *Sozialisten zur Judenfrage: ein Beitrag zur Geschichte des Sozialismus vom Anfang des 19. Jahrhunderts* (Berlin, 1962); Edmund Silberner, *Western European Socialism and the Jewish Problem, 1800–1918: A Selective Bibliography* (Jerusalem, 1955).

5. Qtd. in Silberner, *Sozialisten*, 30.

6. Karl Marx, *Zur Judenfrage*, first published in *Deutsch-Französische Jahrbücher*, 1 und 2. Lieferung (Paris, 1844), here quoted from Karl Marx and Friedrich Engels, *Die heilige Familie und andere philosophische Frühschriften* (Berlin, 1955), 59ff. Translation from Karl Marx, *Selected Writings*, ed. Lawrence H. Simon (Indianapolis: Hackett, 1994), 22–26.

7. Bebel, *Sozialdemokratie und Antisemitismus*, qtd. in Silberner, *Sozialisten*, 204–5.

8. Victor Adler, *Aufsätze, Reden und Briefe* (Vienna, 1929), 3:378. Qtd. in Avraham Barkai, "The Austrian Social Democrats and the Jews," *Wiener Library Bulletin* 24, no. 1 (1970): 32–40, and 24, no. 2 (1970): 16–21.

9. Karl Marx and Friedrich Engels, *Selected Correspondence, 1846–1895* (London, 1943), 471.

10. The school of the "Economists," founded by François Quesnay (1694–1774), adopted this name after the publication of the first volume of his works under the title *Physiocratie* (Paris, 1768).

11. See Dagmar T. Bermann, *Produktivierungsmythen und Antisemitismus* (München, 1971), esp. 65ff.

12. The best-known is Wilhelm Christian Dohm and his book *Über die bürgerliche Verbesserung der Juden* (Berlin, 1781).

13. See Michael A. Meyer, ed., *German-Jewish History in Modern Times* (New York, 1996–98), 3:35ff., 4:34ff., 4:238.

14. Michael A. Meyer, *Response to Modernity: A History of the Reform Movement in Judaism* (New York, 1988), 134.
15. Werner Sombart, *Der moderne Kapitalismus*, vol. 1 (Leipzig, 1902), 392.
16. Max Weber, *Die protestantische Ethik und der Geist des Kapitalismus*, first published in *Archiv für Sozialwissenschaft und Sozialpolitik*, vols. 20–21 (1904–5).
17. Sombart, *Juden*, vii. Translation by Michael Brenner.
18. Werner Sombart, *Die deutsche Volkswirtschaft im 19. Jahrhundert und im Anfang des 20. Jahrhunderts* (Darmstadt, 1954), 455.
19. Werner Sombart, *Die drei Nationalökonomien, Geschichte und System der Lehre von der Wirtschaft* (München, 1930), 331.
20. Werner Sombart, *Der deutsche Sozialismus* (Berlin, 1934), 318 and passim. For a more detailed account of Sombart's ideological conceptions and their fluctuations, see Paul Mendes-Flohr, "Werner Sombart's *The Jews and Modern Capitalism*: An Analysis of Its Ideological Premises," *LBI Yearbook* 21 (1976): 87–107; and Avraham Barkai, *Nazi Economics, Ideology, Theory, and Policy* (New Haven, 1999), 94–99.
21. Max Weber, *Das antike Judentum*, vol. 3 of *Gesammelte Aufsätze zur Religionssoziologie* (Tübingen, 1920).
22. Ibid., 6n.
23. Ibid., 3–4, 360. Translation by Michael Brenner.
24. Ibid., 360. Translation by Michael Brenner.
25. Perhaps most outspokenly by Lujo Brentano, at his time one of the most eminent German scholars of economics and economic history: "This book of Sombart's is one of the most saddening occurrences in German science. If in the previous section [of this essay] I have voiced my disagreement with the teachings of Max Weber, I did so only with great reluctance, because I honor Weber as an extraordinarily spirited man, a man of great learning and inexorable scientific severity. . . . Sombart is different. . . . His book of 1911 . . . is filled with the frivolities of a nonchalant person deeming himself a superman, who contemptuously blows his moody bubbles into the face of the reader who, flabbergasted by his brilliance, is then asked to accept them as 'irrefutably correct' scientific statements" (*Die Anfänge des modernen Kapitalismus* [München 1916], 151f).
26. In his book *Die Zukunft der Juden* (Leipzig, 1912).
27. See Kurt Grunwald, "Europe's Railways and Jewish Enterprise: German Jews as Pioneers of Railway Promotion," *LBI Yearbook* 22 (1967): 192ff.
28. Avraham Barkai, "The German Jews at the Start of Industrialization," in *Revolution and Evolution: 1848 in German-Jewish History*, ed. Werner Mosse, Arnold Paucker, Reinhard Rürup, 123–45 (Tübingen, 1981), 145.
29. I follow the definition of Simon Kuznets in his pioneering studies on the economic development of Jewish and other small religious or ethnic minorities and his model of the "constrains" by which this develop-

Avraham Barkai

ment is determined. For a concise theoretical summary, see S. Kuznets, *Economic Structure of U.S. Jewry, Recent Trends* (Jerusalem, 1972), 10–19. For a more elaborate discussion, see Simon Kuznets's chapter "The Economic Sructure of the Jews," in *The Jews, Their History, Culture, and Religion,* ed. Louis Finkelstein (New York, 1960).

30. For a more detailed account, see Jacob Toury, *Soziale und politische Geschichte der Juden in Deutschland, 1847–1871* (Düsseldorf, 1977); Avraham Barkai, *Jüdische Minderheit und Industrialisierung: Demographie, Berufe und Einkommen der Juden in Westdeutschland, 1850–1914* (Tübingen, 1988); Avraham Barkai, *Branching Out: German-Jewish Immigration to the United States, 1820–1914* (New York, 1994).

31. See Esra Bennathan, "Die demographische und wirtschftliche Struktur der Juden," in *Entscheidungsjahr 1933: Zur Judenfrage in der Endphase der Weimarer Republik,* ed. Werner E. Mosse and Arnold Paucker, 87–131 (Tübingen, 1965), esp. 126–31; Uziel O. Schmelz, "Die demographische Entwicklung der Juden in Deutschland von der Mitte des 19. Jahrhunderts bis 1933," *Zeitschrift für Bevölkerungspolitik* 2 (1982): 31–72.

| 4 |

Jewish Communities
Negotiating Modernity

The Mystical World
of Colonial American Jews

JONATHAN D. SARNA

Early American Jews are not generally associated with the practice of Jewish mysticism.[1] Since there was "no oppression" in colonial America, Jacob Rader Marcus explains in his definitive history, "there was no need here to seek escape through emotionalism, mysticism, or ecstatic flights of the imagination. The colonial Jews never 'illuminated their hearts by beclouding their minds.'"[2]

Most of the Jews who came to the New World belonged instead to the social type now known as "port Jews."[3] They were merchants with far-reaching commercial ties. As such, business dominated their world—so much so that Marcus once called them "a nation of shopkeepers."[4] They also, according to David Sorkin, pioneered aspects of Judaism that we associate with the "origins of the modern Jew": "Virtually all those developments thought to be characteristic of the modern Jew can be found among the port Jews a century or two earlier: the reduction of Judaism to a synagogue-based religion with a growing emphasis on faith as opposed to practice; immersion in the larger Christian culture; the emergence of various forms and degrees of assimilation; and, as a consequence of all of these, the development of a segmental Jewish life and identity."[5]

If one asked, as Michael A. Meyer did of German Jews, what being a Jew meant to the Jews of early America, most historians would not include mysticism as one of the answers.[6] The colonial American Jewish merchants are assumed instead to have been paragons of rationalism—a calculating rather than a mystical group.

This essay challenges that assumption. It argues that messianic hopes and mystical devotions played a larger role in the lives of colonial Jews than generally supposed. In the New World, as in the Old World, the line dividing mystical and magical beliefs from modern thinking was neither as bright nor as well-defined as scholars once imagined.

The spread of Jews to the New World was associated, as early as the seventeenth century, with the hope of messianic redemption.[7] Menasseh ben Israel, the Dutch rabbi who did more than anybody else of his day to promote Jewish settlement in the New World and underscore its religious significance, wrote in 1656 that he "conceived, that our universal dispersion was a necessary circumstance, to be fulfilled, before all that shall be accomplished which the Lord hath promised to the people of the Jewes, concerning their restauration, and their returning again into their own land."[8] According to this hopeful assessment, the Jewish dispersion, furthered by the expulsion from Spain, presaged Jews' imminent ingathering. The traumas that Jews had experienced assumed transcendent significance as part of the divine plan leading up to the return to Zion and the coming of the messiah.

Menasseh ben Israel was, of course, a significant student of mysticism. "I have sworn allegiance to Rabbi Simeon bar Yohai," he wrote, referring to the presumed author of the Zohar, "and I shall not betray my faith."[9] His *Nishmat Ḥayyim*, even if it ignores some central kabbalistic themes, has been described as an "encyclopedia of parapsychology, magic hiromancy and . . . a kabbalistic and philosophical compound of Jewish teachings" on the controversial subject of the eternality of the soul.[10] He concealed his mystical side, however, from some of his non-Jewish friends. Huet, the bishop of Avranches, for example, described him as "a very good man of gentle spirit, easy-going, reasonable and free from many Jewish superstitions and the empty dreams of the Kabbalah."[11] But even non-Jews knew of the rabbi's deep interest in millenarianism and messianism.

The Hope of Israel (1650), Menasseh ben Israel's best-known work, published in Spanish and Latin and eventually translated into English, Dutch, Yiddish, and Hebrew, focuses on the coming of the messiah as it relates to the discovery of the New World and the origins of the American Indians.[12] The preface ("to the courteous reader") explains both the book's title and its objectives:

Jonathan D. Sarna

I prove that the Ten Tribes never returned to the Second Temple, that they yet keep the Law of Moses, and our sacred rites; and at last shall return to their Land, with the two Tribes, Judah and Benjamin; and shall be governed by one Prince, who is Messiah the Son of David; and without doubt that time is near. . . .

I willingly leave it to the judgement of the godly, and learned, what happy worth there is in this my book, and what my own Nation owes me for my pains: It is called *The Hope of Israel;* which name is taken from Jeremiah 14:8: Oh the hope of Israel, the Saviour thereof. For the scope of this discourse is, to show, that the hope in which we live, of the coming of the Messiah, is of a future, difficult, but infallible good, because it is grounded upon the absolute promise of the blessed God.[13]

Like many Christians of his day, Menasseh ben Israel insisted that the Indians found in the New World descended from Adam and Eve and were survivors of the Flood. The alternative—that they descended from a separate act of creation not described in the Bible—was, to him, theologically unpalatable. He also concurred with those who, based on the apocryphal book of Second Esdras, insisted that the Lost Ten Tribes had scattered to the four corners of the earth.[14] Since he argued, based on Isaiah, that "the gathering together of the captivity shall begin . . . in America,"[15] he put forth a conclusion that offered Jews and Christians alike both solace and hope:

The shortness of time (when we believe our redemption shall appear) is confirmed by this, that the Lord has promised that he will gather the two tribes, Judah and Benjamin, out of the four quarters of the world. . . . Whence you may gather that for the fulfilling of that, they must be scattered through all the corners of the world; as Daniel (12:7) says: "And when the scattering of the holy people shall have an end, all those things shall be fulfilled." And this appears now to be done, when our synagogues are found in America.[16]

The synagogues that Menasseh ben Israel had in mind were presumably Zur Israel of Recife and Magen Abraham across the bridge from it on the island of Mauricia (the two were united in 1649).[17] Following the publication of his book, however, many subsequent synagogues in the New World, through the end of the eighteenth century, took on names that reflected the Dutch rabbi's millenarian belief that the colonization of Jews in the New World was both a harbinger and an instrument of messianic redemption. No fewer than four synagogues—in Curaçao, Savannah, Philadelphia, and Jamaica—took as their name the Hebrew title of Menasseh ben Israel's book *Mikveh Israel,* thereby echoing Jeremiah's promise: "O Hope of [*Mikveh*] Israel, Its deliverer in time of trouble."[18] New York's Shearith Israel based its name on the prophecy of Micah: "I will bring together the remnant of [*Shearith*] Israel."[19] The synagogue in Barbados called itself Nidḥe Israel based on the redemptive prophecy of Isaiah:

He will hold up a signal to the nations
And assemble the banished of [*Nidḥe*] Israel
And gather the dispersed of Judah
From the four corners of the earth.[20]

The synagogue in Newport, originally to be called Nefutzei Israel (and, beginning in the nineteenth century, the Touro Synagogue), took as its official name Jeshuat Israel, based on the Psalmist's prophecy: "O that the deliverance of [*Yeshuat*] Israel might come from Zion! When the LORD restores the fortunes of His people, Jacob will exult, Israel will rejoice."[21] All alike demonstrated through their unusual names the mystical significance of New World Jewish communities. They reaffirmed the very point that Menasseh ben Israel had made in his book, that the dispersion of Israel's remnant to the four corners of the world heralded the ingathering of the exiles.

The synagogue of the *Jodensavanne* in the jungle off the Suriname River even more clearly betrays through its name a close acquaintance on the part of local Jews with mystical texts and ideas. The synagogue, consecrated in 1685, was named Berahah VeS[h]alom ("blessing and peace"), which is a highly unusual name for a synagogue, and not based on a scriptural verse.[22] The key to the name lies instead in the Zohar, the mystical Book of Splendor, which asks, "And where is [the Garden of] Eden located? R. Yossi said, in *Aravot* [seventh heaven], for we are taught 'there are [found] the treasuries of good life, blessing, and peace.'"[23] The name provides us with the clearest proof we have that the Jews of Suriname viewed their self-governing community as a Jewish paradise. Indeed, both the synagogue and the town seem to have been modeled on an idealized vision of Jerusalem, akin to Christian efforts to fashion a "new Jerusalem" in New Haven. In mystical terms, Aviva Ben-Ur observes, theirs was a sense "of actualized—as opposed to anticipatory—messianism." Where other New World Jew-

Jonathan D. Sarna

ish communities eagerly looked forward to the coming of redemption, the Jews of Suriname believed that these hopes were already in the process of being fulfilled.[24]

In their private lives too, early American Jews engaged in mystical practices. Jonathan Edwards, the distinguished Protestant theologian, for example, recalled that he "once [1722-23] lived for many months next to a Jew (the houses adjoining one to another), and had much opportunity daily to observe him; who appeared to me the devoutest person that ever I saw in my life; great part of his time being spent in acts of devotion, at his eastern window, which opened next to mine, seeming to be most earnestly engaged, not only in the daytime, but sometimes whole nights."[25] Edwards's Jewish neighbor prayed, as per tradition, toward the east, and his late night devotions would most likely have been the mystical rite, developed in the sixteenth century, known as tikkun ḥatsot, "prayers recited at midnight in memory of the destruction of the Temple and for the restoration to the Land of Israel."[26] Since Edwards was living at the time on the estate of Thomas Smith, having befriended Madame Susanna Smith and her son, John, we know from the tax assessment list for that year that the Jew in question was named Lousada (Louzada), scion of a well-known Sephardic merchant family.[27] How many other colonial Jews filled their public lives with business but spent hours of their private time devoutly communing with God we do not know.

Ezra Stiles, pastor of the Second Church of Newport and later president of Yale University, provides broader evidence of mystical beliefs and practices among Jews. "This day," he reported to his diary on August 10, 1769, "one of the Jews shewed me a computation of one of the present Rabbins of Germany: wherein he makes Time, Times, and half [Daniel 7:25, 12:7], to denote the space from the last Destruct[ion] of the Temple to its Restora[tion] & Return of XII Tribes. Time he call 'Seventy Semitots' or 490 years, Times 980, half 245, total 1715 years, ending he says, A.D. 1783, when the Messias is expected." Others, including Gershom Seixas, ḥazzan of Shearith Israel, supplied alternate dates, but there can be little doubt that messianic speculation among Jews was rife.[28]

Stiles, a Christian Hebraist, was particularly fascinated by the mystical texts of the Jews, and owned a copy of the Zohar. Like many devout Christians of his day, he imagined that the kabbalah concealed hidden trinitarian teachings. He inquired about this of every visiting Jew whom he considered knowledgeable enough to enlighten him upon the subject, and also corresponded on these subjects with his friend, the itinerant Sephardic ḥakham, Raphael Haim Isaac Carigal.[29]

Others too discussed kabbalah in early America. At least two converts, Isaac Miranda and Judah Monis, owned their own copies of kabbalistic writings.[30]

Finally, we learn from Stiles of a curious mystical practice that seems to have been widely observed by Newport Jews, at least during thunderstorms: "The Jews are wont in Thunder Storms to set open all their Doors and Windows for the coming of Messias. Last Hail Storm, 31 July [1769], when Thunder, Rain & Hail were amazingly violent, the Jews in Newport threw open Doors, Windows, and employed themselves in Singing & repeating Prayers, &c., for Meeting Messias."[31] A century earlier, a Greek Catholic priest in eastern Europe, describing the enthusiasm surrounding the false messianic claims of Sabbatai Sevi, reported what may be a related practice: "whenever a cloud appeared over some city, they [the Jews] would boast before the Christians and say that the messiah would soon take them to dwell in Palestine and in Jerusalem." Gershom Scholem shows that "the expectation of being transported on the clouds of heaven seems to be authentic . . . the motif occurs in a midrashic source [Pesiqta Rabbathi, I] . . . the belief was current not only in Russia and Poland, but also in Germany and Turkey. . . . The Sabbatian enthusiasts were not the first to believe in a miraculous journey to the Holy Land on the clouds of heaven."[32]

While none of Scholem's sources specifically mention thunderstorms, the Jews of Newport, many of them with roots on the Iberian Peninsula, were apparently heir to an authentic mystical tradition. Notwithstanding their deep involvement in the North Atlantic trade, their close interactions with non-Jews, their linguistic and cultural assimilation, and other evidences of "modernity" characteristic of port Jews, they nevertheless upheld this mystical tradition, even though it presumably brought a good deal of rainwater into their homes. Menasseh ben Israel's *Hope of Israel* and the very name of their own synagogue, Jeshuat Israel, likely steeled their resolve amidst the thunder, the hail, and the rain. They believed—more fervently, perhaps, than historians realize—that "deliverance" was near.

Messianic expectations, mystical devotions, and magical beliefs: contrary to what previous scholars have imagined, these all formed part of the cultural and religious worlds of early American Jews. As the "hope of Israel," they were instruments of messianic redemption. As "port Jews" they were harbingers of modernity. Their identity, like that of their non-Jewish counterparts, was shaped by multiple and conflicting impulses.[33]

Jonathan D. Sarna

NOTES

1. Given the close family ties and remarkable geographic mobility of Jews in the Caribbean and North American Jewish communities of the seventeenth and eighteenth centuries, I consider them here as a group.

2. Jacob R. Marcus, *The Colonial American Jew, 1492–1776* (Detroit: Wayne State University Press, 1970), 962. Marcus explicitly contrasts Jews with their non-Jewish colonial counterparts.

3. David Sorkin, "The Port Jew: Notes toward a Social Type," *Journal of Jewish Studies* 50 (Spring 1999): 87–97; Lois Dubin, *The Port Jews of Habsburg Trieste: Absolutist Politics and Enlightenment Culture* (Stanford: Stanford University Press, 1999); David Cesarani, ed., *Port Jews: Jewish Communities in Cosmopolitan Maritime Trading Centres, 1550–1950* (London: Frank Cass, 2002); Jonathan D. Sarna, "Port Jews in the Atlantic: Further Thoughts," *Jewish History* 20 (2006): 213–19.

4. Marcus, *Colonial American Jew*, 1339.

5. Sorkin, "Port Jew," 96–97.

6. Michael A. Meyer, *The Origins of the Modern Jew: Jewish Identity and European Culture in Germany, 1749–1824* (Detroit: Wayne State University Press, 1967), 8–9.

7. Abraham Farisso associated the discovery of the New World with the hope for Israel's redemption as early as 1525, but his work preceded the emergence of Jewish communities there. See David B. Ruderman, *The World of a Renaissance Jew: The Life and Thought of Abraham ben Mordecai Farissol* (Cincinnati: Hebrew Union College Press, 1981), esp. 137. For this and other examples, see Noah J. Efron, "Knowledge of Newly Discovered Lands Among Jewish Communities of Europe (From 1492 to the Thirty Years' War)," in *The Jews and the Expansion of Europe to the West 1450–1800*, ed. Paolo Bernardini and Norman Fiering, 47–72 (New York: Berghahn Books, 2001); and Abraham Melamed, "The Discovery of America in Jewish Literature of the 16th and 17th Centuries," in *Following Columbus: America 1492–1992* [in Hebrew], ed. Miriam Eliav-Feldon, 443–64 (Jerusalem: Mercaz Shazar, 1996).

8. Menasseh ben Israel, *Vindiciae Judaeorum* (1656), 37, reprinted in Lucien Wolf, *Menasseh ben Israel's Mission to Oliver Cromwell* (London, 1901), 143; see also Jonathan I. Israel, "Menasseh ben Israel and the Dutch Sephardic Colonization Movement of the Mid-Seventeenth Century (1645–57)," in *Menasseh ben Israel and His World*, ed. Yosef Kaplan et al. (Leiden: Brill, 1989), 139–42. For a readable but dated biography, see Cecil Roth, *A Life of Menasseh ben Israel: Rabbi, Printer and Diplomat* (Philadelphia: Jewish Publication Society, 1934).

9. Joseph Dan, "Menasseh ben Israel: Attitude towards the Zohar and Lurianic Kabbalah," in Kaplan, *Menasseh ben Israel and His World*, 200n3.

10. Rivka Schatz, "Menasseh ben Israel's Approach to Messianism in the Jewish-Christian Context," in ibid., 247 (quoted); and Moshe Idel, "Kab-

balah, Platonism and Prisca Theologia: The Case of R. Menasseh ben Israel," in ibid., 207–19 (esp. n63). For the context of *Nishmat Ḥayyim*, see Alexander Altmann, "Eternality of Punishment: A Theological Controversy with the Amsterdam Rabbinate in the Thirties of the Seventeenth Century," *Proceedings of the American Academy for Jewish Research* 40 (1972): 1–40.

11. Menasseh ben Israel, *The Hope of Israel*, ed. Henry Mechoulan and Gerard Nahon (London: Oxford, 1987), 25.
12. Benjamin Schmidt, "The Hope of the Netherlands: Menasseh ben Israel and the Dutch Idea of America," in Bernardini and Fiering, *Jews and the Expansion of Europe*, 102n12.
13. Ibid., 102.
14. Richard H. Popkin, "The Rise and Fall of the Jewish Indian Theory," in Kaplan, *Menasseh ben Israel and His World*, 63–82.
15. Menasseh ben Israel, *The Hope of Israel*, 145.
16. Ibid., 158.
17. Arnold Wiznitzer, *Jews in Colonial Brazil* (New York: Columbia University Press, 1960), 77–78, 130–35.
18. Jeremiah 14:8 in the New JPS translation. For the history of these synagogues, see Isaac S. and Suzanne A. Emmanuel, *History of the Jews of the Netherlands Antilles* (Cincinnati: American Jewish Archives, 1970), 1:51n2, which suggests that the name in Curaçao dates to 1651; Saul J. Rubin, *Third to None: The Saga of Savannah Jewry 1733–1983* (Savannah, Ga.: S. J. Rubin, 1983), 5, which dates "Mickva Israel" in Savannah to 1735; Edwin Wolf 2nd and Maxwell Whiteman, *The History of the Jews of Philadelphia from Colonial Times to the Age of Jackson* (Philadelphia: Jewish Publication Society, 1975), 115, which dates Philadelphia's "Mikve Israel" to 1782; and Jacob A. P. M. Andrade, *A Record of the Jews in Jamaica from the English Conquest to the Present Times* (Kingston: Jamaica Times, 1941), 45–46, which dates "Mikveh Yisroeil" in Spanish Town, Jamaica (an Ashkenazi synagogue) to 1796.
19. Micah 2:12. The name seems originally to have been Shearith Jacob (following Micah 5:6–7), but by 1728 the name Shearith Israel had been adopted. See Jacob R. Marcus, *Studies in American Jewish History* (Cincinnati: HUC Press, 1969), 45; and David de Sola Pool, *An Old Faith in the New World: Portrait of Shearith Israel, 1654–1954* (New York: Columbia University Press, 1955).
20. Isaiah 11:12. The origin of the synagogue is unknown but has been dated to 1654; see Mordecai Arbell, *The Jewish Nation of the Caribbean* (Jerusalem: Geffen, 2002), 198.
21. Psalms 14:7. Nefutzei Israel presumably was based on 1 Kings 22:17 with its promise that the scattered of Israel would "return. . . home in safety." The name seems to have been changed between 1764 and 1765; see Theodore Lewis, "Touro Synagogue—National Historic Site," *Newport History* 48 (Summer 1975): 283.

22. The Jews of St. Thomas employed the same name for their congregation, founded in 1796. See Judah M. Cohen, *Through the Sands of Time: A History of the Jewish Community of St. Thomas, U.S. Virgin Islands* (Waltham: Brandeis University Press, 2004), 15–18.

23. Zohar, Midrash Hane'elam, Genesis, p.125a (see also T. B. Hagigah 12b): "V'eden b'ayzeh maqom hu'? . . . R. Yose 'amar ba'aravot hu', deha' tenan: sham ginzei hayyim tovin berakhah veshalom."

24. I draw here upon the brilliant analysis of Aviva Ben-Ur in "Still Life: Sephardi, Ashkenazi and West African Art and Form in Suriname's Jewish Cemeteries," *American Jewish History* 92 (March 2004): 40–46.

25. Jonathan Edwards, *Religious Affections*, ed. John E. Smith (New Haven: Yale University Press, 1959), 165. Edwards's judgment on the Jew was negative: "Experience shows that persons, from false religion, may be inclined to be exceeding abundant in the external exercises of religion."

26. *Encyclopedia Judaica* (Jerusalem, 1971), 15:1139; Gershom Scholem, *On the Kabbalah and Its Symbolism* (New York: Schocken, 1960), 146–50.

27. George M. Marsden, *Jonathan Edwards: A Life* (New Haven: Yale University Press, 2003), 47–48. For details concerning the Smith family, see the biographies of William and John in Franklin Bowditch Dexter, *Biographical Sketches of the Graduates of Yale College, October 1701–May 1745* (New York: Henry Holt, 1885), 207–11, 359–60, esp. 359. I am grateful to Professor Louis Hershkowitz for providing me with information from the New York Tax Assessment list, January 1722–February 1723 (Hershkowitz to Sarna, April 22, 2004). On the Lousada family, see Robert Zassler, "About Jews in the Colonial New Brunswick Area," posted at http://home.earthlink.net/~etzahaim/ceajhist2.html; "Lousada," *Universal Jewish Encyclopedia* (1942), 7:210; and Marcus, *Colonial American Jew*, 332–33. For a genealogy, see Malcolm Stern, *First American Jewish Families* (Baltimore: Ottenheimer, 1991), and www.geocities.com/wdavid5961/Descendants_of_Jacob_De_Lousada.html.

28. Franklin Bowditch Dexter, *The Literary Diary of Ezra Stiles* (New York, 1901), 1:19; Jacob R. Marcus, *The Handsome Young Priest in the Black Gown: The Personal World of Gershom Seixas* (Cincinnati: American Jewish Archives, 1970), 58–62; Raphael Mahler, "The Historical Background of Pre-Zionism in America and Its Continuity," in *A Bicentennial Festschrift for Jacob Rader Marcus*, ed. Bertram W. Korn, 347–54 (New York: Ktav, 1976).

29. Marcus, *Colonial American Jew*, 1104–7; Arthur A. Chiel, "Ezra Stiles—The Education of an 'Hebrician,'" *American Jewish Historical Quarterly* 60 (March 1971): 235–41; Arthur A. Chiel, "The Rabbis and Ezra Stiles," *American Jewish Historical Quarterly* 61 (June 1972): 294–312.

30. Marcus, *Colonial American Jew*, 1075, 1081, 1083, 1102.

31. Dexter, *Literary Diary of Ezra Stiles*, 1:19.

32. Gershom Scholem, *Sabbatai Sevi: The Mystical Messiah* (Princeton:

Princeton University Press, 1973), 594–95. Thanks to Jonathan Schorsch for pointing me to this source.

33. For parallels, see David D. Hall, *Worlds of Wonder, Days of Judgment: Popular Religious Belief in Early New England* (Cambridge: Harvard University Press, 1989); and Jon Butler, *Awash in a Sea of Faith: Christianizing the American People* (Cambridge: Harvard University Press, 1990).

Public Faith and Private Virtue

Cincinnati's American Israelites

KARLA GOLDMAN

As a major nineteenth-century urban center that arose as a gateway to the West, Cincinnati served as an early incubator of American Jewish life and identity. Led by the indefatigable Rabbi Isaac Mayer Wise, prosperous Cincinnati Jews strove to create the patterns and institutions that could define a universal American Judaism. They ultimately succeeded in creating the first successful national institutions of American Jewish life: the first federation of American synagogues and the first long-lasting American institution for rabbinical education.

As the foremost historian of the Jewish Reform movement and Hebrew Union College, Michael Meyer has documented the efforts of Wise and a dedicated community of midwestern and southern Jews to create an institutional base and spiritual leadership for an American Israel. Meyer's work offers a guide to understanding the key role that the early Cincinnati-based institutions of Reform Judaism came to play in shaping American Judaism. Meyer has shown us that, despite the grandiloquent rhetoric that accompanied the founding of the Hebrew Union College, the school was in fact established on the flimsiest of material foundations.[1]

And yet, the laymen and laywomen of the "west and south" who donated their money and energy to this fledgling institution were singular in their willingness to look beyond themselves and their moment to build an institution that they hoped would secure the future of American Judaism. True, they knew that they could rely upon the tireless Isaac M. Wise both to represent this movement and to do much of its heavy lifting. Still, Wise's presence does not offer a sufficient explanation for why Cincinnati's mostly Jewishly ignorant laymen took on so much of the responsibility for creating an institutional basis for American Judaism.

The present inquiry builds upon Meyer's work to consider the question posed by one nineteenth-century observer of Cincinnati's success in training American rabbis: "Why is it that the Israelites of Cincinnati wield stronger and more popular influence as leaders and starters of religious enterprise in American Judaism than the other large Hebrew communities?"[2] What motivations—beyond the future preservation of Judaism in the United States—resulted in the location of American Judaism's earliest national institutions in Cincinnati? What did the creation of these institutions mean for the American and civic identities of their founders? We will see that nineteenth-century Cincinnati Jews drew upon the cultural discourse of their era and locale to position themselves and their institutions as guarantors of American civilization. Playing off the city of Cincinnati's self-identification as a leading exemplar of material and moral progress, local Jews believed that their institutional activism enriched their city in ways that, as American Jews, they felt uniquely qualified to do.[3]

The impulse to establish nineteenth-century Judaism as an impressive and respected local communal presence was seen in cities throughout the United States where Jews looked to their synagogues, religious leaders, and rituals to establish their credentials as respectable citizens. Nineteenth-century synagogue dedications invariably brought forth grand rhetoric. The Jewish and often secular press went to some lengths to describe these new edifices, whether characterized as magnificent and awesome, or "neat and respectable," as ornaments of their cities and monuments to American Judaism. The presence of many non-Jewish guests was always noted and generally included municipal officials and the clergymen of the city. The gentiles who attended these events were usually identified in accord with their intelligence, prominence, sincerity, and elite status, or the fact that they had contributed to the synagogue building fund. Almost all of them, it seems, came away deeply impressed by the solemnity and awesomeness of the occasion and suitably convinced of the purely rational basis of Jewish practice. They also had the welcome sense, articulated by Tennessee governor John C. Brown at such an occasion, that "the Israelites were among the best citizens of the city and state."[4]

Impressive synagogue buildings seemed to hold a wondrous power to transform the civic identities of a community's Jews. In an 1875 speech, Nicholas Scharf of Vicksburg, Mississippi, recalled less auspicious days when the Jewish community used to welcome the high holidays in decrepit old storerooms. Scharf recalled "feeling ashamed to be seen by our Christian brethren to enter such a place used for a house of worship." This shame was exacerbated by the "disorderly scenes, the disturbances, etc., that made our service a burlesque and would shock the sensibilities of any one." In more recent years, according to Scharf, the Jews of Vicksburg had been blessed to build a synagogue that was a true "ornament to the city." The result was that now, "We need not stealthily nor shamefully enter its holy portals, but boldly and with pride hold" religious services. The worship itself, moreover, in keeping with its refined synagogue home, had progressed far from the chaotic "davening" of former days: "How orderly and how edifying is our service; how beautiful and soul stirring our choir."[5]

All these transformations of practice and setting had, Scharf was convinced, taught the broader community important lessons about Jews: "Our temple, so frequently visited by strangers of other denominations, by men of intelligence and prominence, has it not learned them that we Jews have souls—have honor, believe in God and are taught to love our neighbor as ourselves?" But Vicksburg's fine temple and refined worship had done more than teach non-Jews about Judaism; it had also transformed the civic identities of its members. "Has the expounding of our faith not elevated us as citizens and taught our neighbors that a Jew is entitled to the same respect, honor, and position as any other man?" Scharf asked. He went on to point to the many members of the congregation who held positions of "honor and trust" in the city and indicated that "the proper manifestation of religion is often judged as one of the fundamental assurances and safeguards of private virtue and public faith." By establishing a public faith, the Jews of Vicksburg had, in Scharf's view, assured the place of their community "in the estimation and judgment of our Christian brethren."[6]

Cincinnati Jews, no less than those of Vicksburg and numerous other cities, derived a high sense of civic and social status from their grand postbellum synagogues, and from the prosperity and respectability of many in their midst. They took special pride in the honor accorded to their rabbis by the broader community. Max Lilienthal of the Bene Israel congregation was especially noted for his dedication to the wider community, serving on the city school board and on the Board of Regents of the University of Cincinnati. He was reputed to be the first rabbi to speak from an American Christian pulpit and was

one of the speakers at the 1871 dedication of Tyler Davidson Foun-
tain, erected as the elegant centerpiece of downtown Cincinnati. The
tremendous esteem with which Lilienthal was regarded by the larger
community was demonstrated in 1868, when he announced his intention to leave the city for a prestigious position in New York City.
Protests from his congregation were supplemented by a letter signed
by sixteen of Cincinnati's most prominent citizens, insisting that the
rabbi was too important a leader for the community to lose. At a meeting of non-Jews held at the home of a respected local judge, Lilienthal
finally consented to stay.[7]

In the wake of his decision and presumably as part of the negotiations to get him to stay, Lilienthal's congregation immediately
pushed forward the construction of their new temple building (a project that had stalled at the stage of digging a huge hole in the ground
some years earlier). With the 1869 dedication of the new building, the
congregation moved forward on a number of ritual reforms, as the
congregation's president declared their understanding that "the public
at large will judge our religion according to the decency we display on
every public occasion." The congregation's president seemed to raise
the emphasis on order and decorum to almost a religious duty as he
declared, "Our members seem to have but one aim before them, that
of elevating our beloved Congregation and Judaism in general in the
eyes of all men."[8]

In this desire, the Jews of Cincinnati were, like the Jews of Vicksburg and elsewhere, affirming their hope that grand synagogues and
impressive rabbis would secure for them the regard and esteem of
their non-Jewish neighbors. One could probably see the additional effort of creating national institutions of Jewish life solely in this light.
Yet inquiry into the way that Cincinnati Jews extended the vision of
what their aspirations might mean for their community, their city, and
their nation offers important insight into the larger significance of
their efforts in defining themselves as American Jews.

Not surprisingly, Isaac Mayer Wise offered the clearest articulation of the idea that building monuments of American Judaism was
about far more than gaining their neighbors' esteem. Hyperbolic rhetoric was a standard accompaniment to synagogue dedications, and Wise
did not stint in describing his congregation's new building in 1866 or
its potential effect on the future of American Judaism: "Posterity will
point with just pride to this noble edifice and say our fathers erected
this rock and center to a holy cause, to divine worship, to the glory of
our sacred religion." In Wise's eyes, his temple—his "Alhambra,"—a
striking agglomeration of Moorish, romantic, and neoclassical archi-
tectural elements, represented a unique harmonious synthesis of the

different historic civilizations and cultural values that were reaching their apogee in Cincinnati. It embodied, simultaneously, "veneration for the name of Israel; a monument of modern architecture, of American art, and of the progress of both civil and religious liberty, mental culture, and religious sincerity."[9]

Wise elaborated upon this story in an 1869 article that he wrote about the city intersection where his temple had staked its $263,000 claim, titled "Religious Liberty, Corner of Eighth and Plum Streets, in Cincinnati." Wise suggested that if his readers' imaginations were "sufficiently vivacious, expansive and soaring" to be able to envision this corner they might "form a correct and concrete idea of civil and religious liberty," seeing in this particular intersection "a picture to which the world at large can offer no parallel, no precedent, no comparison."[10]

Wise went on to describe the buildings that defined the intersection in question. On one corner, the city building embodied the physical representation of "civil liberty." On the second corner, Wise described the Catholic "archbishop's cathedral," with its magnificent porch and tower, standing as a loud protestor, seeking to resist the civil and religious liberty proclaimed on the opposing corner. Crossing the street again, Wise came to his own "gorgeous temple of K. K. Benai Yeshurun, a monument of three thousand years of history, pointing heavenward with its two minarets." Crossing once more, Wise pointed to the new and radical Unitarian Church, which, like the synagogue, depended upon "liberty's right arm" to protect its freedom of expression. The adjoining Scotch Presbyterian church resisted both the decorousness and the rationality of its neighbors with its fiery Lord standing by ready to "burn all sinners even to the center of the earth." It too, however, relied upon the American tradition of religious liberty that allowed those on each corner to proclaim, "I am as I please to be."

The Jewish contribution to this collection was not to be missed. B'nai Yeshurun stood out for more than its striking Moorish departure from familiar forms of Cincinnati architecture. More important, the liberty represented by this street corner resonated most loudly in the unprecedented freedom and prosperity afforded to Judaism in its American context. Jews stood together with the Unitarians in finding a fertile home in the unique soil of American religious liberty. It was, however, the exotic Jewish presence that, Wise suggested, saved American religious liberty from being merely a bland concoction and Eighth and Plum from being just another street corner. With its presence, the pluralism and coexistence represented in this Cincinnati street scene marked one of the signal achievements of American civilization. "So it looks in Cincinnati, corner Eighth and Plum streets," Wise concluded, "It is the most striking monument of civil and religious liberty in this or any other country. It is the most telling demonstration of the spirit of our age and the freedom of our country." It is important to see Wise's rhetoric not just as grandiosity or hyperbole but also as part of an effort to put Judaism at the center of a cultural dialogue about the nature of western civilization.

Historians have noted that the cultural discourse of late-nineteenth-century white middle-class Americans revolved around constant reference to the meaning of manhood, race, and civilization. White American civic, religious, and intellectual leaders identified their cultural ideals with the poised self-control and rational mind of white men, while relegating the world of feelings, bodies, and uncontrolled passions to women and what were deemed lower, more primitive races.[11] Wise and his followers took advantage of this general cultural discourse and the particular inclination of those in Cincinnati to see their city as a community that pioneered the journey from savagery to civilization.[12] They used these cultural contexts to portray their own work of building institutions for American Judaism as constitutive participation in the building of western civilization.

In 1872 a group of Cincinnati laymen began a formal push to realize Wise's decades-old dream of creating a union of Jewish congregations that could provide the institutional basis necessary to support a rabbinical school in the United States. In many ways, this initiative represented an extension of the familiar local efforts that numerous Jewish communities had made to establish themselves on the American landscape. The work of creating a rabbinical school, another dream of Wise's, was often spoken of as akin to the erection of a metaphorical synagogue building, such as when Wise said of the prospective college, "It will be the grandest temple ever built. It will be the most gorgeous structure of the Hebrew mind, the most lasting monument of the American Israel."[13] Grand as were many American synagogues, the envisioned rabbinical college would extend the vision of Judaism's contributions to American civilization even further.

Read within the context of civilizational discourse, the emphasis of Reform's institutional builders on the enlightened rationality of the Judaism represented by the college becomes quite suggestive. Wise placed Judaism explicitly within a hierarchal cultural model. He wrote repeatedly about the "sublime, universal, tolerant, humane, and divine" character of the "Hebrew people in Palestine." While he acknowledged that the Diasporic cultures in which it had existed subsequently had diverted Judaism from its "pristine purity," he argued that it would still take western civilized society many decades or even centuries to "regain the manhood, the moral and mental freedom of the ancient Hebrews of Palestine."[14] Wise believed that the true ideal of civilization was to be found in the Jewish past. When another writer slurred the ancient Hebrews as barbarians (a loaded term in the field of cultural discourse), Wise responded acidly: "those Jews were men, it appears when your ancestors were yet baboons, for all we know, and laid the foundation to the world's civilization when your ancestors were cannibals."[15]

Wise and his coworkers did not hesitate to bring this discourse of civilization into their arguments for the college. Moritz Loth, the principal lay leader involved in the push for a congregational union and its first president, presented the college as leading to an epoch "from which a more glorious civilization will spring," one aspiring to the model of ancient Israel but marked by the refinements of nineteenth-century bourgeois culture.[16] Arguments about the character of the men who would be able to build this civilization hewed closely to the model of consummate self-control that was indelibly associated with the triumph of Anglo-Saxon Protestant culture in the public mind. On more than one occasion in the years leading up to the creation of the college, *The Israelite* challenged its readers to show themselves "perfect [or 'complete'] masters of their passions."[17] The model of cultivated Jewish behavior that Loth attributed to the Ten Commandments likewise fully embraced the values identified within prevailing cultural discourse as behaviors identified with cultivated white men: "It is the duty of all to train themselves to self-restraint, to self-denial and exertions of noble achievements."[18]

Out of this denial of one's personal and often irrational desires would arise the edifice of a rational and ennobling modern Judaism that would authentically echo the essential model of ancient Jewish civilization, identified as the true "foundation of civilized society." The maturation of this effort, the creation of institutions that would elevate all American Jews was also identified with the gendered ideal of the prevailing cultural discourse of civic engagement. In creating such institutions, Wise argued, American Jews "will have arrived at the point of manhood, of co-operation of general interests, of true citizenship in the community of Israel."[19] It would "prove to ourselves and to our neighbors that we have arrived at the age of manhood, capable and willing to take care of our own sacred affairs." Not only would those creating these institutions prove their manhood, enabling them to become a "living power in the land"; the students under their care would likewise be enabled to become "men, citizens, and Israelites in the noblest sense of these terms."[20]

Despite the lowly origins of most of its prospective students, and what Meyer has shown us were the questionable financial groundings of the new venture, expectations for the new college were little short of messianic in presenting a vision of what a virile Judaism as realized in Cincinnati could bring to western civilization. Wise and his supporters portrayed an American Judaism that both drew upon and reinforced the deepest sources of western civilization upon which their city stood. The success of the institutions that they created supported the desire of Cincinnati's leaders to see their city as a national leader in the refinement of material and moral civilization. And thus Cincinnati's Jewish leaders, one-time impoverished Jewish peddlers from southern Germany, could become not only prosperous merchants and community leaders but also exemplary white citizens of Cincinnati.

Not surprisingly, the new college was inaugurated with great fanfare. The *Israelite* could not find terms superlative enough to describe the full effect of the ceremonies, setting, and gathered assemblage, presenting as it did "a panorama . . . which no pen can describe, no artist paint, and no eloquence reproduce."[21] The new Hebrew Union College with its scraggly band of students meeting in a cramped synagogue basement did not quite match the high-flying rhetoric used during the college's dedication, but Cincinnati Jews and Isaac Mayer Wise were in it for the long haul. From 1875 to 1876, as the first year of the preparation course of the Hebrew Union College was in session, fund-raising accelerated with Cincinnati Jews contributing $23,000 of the $26,500 raised during that period. Wise prepared and enforced a highly demanding curriculum. Lay leaders including Moritz Loth attended assiduously to the physical and cultural needs of the young students.[22]

Eight years later, four young men were ordained in the sanctuary of Wise's ornate temple. On this occasion, the high-flying rhetoric accompanied what seemed a truly momentous achievement—the creation of rabbis for an American Israel. This harmony would dissipate in a matter of hours once the traditional rabbis in attendance were confronted with a decidedly unkosher celebratory repast, but for the moment, it seemed that the grandeur ascribed to the event actually bore some relationship to reality.

Although the ordination obviously represented a deeply symbolic milestone in the development of American *Judaism*, speakers at the event also pointed to the significance of this event within the context of *American* culture. Visiting New York rabbi Kaufmann Kohler, acknowledging perhaps that both New York and Philadelphia had failed in their attempts to establish schools of rabbinical training, spoke of the rarified cultural air of Cincinnati. "Where on this blessed continent," Kohler asked, "is there a city so broad and liberal in their social views where a community in which such sweet harmony exists among the various sects, where Jewish Temples and Catholic, Methodist and Unitarian Churches so fraternally grasp each other's hand to let people feel they all walk under one paternal roof, beneath the broad canopy of heaven?" His observation, presumably unconsciously, echoed Wise's description from fifteen years before of the pluralistic religious civic intersection prevailing just outside the temple door.

In Wise's Cincinnati, Jewish achievements were seen not just as reflective of American opportunities but as singular American contributions. Even before the college had been established, Wise had argued that the creation of the school in Cincinnati would allow American Jews to "fulfill in America what the schools of Samuel, Ezra, and Jamnia did in the East." American rabbis would be able to train American Jews to a true understanding of Sinai's laws and to observe "them in their full meaning" so that "the Israelites will become exemplary citizens" and a "living power in the land." The significance of this achievement would redound far beyond the Jewish community and far beyond Cincinnati: "This college brings down the Shechinah [God's presence] not only upon this city, but upon the American Israel, upon this great and glorious land, so the glory shall return to Zion."[23]

Cincinnati Jews were forwarding a special kind of Americanization. They sought to secure an elevated place in their community's cultural hierarchy of values, race, and class by advancing distinctive Jewish institutions and identities. By creating organizations that gave a modern face to an ancient culture that they identified as the basis of contemporary American values, they placed themselves as prime guarantors of the special place that Cincinnati set for itself as a unique home for material and moral progress. There was nothing parochial about their intentions or their achievements. They had no doubt that the singular ornaments that they contributed to their city and nation defined and elevated not only themselves but also everyone in their neighborhood. As one proud observer at the first ordination noted, "This is the greatest day of civilization I have lived to see."[24]

NOTES

1. See Michael A. Meyer, "A Centennial History," in Hebrew Union College–Jewish Institute of Religion at One Hundred Years, ed. Samuel E. Karff (Cincinnati: Hebrew Union College Press, 1976), esp. 7–43; Michael A. Meyer, Response to Modernity: A History of the Reform Movement in Judaism (New York: Oxford University Press, 1988), esp. 260–63.

2. Israelite, June 1, 1883.

3. Andrew R. L. Cayton, Ohio: The History of a People (Columbus: Ohio State University Press, 2002); Henry D. Shapiro and Jonathan D.

Sarna, eds., *Ethnic Diversity and Civic Identity: Patterns of Conflict and Cohesion in Cincinnati Since 1820* (Urbana: University of Illinois Press, 1992), xii–xiii, 4.

4. *Israelite*, October 12, 1855, January 11 and November 21, 1856, October 23, 1857, April 16, 1858, July 5, July 26, and October 3, 1872.

5. *American Israelite* (Wise's newspaper, the *Israelite*, was renamed the *American Israelite* in 1874), April 30, 1875.

6. *American Israelite*, April 30, 1875.

7. Jonathan D. Sarna and Karla Goldman, "From Synagogue-Community to Citadel of Reform: The History of K. K. Bene Israel (Rockdale Temple) in Cincinnati, Ohio," in *American Congregations*, ed. James P. Wind and James W. Lewis, 176–77 (Chicago: University of Chicago Press, 1994); Jonathan D. Sarna and Nancy H. Klein, *The Jews of Cincinnati* (Cincinnati: Center for the Study of the American Jewish Experience, 1989), 50; Barnett R. Brickner, "Jewish Community of Cincinnati Historical and Descriptive, 1817–1933" (PhD diss., University of Cincinnati, 1933), 326. David Philipson, *Max Lilienthal, American Rabbi, Life and Writings* (New York: Bloch Publishing, 1915), 96–125.

8. Sarna and Goldman, "From Synagogue-Community," 177.

9. Isaac M. Wise, "The Principles of the Model-School in Israel," *Israelite*, August 31, 1866, 4.

10. "Religious Liberty, Corner of Eighth and Plum Streets, in Cincinnati," *Israelite*, October 15, 1869.

11. Gail Bederman, *Manliness and Civilization: A Cultural History of Gender and Race in the United States, 1880–1917* (Chicago: University of Chicago Press, 1995); Beryl Satter, *Each Mind a Kingdom: American Women, Sexual Purity and the New Thought Movement, 1875–1920* (Berkeley: University of California Press, 1999); Louise Michele Newman, *White Women's Rights: The Racial Origins of Feminism in the United States* (New York: Oxford University Press, 1999).

12. Cayton, *Ohio*, 98.

13. *Israelite*, May 29, 1874.

14. *Israelite*, November 5, 1872.

15. *Israelite*, July 26, 1872.

16. *UAHC Proceedings*, March 24, 1873 (Cincinnati: Bloch & Co., n.d.), vii.

17. *Israelite*, September 19, 1873; *American Israelite*, October 15, 1875.

18. *UAHC Proceedings*, 10, 37.

19. *Israelite*, October 18, 1872.

20. *American Israelite*, April 30, 1875, September 3, 1875.

21. Meyer, "Centennial History," 7.

22. *UAHC Proceedings*, volume 1.

23. *American Israelite*, October 8, 1875.

24. "Reflections on the Council," *Israelite*, July 20, 1883, 4.

Gender, Antisemitism, and Jewish Identity in the Fin de Siècle

Paula E. Hyman

When Michael Meyer published his pathbreaking book *The Origins of the Modern Jew* in 1967, he initiated a scholarly investigation of the nature of Jewish identity in Germany. Jewish self-consciousness, the very recognition that there was a choice as to how to be Jewish, he asserted, was a hallmark of the modern period. As he made clear in his subtitle—"Jewish Identity and European Culture in Germany, 1749–1824"—he was concerned with the period in which he deemed modern Jewish identity, with all its self-consciousness, to have emerged and with the site of its first articulation. As an intellectual historian, he was interested in the varieties of ideas that articulate Jews, some of whom were affiliated with an ideological movement, proffered as reasons to be or not be Jews in the context of the emerging modern German nation. He chose to focus on the individual bearers of those ideas rather than on the abstract ideas themselves.

Although few historians at the time were alert to the significance of gender in the formation of modern Jewish identities, Meyer paid some attention to the phenomenon of the "salon Jewesses," a small number of prominent German Jewish women who chose, for the most part, to defect from Judaism. Focusing on Dorothea Mendelssohn, Henriette Herz, and Rahel Varnhagen, he noted that they had little Jewish education and that they found in romantic Christianity the spirituality that, to them, was absent in Judaism. For Meyer, however, their gender was virtually incidental. His conclusion could apply equally to men and to women: "Born Jews in a romantic age, they could draw spiritual sustenance only from foreign wells."[1]

In his later work on religious reform, however, Meyer noted that German reformers, such as Abraham Geiger and Samuel Adler, were aware of the need to address the specific disabilities that women suffered in divorce law and in their secondary status in the synagogue. As German Jews constructed a form of Jewish identity consonant with the modern world, the place of women had to be reconsidered. While not at the forefront of their concerns, the rights of women were a corollary of their desire to refashion Judaism and Jewish identity.[2]

Although a variety of approaches to Jewish identity found expression in the eighteenth century and the first half of the nineteenth, the issue was by no means resolved as Jews confronted the twentieth century. Indeed, the issue of gender loomed even larger in the fin de siècle than it had two generations earlier. In Germany in particular, the rise of romantic nationalism and modern political antisemitism directed at Jews who regarded themselves as loyal German citizens, and culturally German to boot, subjected German Jews and their identity to constant scrutiny. A parallel phenomenon existed in Austria and to a lesser degree in France. In the forty years since the appearance of *The Origins of the Modern Jew*, scholarly focus on Jewish identity has shifted to the fin de siècle. Moreover, gender and postcolonial theories that have highlighted the linkage of race and masculinity in the late nineteenth century have illuminated not only antisemitic stereotypes but also Jewish reformulations of their identities.

In the modern period, ironically, Jews were less prepared for antisemitism than they had been in medieval and early modern times, when the master narrative of their faith explained why they suffered at the hands of gentiles. I find the following anecdote to best convey how traditional Jews dealt with the disparity between their inner sense of superiority and the reality of their subordinate status in the real world. It is a story told by Solomon Maimon, an eighteenth-century Polish Jew who tried, rather unsuccessfully, to transform himself into a German philosopher. In his memoirs, published in 1792–93, Maimon recounts the following story:

> Prince Razivil . . . came one day with his whole court to hunt in the neighbourhood of our village. Among the party was his daughter. . . . The young princess . . . betook herself with the ladies of her court . . . to the very room where as a

boy I was sitting behind the stove. I was struck with astonishment at the magnificence and splendour of the court,
gazed with rapture at the beauty of the persons and at the
dresses with their trimmings of gold and silver lace. . . . My
father came just as I was out of myself with joy and had bro-
ken into the words "Oh, how beautiful!" In order to calm
me and at the same time to confirm me in the principles of
our faith, he whispered into my ear, "Little fool, in the other
world . . . the princess will kindle the stove for us."[3]

This religious solace available to traditional Jews, not yet touched by
Enlightenment thought and by civic emancipation, no longer appeased
the secularly educated Jewish citizens of central and western Europe at
the end of the nineteenth century. In the fin de siècle, psychologically
vulnerable European Jews were surprised to discover that their status
as full members of the bourgeoisie was under assault. In France they
had been emancipated a century before. In Germany and Austria they
had enjoyed the advantages of citizenship only for about a generation,
but their economic success and adaptation to urban culture were apparent well before the achievement of political equality. Even as early
as the first few decades of the nineteenth century, as the historian David Sorkin has pointed out, they identified with the *Bildungsbürgertum*
(the middle classes whose status depended on their education) and
saw themselves as respectable representatives of the best in German
culture.[4]

    In speaking of the effect of antisemitism on Jewish identity I am
not referring here specifically to the political usage of antisemitism in
the last quarter of the nineteenth century. German-speaking Jews, as
well as French Jews, initially saw that phenomenon as temporary, a
recurrence from the past of antisemitic attacks, not as a modern transformation of an earlier scourge. They were concerned with the emergence of political antisemitism but felt that their newly acquired political status offered them protection, as did their defense organizations,
such as the German Centralverein deutscher Staatsbürger jüdischen
Glaubens, established in 1893. By 1916 the Centralverein, through its
institutional memberships, claimed to speak for two hundred thousand German Jews. That organization, and others like it, offered rational refutations of antisemitic invectives and asserted the fundamental
right of Jews to be citizens of their respective countries.[5]

    Central European Jews had to contend not only with the per-
petuation of old stereotypes but with a new critique of Jews' claim to
bourgeois respectability—the rise of racist conceptions of Jews. This
racist critique focused on the Jews' bodies, and especially on the very

masculinity of Jewish men.[6] In this article I address the question of how to evaluate the social and political consequences of negative stereotypes as seen by the victims themselves. To what extent did antisemitic depictions of Jews affect their identities and behavior? How can social historians integrate a "cultural studies" approach into our investigations of lived historical experience? The subject of representations of Jews, and the ways those representations were gendered, is important for the study of antisemitism, the linkage of antisemitism and misogyny, and the nationalist self-conceptions of Germans and Austrians, particularly in the fin de siècle. While these representations played a pivotal role in those three areas, I suggest that their effect on central European Jews themselves is less certain. Scholars sometimes give far too much play to the exceptional and lose sight of the reactions of ordinary people.

It is also appropriate to underline here that images must be approached with some skepticism. We often do not know how many people they reached or precisely how contemporaries interpreted them. In the case of images of Jews, we do not know how Europeans who were acquainted with Jews reconciled the images with the real people who were their neighbors. It does seem likely, however, given the pervasiveness of the imagery, that the negative tropes of female and male Jews that became common in literature and journalistic writing reflect a cultural "take" on the Jew that goes beyond the particular novel, article, or caricature. The very repetition of stereotypes in the popular media confers legitimacy upon them and provides a template for placing individuals within a category. Homi Bhabha, perhaps the best known contemporary theorist of colonialism and postcolonialism, has made the point that stereotypes blur differences and vacillate between what is commonly known and what must be endlessly repeated.[7]

In the past decade, scholarly attention to fin de siècle references to the "feminization" of Jewish men has proliferated. To a considerably lesser extent, the image of the Jewish female in art, theater, and literature has also been explored. The 1990s produced a cottage industry of examining how Europeans looked at the Jewish body. Among American scholars Sander Gilman has taken the lead in pointing out how Jewish men were portrayed as displaying characteristics that they shared with women.[8]

These feminine characteristics ascribed to Jewish men were far-reaching. Some were physical: male Jews were weak and rounded, ugly and ill formed, awkward, and incapable of performing the hard work required of productive citizens. There were racist thinkers who repeated the medieval charge that Jewish males had a peculiar odor, reminiscent of menstruation, that proved their similitude to women.

Paula E. Hyman

Jewish men, it was claimed, suffered from the same mental illnesses, or weaknesses, that supposedly plagued the female sex. Like women, for example, they were prone to hysteria. And they were far more likely to suffer from other mental diseases, especially neuroses, than were other men.[9]

But the feminine attributes discerned in Jewish men were moral as well, aspects of basic character. Jewish men were represented as materialistic, manipulative, and lacking in moral vigor and honor. They were crafty, not straightforward, honest, and courageous like true men. Moreover, their manipulativeness emerged clearly in the way they used language. As Gilman concluded in his massive study of Jewish self-hatred, in the eyes of their detractors, "Jews, when oppressed, can attack only verbally. In this, they are like women, whose lack of strength is compensated for by their wit." In fin de siècle Europe, Jews became the touchstone for general anxieties about the nature of masculinity in the modern world.[10]

Most influential in depicting the feminization of Jewish men in the fin de siècle was the young philosopher and convert from Judaism Otto Weininger. In his magnum opus, *Geschlecht und Charakter* [Sex and Character], which appeared in 1903, Weininger offered a misogynist analysis of gender distinctions that posited an analogy between Jews and women. Weininger stressed that the Jews as a race incarnated female principles. As he put it, Jews were "among those nations and races whose men . . . are found to approach so slightly and so rarely to the ideal of manhood." He found Judaism to be "saturated with femininity, with precisely those qualities the essence of which [are] . . . in the strongest opposition to the male nature." Like women, Jews had no personalities of their own, no moral sensibility, and no capacity for genius. They were cowardly. Defining Judaism as "the spirit of modern life," Weininger was able to link his disparagement of Jews and women with the concern about the degeneration of European culture and society in his own time."[11]

Weininger's work achieved popularity in its own time, and also subsequently. Although turgid, it was bold and inflammatory (and the author's suicide shortly after its publication certainly did not detract from its infamy). What is more important for any assessment of the widespread intellectual acceptance of both antisemitism and misogyny is the fact that intellectual luminaries such as Sigmund Freud and the philosopher Ludwig Wittgenstein grappled seriously with Weininger's insights. By 1922 the book had appeared in twenty-three editions.[12] The notion that women and Jews shared a common moral and physical weakness became part of central European conventional wisdom.

The image of the Jewish woman in the fin de siècle has attracted scholarly attention only recently. In part, this reflects the fact that feminist scholars came late to this subject, and in part, it reflects the fact that European attitudes to "the Jewess" were traditionally more complicated, more ambiguous, than to the Jewish man. The qualities associated with Jewishness—all negative—were located in the male. When Europeans wrote about Jews, as they did with astonishing frequency from the early eighteenth century until the Holocaust, they focused on Jewish men. As Sander Gilman stated with his customary assurance, "The Jew is always defined as masculine [male]," and his view has been widely accepted.[13] When Europeans referred to the superstitiousness of traditional Judaism, they most often pictured bearded men, wrapped in strange prayer shawls, not women. When they portrayed the Jews' exploitation of the simple peasant or the rapaciousness of Jewish capitalists, who were considered the figures behind the new economic system's growth, they singled out male Jews.

European social and political critics did not entirely ignore Jewish women, but for much of the eighteenth and nineteenth centuries their Jewishness was very much secondary to their femaleness. The Jewess was a member of a subordinated and stigmatized group, but her femaleness trumped her Jewishness. Femaleness was double-edged, dangerous but also alluring. Jewish women were pictured in two contradictory ways—as "la belle juive" and "la femme fatale." The "belle juive," the "beautiful Jewess," was exotic, in an Oriental way, and most often portrayed as desirable. When a Jewish woman was portrayed as a femme fatale, generally later in the nineteenth century, her Jewishness disappeared in her quintessential seductive qualities as a female.[14]

In the fin de siècle, negative qualities began to be attached to Jewish women that combined male-based antisemitic stereotypes with general features of female allure and danger. The Jewish woman's image thus combined both positive and negative traits. The female in general was still seen as seductive, and of course necessary, but the emergence of increasingly visible and assertive "New Women" led to depictions of women as dangerous, challenging men's hegemony in professional and cultural life. To shift the focus to fin de siècle Vienna for a moment, Gustav Klimt's portraits of Jewish women and use of Jewish women as models in some of his paintings disseminated the idea that the Jewess incarnated the modern femme fatale. It should be noted that Klimt, after all, was widely criticized in the fin de siècle for undermining traditional values by celebrating the seductive femme fatale. One critic of his painting of Judith, the Jewish heroine of the Apocrypha, commented that his Judith was dressed as a beautiful, fiery-eyed Jewish woman from the fashionable Viennese district of the

Ringstrasse. In the European imagination, then, the Jewish woman, however desirable, was a symbol of difference and of the exotic. Her difference was summed up in references to her "Orientalism."[15]

The Orientalization of the Jewish female was not necessarily an antisemitic act but a reflection of the fact that, however much Jews acculturated to the surrounding culture, as long as they remained Jews—and sometimes even after they converted—they were seen as Other. Indeed, the fact that Jewish women were stereotyped as Oriental should be recognized as a form of colonialism, in this case internal colonialism. Although postcolonial theorists have not applied their insights to the situation of European Jews in the century of enlightenment and emancipation, some historians of Jews and Judaism have done so. In *Defenders of the Faith*, his 1994 book on Jewish doctors and race science, John Efron suggested that "the categories of 'empire' and 'colonized' need to be expanded to include groups such as Jews."[16] A few years later, Susannah Heschel called for the application of postcolonial theory "to illuminate the situation of Jews as a marginal minority group within a broader Christian or Muslim society" and proceeded to do so in her study of the nineteenth-century German Jewish scholar Abraham Geiger.[17] I borrowed the term "internal colonialism" from Jonathan Hess, who, in his book *Germans, Jews, and the Claims of Modernity*, persuasively linked the late-eighteenth-century debates about the nature of Jews and their status in Germany to the issue of colonialism, labeling German attitudes toward Jews and Judaism a form of internal colonialism.[18] The stereotyping of Jewish women as Orientals is yet another example of internal colonialism that denies the possibility of accepting the Jews as potential Germans or real Frenchmen or Englishmen and also denies the value of their difference. If we accept the position of nineteenth-century western and central European Jews as internal colonials, then their acculturation can be seen as mimicry in which the Jew is the Other, or in Bhabha's terms, "a subject of difference that is almost the same but not quite."[19]

The perception that the Jewish woman was "almost the same but not quite" acquired a darker cast at the end of the nineteenth century and the beginning of the twentieth than had been the case previously; the danger associated with the seductive female was connected more firmly with specifically antisemitic elements. The dark and beautiful exotic Jewish woman was frequently depicted as a purveyor of disease—that is, syphilis. Here she was seen as parallel with the male Jew, who had been depicted in popular culture as the primary transmitter of the disease since the fifteenth century, when syphilis first appeared in Europe. According to Gilman, Sarah Bernhardt came "to represent the embodiment of [the] destructive stereotype [of the Jewish woman]."[20] Bernhardt, in the words of a contemporary French critic writing in the 1890s who focused on tuberculosis rather than syphilis, was one of "those lean actresses, the Rachels and Sarahs, who spit blood."[21] Jewish women were also recognized as an important component of those modern European women who sought to assume public roles as social welfare workers, philanthropic activists, and social critics and hence were considered a threat to those who supported a social order in which women were limited to domestic pursuits.[22] One might expect that if Jewish men were perceived as feminized, modern Jewish women would be depicted as masculinized. Yet, that trope did not figure in an overt way in representations of Jewish women (despite the fact that Sarah Bernhardt wore trousers).

Instead, the development of racist thought, and its inclusion within the new versions of antisemitism, facilitated the application of negative stereotypes of "the Jew" to Jewish women. In the period of the rise of political and racial antisemitism, especially in Germany and France, antisemitic caricature began to depict Jewish women as grotesque, rather than beautiful, figures. Previously, caricatures had focused primarily on male Jews and presented few Jewish women, as opposed to Jewish men, with the visible physical symbol of Jewishness: the hooked nose. The newly caricatured Jewish female was fat and unattractive, and sported a prominent nose. Like her husband, she was driven by her desire for wealth and status, and she mangled her country's language. The most striking caricature, from Eduard Fuchs's 1921 Die Juden in der Karikatur, was published in Amsterdam in 1895. Titled "Kurgäste," it depicted a family of corpulent, overdressed Jewish bourgeois sauntering through, and totally out of place at, a spa. The caricature virtually screams that these excessive people do not belong.[23] A caricature from 1907 also focused on Jews, including fat Jewish women, dominating the public space—in this case the opera. Since one of Wagner's operas was being staged, the presence of Jews was presented as particularly inappropriate, and perhaps dangerous for German culture. Caricatured Jewish women appear in the newspaper illustrations that proliferated during the Dreyfus Affair and in German satirical journals like Fliegende Blätter and Simplicissimus (but still much more rarely than male Jews).[24]

What should be clear from this brief survey of images of Jewish women in western and central Europe before World War I is that a variety of images coexisted at any one time in literature, art, and satire, with negative images appearing frequently only with the rise of modern antisemitism at the end of the nineteenth century. What they all have in common—even the most admiring descriptions of "la belle juive"—is that they define the Jewish woman as a recogniz-

Paula E. Hyman

able entity, the foreigner in our midst. And, by the end of this period, she bears both negative Jewish traits, such as materialism, dishonesty, and sometimes ugliness, as well as negative female traits, such as excessive sexuality and inappropriate assertiveness, that is, lack of the demure submissiveness that had characterized bourgeois women (at least in theory). Only in the fin de siècle do the images of Jewish women approach the vilification that had long characterized the depictions of Jewish men. Antisemitism transformed Jewish women from women into Jews.

We return now to Jewish men. It is clear that the stereotype of the feminization of the Jewish male was widely accepted in intellectual as well as popular culture in the fin de siècle. How Jewish spokesmen, and ordinary Jews, responded to this disparagement of Jewish masculinity is less clear. In their traditional communities before emancipation, as Daniel Boyarin has pointed out, Jews had seen attributions to gentile males of the qualities of brute strength, violence, and willingness to engage in battle as *goyim nakhes*, pleasure for gentiles. Jews did not consider these qualities appropriate for Jewish men.[25] Even as they began to acculturate at the beginning of the nineteenth century, Jewish men identified selectively with a more cerebral form of masculinity—Enlightenment rationality and the *Kultur* of the *Bildungsbürgertum*. During the course of the century acculturation did lead, however, to Jews' internalization of the gender norms of the larger society. According to those norms, the male was depicted as strong and powerful but also rational, responsible for economic and political life. The female was physically weak and emotional but responsible for the moral and spiritual quality of the home as well as its orderly functioning.

Historians have focused on the striking responses of some prominent Jewish intellectuals and public figures who internalized the disparagement of their masculinity. Otto Weininger, for example, has received extraordinary, and to my mind undeserved, scholarly attention in the last twenty years or so.[26] Sigmund Freud's shame at his father's accommodation to a symbolic attack on his manhood has been repeatedly cited.[27]

Walther Rathenau, the German Jewish industrialist, intellectual, and politician, also accepted the prevailing cultural critique of the Jewish male. When he was thirty, in 1897, he wrote an anonymous essay on the Jewish question, which he titled "Hear, O Israel." He was concerned about the persistent Otherness of Jews within German society, and he blamed Jews themselves for their lack of social acceptance. Focusing on the physical awkwardness of Jews, he called on Jews to remake themselves. "Look in the mirror!" he exhorted his fellow Jewish men. "If you recognize your poorly constructed frame—the high shoulders, the clumsy feet, the soft roundedness of form—as signs of bodily decadence, you will, for a few generations, work for your external rebirth."[28]

The pervasiveness of antisemitic stereotypes, of race thinking in fin de siècle central Europe, is also evident in some memoirs of Jewish men. I have not read enough of them to generalize, but it is worth remarking that some young German Jewish men were convinced—to their chagrin—that their Jewishness was stamped on their faces. In his memoirs Richard Lichtheim, born in 1885, commented that when he looked in the mirror, to his dismay a Jewish face stared back.[29] When I looked at the photograph of Lichtheim, which served as the frontispiece of his book, I saw a rather typical-looking German. The critic Moritz Goldstein reflected in the 1950s on the origins of his famous article of 1912, "Deutsch-jüdischer Parnass," which called on German Jews to recognize that Germans resented the Jews' prominent role in German culture and should go their own way. He located his own awareness of the pervasiveness of German antisemitism at the time he began university, and recognized its connection to masculinity. As Goldstein wrote,

> At my own Berlin University I learnt that there were student clubs which not only excluded Jews but strictly refused to accept the challenge to a duel from a Jew or, as it was called, "to give satisfaction." Since it was academic usage to take revenge for any offence . . . by an immediate invitation to a fight with pointed weapons (which usually led to no more than the much coveted face scars or *Schmisse*), this refusal implied, and was meant to imply, that the Jew was a creature without "honour." I was too much of a German student to laugh at so childish a concept of honour; I felt deeply hurt.[30]

Arthur Ruppin, an important sociologist and demographer of the Jews, encountered antisemitism earlier in his youth than did Goldstein. Born in a small town in Posen in 1876, he moved to Magdeburg with his family when he was sixteen and was exposed to antisemitism when he entered the municipal secondary school there. At university, in Berlin and Halle, antisemitism was also palpable. He mentions specifically the exclusion of Jews from student associations. In the diary that he kept as a youth there are many references to antisemitism, even to an 1893 conversation with a friend to the effect that perhaps one day the Jews would be thrown out of Germany. He became active with the Zionist movement in Palestine before World War I.[31]

The most common response of Jewish men to their recognition that their masculinity was under attack was not to question the cultural construction of masculinity in the larger society but to establish their own organizations that enabled the display of their masculinity. Jewish men, like the Jewish community as a whole, indulged in mimetic behavior. The growing exclusion of Jewish students from fraternities at universities by the end of the nineteenth century, and the open refusal of German students to include them in the circle of those with whom one would duel, led to the establishment of Jewish fraternities and student clubs. Likewise, as young Jews were turned away from German youth groups that stressed hiking and physical exercise, Jews formed their own groups with similar agendas.[32]

The Zionist movement, itself a product of the fin de siècle, formulated the most direct Jewish response to this antisemitic disparagement of Jewish masculinity and the Jewish male body. Zionists concurred with antisemites and many race scientists that Jews were unhealthy in body and mind. They attributed Jewish frailty and the lack of manliness necessary for men to participate as equals in European society to the deleterious effects of two thousand years of living in the Diaspora as a despised and powerless minority. By creating the "New Jew," Zionism would restore manliness to the Jewish male. It was Max Nordau, one of the early Zionist leaders and an influential European intellectual who had written on degeneracy, who specifically addressed the image of the weak Jewish man. Beginning in 1900, he popularized the concept of *Muskeljudentum*, muscular Jewry. Only through conscious effort initiated in the Diaspora could the Jews reverse the process of degeneration they had suffered and achieve the physical strength that characterized healthy men. To realize these goals, the Zionist movement sponsored sports and gymnastic clubs to remake Jewish bodies along with Jewish minds, and Nordau specifically touted the Jewish need for gymnastics to build healthy Jewish bodies to complement strong Jewish minds.[33]

The concern among Jewish intellectuals and communal leaders about the feminization of Jewish men—both as antisemitic charge and as perceived reality—led, incidentally, to a reinforcement of prevailing gender norms. This is most evident among Zionists, who wrote regularly about their social vision.[34] The Zionist "New Jew" was a distinctly male creature, a vigorous, sun-tanned pioneer who was building the new land. Women pioneers were not represented in Zionist publicity. Women appeared only as symbols, of Zion, for example, much as Marianne was the symbol of modern France. Indeed, in the Zionist *yishuv* in Palestine, women confronted significant opposition to their participation in the agricultural work that was the center of the movement's efforts to settle the land.[35] Like other nationalist movements of the time, Zionism also presupposed a linkage between masculinity and civic consciousness. Male activists were responsible for the direction of the nation, and full participation in the public life of the nation was limited to men alone. Theodor Herzl's 1902 utopian novel *Altneuland* accepts the political equality of women—it is utopian, after all—but once the new society is realized women sensibly choose to devote themselves to their domestic responsibilities in place of civic participation.[36] When women's role in Zionism was mentioned in nonfiction writing, it was limited to fundraising for the movement in the Diaspora, serving as helpmeets to male pioneers, and subsequently giving birth to and raising children with an appropriate Jewish nationalist spirit. The majority of Jews living in western and central Europe, however, were not attracted to Zionism and hardly refashioned their identities in its image.

It appears that one response of German and Austrian Jews to the cultural pervasiveness of antisemitism was to leave Judaism and the Jewish community, converting to Christianity or becoming *konfessionslos*. We know that the rate of conversion increased in this period, with male converts outnumbering female.[37] In the absence of anthropological studies, we cannot know with any certainty what precipitated their conversion, although most scholars of the phenomenon agree that it was not religious faith. Because it was impossible for people of different religions to marry in Germany and Austria, conversion could occur for the purpose of enabling intermarriage. This may be interpreted as a marker of acculturation and integration, not necessarily a flight from Judaism precipitated by antisemitism.

There are no female parallels to Rathenau or Ruppin, perhaps because the obstacles to women as intellectuals and political or business leaders were formidable.[38] Investigations of the impact of this charge of the feminization of Jewish men have concentrated almost exclusively on a small group of intellectuals. However, there has been virtually no exploration of the effects of this charge or of the disparagement of Jewish women on the construction of Jewish women's identity and on their participation in public activity in the fin de siècle. There is evidence that both within the larger society and in the Jewish community, Jewish women were at least as conscious of disabilities resulting from their status as women as of their stigmatization as Jews. Central European Jewish women seem not to have retreated into the home and into maternal roles to counter misogynistic and antisemitic criticism of their prominence in the public sphere. In fact, within the Jewish community they seem to have asserted their right to address public issues and to be granted recognition as partners in formulating policy

Paula F Hyman

on matters of Jewish communal concern. That is, far from refraining from challenging male Jewish communal leaders in order to protect their presumably fragile sense of masculinity, women challenged their own exclusion from positions endowed with decision-making power.

Jewish women's entry into political life displayed both their independence and their resolve to speak out on issues they deemed central to them as women. Both in Germany and internationally they spoke out about what was then called "white slavery," the international sex trade in women, and specifically about the participation of Jews as pimps and prostitutes (the latter always conceived as victims).[39] The Jüdischer Frauenbund, the national German organization of Jewish women founded in 1904, offers an instructive example of Jewish women's activity and self-definition.[40]

White slavery assumed a prominent place on the agenda of the Jüdischer Frauenbund, stimulating it to respond creatively to the needs of less fortunate Jewish females and to assert its own goals. The organization established the first Jewish home in Europe for sexually delinquent girls and unmarried mothers, campaigned to provide better recreational and educational facilities for girls, and pressed the male leaders of their community to do more to rescue potential victims of white slavery and to address the social conditions that fostered prostitution. Bertha Pappenheim, the president of the Frauenbund, made several fact-finding trips to Galicia, the Balkans, Russia, and the Ottoman Empire in the years before World War I to investigate the socioeconomic conditions of the Jewish population, with special attention to the situation of women. Their work on the issue of white slavery emboldened leaders of the Frauenbund in 1907 to propose that the Jewish Committee to Combat White Slavery elect women to its board of directors as full members and not merely as honorary delegates. That same year the Frauenbund made it clear to the general Jewish philanthropic organization, the Hilfsverein, that in exchange for its participation it expected to be involved in decision making. Pappenheim was also willing to publicly criticize Jewish law on women, though she was herself an Orthodox Jew. She stated in 1907 that "in the eyes of Jewish law woman is not an individual, not a personality, but is judged and acknowledged only as a sexual being."[41] Under Pappenheim's leadership the Frauenbund went on to campaign vigorously for female suffrage within the Gemeinde, the formal community of German Jewry in every locale in which there was a Jewish collectivity. Ultimately, it became the first religious women's organization in Germany to demand suffrage both in its own community and in the state.

Modern Jewish women who transgressed bourgeois norms certainly created a sense of unease. Jewish women who crusaded to end the Jewish involvement in white slavery, for example, were criticized for airing dirty laundry in public and for publicly campaigning vigorously for female suffrage within the *Gemeinde* and for equality within Jewish communal institutions. Although the male leaders of Jewish communal institutions were, not surprisingly, reluctant to accord women actual power within their ranks, they were eager to mobilize women's participation particularly in philanthropic organizations, whose work was deemed to fall within women's natural domain. By the 1920s a full range of European Jewish organizations—from Zionist to religious to philanthropic—made efforts to engage women in their activity.[42]

The absence of Jewish women from the ranks of those anguished by antisemitic stereotyping led me to rethink the responses of Jewish men. In their daily activity, most Jewish men also seem not to have been preoccupied with their purported lack of masculinity. They continued to find success in business, where social restrictions were less palpable than in the professions, and in intellectual pursuits. In France, in particular, the civil service and political positions were wide open to them.[43] They participated actively in German, Austrian, and French cultural life. Within the Jewish community, particularly in Germany and Austria, they continued to design campaigns to refute antisemitic charges and to promote pride among Jews through their national voluntary organizations, the Centralverein and the Österreichisch-Israelitische Union.[44] Although the Centralverein had often exhorted Jews to behave with self-discipline and refinement so as not to give fuel to antisemites, its message to German Jewry combated the traditional Jewish policy of public silence. It called on German Jews to affirm their Jewishness in public and to defend themselves against antisemitic statements. In France, where Jews confronted the assertive antisemitism of the Dreyfus Affair, and have conventionally been depicted as its passive victims, the scholar Pierre Birnbaum has demonstrated in his foray into local archives throughout France that Jews aggressively called on governmental authorities to protect their civic rights, their persons, and their property. When subject to rioting in early 1898, a few Jews also intervened physically, challenging antisemitic demonstrators.[45]

Jewish identities in fin de siècle Europe were variegated and shifting. They were highly gendered and affected by geographical and social location. As I have argued elsewhere, Jewish men were anxious about their status in the larger society, which often did not live up to their expectations, particularly as antisemitism became more pervasive. They often expressed their anxieties in discussions of the failures of Jewish women to carry out their responsibilities as agents both of acculturation and of boundary maintenance.[46] Some Jewish men

Paula E. Hyman

worried about their depiction in popular culture and intellectual discourse. Although they did not embrace women's more public roles within the Jewish community, neither were they staunch opponents of the changes in women's roles that occurred in the early twentieth century. Jewish women, on the other hand, seem to have been concerned primarily with enhancing their status as women and participating fully in social welfare and civic life.

I am not disavowing the many insights that cultural analysts have provided in our quest to understand the status of Jews in European societies and the meanings attached to the representation of the Jew by nationalists, antisemites, and Jews themselves. The gender difference in representations of Jews has been important in my own understanding of the construction of modern Jewish identities and my interpretation of the project of assimilation—that is, the official communal policy of self-definition vis-à-vis the larger society. But an examination of the behavior and activity of the majority of Jewish women and men in western and central Europe suggests that, however hurtful Jews found the antisemitic imagery that was pervasive in their societies, that imagery was central neither to the fashioning of their Jewish identities nor to their self-presentation in the larger society.

NOTES

1. Michael A. Meyer, *The Origins of the Modern Jew: Jewish Identity and European Culture in Germany, 1729–1824* (Detroit: Wayne State University Press, 1967), 114. For later work on the salon Jewesses, see Deborah Hertz, *Jewish High Society in Old Regime Berlin* (New Haven: Yale University Press, 1988).

2. Michael A. Meyer, *Response to Modernity: A History of the Reform Movement in Judaism* (New York: Oxford University Press, 1988), 139–40. Meyer notes that the reformers meeting in Breslau did not have time to discuss the preliminary report on the status of women.

3. Solomon Maimon, *An Autobiography*, trans. J. Clark Murray (Urbana: University of Illinois Press, 2001), 25–26.

4. David Sorkin, *The Transformation of German Jewry, 1780–1840* (New York: Oxford University Press, 1987).

5. Ismar Schorsch, *Jewish Reactions to German Anti-Semitism, 1870–1914* (New York: Columbia University Press, 1972); Jehuda Reinharz, *Fatherland or Promised Land: The Dilemma of the German Jew, 1893–1914* (Ann Arbor: University of Michigan Press, 1975). The statistic on 1916 affiliation is from Schorsch, 119. See also Jacob Toury, "Defense Activities of the Oesterreichisch-Israelitische Union before 1914," in *Living with Antisemitism: Modern Jewish Responses*, ed. Jehuda Reinharz, 167–92 (Hanover: University Press of New England, 1987).

6. See Sharon Gillerman, "More Than Skin Deep: Histories of the Modern Jewish Body," *Jewish Quarterly Review* 95, no. 3 (2005): 470–78; and John M. Hoberman, "Otto Weininger and the Critique of Jewish Maculinity," in *Jews and Gender: Responses to Otto Weininger,* ed. Nancy Harrowitz and Barbara Hyams, 141–53 (Philadelphia: Temple University Press, 1995).

7. Homi Bhabha, "The Other Question . . . Homi K. Bhabha Reconsiders the Stereotype and Colonial Discourse," *Screen* 24, no. 6 (1983): 18–36.

8. Of Gilman's many works, the most influential insofar as Jewish identity is concerned have been *Jewish Self-Hatred: Anti-Semitism and the Hidden Language of the Jews* (Baltimore: Johns Hopkins University Press, 1986), *The Jew's Body* (New York: Routledge, 1991), and *Freud, Race, and Gender* (Princeton: Princeton University Press, 1993).

9. In addition to Gilman's publications listed earlier, see his *Difference and Pathology: Stereotypes of Sexuality, Race, and Madness* (Ithaca: Cornell University Press, 1985); Jay Geller, "(G)nos(e)ology: The Cultural Construction of the Other," in *People of the Body: Jews and Judaism from an Embodied Perspective,* ed. Howard Eilberg Schwartz, 250–53 (Albany: State University of New York Press, 1992); and John Efron, *Defenders of the Race: Jewish Doctors and Race Science in Fin de Siècle Europe* (New Haven: Yale University Press, 1994), 26–27. Jacques Le Rider's *Modernity and Crises of Identity: Culture and Society in Fin de Siècle Vienna,* trans. Rosemary Morris (New York: Continuum Publishing Company, 1993; French original Presses Universitaires de France, 1990), makes a strong argument, from a psychological and psychoanalytical perspective, for the linkage of concerns about Jewishness and femininity in discussions of European degeneracy. See esp. 165–83. George Mosse pioneered in noting that the Jewish male's body was feminized and that Jewish masculinity was thereby challenged. See his *The Crisis of German Ideology: Intellectual Origins of the Third Reich* (New York: Grosset and Dunlap, 1964), esp. 140; *Nationalism and Sexuality: Respectability and Abnormal Sexuality in Modern Europe* (New York: Howard Fertig, 1985), 36–37, 133–52; and *The Image of Man: The Creation of Modern Masculinity* (New York: Oxford University Press, 1996).

10. The quotation is from Gilman, *Jewish Self-Hatred,* 258.

11. Otto Weininger, *Sex and Character,* reprint of the authorized translation of the 6th German ed. (New York: AMS Press, 1975). The direct quotations can be found on pp. 302, 306, 329; this passage summarizes material from pp. 302–30.

12. Jacques Le Rider, *Le cas Otto Weininger: racines de l'antiféminisme et de l'antisémitisme* (Paris: Presses Universitaires de France, 1982); Harrowitz and Hyams, *Jews and Gender.*

13. Sander Gilman, "Salome, Syphilis, Sarah Bernhardt, and the 'Modern Jewess,'" in *The Jew in the Text: Modernity and the Construction of Identity,* ed. Linda Nochlin and Tamar Garb, 97–120 (London: Thames and

Hudson, 1995), 98.

14. Luce A. Klein, *Portrait de la juive dans la litterature française* (Paris: Editions Nizet, 1970), 55–73, 94–95. See also Florian Krobb, *Die schöne Jüdin: Jüdische Frauengestalten in der deutschsprachigen Erzählliteratur vom 17. Jahrhundert bis zum Ersten Weltkrieg* (Tübingen: Max Niemeyer Verlag, 1993.

15. *Gustav Klimt und die Frauen* (Vienna: Verlag Cristian Brandstätter, 1994), 88–89. The depiction and critique of Judith I (1901) is part of a chapter titled "Fatale Frauen: Die Omnipotenz des Weiblichen," 84–89.

16. Efron, *Defenders of the Faith*, 3.

17. Susannah Heschel, "Jewish Studies as Counterhistory," in *Insider/Outsider: American Jews and Multiculturalism*, ed. David Biale, Michael Galchinsky, and Susannah Herschel, 101–15 (Berkeley: University of California Press, 1998), 104; Susannah Heschel, *Abraham Geiger and the Jewish Jesus* (Chicago: University of Chicago Press, 1998).

18. Jonathan Hess, *Germans, Jews, and the Claims of Modernity* (New Haven: Yale University Press, 2002).

19. Homi Bhabha, "Of Mimicry and Man: The Ambivalence of Colonial Discourse," in *The Location of Culture* (London: Routledge, 1994), 86. Bhabha, of course, was not referring specifically to the Jew.

20. Sander Gilman, "Salome, Syphilis, Sarah Bernhardt," 111.

21. Anatole Leroy-Beaulieu as cited in ibid., 111.

22. Marion Kaplan, *The Making of the Jewish Middle Class: Women, Family, and Identity in Imperial Germany* (New York: Oxford University Press, 1991), 202–27.

23. Eduard Fuchs, *Die Juden in der Karikatur* (München: Verlag Albert Langen, 1921). The caricature Kurgäste is on p. 191.

24. Ibid.; Norman Kleeblatt, ed., *The Dreyfus Affair: Art, Justice, Politics* (Berkeley: University of California Press, 1987).

25. Daniel Boyarin, *Unheroic Conduct: The Rise of Heterosexuality and the Invention of the Jewish Man* (Berkeley: University of California Press, 1997).

26. See, e.g., Jacques Le Rider, *Cas Otto Weininger* and his *Modernity and the Crisis of Identity*; Harrowitz and Hyams, *Jews and Gender*. On the linkage of antifeminism and antisemitism, in addition to Le Rider's *Modernity and Crises of Identity*, see Shulamit Volkov, "Anti-Semitism as a Cultural Code—Reflections on the History and the Historiography of Antisemitism in Imperial Germany," *Leo Baeck Institute Yearbook* 23 (1978): 25–46.

27. See, e.g., Peter Gay, *Freud: A Life for Our Time* (New Haven: Yale University Press, 1988), 11–12.

28. Walther Rathenau, "Höre, Israel!" *Zukunft* 18 (March 16, 1897): 454–62, as cited in Robert A. Pois, "Walther Rathenau's Jewish Quandary," *Leo Baeck Institute Yearbook* 13 (1968): 121.

29. Richard Lichtheim, *Rückkehr: Lebenserinnerungen aus der Frühzeit des deutschen Zionismus* (Stuttgart: Deutsche Verlags-Anstalt, 1970).

30. Moritz Goldstein, "German Jewry's Dilemma before 1914," *Leo Baeck Institute Yearbook* 2 (1957): 236–54, here 237. Goldstein was thirty-two years old when he published his article in the first issue of the journal of cultural criticism *Kunstwart*.

31. Arthur Ruppin *Erinnerungen. I: Jugend-und Studentenzeit 1876–1907* (Tel Aviv: Verlag Bitaon, 1945), 61–62, 131–36.

32. Konrad Jarausch, *Students, Society, and Politics in Imperial Germany: The Rise of Academic Illiberalism* (Princeton: Princeton University Press, 1982), 271–72; and Mosse, *Crisis of German Ideology,* 135.

33. Max Nordau, "Muskeljudentum," *Jüdische Turnzeitung,* June 1900; reprinted in his *Zionistische Schriften* (Köln: Jüdischer Verlag, 1909), 379–81. See also David Biale, *Eros and the Jews: From Biblical Israel to Contemporary America* (New York: Basic Books, 1992), 177–79; George Mosse, "Max Nordau, Liberalism, and the New Jew," *Journal of Contemporary History* 27, no. 4 (1992): 565–81; and Michael Berkowitz, *Zionist Culture and West European Jewry before the First World War* (Cambridge: Cambridge University Press, 1993), 107–9.

34. See, e.g., the Yiddish pamphlet *Di yudische froy un der tsionizm* (Warsaw: Druckerei "Hazefira," 1918), which included an essay by Martin Buber. The articles seem to have been aimed at a western-educated audience and then were translated into Yiddish.

35. Sylvie Fogiel-Bijaoui, "On the Way to Equality? The Struggle for Women's Suffrage in the Yishuv, 1917–1926," in *Pioneers and Homemakers: Jewish Women in Pre-state Israel,* ed. Deborah Bernstein, 261–82 (Albany: State University of New York Press, 1992).

36. Theodor Herzl, *Old-New Land,* trans. Lotta Levenson (New York: Bloch Publishing, 1941), 75–77. "Old maids," however, were recruited to administer public charities.

37. Todd M. Endelman, "The Social and Political Context of Conversion in Germany and England, 1870–1914," in *Jewish Apostasy in the Modern World,* ed. Todd M. Endelman, 83–107 (New York: Holmes and Meier, 1987).

38. Sander Gilman cites the example of Else Croner, who in a 1913 book defended the "Modern Jewess" [of Germany] but located the source of the contemporary negative images of the Jewish female in East European Jewish women. Gilman, "Salome, Syphilis, Sarah Bernhardt," 115–19.

39. Paula Hyman, "The Jewish Body Politic: Gendered Politics in the Early Twentieth Century," *Nashim* 2 (1999): 37–51.

40. Marion Kaplan, *The Jewish Feminist Movement in Germany: The Campaigns of the Jüdischer Frauenbund, 1904–1938* (Westport, Conn.: Greenwood Press, 1979).

41. Bertha Pappenheim, "Zur Sittlichkeitsfrage" (1907); reprinted in *Sisyphus: Gegen den Mädchenhandel—Galizien,* ed. Helga Heubach (Freibach: Kore Verlag, 1992), 114.

42. Paula Hyman, "The Transnational Experience of Jewish Women in Western and Central Europe after World War I," in *European Jews and*

Jewish Europeans between the Two World Wars, ed. Raya Cohen, 21–33 (Tel Aviv: Tel Aviv University, 2004).

43. Pierre Birnbaum, *Jews of the Republic: A Political History of State Jews in France from Gambetta to Vichy*, trans. Jane Marie Todd (Stanford: Stanford University Press, 1996).

44. Arnold Paucker, "The Jewish Defense against Antisemitism in Germany, 1893–1933," in *Living with Antisemitism: Modern Jewish Responses*, ed. Jehuda Reinharz, 104–32 (Hanover: University Press of New England, 1987).

45. Pierre Birnbaum, *The Anti-Semitic Movement: A Tour of France in 1898*, trans. Jane Marie Todd (New York: Hill and Wang, 2003), 309–31. Steven Wilson had made a similar argument in *Ideology and Experience: Antisemitism at the Time of the Dreyfus Affair* (Rutherford, N.J.: Fairleigh Dickinson University Press, 1982).

46. Paula Hyman, *Gender and Assimilation in Modern Jewish History: The Roles and Representation of Women* (Seattle: University of Washington Press, 1995), esp. 154–60.

16

Apprenticeships in Work and Love

Jewish Youth Growing Up in Imperial Germany

MARION KAPLAN

During a long career of contemplating "our humanness," Sigmund Freud, an articulate and expert witness to the bourgeois norms of his era, designated work and love as the two indispensable components of a happy and well-adjusted life.[1] It is not surprising, therefore, that in search of psychological and material fulfillment, Jews like other middle-class Germans aspired to solid, well-paying jobs or careers and solid, well-endowed, and satisfying marriages. What kinds of apprenticeships would pave a pathway to these goals? At first glance, the term "apprenticeship" may appear a bit incongruous. While one can imagine a class-appropriate and gendered apprenticeship in which young Jewish men and women gained sufficient skills for a job or a career, how did they "train," as it were, for love? And, how was "love" defined? In 1910 Freud defined "normal" love as both "tender" and "sensual." Although many poets and writers before him had brought affection and physical love together, at the end of the nineteenth century "sexual satisfaction was becoming as much an ingredient in the definition of true love as affection and permanent commitment."[2] And yet, gender affected the ways in which one learned about "love." Whereas young women were socialized to focus on romance, young men could engage in romantic and sexual episodes.

Looking back on their "adolescence," often "a new and . . . disquieting concept in the late nineteenth century," German Jews discussed their instruction in housework and careers but rarely provided similar details with regard to their initiation into sexual love.[3] A few sources, unusual in their depth of detail, will allow us to look at how some young Jewish women and men first encountered and experienced work and love. We will note that young Jewish middle-class men entered both "apprenticeships" far more easily and learned more about these worlds than did similarly situated young women, often leaving the latter at a disadvantage as they embarked upon adult jobs and marriage.

EARLY EXPERIENCES WITH WORK

Location heavily influenced the kinds of work children and young adults could do. Rural children, generally less privileged than middle-class, urban children, often began informal apprenticeships while still in elementary school. They helped in the family shop or business, running errands, cleaning up, or serving customers. Work, like most areas of life, was gendered. Livestock dealers expected daughters to help in the house and sons to help in the stables. They took sons along when they visited peasants, and when these boys finished lower school, some joined the business. One boy from Ellar (Hesse) entered his father's cattle business in 1901 at the age of fourteen. He and his seventeen-year-old brother bought and sold cattle at the markets. Three years later, he functioned as a full-fledged cattle dealer.[4] In the village of Rülzheim (near Mannheim) the four Friedhoff children, born between 1896 and 1907, helped run the family hotel and kosher butcher shop. The girls assisted the two maids with the weekly laundry. This included pumping and carrying water from a well, soaking the wash in hot water on Sunday and then boiling and scrubbing it on Monday. The sons visited customers to announce when their father bought a calf, when meat would be available, and the price at which it would be sold. As a sixteen-year-old, another son learned how to be a "professional" butcher, helping his father's friend butcher goats.[5]

The Friedhoffs also illustrate how some rural families scraped together enough to furnish each of their two sons and two daughters with a formal apprenticeship or some instruction beyond lower school. Although the parents had only completed *Volksschule* themselves, they supported their oldest son's apprenticeship even during a period of financial struggle. However, they could only manage to apprentice him in a small town department store, not in a post he considered crucial to a better career. Although he later became a prosperous tobacco manufacturer, he felt he had succeeded "despite his lack of better training."[6] The parents also managed to send one daughter to a business school to learn how to run a small guesthouse. Toward the end of World War I, the two sisters had enough hotel experience and business training to open an inn for Jewish soldiers. The youngest son benefited from his parents' later prosperity. They sent him to gymnasium in another town, forfeiting his assistance in the hotel as well as paying for his room and board with a family that kept a kosher kitchen.

Families expected rural and urban girls to help out around the house or, among the wealthier, at the very least to know how the household functioned so that they could oversee a maid—usually just one for all the necessary chores. Most girls observed their mothers as they completed household tasks, although these were rarely dignified with the term "work." Girls helped out increasingly as they got older, sometimes taking over the household entirely if their mothers got sick or died. In the early decades of the imperial era, most housewives still produced their own clothing or hired an occasional seamstress or laundress. They also mended, shopped, cooked, baked, preserved, and canned. Homes, grimy from wood- or coal-burning stoves, required special care. Ornaments needed to be dusted and burnished. Rural women had even more to do, including raising some of the family's produce. In families that could afford some household help, girls also learned from servants.

Toward the turn of the century, the increasing availability of running water and new appliances, as well as canned foods and manufactured clothing reduced the time housewives spent as producers and increased their work as consumers. Now families and future spouses also expected young women to handle consumption and budgeting in order to run a household. In addition, middle-class housewives had to present the family in its best light. Not only did housework produce some of the basics, efficient consumption could also fill the gap between aspirations and economic stringencies. Helene Eyck (born in 1859) wrote diary entries in the 1880s and 1890s that show the housework involved in balancing a limited budget while trying to provide "class appropriate" perks, like dance lessons, to her children. She also tried to pass on the virtues of thrift and organization to her daughters, whom she expected would marry and become housewives themselves.

While rural boys and girls worked alongside their parents, and most urban middle-class daughters also spent their "apprenticeships" at home, a large majority of city and small town Jewish boys looked for an apprenticeship in a store or business after the equivalent of a high school education. Their choice of an apprenticeship often depended upon family connections, sometimes as a result of antisemitism and other times as the easiest and most obvious path. Thus, Jewish boys frequently found employment among relatives, friends, or distant acquaintances. Victor Klemperer's father had known one of the owners of Victor's firm, probably facilitating the boy's entry into his apprenticeship. Young Hugo Marx (born in 1892) apprenticed at a bank due to his uncle's connections. Although he quickly grew to hate the job, he stayed for a year and a half because his family saw the position "as a favor" and because the bank "put up with" him to please his uncle.[7] When he finally quit, he lasted only two months in the next job until another uncle promised to support his legal studies.[8]

Generally, apprentices spent three years learning a trade while earning only their room, board, and a bit of pocket money. By 1900 some boys might also attend a few night school courses—such as arithmetic, bookkeeping, business correspondence, and foreign languages—at a local business school. These schools had grown from about 50 in 1870 to 750 by the beginning of the war as part of the growing professionalization of business. Those with "solid" training could aspire to better positions, relatively good pay and working conditions, and possibly even to independence. During his apprenticeship, described in more detail in the next section, Victor Klemperer (born in 1881) met such men: they "had very good manners, including the tone of the educated middle class."[9] Those with no more than an elementary education and a minimal apprenticeship constituted a lower class of assistants whose poor pay and conditions reflected their lack of education and skills and who "in the struggle around working conditions [were] in part worse off than laborers."[10]

Whether or not apprenticeships bore fruit, the adults involved believed that inculcating the value of work mattered most of all. Hard work would be rewarded but was also a reward in itself. Values such as initiative, hard work, and self-discipline played a formative role in bourgeois or aspiring bourgeois childhoods. The "gospel of work" was almost "exclusively a bourgeois ideal," Peter Gay reminds us, because the "aristocrats did not value it and the working poor did not need it."[11] Parents, especially fathers, set an example in the world of paid employment. Children appreciated the long hours that their fathers worked and acknowledged this in their memoirs. Julius Frank's father, a cattle dealer, rose at 3 A.M. to feed and milk the cows.[12] Another cattle dealer, the father of ten, "arrived home exhausted from too much hard work."[13] Both the fathers and their sons saw work and character as closely linked. Conversely, and like many other bourgeois men, they worried that idleness presented a danger to virility, that sloth was unmanly.[14] In fact, part of their masculinity training included the notion that a "real man" worked hard.[15] These fathers impressed their children with their work habits.[16] Of those who achieved success in the workday world, some thanked God for their good fortune, but most attributed it to hard work.[17] The son of a Hessian-Jewish cattle dealer recalled his father's motto: "He who rests, rusts."[18]

GROWING UP: FORMAL APPRENTICESHIPS IN THE WORLD OF WORK

While daughters might demand or need jobs, middle-class parents considered employment a necessity for boys and marriage women's ultimate goal. Children thus learned how to be gendered grown-ups. Thus, girls generally did not seek formal apprenticeships. As we have seen, they learned household-related skills at home. They might also take gender-tracked classes at school, particularly sewing and embroidery. Middle- and upper-middle-class girls could, further, attend "household" or finishing schools or learn the basics of housewifery during the first months of marriage.[19] Boys' careers, on the other hand, took careful planning.

For most Jewish boys, this generally meant a formal commercial apprenticeship, the field in which about two-thirds of Jewish Germans worked.[20] Sometimes, these decisions could cause acute tension, for example, when families insisted that their (unwilling) sons follow in their fathers' footsteps or proceed toward their parents' goals.[21] In the 1890s Lotte Paepcke's grandfather apprenticed her father in the leather trade so that he would eventually take over the family shop. The young man loved the piano. The battle between "*Lied und Leder*" (song and leather) ended with a three-year apprenticeship to a Jewish leather merchant.[22] At the turn of the century, Carl Cosmann hoped to study medicine. His father, a merchant who had acquired real estate, insisted that he become a lawyer in order to help with the property.[23] Sons who refused the paths that families cleared for them caused parental anxiety and displeasure. In the 1890s Jacob Epstein had hoped that his oldest son would enter his flourishing business. The young man preferred collecting minerals and volunteering at zoological institutes. His father contributed to his upkeep but felt profoundly disappointed.[24]

Since such a large proportion of Jewish males engaged in some form of commerce, the example of three commercial apprentices gives us some idea of how these young men spent their workdays and how they perceived their prospects. Julius Berger, who apprenticed in Berlin in 1875 at the age of twelve, Victor Klemperer, who apprenticed

there in 1897 at sixteen, and Adolf Riesenfeld, who apprenticed in Breslau in 1899, were typical of urban commercial clerks. A "clerk from
the province," Julius Berger secured an apprenticeship in a leather
wholesale house. He worked all day packing, unpacking, examining,
and readying leather. Still of school age, he had to attend night school.
His income, twenty marks monthly, covered the room and board that
he took at his aunt's home. There he slept in a windowless room with
five cousins. Berger labored long hours and walked to work to avoid
the expense of public transportation. He had very little pocket money.
(He spent almost the entire three marks a month his father sent him
on shoe repairs.)[25] Berger loved the city, but despite this he returned
to his provincial hometown in West Prussia at sixteen after completing his apprenticeship. He joined his father's business and later made
millions.[26]

Whereas Berger offered an outline of his activities and his thrift,
Klemperer devoted a considerable portion of his autobiography (based
on diary notes) to the early exhilaration and later frustration of his
apprenticeship in a Berlin export firm. Right before leaving school,
he had written an essay describing the businessman as someone who
could conquer the world, someone who carried not only business but
also culture abroad. His older brother, sensitive to antisemitism, read
the essay before Victor handed it in, "afraid that [Victor] might speak
inappropriately about money."[27] He expected his younger brother to
make a good living. Yet, sensitive to how an antisemitic teacher might
construe the essay, he certainly did not want Victor to write about
money.

At first Klemperer embarked on an exciting adventure. He met
new people, mostly from the middle and lower middle classes, one of
whom became a lifelong friend. His officemates were Jews and Christians. He could recall no issue arising from the religious differences.
The job demanded ten hours of work, from 8 A.M. to 1 P.M. and then
from 3 P.M. until 8 P.M., six days a week. He had to attend business
school two hours a week for further education, in his case, to improve
his handwriting. His business did not yet use typewriters, and he
had been told his handwriting would be an obstacle to his career success.[28]

The work challenged Klemperer, and he enjoyed the income, fifteen marks a month in the first year. He could look forward to twenty
marks in the second, and thirty in the third year, by which time he
would be doing the work of fully trained personnel. He also reveled in
the feeling of independence from his family that his new status provided, the business English he studied at night, and the conversations
with coworkers during breaks (when they were permitted to talk) and

behind warehouse shelves (when they were not).[29] These chats not only provided collegiality but offered important business gossip, such as salary conditions, who had been hired in neighboring firms, career problems, and prospects. His work consisted of examining newly arrived shipments, learning about the stock, writing lists of entries, and filling shipping orders.

Boredom soon set in. After one year, Klemperer would awaken on Monday mornings feeling he was about to embark on a six-day jail sentence. He had tired of handling the vases, photo albums, picture frames, and ashtrays—the "culture"—he had to send abroad. His illegible handwriting kept him in the warehouse long after he should have made it to the front offices, and he began to worry. Would he always be stuck in the warehouse? Moreover, he saw no future in this firm since it, like many similar firms, had few permanent employees, relying on cheap apprentices for most of the work.

Klemperer worried that his life would consist of this futile work and that he would never be happy if he did not feel devoted to his work. He debated his lot with his close friend and coworker Hans Meyerhof. The latter contended that one fulfilled oneself outside of work: "Look at [my] Papa; he sells nails . . . and has his gymnastics club, his Freemason lodge and preaches, philosophizes, and debates and is happy." Meyerhof presumed that most people toiled ten hours a day in monotonous jobs. Klemperer's unhappiness grew until he finally left the apprenticeship after a thirty-one-month stint. He was lucky. His highly successful brothers supported his further university education, hoping that he too would enhance the family's prestige.[30]

Adolf Riesenfeld (born in 1884) was not as lucky. He remained in business for the rest of his life. Unlike Klemperer, who had completed the exam for the military's "one-year volunteers," the minimum for good bourgeois schooling, Riesenfeld had not. Riesenfeld had fled his unhappy experiences at school to be an apprentice to his father in 1899. He believed that his lack of certification later played a role in his social acceptance—or lack of it—in the business and social worlds. Had his apprenticeship brought him joy, he might have felt differently. But now he had to contend with his father with whom he had a strained relationship at work as well as at home. His one-and-one-half-year apprenticeship as a shipping agent in his father's dispatching firm resulted in "a chain of bitter experiences . . . the saddest time of my whole life."[31] He earned less and worked longer hours than Klemperer. In 1899 he took home five marks per month and his day started at 7 A.M. and finished at 9 P.M. with a ninety-minute lunch break. He completed his apprenticeship in another business and came back to more *Sturm und Drang* in his father's business. Ultimately, he

Marion Kaplan

inherited the business but not before his father made him purchase a portion of it.

Escaping the tedium of their jobs, apprentices sought amusement in the big city. Despite his poverty, Julius Berger managed to go to the theater on Sundays, paying twenty-five pfennig for a standing room ticket.[32] Adolf Riesenfeld, although miserable in his apprenticeship, took pleasure in the books he borrowed from a lending library, the theater, and the relatively new thrill of bike riding. He also visited friends and joined a club of about twenty young men who discussed literature and general issues of interest to them, such as platonic and nonplatonic friendships and free love. The weekly meetings provided him with a social life and a "ray of hope" beyond the humdrum of work.[33] Victor Klemperer used the remainder of his weekly income—after depositing part of it in a savings bank—to visit the opera (standing room), theater, comedies, and cafés.[34] He also enjoyed riding his new bicycle on weekends in addition to riding it to and from work twice daily. Apprenticeship afforded young men their first semi-independence from their families and their first step into the adult world of work and entertainment.

Jewish families provided crucial support for enterprising male progeny. Not only did they arrange apprenticeships, but some passed on the family's business, and the more well established provided money to set up or expand their sons' businesses. A glance at Jewish textile entrepreneurs in Silesia shows a pattern of family businesses passed on in the same family from generation to generation.[35] Extended families also assisted young men. Some German Jews had relatives in England and the United States, countries still more economically advanced than Germany. There, boys learned newer commercial methods and made contacts. Relatives eased the way: "No wonder that the young Jew was ready sooner to go abroad—whether into an apprenticeship or on a business trip."[36] As Germany became more involved in international trade, Jews could take advantage of their connections abroad to enhance business at home.[37]

EARLY SEXUAL EDUCATION AND EXPERIENCE

Although parents worried about and addressed children's schooling, career training, and cultivation, they generally avoided sex education or conversations about the opposite sex. General advice literature, on the other hand, urged candor, telling parents to "establish a trusting friendship with their son and daughter, and acquaint them, as friends, with their desires and urges."[38] Such counsel notwithstanding, most parents, if they dealt with sex education at all, often did so with embarrassment and avoidance. There seems to have been little distinction between the way village and urban parents treated the topic. Gender also made little difference: sons and daughters both record their parents' reticence.[39] However, gender certainly influenced what children learned on their own.

The stork story appears in many children's and parents' memoirs, not only as the source of the new baby but of the painful "bite" that caused the mother to take to her bed. In a Bavarian village, young Alex Bein (born in 1903), believed that the stork that had brought him a brother had also bitten his mother. His mother's leg needed to heal, so she had to stay in bed. In Cologne Jenny Wieruszowski explained her bed rest after childbirth (in 1896) to her two small children by saying she had been bitten by a stork.[40] A few years later, her oldest daughter, not yet ten, told her mother she no longer believed in the stork. Jenny did not insist on the stork but explained to the child that she was too young to understand these issues: "I tried so hard to keep the children completely innocent," she wrote in her diary.[41] Some years later, one of the older girls announced: "I only know that the baby comes from the mother and that the man plays some kind of role in the process." Her mother replied: "I advised her to calm down since this was the most important [piece of information] and that it was only necessary to know more details once one was older and more mature."[42]

Similarly, when Margarete Sallis (born in 1893) revealed to her mother that friends had told her the stork was a fairy tale but had failed to inform her what actually happened, her mother appeared "visibly relieved" that Margarete did not know and she could therefore avoid the specifics of the subject. Sallis later realized, "Even otherwise enlightened people and rational thinkers love to avoid unpleasant conversations and to 'gloss over them.'" Writing to a more sexually educated readership many years later, Sallis admitted, "At that time, it seemed to me that these processes were of a purely biological nature and they did not seem so terribly important to know about in exact detail."[43]

Such avoidance heightened curiosity and anxiety in some and lessened these feelings in others, but it surely reinforced ignorance in all. Until the age of twenty, in 1913, Sallis thought that babies emerged from the navel.[44] Some years earlier, thirteen-year-old Toni Ehrlich told her recently engaged twenty-year-old sister that "the most beautiful profession of all is that of the marriage registrar, because he creates life." Her sister did not correct her, admitting only later that during her engagement she believed a passionate kiss could make her pregnant.[45]

Girls fared no better at school than at home. In Berlin, Alice Salomon (born in 1872) attended a girls' school, associating only with girls and women teachers:

> I cannot remember that we ever had a male teacher with whom we would have been able to flirt. Love and sexuality were entirely outside our horizon. There was no co-education, no co-ed sport . . . no cinema. The newspapers, too, were far more reserved than today. . . . With regard to what I knew about sexuality and marriage, I might as well have grown up on an island inhabited only by the female members of our species . . . when we encountered the physical consequences of puberty, we regarded them as an annoyance. We did not discuss sexuality.[46]

Men also wondered at this "atmosphere of naiveté . . . in which we grew up and remained for a rather long time."[47] Norbert Elias (born in 1897) recalled his father's palpable discomfort when he tried to discuss sex with him: "I remember . . . a very remarkable attempt he made to 'enlighten' me . . . on sexual matters. One can hardly imagine that today. He obviously felt that it was his duty. I still remember that it was awkward. It was not something he liked doing, but he felt he had to do it."[48] For Paul Friedhoff (born in 1907), sex education came from an encyclopedia that he received on his Bar Mitzvah: "Some of my friends and I would hide out in corners in order to inspect the illustrations . . . and to read things about which our parents refused to enlighten us."[49] Similarly, school authorities appeared uncomfortable with male adolescent behaviors. They either ignored sexual education or left it to the clergy. Joachim Prinz (born in 1902) recalled a Catholic priest who gave a monthly lecture in his school about the "sin of masturbation." Although Prinz's face reddened, he relaxed when he realized that the priest was "after all, not my priest; my rabbi never talked about it."[50]

Nor did Jewish organizations offer adequate alternatives for young women and men to meet and learn about one another, even in platonic relationships. In the early decades of the imperial era, Jewish adolescents were left to their own devices or to small, local organizations. Non-Jewish teens lived in equal isolation: despite the growth of associational life, only about 20 percent of all German teens belonged to any organization at all.[51] After the turn of the century, however, Jewish options increased, as Jewish teens joined developing German groups and Jewish organizations. In 1907 several orthodox youth groups banded together, and the largest Jewish youth organization, the Association of Jewish Youth Clubs of Germany (Verband der jüdischen Jugendvereine Deutschlands), established itself in 1909.[52] It attracted teenagers of both sexes, a separate group of eighteen- to twenty-five-year-olds, and young men, generally white-collar employees, up to the age of thirty-five.[53]

Although Zionism had barely attracted ten thousand members to its fold by 1914, it had particular success among the young. The Blau Weiss, a youth group established in 1912, promoted Jewish nationalism and cultural Zionism. Its members believed that nature and outdoor activities could heal the Jewish soul and create strong Jewish bodies that would make Jews proud of themselves. It appealed to teenage girls and boys who rejected "bourgeois" values and their parents' attempts to acculturate to German society. Instead, Blau Weiss opted for (in fact, also acculturating to) the German youth movement's penchant for hiking, camping, and a sense of community. The Zionist youth movement thus provided an opportunity for young people to enjoy one another's company, but according to Joachim Prinz, it maintained a strict ethos of celibacy. At fifteen, he had a girlfriend, but, he recalls, "I did not think of sexual activities, for I was a member of a youth movement that frowned on such things."[54] Later, however, he met his future wife in this Zionist group. Notwithstanding his ardent loyalty to Zionism "at a time when 'physical purity' was one of the great goals of the Youth Movement, I was already deeply in love with Lucie and we had a rather active sex life together."[55]

Despite their lack of information, boys and girls engaged in a spectrum of sexual experiences and experiments. A few examples from diaries and memoirs offer indications as to what some individuals felt. Margarete Sallis, for example, not only showed interest in sexuality and her changing body but also happily flirted with men. Her memoirs, unusually candid for a woman, recall that when her parents went out, she would put her hair up, undress, and drape herself in her mother's jewelry, lace and scarves. Admiring her developing body in the mirror, she would relish the "the joy of exploring her own body."[56] Sallis also had a few relationships in her teen years even if the "facts of life" remained foreign to her. Her first love, a tutor in her uncle's employ, aroused her desire. After an agreement between her parents and the young man that an engagement would follow her *Abitur*, "all reservations fell away [and] a very exciting time began. The longing 'for more' and the certainty of 'never enough' grew in quick kisses and necking in . . . dark theater loges, on walks, and on the way home at night." The engagement never took place, and she "longed for his kisses and for the masculine closeness that had come into my life."[57] Later, she could only marvel at her ignorance and at her luck: "several times, I must have had a guardian angel on my adventurous and dangerous path because the men involved were so incredibly decent."[58] Despite her early experiences of desire, she naively believed the doctor who told her she was "frigid" when she discussed her reactions to her husband. Only after her husband's death, when she slept with another man, did she discover that she "was by no means frigid . . . it was as if something had opened up."[59]

Whereas adolescents like Sallis engaged in acceptable schoolgirl crushes, boys more likely joined in sexual discussions and actual sexual play. In a memoir written late in his life, Joachim Prinz recalled "sex games among us and our friends. . . . There was a lot of laughter about it. Nobody really took it terribly seriously, and all this was done as though it were a matter of natural routine." Contradicting himself as to how "routine" this was, his next sentence continues: "Neither of my parents ever spoke to me about sex."[60] Adolf Riesenfeld detailed his early sexual education and initiation in a diary written while he was a soldier during World War I. There he analyzed his sexual development with great contrition. The diary is unusual in its explicitness, though not in the guilt that enshrouds it. Moreover, he expected his children to read it and hoped they might understand his youthful foibles. At first, he showed little curiosity about relationships with the opposite sex and more interest in the sexual experimentation occurring among his male friends in his Breslau gymnasium. His personal sexual experimentation started at around age ten. Of an era in which masturbation was considered "the secret vice," "self-pollution," and a "secret sin of youth," he wrote of his own masturbation and school boy chatter: "my sources were . . . mostly dirty."[61] By age eleven his "fellow students were well informed about the basics of this problem, and the one boy who had grown up in complete innocence met with unmitigated mockery."[62]

The rituals of their emerging masculinity included more serious sexual play, first among the boys and later with women. Riesenfeld wrote:

Already in the *Quarta* [age 12], the sexual moment prevailed in our conversations. In darkness, we indulged in lustful fantasies, approached and touched each other's genitals and by the *Untertertia* [age 13], this had almost turned into a system and had, like an epidemic, taken hold of almost the entire class. Led by some precocious boys, of whom I was one, the more innocent minds of other students were poisoned, and the triumph to have moved one of them to the exchange of sexual touching filled us with a satisfaction similar to that of appropriating a woman later. As a matter of course we then masturbated and, later on, the first attempts at genuine heterosexual play led some (according to the students themselves) to full intercourse at the age of 14. In the *Quarta*, I limited myself to running after some little girls together with my buddies, to rifling through books for their sexual contents, and to looking with lascivious intentions at pictures in shop windows.[63]

Occasionally female servants gave their young male charges their views of relations between the sexes. And this could include sexual play. When Joachim Prinz and his two brothers, all born between 1902 and 1905, were young children, the two young girls who took them on long walks introduced them "to sexual experiments of which we understood very little."[64] Adolf Riesenfeld's diary echoes Joachim Prinz's experience. He declared that at an early age, perhaps six or seven, the maid who often took him into her bed planted the "seed to an early sexual maturity" in him, that is, made him sexually curious and involved.[65]

Growing Up: Relationships with the Opposite Sex

In an era when most middle-class marriages distinguished themselves from those above and below them on the class hierarchy through parental involvement in marriages, including financial considerations, families assumed their children would enter arranged marriages relatively inexperienced and would adjust to their new partners emotionally and sexually. Here, as in other situations, gender played a role in the extent to which young men and women gathered heterosexual experience before marriage. Women were often more closely chaperoned and were expected to show restraint, while men had freer rein.[66] In fact, our diarists reflect a "thoroughly Victorian location of desire within the specifically male body."[67]

The almost compulsory dance lessons to which bourgeois parents sent adolescents in order that they learn social graces, master the dance skills they might need later in life, and meet the "right" partners provided an important forum for meeting the opposite sex. But parents were not the only ones to understand the significance of these situations. Even young single men like Klemperer and Riesenfeld took Sunday dance lessons. Riesenfeld believed he had acquired some poise and met "appropriate" young ladies at an all-Jewish dance class in Breslau. Donning a tuxedo, white gloves, cummerbund, and patent leather shoes—all bought on credit, since he earned only sixty marks a month—he first mastered lessons in deportment: "I enjoyed them with sincerity and deliberation since I indeed lacked societal skills." Riesenfeld wrote that he lived for the dance evenings. He would later meet his wife there.[68] After polishing their manners, the men dressed and gallantly greeted the young women's mothers. Then, they bowed to the young ladies dressed in "cloud[s] of white, pink, and blue."[69] If dating ensued, parents could rest assured that partners came from an appropriate class background. Still, middle-class girls were carefully chaperoned and protected. Thus, middle-class boys in search of sexual experience looked elsewhere. Often they did not have far to go.

Female servants were the most vulnerable and accessible women available to middle-class men. Whether or not numerous sexual encounters occurred between teenage boys and servants—certainly a widespread Victorian and Wilhelmine belief and one the Nazis would later attribute to all Jewish males—it is rare to find these trysts recorded.[70] Here, of course, gender and class intersected, with young middle-class men taking advantage of women of lesser means and lesser power within the men's own homes. Two rare memoirs, those of Joachim Prinz and Adolf Riesenfeld, offer some insight into these relationships. Interestingly, and perhaps guiltily, both men attributed their sexual experiences to the young women's initiatives. While women's initiatives are not impossible to imagine, the defenselessness of such young women and the number of domestics with illegitimate children suggests less volition on their part in general than our particular memoirists admitted or even realized. When Joachim Prinz entered puberty, he claimed that the "young girls who took care of us children took care of that. . . . I still remember how one of them introduced me to the secret world of sex, willingly and joyfully offering her services as a matter of course. She was not much older than we were, but certainly much more knowledgeable."[71] Riesenfeld also described his adolescent attempts to learn about sex from the servants in his home. He would talk with them about sex, and two of them allowed him to touch their breasts. One night, when he was fourteen, they invited him to their room. He could hardly wait until his father fell asleep. He recalled: "Feverish excitement took hold of my entire organism. . . . I waited hour after hour." By the time he managed to get to their room, they had fallen asleep.

Riesenfeld wrote that he suffered from his unfulfilled sexual desires. He did have girlfriends, but he saw them in other young people's homes. They might kiss occasionally, but his first serious kiss came at age twenty.[72] By the end of 1906, at twenty-two, he still had not slept with a woman. While courting his future wife, he met with working-class women for some "affection" but not for sex—at least as he defined it.[73] Long days of work, evenings spent with his future wife or at his club, concerts, theater, and reading filled his time. He also played tennis, swam, skated, and took dance lessons.[74] Still, as almost all of his male friends had experienced sex with prostitutes, he felt forced to consider this available alternative as well. Yet, he "suffered terribly from sexual abstinence based . . . on my great shyness. My sense of hygiene, the fear of infection, romantic ideas about love and frugality prevented me from taking recourse to prostitution. Nevertheless, I was often close to quenching my burning desire at this impure source. Of course I discussed this inexhaustible topic in the greatest detail in my club; my more experienced friends pitied me, sought to help me, mocked me, or complained that there was too much talk about these things."[75]

Not all young men observed the rules that Riesenfeld had set for himself with regard to prostitutes. At about age seventeen, Victor Klemperer described the "sexless beings" (girls) he met at dance lessons in 1898. Like other gymnasium pupils whose sexual activities centered almost entirely on prostitutes, he and his friend had already "had our experiences in the prostitute-filled areas surrounding the Hallesches Tor and discussed these in great detail." Indeed, our two male memoirists recall their conversations with other men about sex as much as the sex itself. These visits to prostitutes, then, appear to have been as much an exercise in male bonding as in sexual experimentation.[76] In neither case did their stories or memories linger on the fate of the women themselves.

At age twenty-two, in 1906, Adolf Riesenfeld had his first complete sexual experience. He slept with Hedwig, one of the two servants in his father's house, and was ecstatically happy. The next day he reported his exploit to his Jewish girlfriend, Mieze, and "I assume[d] that she did not take this too tragically. As a bright girl she knew that a young man of almost 23 years had a right to a sex life that she did not want to grant me."[77] Mieze's "agreement" and Riesenfeld's assumption reflected their class and gender positions. Riesenfeld would have most likely been shocked and, possibly, dismayed had Mieze "granted" him sex. Like most middle-class men, he assumed that he could sleep with women of the lower classes but not with those of his class: "The girls of their own class were counted as treasures to be protected and retained as a form of wealth . . . their erotic innocence was to be hoarded, not spent."[78]

Riesenfeld found his first long-term lover only after his formal engagement to Mieze. He was very fond of Hanne, a non-Jewish coworker who came from modest circumstances, and he claimed to have informed her of his engagement.[79] To maintain this relationship, he actually moved to a different lodging when his landlady forbade female visitors. At Christmas, he visited Hanne at home with her family: "I dutifully admired the decorated Christmas tree . . . and I enjoyed being in this very proper small home." When he finally left Dresden he worried that Hanne might be pregnant, but she was not. In his diary, he told himself that he would have helped her out.[80] Riesenfeld waited almost five years, until he felt financially secure, to marry Mieze. Only then could their sex life begin. Much later (1942), he reflected: "Surely, the young people of today who tend to view these things very rationally and do not usually wait for the religious or secular wedding before taking up marital relations, are in a better position than we were."[81]

Klemperer's, Prinz's, and Riesenfeld's histories suggest that despite parents' reluctance to educate either gender with regard to sex, boys ultimately gathered more experience than girls. No Jewish women describe comparable sexual experiences either at school or at home. This does not mean that women's sexuality was completely ignored or that women remained completely inexperienced. Käthe Frankenthal (born in 1889), a nonconformist in every way, had several boyfriends during her university studies. When it came time to consider marriage, however, she decided to remain single. Reporting that she was satisfied with her sex life, she wrote that a husband "would not have relieved me of the small difficulties of daily life, he would have increased them." What she really needed was a housekeeper, she concluded, adding, "Many career women of my generation held similar attitudes on these questions."[82] Whereas Frankenthal's sexual experiences can not be generalized to most other female students in the era before World War I, the discreetness with which she alluded to her sexual affairs can be.[83]

This discretion reflected individual attitudes toward privacy as well as personal refinement. In addition, neither women nor men wrote very much about their own sexuality in memoirs meant for their children. Still, the more outspoken examples appear in diaries or memoirs written by men. They show off a kind of appropriate "masculinity" even for their sexually inhibited times. Their boyish longings and experimentation proved they were "real boys," and their later familiarity and skill with sex underlined that they were "real men." In fact, these memoirs suggest that boys and young men could accomplish sexual apprenticeships in a variety of ways and that, as adults, they understood their apprenticeships in "masculinity" to be acceptable enough to write about—in the past tense.

Few men and women, however, openly and defiantly challenged sexual and marital norms in their own day. A significant portion of those who did so—not as a political or sexual "statement" but as a way of life—would later marry out of their faith. In Breslau, for example, between 1874 and 1894, 37 percent of Jewish women and almost half of Jewish men who entered a mixed marriage lived together before marriage.[84] Intermarriages often had very romantic beginnings. Unlike intra-Jewish marriages, in which Jewish families and friends tried to bring "suitable" young people together, these couples fell in love on their own.[85] Then they confronted parents who faced the marriage either reluctantly or with intense opposition and overcame these obstacles to achieve a happy ending—or at least a happy beginning.

Victor Klemperer and his love, Eva, were two such strong-willed young people. He was Jewish, she Christian. Klemperer recalled his first meeting with his future wife in 1904: "there was an immediate feeling of belonging together." Although the son of a bourgeois family, he preferred a more bohemian lifestyle. He was a twenty-two-year-old university student, and Eva, a few months younger, was a pianist. She played piano for him, and he read poetry to her. They shared a love for the French and Italian languages and both hated English. Both believed they would be lifelong partners after knowing each other for thirteen days. When they went on a three-day holiday in the summer of 1904, they bought fake weddings rings to avoid embarrassment. When they found it increasingly painful to separate daily, they decided to live with each other. They chose free love, considering marriage "bourgeois": "We were both very young and felt that we stood at the beginning of our development. As long as we felt that we were on the same path, we wanted to stick together, and not a moment beyond that. This alone seemed moral to us. To wait for the consent of family and state we called cowardice and, judging from very close experiences, we both thought very little of marriage."[86] Almost thirty-five years later, Klemperer addressed Eva, then his wife, directly in his memoir: "I have always loved you with the same passion. I only felt well when you were very close to me, when, from time to time, I could lay my hand on your arm."[87]

Their families objected to the relationship. Hers, although impoverished, stemmed from the nobility and scorned his Jewish background. His had no difficulty accepting her religion—his brothers had also intermarried—but preferred a woman with money. Moreover, Klemperer's parents worried that Eva would keep him from studying. The couple married in 1906 only so that Victor could be certain that his family would no longer try to destroy his relationship. His family did not attend their wedding but later insisted that they move into a less bohemian apartment and then paid for it. Romantics both, they had the date they met in 1904 engraved in their wedding rings rather than their legal marriage date. Their deep and tender relationship later nurtured them through the horrors of the Nazi years.[88]

Of course there were other Jews too who flouted sexual taboos. Some women even had children out of wedlock. These issues, not generally discussed in the memoirs of middle-class families, can be found in statistical surveys.[89] If illegitimacy rates are any indication of premarital sex in an age of insecure birth control, then the relatively low Jewish rates indicate fewer premarital sexual unions than in the non-Jewish population. For example, between 1882 and 1901, about 3 percent of Jewish births in Prussia compared to 8 percent of non-Jewish births were illegitimate. Most of these occurred in big cities. Still, illegitimacy rose during the imperial era so that between 1900 and 1915 5 percent of Jewish births in Prussia were out of wedlock.[90] In actual numbers, this meant that in a city like Hamburg between 1900 and 1912, 247 babies were born out of wedlock.[91] Where orthodoxy still controlled Jewish youth, in the provinces of West Prussia or Pomerania, for example, illegitimacy remained very low.[92] Yet, even among the orthodox, "premarital sex was less rare than before, especially among male youth, although the great majority practiced scrupulous restraint."[93] Moreover, in rural areas, if a pregnancy resulted from premarital sex, the parents and community frequently stepped in to "legitimize" the child. For example, in the village of Rülzheim in the Palatinate, most people expected one young Jewish couple who had been courting for a long time to marry. When the young woman became pregnant and the man resisted the marriage, the woman's parents threatened court proceedings. The marriage produced three sons.[94]

In conclusion, Jewish middle-class boys and young men acquired more exposure to the worlds of work and sexual apprenticeships than did women. Early work apprenticeships, both informal and formal, allowed men to rise in business careers, while "no one thought of giving a girl a career as her purpose in life."[95] Similarly, while Jewish parents appeared reluctant to educate either boys or girls in sexual knowledge, boys attained more sexual experience on their own than did girls. In imperial Germany then, not only did the political and family law systems discriminate against women but women's lack of economic competence and sexual enlightenment heightened male dominance within the family.[96] Thus, more male knowledge equaled more male power.

To return to Freud's components of a happy, well-adjusted person, it appears that young Jewish men entering marriage held the obvious advantage of knowing the worlds of work and of sexuality far better than their wives. For women, marriage would continue their perfunctory introduction to (house)work and only begin their apprenticeship in physical love.

NOTES

Many thanks to Renate Bridenthal, Ruth Kaplan, and Douglas Morris for their ongoing loyalty and support and their exacting and talented editing and to Katja Vehlow for her help in translating.

1. C. Hazan and P. R. Shaver, "Love and Work: An Attachment-Theoretical Perspective," *Journal of Personality and Social Psychology* 59, no. 2 (1990): 270–80.
2. Peter Gay, *Schnitzler's Century: The Making of Middle-Class Culture* (New York: Norton, 2002), 59.
3. Claudia Nelson and Lynne Vallone, eds., *The Girl's Own: Cultural Histories of the Anglo-American Girl, 1830–1915* (Athens: University of Georgia Press, 1994), 3.
4. Louis Liebmann, memoirs, 13, Leo Baeck Institute, New York (hereafter cited as LBI).
5. Bernhard Kukatzki, ". . . *das einzige Hotel in der ganzen Gegend, das koscher geführt wurde: Das Hotel Victoria in Rülzheim*" (Schifferstadt: Bernhard Kukatzki, 1994), 12–13.
6. Kukatzki, *Hotel*, 14.
7. Hugo Marx, *Werdegang eines jüdischen Staatsanwalts und Richters in Baden (1892–1933)* (Villingen: Neckar Verlag, 1965), 48.
8. Marx, *Werdegang*, 53.
9. Victor Klemperer, *Curriculum Vitae: Jugend um 1900* (hereafter cited as *CV*), vol. 1 (Berlin: Siedler Verlag, 1989), 142.
10. Manfred Horlebein, "Kaufmännische Berufsbildung," in *Handbuch der deutschen Bildungsgeschichte*, vol. 4, ed. Christa Berg (Munich: C. H. Beck, 1987–91), 405.
11. Gay, *Schnitzler*, 198.
12. Monika Richarz, ed., *Jüdisches Leben in Deutschland: Selbstzeugnisse zur Sozialgeschichte im Kaiserreich* (Stuttgart: Deutsche Verlags-Anstalt, 1979), 191.
13. Liebmann memoirs, 8.
14. Gay, *Schnitzler*, 196.
15. For similar attitudes among non-Jewish men, see Ute Frevert, *"Mann und Weib, und Weib und Mann": Geschlechter-Differenzen in der Moderne* (Munich: C. H. Beck, 1995), 144–49.
16. Some women noted their fathers' work habits as well. Brigitte Fischer, the daughter of the famous Berlin publisher, carefully observed her very busy father and believed she modeled her later life on his diligence. Fischer, *Sie schrieben mir: Oder, Was aus meinem Poesiealbum wurde* (Zu-

rich: W. Classen, 1987), 52.

17. Richarz, *Kaiserreich*, 89–90, 247 (God), 248–49.

18. Liebmann, memoirs, 7, 14.

19. Rahel Straus, *Wir lebten in Deutschland: Erinnerungen einer deutschen Jüdin* (Stuttgart: Deutsche Verlags-Anstalt, 1962), 119.

20. In 1895, 69 percent of Jewish men engaged in commercial activities. The figure dropped to 64 percent in 1907. *Zeitschrift für Demographie und Statistik der Juden* (hereafter cited as *ZDSJ*), January–March 1919, 2, and *ZDSJ*, July–August 1911, 97–112, respectively. At these times about 10 percent of the general population had commercial careers.

21. Gunilla-Frederike Budde, *Auf dem Weg ins Bürgerleben: Kindheit und Erziehung in deutschen und englischen Bürgerfamilien, 1840–1914* (Göttingen: Vandenhoek and Ruprecht, 1994), 409.

22. Lotte Paepcke, *Ein kleiner Händler, der mein Vater war* (Heilbronn: Salzer, 1972), 14. See also Andrea Hopp, *Jüdisches Bürgertum in Frankfurt am Main im 19. Jahrhundert* (Stuttgart: F. Steiner, 1997), 58–59, for another example of a son who had to go into the family business.

23. Michael Zimmermann and Claudia Konieczek, eds., *Jüdisches Leben in Essen 1800–1933* (Essen: Klartext, 1993), 13.

24. Hopp, *Bürgertum*, 174.

25. Richarz, *Kaiserreich*, 251–53.

26. Ibid.

27. Klemperer, *CV*, 134.

28. Ibid., 150.

29. Ibid., 147.

30. Ibid., 141.

31. Adolf Riesenfeld, diary, entry of January 9, 1917, LBI.

32. Richarz, *Kaiserreich*, 251–53.

33. Riesenfeld diary, entry of November 1, 1917.

34. Klemperer, *CV*, 158–59.

35. John Foster, "The Jewish Entrepreneur and the Family," in *From the Emancipation to the Holocaust: Essays on Jewish Literature and History in Central Europe*, ed. Konrad Kwiet (New South Wales: University of New South Wales, 1986), 17.

36. Arthur Prinz, *Juden im Deutschen Wirtschaftsleben, 1850–1914*, ed. Avraham Barkai (Tübingen: J. C. B. Mohr, 1984), 9–10.

37. Prinz, *Juden im Deutschen Wirtschaftsleben*, 9–10.

38. Gay, *Schnitzler*, 89.

39. Peter Gay, however, suggests that young men may have been slightly more aware of the physical differences between the sexes, noting "middle-class young women were more likely to be 'protected' from the facts of gender differences and their implications than were young men." *Schnitzler*, 91.

40. Jenny Wieruszowski, diary, entry of May 7, 1896, LBI.

41. Ibid., entry of October 7, 1900.

42. Ibid., entry of June 12, 1908.

43. Margarete Sallis, memoirs, 23, LBI.
44. Ibid., 22.
45. Toni Ehrlich, memoirs, 55, LBI.
46. Alice Salomon, *Charakter ist Schicksal: Lebenserinnerungen* (Weinheim, 1983), 24.
47. Alex Bein, *Hier kannst Du nicht jeden grüßen: Erinnerungen und Betrachtungen*, ed. Julius H. Schoeps (Hildesheim: Olms, 1996), 15.
48. Norbert Elias, *Reflections on a Life* (Cambridge: Polity Press, 1996), 8.
49. Kukatzki, *Hotel*, 19.
50. Joachim Prinz, *Rebellious Rabbi: An Autobiography—the German and Early Years*, ed. Michael A. Meyer (Bloomington: Indiana University Press, 2007), 22.
51. Christa Berg, "Familie, Kindheit, Jugend," in C. Berg, ed., *Handbuch der deutschen Bildungsgeschichte*, 6 vols. (Munich: C. H. Beck, 1991), 128.
52. It had twenty-five branches in 1909. Offering lectures and discussions about Jewish history and religion, it grew to twenty thousand members by 1916. Steven Lowenstein, "The Community," in *German-Jewish History in Modern Times*, vol. 3, ed. Michael A. Meyer, 150 (New York: Columbia University Press, 1997); Herbert Strauss, "The Jugendverband," *Leo Baeck Institute Year Book 6* (1961). See also Friedrich Brodnitz, ed., *Gemeinschaftsarbeit der jüdischen Jugend* (Berlin: Zentralwohlfahrtsstelle der deutschen Juden, 1937), 65.
53. The B'nai B'rith and the Central Verein supported the younger groups, hoping to instill a strong Jewish identity in young Jewish males—"then, each of our children will form his own defense association and will carry out his own defense." They also hoped to combat Zionism in Germany. Chaim Schatzker, *Jüdische Jugend im zweiten Kaiserreich* (Frankfurt am Main: P. Lang, 1988), 235.
54. Prinz, *Rebellious Rabbi*, 35.
55. Ibid., 54. I am not suggesting by this example, however, that such groups equalized sexual experiences for boys and girls.
56. Sallis memoirs, 24 (1904–7).
57. Ibid., 31.
58. Ibid., 23.
59. Sallis, *Ich habe mein Land gefunden: Autobiographischer Rückblick* (Frankfurt am Main: J. Knecht, 1977), 70, 111.
60. Prinz, *Rebellious Rabbi*, 22. Prinz's attitudes were sexually far more liberal than those of the majority of his contemporaries. After World War I, he seems to have fit in well with the freer sexual culture of Weimar Berlin. His memoirs, dictated in later life after the sexual "revolution" of 1968, may have benefited from the opportunity to be more frank about his own sexuality as a result of a more liberal sexual culture in the United States.
61. Peter Gay, *The Bourgeois Experience*, vol. 2, *The Tender Passion* (New York: Oxford University Press, 1986), 133, 287; Karl Oppel, *Das Buch der Eltern* (Frankfurt am Main: Diesterweg, 1906), 377.

62. Riesenfeld diary, entry of December 7, 1916.
63. Ibid.
64. Prinz, *Rebellious Rabbi*, part 1, 3.
65. Riesenfeld diary, entry of February 17, 1916.
66. This restraint was often because of enforced ignorance. In England, e.g., scholars note that in the early twentieth century "girls [were] kept in astounding ignorance about their sexuality." Carol Dyhouse, *Girls Growing Up in Late Victorian and Edwardian England* (London: Routledge 1981), 21.
67. Claudia Nelson, "Vegetarianism and Social Reform" in Nelson and Vallone, *The Girl's Own*, 13.
68. Riesenfeld diary, entry of November 8, 1917.
69. Ibid., entry of February 12, 1941.
70. E.g., see ibid., entry of December 21, 1916.
71. Prinz, *Rebellious Rabbi*, part 1, 21.
72. Riesenfeld diary, entry of November 8, 1917.
73. Ibid., entry of November 24, 1941.
74. Ibid.
75. Ibid., entry of December 2, 1941.
76. Klemperer, *CV*, 171.
77. Riesenfeld diary, entry of January 1, 1942.
78. Leslie Williams, "The Look of Little Girls: John Everett Millais and the Victorian Art Market," in Nelson and Vallone, *The Girl's Own*, 128.
79. Riesenfeld diary, entry of January 6–7, 1942, chap. 17.
80. Ibid., chap. 16–18.
81. Ibid., entry of January 16, 1942.
82. Käthe Frankenthal, *Der dreifache Fluch: Jüdin, Intellektuelle, Sozialistin: Lebenserinnerungen einer Ärztin in Deutschland und im Exil* (Frankfurt am Main: Campus, 1981), 110. Other Jewish women (mostly of the lower [*unterbürgerlich*] and petty bourgeois [*kleinbürgerlich*] classes) lived with their Jewish partners before marriage. Till van Rahden found that in Breslau between 1874 and 1894, 5 percent of partners in marriages with two Jewish partners lived together before their weddings. Till van Rahden, *Juden und andere Breslauer: Die Beziehungen zwischen Juden, Protestanten und Katholiken in einer deutschen Großstadt von 1860 bis 1925* (Göttingen: Vandenhoeck and Ruprecht, 2000), 164.
83. Harriet Freidenreich, *Female, Jewish, Educated: The Lives of Central European University Women* (Bloomington: Indiana University Press, 2002), 253n79. Even in the radical and intellectual circles in England in which Olive Schreiner participated in the 1880s and 1890s, "the discussion of female sexuality remained hedged around by limitations and inhibitions." Dyhouse, *Girls*, 160.
84. Van Rahden, *Juden*, 164.
85. Marion Kaplan, *The Making of the Jewish Middle Class: Women, Family, and Identity in Imperial Germany* (New York: Oxford University Press, 1991), chap. 3; Kirstin Meiring, *Die Christlich-Jüdische Mischehe in*

Deutschland, 1840–1933 (Hamburg: Dölling and Galitz, 1988), 110–17.

86. Klemperer, *CV*, 383–90, 392, 398–99, 403–4.

87. Ibid., 383–85.

88. Ibid., 393–404, 406.

89. In Prussia, e.g., Jewish rates of illegitimacy between 1900 and 1914 averaged under 5 percent. Christian rates were higher. *ZDSJ*, April 1906, 61–62, and April–June 1916, 31.

90. Richarz in Meyer, *German-Jewish History*, 3:11.

91. Sabine Knappe, "Jüdische Frauenorganisationen in Hamburg zwischen Assimilation, jüdischer Identität und weiblicher Emanzipation während des Kaiserreichs" (master's thesis, University of Hamburg, 1991), 100.

92. Arthur Ruppin, *Die Juden der Gegenwart* (Berlin: S. Calvary, 1904), 244–45.

93. Mordechai Breuer, *Modernity within Tradition: The Social History of Orthodox Jewry in Imperial Germany* (New York: Columbia University Press, 1992), 7.

94. Kukatzki, *Hotel*, 16.

95. Anna Kronthal, *Posner Mürbekuchen: Jugenderinnerungen einer Posnerin* (Munich: Karl Wehrle, 1932), 73.

96. Ute Frevert, *Women in German History*, trans. Stuart McKinnon-Evans (Oxford: Berg, 1988), 322; Ute Gerhard, *Verhältnisse und Verhinderungen. Frauenarbeit, Familie und Rechte der Frauen im 19. Jahrhundert* (Frankfurt am Main: Suhrkamp, 1978), section 4, "Die Rechte der Frauen."

Lukewarm Establishment or Militant Religious Ideology?

German Liberal Judaism in the 1920s

STEVEN M. LOWENSTEIN

Almost from its inception, German Liberal Judaism fought a battle on two seemingly opposite fronts. On the one hand, Reform leaders desired to change many aspects of traditional Judaism, which they saw as outdated or offensive to the true spirit of Judaism. In this effort they challenged the large body of older traditionalists who they felt lacked secular culture and who seemed superstitious or mechanical in their religious observance. There was, however, a second target group, which Reform Jewish leaders desired to transform. This group consisted of young, often well-to-do, Jews with a secular education who had turned their back on all Jewish traditions, stayed away from the synagogues, and sometimes abandoned Judaism altogether. In the eyes of the leaders of Reform, these people had a superficial view of Enlightenment but could be won back to Jewish religious life, if that life were made more attractive to them. This second challenge was often labeled "the overcoming of indifference."

Although the two struggles of Liberal Judaism seem, at first glance, to involve separate goals, they were actually closely related. The more that Reform Jewish leaders looked at the defectors "on the left," the more they felt that Judaism could not afford to leave tradition as it was. The conservative task of winning back the disaffected helped to accentuate the progressive task of moving Judaism forward, away from tradition. Liberal Judaism was often faced with the dilemma that every move to assuage traditionalist feelings could antagonize the "indifferent" whom the movement wished to attract back to Judaism, while every innovation designed to appeal to the disaffected would antagonize traditionalists, including the moderates within the movement.

In the 1920s, German Liberal Judaism faced this same dilemma in a new and even more complex form. In part, Jewish Liberalism was a victim of its own success. The great majority of German Jews during the Weimar Republic had abandoned the practices and beliefs of Orthodox Judaism. Liberal Jews had gained control of the administration of most urban Jewish communities in Germany and had built impressive Liberal synagogues with organs, choirs, and an aesthetically pleasing service. Most German Jews would probably have identified themselves as Liberal Jews. But the Liberal Jewish religious movement was not nearly as strong as its apparent majority status seemed to indicate. On the one hand, it still faced militant ideological opponents; on the other hand, its own constituency consisted of a small number of the committed and a much larger number of the lukewarm and indifferent.

Although they had become a relatively small minority, traditional Jews had certainly not disappeared from the German Jewish scene. Despite ideological divisions between separatists and communal Orthodox, traditional Jews retained a strong degree of confidence in the rightness of their cause, a commitment to a somewhat modernized traditional way of life and claimed, in the name of freedom of conscience, consideration for their institutions by the Liberal majority.[1] While claiming consideration for their own constituency, most Orthodox Jews continued to fight all Liberal religious innovations with considerable militancy.[2] But although the Orthodox remained ideologically and politically active in the Jewish communities, their numbers were in decline. However, Liberal Judaism faced a new, highly active opponent in the new Zionist movement. The Zionists had strong support among young people and among the growing numbers of immigrants from eastern Europe. The movement challenged Liberal dominance in the Jewish communities.

On the other front, religious indifference was stronger than ever. Most of those who supported the Liberals against their Jewish opponents were not themselves committed Liberal Jews. Not only their Orthodox opponents, but also Liberal leaders themselves pointed out that the magnificent "organ synagogues" were filled only on the high holidays and were often virtually empty on the Sabbath.[3] Beyond agreeing

Steven M. Lowenstein

with the Liberal movement in its rejection of Orthodoxy, most German Jews played little part in the religious life that Liberal Judaism offered as an alternative.[4] Meanwhile intermarriage rates were increasing and growing numbers of German Jews (like their non-Jewish neighbors) were disaffiliating with all religion and withdrawing from their religious communities.[5]

So despite the apparent numerical strength of their adherents, many Liberals saw their movement as being in crisis.[6] They feared the militancy of their opponents, but were even more concerned about the difficult struggle to win back the large numbers of Jews who had simply lost interest in religion. This struggle required both a stronger sense of self-definition and the creation of new forms of religious activity, which would be attractive to those who had become estranged.

Part of the problem of self-definition was exemplified by the label "Liberal" itself. The term had replaced the nineteenth-century label "Reform," which now was applied mainly to the radical Reformgemeinde in Berlin. "Liberal" was a political term often used to label one of the two main Jewish parties that struggled for dominance in late nineteenth-century communities—the Liberals (Reformers) and the Conservatives (Orthodox). One could vote for the Liberals in communal elections without participating in religious worship, study, personal religious practice, or even believing in God. But the Liberal label was not only used to describe the religious movement in juxtaposition with the Orthodox. It was also the name given to the non-Zionist approach to the growing problem of antisemitism. The defense organization Central-Verein deutscher Staatsbürger jüdischen Glaubens had more members and inspired more action than the Vereinigung für das Liberale Judentum. For many German Jews of the early twentieth century, the chief debate was not between orthodox and liberal forms of religious Judaism but between the German-Jewish ideology of the Central-Verein and the militant Jewish nationalism of the Zionists. Although not unanimous on the matter, most leaders of German religious liberalism strongly opposed Zionism and supported the ideology of the Central-Verein for both "political" and religious reasons.[7] In the 1920s, German Jewish liberalism found itself fighting on three fronts: against militant Zionism, against the renewed claims of Orthodoxy, and against the gains of indifference and secularism in German Jewry.[8] Liberal Judaism needed to stake out its claim as a religious movement against other religious movements, but also against *Verwaltungsjudentum, Vereinsjudentum,* and *Wohltätigkeitsjudentum* (administrative Judaism, club Judaism, and charity Judaism).[9] Throughout the 1920s, articles on how the liberal religious ideology could attract the disaffected filled the pages of the *Jüdisch-Liberale Zeitung* alongside more polemical articles against liberalism's opponents in the Jewish political arena.

There were other problems of self-definition besides the difficulties raised by the use of the term "liberal" by Jews who had little or no religious interest. How was one to clarify the mission of a movement whose message was subtle and whose views spanned a broad spectrum?[10] Although some argued that belief in ethical monotheism was enough to qualify one as a religious Jew, many felt that Liberal Judaism required more, and they tried to define its religious nature. Some continued to rely on the rationalist philosophies and evolutionary ideas of the nineteenth century, but a substantial number of Liberal writers proclaimed that religious ideas must change to accommodate the new respect for the irrational and the emotional in religion. The materialism and "scientism" of the nineteenth century were often explicitly rejected.[11] Subjectivity was given as high regard as objectivity. The rhetoric of many of the essays in the *Jüdisch-Liberale Zeitung* is indicative of this new attitude. Writers wrote of "warmes religiöses Empfinden" (warm religious experience), "lebendige Kraft der Überzeugung" (the living power of convictions), "Herzensfrömmigkeit" (piety of the heart), "Innerlichkeit" (inwardness), and "suchender Inbrunst" (searching fervor). They called for a deepening and a renewal of Judaism.[12] One leader even suggested changing the name of the movement from Liberal Judaism to Vereinigung für die religiöse Erneuerung im Judentum (Union for Religious Renewal in Judaism).[13]

When it came to practical innovations rather than matters of personal spirituality, the Liberal movement had a much more difficult time in clarifying its position. It was easier to reject Orthodox ideas of the immutability of Jewish ritual and law than it was to formulate what the religious practice of Liberal Jews ought to be. Often, Liberal Jews were accused of being purely negative, stating what they did not believe and did not practice rather than what their positive values were. But their first attempt to state the religious platform of the movement in positive terms, the *Richtlinien zu einem Programm für das liberale Judentum* (Guidelines for a platform for Liberal Judaism) of 1912, highlighted the difficulties of such an effort. While arousing vehement opposition from Orthodox (and a few moderate Liberal) rabbis and leaders, the guidelines were unsuccessful in promoting consensus on Liberal belief and practice. In the end, obedience to the *Richtlinien* was left up to the conscience of the individual. Throughout the 1920s leaders of Liberal Judaism continued to discuss the ideas of the *Richtlinien*, which some hoped to revive and others rejected. Some argued that as a movement based on freedom and development, Liberal Judaism could not have fixed rules.[14] This widespread point of view rendered the formulation of Liberal Jewish practice almost impossible.

Compared to American Reform Judaism, the Liberal Jewish movement seemed rather traditionalist—especially in practice. In part this was because German Jewry did not have the organized equivalent of American Conservative Judaism, although there were periodic attempts to create a *Religiöse Mittelpartei*.[15] In addition, the centuries-long traditions of many of the German communities and synagogues made many members reluctant to tamper with historical precedents.[16] A more weighty reason, however, was the contrast between the way religious life was organized in America and Germany. Unlike the absolute freedom American Jews had in forming their own congregations, German Jews were generally required to belong to the Jewish community of their locality.[17] The *Einheitsgemeinde* (unified community) paid the rabbis, built and subsidized the main synagogues, and provided religious education and social welfare to all Jews in the city. Since working through the *Einheitsgemeinde* required procuring a considerable degree of consensus, Liberal Jews moderated their radicalism in setting up their religious institutions. Although Reform synagogues generally had organs, mixed choirs, and some German prayers, most of the prayers were in Hebrew, men kept their heads covered, and women sat separately from men. In many cases Liberal rabbis, bowing to pressure from the *Einheitsgemeinde* or based on their own convictions, lived their lives according to halakhic norms little different than those of the Orthodox. This personal traditionalism in religious practice came under increasing criticism in the 1920s.[18] By the mid-1920s many Liberal Jews began to question the *Einheitsgemeinde*, which they had previously supported as the best vehicle for spreading their beliefs. Some even referred to it by the negative label of *Zwangsgemeinde* (coerced community) and saw it as muffling attempts to put through needed innovations.[19]

Many of the innovations of nineteenth-century German Liberal Judaism had been in the direction of greater aesthetics, formality, and respectability in the synagogue service. The organs, choirs, sermons, and imposing buildings of the great urban synagogues had successfully turned prayer into an aesthetic experience. It had gotten rid of the "disorder" of the traditional service with its loud individual prayer and cacophony. But it had also reduced the lay worshippers into a passive "audience" who listened in silence to the service carried out by rabbis, cantors, and choirs. More and more Liberal writers began to see the turn to "aesthetic Judaism" as a barrier rather than a boon to religious fervor.[20] Almost every proposal for change aroused discussion and often opposition within the movement, but in the course of the 1920s certain innovations were attempted on a wide basis.

The practical innovations, which various groups of Liberals proposed or implemented, cut in opposite directions. On the one hand, they revived traditional ceremonies, holidays, and observances, which had been dropped by most non-Orthodox Jews. Not only was there a repeated campaign to get families to switch from Christmas to Chanukah observances, but there were also attempts to revive the holidays of Shavuot, Sukkot, and Simchat Torah as well as the penitential Selichot service before the High Holidays.[21] Some proposed innovations were "tradition-neutral," such as the desire for smaller synagogues and the substitution of communal choral singing for passive listening to the choir.

Proposals to reanimate Sabbath observance combined both a revival of tradition and nonhalakhic innovation. It was recognized by almost all discussants that for most German Jews, Saturday was a day of work and shopping, while Sunday was the actual day of rest. Many writers proposed the creation of Sunday synagogue services, which would not be Sabbath services but would provide weekly inspiration to many individuals that could not attend services on Saturday. Despite the fact that such proposals had aroused anti-Liberal feelings, and even Liberal election defeats, at the beginning of the twentieth century, many writers felt that the principle of providing worship opportunity to the alienated Jewish masses outweighed any potential "political" loss.[22] A less radical, but still nonhalakhic, solution was the institution of late Friday evening services after the close of business hours, during the winter when the Sabbath began early. Such Friday night services were the main locus of many of the most innovative Jewish worship experiences in Weimar Germany.[23] The same combination of traditional and nonhalakhic elements can be said for the plans to create a unified Liberal German prayer book—the *Einheitsgebetbuch*, which was finally issued in 1929 after many years of discussion.[24]

In their diagnoses of what kept most Jews from the synagogue, many writers found aspects of the tradition to be the problem. There were frequent calls for the elimination of repetition in the liturgy, the shortening of the service, and the use of more vernacular prayers. Some complained about the boring, routine sermons, and others suggested abandoning many of the traditional melodies, which no longer spoke to moderns. There were frequent complaints about the place of women in the synagogue and calls for the abolition of separate seating for the sexes. Mixed seating became the mode in the innovative

Synagogenverein Norden in Berlin and was introduced into the Prinz-regentenstraße Synagogue built in western Berlin in 1930.[25]

Unlike earlier periods in which German Reform was the undisputed leader of world progressive Judaism, in the 1920s the influence of English-speaking Reform and Liberal Judaism was being felt in Germany.[26] A number of German Liberal leaders looked to the large and lively American Reform Jewish movement as a successful model to emulate, though others had their reservations. The new Liberal Jewish Movement in England, headed by Lily Montagu and Claude Montefiore, was in close contact with the German movement. The World Union for Progressive Judaism, which met for the first time in London in 1926 (and then met in Berlin in 1928), became a force for the exchange of ideas between German- and English-speaking Liberal rabbis. In general, the World Union was a force encouraging those trends in German Liberal Judaism, which desired both deepened religious faith and a move in a less traditional direction.[27]

Those proposing new innovations often faced a practical problem. In the words of one Liberal writer about the Liberal synagogue: "Those who come don't want reform, those who want reform don't come."[28] Pressure for change came from all directions in the 1920s. While most of those who wrote in the *Jüdisch-Liberale Zeitung* leaned toward less attention to tradition and more innovation, others called for a revival of traditions that had previously been dropped. Those calling for preservation or restoration of traditions came not only from the Orthodox and those who created the *Mittelpartei* but also from within the Liberal movement itself. The spectrum within the movement was broad and was, perhaps, becoming broader.[29] The disagreements were not only about the question of Jewish nationalism (Zionism and its offshoots) as some writers imply. They also included disagreements over religious matters such as degree of innovation in the liturgy, the value of the Hebrew language, the desirability of halakhic observance, and the institution of Sunday services. These disagreements divided both rabbis and lay people, though the lay leaders of the movement seem to have been to the left of the rabbis.[30] While some Liberal leaders were calling for less attention to traditional forms and more attention to the eternal spiritual content of Judaism, other liberal rabbis were defending the tradition and calling for a return to more traditional practice.[31]

In the end, there was more excitement and discussion than there was actual change. Many of the changes that were successfully implemented were not very radical (late Friday evening services, the new *Einheitsgebetbuch*). When the Prinzregentenstraße Synagogue in Berlin became the first major communal synagogue to seat men and women together, this was considered a very radical move by many, even within the Liberal movement. The Liberal rabbinical opinions on the matter were almost evenly split (with a few intermediate opinions like that of Leo Baeck that the synagogue should have both mixed and gender-segregated sections).[32] Attempts at creating some type of *religiöse Feierstunde* (religious solemnities) in synagogues on Sunday morning or afternoon proceeded with great caution to ensure that they did not seem to be Sabbath services.[33] In general it was easier to implement changes in small groups (like the Berlin Liberale Synagoge Norden) than in the organized community as a whole. The large urban *Einheitsgemeinde* was generally a hindrance to change, since every slight innovation had to go through discussion by divided and politicized communal boards. More radical changes were frequently discussed in the pages of the *Jüdisch-Liberale Zeitung*, but they were almost never implemented, in part because they came from radical forces within the movement.[34]

One has the impression that the idealism and religious conviction that manifested itself in the crisis years of 1919 to 1923 began to subside with the relative prosperity of the mid-1920s. The *Jüdisch-Liberaler-Jugendverein* (ILI), which began with high enthusiasm and religious fervor in the early Weimar period, seemed more routine in its attitudes by 1929.[35] It never procured the adherence of more than a tiny portion of the non-Orthodox, non-Zionist German-Jewish youth. In general, religious liberalism never captured the attention of the German-Jewish public the way more secular non-Zionist movements like the Central-Verein (CV) did. Those Liberal Jews who emphasized the religious nature of Judaism were often more militantly anti-Zionist than the CV, which tried to work with the Zionists in the Keren Hayesod and the Jewish Agency during the 1920s.[36]

But the "renaissance" of German Jewry in the 1920s and the "cultural revival" of the first years of Nazi rule were marked much more by the feelings of peoplehood and Jewish nationalism proclaimed by the Zionists than by the universalized and Germanized spirituality championed by the militant leaders of religious liberalism.

NOTES

1. One of the first Orthodox leaders to use the argument that Orthodox independence needed to be respected was Samson Raphael Hirsch in his arguments in favor of the right to withdraw from the official Jewish community without leaving Judaism. This argument helped him gain the support of secular Liberal Jewish politicians like Eduard Lasker. In the 1920s Orthodox leaders frequently used their right of freedom

of conscience to ensure that their religious practices were respected. Liberal Jewish leaders generally accepted the argument but argued in return that Orthodoxy needed to respect the freedom of conscience of Liberal and nonobservant Jews, something the Orthodox were reluctant to concede.

2. This Orthodox militancy expressed itself on a number of occasions, especially during the Richtlinien controversy of 1912. In the 1920s, Orthodox Jews, usually in alliance with the Zionists, tried to roll back earlier concessions they had made or to heighten the strictness of the enforcement of Jewish practice in community institutions. Attempts or successful actions to institute greater traditions included the reestablishment of a rabbinical court for monetary matters (*Bet Din*) in Berlin, the requirement that boys at community religious schools cover their heads during lessons, the abolition of female solos in the Königsberg choir, the closing of Jewish cemeteries on the Sabbath, the switch from a German to a Hebrew version of the Chanukah hymn "Ma'oz Tzur," the switch from a three-year to a one-year Torah cycle in Dresden, and the moving of the reader's desk back to the middle of the synagogue in the old synagogue of Berlin. *Jüdisch-Liberale Zeitung*, December 30, 1921, November 17, 1922, November 28, 1924, January 2, 1925, July 26, 1926, and September 14, 1928.

3. Ibid., June 18, 1926, January 7, 1927.

4. There are various ways of gauging the high level of religious indifference among German Jews in the 1920s; most of them qualitative rather than quantitative. Some of the rare bits of quantitative information come from Hamburg, where one could affiliate with one of three competing religious associations in addition to belonging to the overall Hamburg Jewish community. Sixty-five percent of Hamburg Jews in the 1920s did not belong to any of the religious associations; 1,579 paying member units representing some 5,000 individuals belonged to the Orthodox Synagogenverband, while the Liberal Tempelverband had 453 member units representing 1,135 individuals and the Neue Dammtor synagogue, which stood between the Orthodox and Liberal groups, had 398 members, representing 1,130 individuals. Though the Orthodox represented only about one in every four Hamburg Jews, they were a clear majority of those who affiliated with a religious association. In the mid-1920s, 20.6 percent (984) of married Jews in Hamburg were living in an intermarriage. Of the 3,782 in-married couples, 30 percent had not had a religious wedding, 32 percent had had an Orthodox ceremony, 20 percent had been married in the Liberal temple, and 18 percent had been married in the Neue Dammtor synagogue. See Ina Lorenz, *Identität und Assimilation: Hamburgs Juden in der Weimarer Republik* (Hamburg: Hans Christians Verlag, 1989), xciii–xciv, lviii, lxxvii.

5. The Jewish intermarriage rate in Germany increased from 12.85 percent in 1920 to 23 percent in 1932 (mainly because of a decline in homogeneous Jewish marriages rather than an increase in the number of mixed

ones). See Steven Lowenstein, "Jewish Intermarriage and Conversion in Germany and Austria," *Modern Judaism* 25 (2005): 23–61.

6. The question of a crisis of German Jewish Liberal Judaism is discussed in issues of the *Jüdisch-Liberale Zeitung* on March 18 and September 30, 1921, and April 21 and April 28, 1922.

7. Usually the Orthodox joined with the Zionists in opposing "assimilationist" Liberal practices such as the use of the organ and the German language in the synagogue services. There were occasional electoral alliances between the "religious" Liberal and Conservative (Orthodox) parties against the "secular nationalist" Zionists. As far as I can tell there was never a Zionist-Liberal alliance against the Orthodox.

8. It is important to note that the struggle against conversion to Christianity receded rapidly during the 1920s in the face of growing secularism and assimilation. While the percentage of those who withdrew from the Jewish community to become unaffiliated or married non-Jewish spouses without converting to Christianity increased, the number of Jews who converted to Christianity declined. This was caused in part by the growth of secularism in German society. (The number in Germany of those not listed as belonging to a specific religion, increased from 212,038 in 1910 to 1,140,957 [*Gemeinschaftslose*] in 1925 and 2,437,043 [*Gemeinschaftslose*] in 1933.) Another important factor was the disappearance of the religion-based governmental discrimination of the German Empire, which induced many men to convert to gain government or university positions. In Weimar Germany such conversions were neither legally necessary nor were they much help in the face of the growth of racial antisemitism.

9. Salomonski, "Die Erneuerung des Judentums," *Jüdisch-Liberale Zeitung*, August 17, 1928, 3.

10. In contrast to American Reform Judaism with its clear, if controversial, Pittsburgh platform of 1885, German liberalism had never taken a clear stance on such basic matters as the continued applicability of the kosher laws or regulations for Jewish marriage and divorce.

11. *Jüdisch-Liberale Zeitung*, July 2, 1926. The author spoke of the need not only for belief in God but for "Erleben Gottes in tiefster Seele, das Empfinden Gottes in tiefinnersten Gemüte" (the experience of God in the deepest soul, the experience of God in the deep, innermost feelings).

12. *Jüdisch-Liberale Zeitung*, December 30, 1921, November 3 and November 17, 1922, March 2, April 13, April 27, and December 28, 1923, and March 1, 1924.

13. Ibid., February 16, 1924.

14. Ibid., April 28 and November 2, 1922, May 2, 1924, February 20, 1925, and July 23, 1926. Many Liberals spoke out against any "new Schulchan Aruch."

15. Though there was a contrast between the more traditional Jüdisch-Theologisches Seminar in Breslau and the more progressive (though officially nondenominational) Hochschule für die Wissenschaft des Juden-

tums in Berlin, graduates of both seminaries belonged to the Verband liberaler Rabbiner and the Vereinigung für das liberale Judentum. The first attempt to create a religious *Mittelpartei* in Berlin took place in 1909, but it was short-lived. In the early 1920s there is discussion of a middle trend (*mittlere Richtung*) and eventually the founding of a new Religiöse Mittelpartei für Frieden und Einheit der Gemeinde for the elections to the Preussischer Landesverband jüdischer Gemeinden in 1925. The Liberal leadership generally related to this new party with hostility and saw it as a disguised form of conservatism. *Jüdisch-Liberale Zeitung*, January 27, 1922, January 19, 1923, January 2, 1924, January 16 and February 20, 1925, December 31, 1926, and February 4, February 11, and February 25, 1927. At times the *Mittelpartei* engaged in strong attacks against Liberal Judaism.

16. A widespread term to describe the reluctance to tamper with tradition was *Pietät*, which is definitely not synonymous with its English cognate *piety. Pietät* implied respect for the ways of one's parents, the desire to preserve things hallowed by the past, and a sentimental attachment to tradition. Many writers describing German Jewish religion in the twentieth century state that worshippers were often more motivated by *Pietät* than by real religious fervor.

17. The Prussian Secession Law of 1876 (and similar laws in a few other states, notably Hessen) permitted individuals to withdraw from the official Jewish community without leaving the Jewish religion if they filed an official declaration stating that belonging to the community violated their conscience. Until that exception was passed, Jews who wished to be free of their communal taxes had to withdraw from Judaism altogether. During the Weimar Republic withdrawal from the community no longer required a declaration of conscientious reasons for withdrawal.

18. *Jüdisch-Liberale Zeitung*, November 3, 1922, May 2 and December 19, 1924, February 20, 1925, and October 15, 1926.

19. Ibid., May 2, May 29, July 2, and October 15, 1926.

20. Ibid., April 22, 1922, March 1, 1924.

21. Ibid., December 16, 1921, September 8, October 1, and October 8, 1926.

22. Ibid., December 29, 1922, and May 18 and June 22, 1923.

23. The introduction of late Friday evening services is only one of a great number of parallels between developments in German Liberal Judaism and developments in American Jewry around the same time. Another parallel is the growing influence of and increasing dissension about Zionism within Reform Judaism. One of the small innovative congregations that implemented both late Friday evening services and mixed seating of the sexes was the Liberale Synagoge Norden in Berlin about which Michael Meyer wrote in detail in "*Gemeinschaft* within *Gemeinde:* Religious Ferment within Weimar Liberal Judaism," in *In Search of Community: Jewish Identities in Germany and Austria, 1918–1933*, ed.

Michael Brenner and Derek Penslar, 15–35 (Bloomington: Indiana University Press, 1998).

24. *Jüdisch-Liberale Zeitung*, October 23, 1922, May 2, 1924, and March 15, 1929. It is interesting how little discussion the *Einheitsgebetbuch* engendered in the columns of the *Jüdisch-Liberale Zeitung*.

25. Ibid., December 29, 1922, November 5 and November 19, 1926, and February 22, 1929.

26. While the terms "Liberal" and "Reform" are generally used as synonyms in this article, they denoted two different movements in England. The term "Liberal Judaism" was applied to the less traditional of the two movements, and it was British Liberal Judaism, which had close ties with German Liberal Judaism.

27. Some moderates demonized the World Union. In Cologne in December 1926, the newly formed Jüdisch-religiöse Mittelpartei für Frieden und Einheit in der Gemeinde warned in an election flyer of a "mächtiger, über reiche Geldmittel verfügender innerer Feind" (a powerful internal enemy possessing rich monetary resources) that wished to destroy the bases of the Jewish religion. This internal enemy was "International London Liberalism," in other words, the new World Union for Progressive Judaism. The leaflet claimed that this new heresy had nothing to do with the organic development preached by earlier Liberal leaders like Geiger and Zunz or Hermann Cohen. They went so far as to warn that the new group was "a Jewish-Christian tinged deistic sect." *Jüdisch-Liberale Zeitung*, December 31, 1926, and February 25, 1927.

28. Rabbi L. Fuchs (of Chemnitz) "Zum Einheitsgebetbuch," *Jüdisch-Liberale Zeitung*, October 13, 1922: "Die zur Synagoge kommen, wollen keine Reform; und die eine wollen, kommen nicht!" Similar statements are found in an article dated October 15, 1926.

29. There are a number of discussions of the broad spectrum of views within the German Liberal Judaism. See, e.g., *Jüdisch-Liberale Zeitung*, May 12, 1922, May 11, 1923, August 31 and September 6, 1928, and May 31, 1929. A writer in May 1922, analyzing a Liberal rabbinic conference, delineates several groups within the Liberal rabbinate moving from most to least traditional: (1) Wiener-Goldmann-Fuchs, (2) Leo Baeck as a transition, (3) Lewkowitz-Vogelstein-Samuel, and (4) Kellermann (the rabbi of the *Reformgemeinde*). In his opening remarks at the annual conference of the Liberal rabbinic association in May 1929, Rabbi Caesar Seligmann stated, "Complete unity [*eine restlose Einheit*] cannot be established even within our rabbinical association considering our internal disquiet [*Unruhe*] and search for new paths. Three or even two decades ago there was only one opinion and trend [*Meinung und Richtung*] among us [Liberal rabbis]. Today that has changed and maybe that is a sign of stronger vitality. Movement [*Bewegung*] is always and everywhere more valuable than undisturbed quiet."

30. Editorials in the *Jüdisch-Liberale Zeitung*, especially in the second half of the 1920s, criticized the inconsistency or moderation of the Liberal

rabbinic organization frequently. See *Jüdisch-Liberale Zeitung*, May 12 and November 3, 1922, and April 1 and April 8, 1927. According to Avraham Barkai, most rabbis refrained from participating in activities of the Vereinigung für das liberale Judentum (and by implication in the *Jüdisch-Liberale Zeitung*) after the newspaper blasted their moderate attitude toward Zionism in March 1927. Avraham Barkai, "Between *Deutschtum* and *Judentum:* Ideological Controversies within the *Central Verein*," in Brenner and Penslar, *In Search of Jewish Community*, 74–91, esp. 84–85. This would imply that the columns of the *Jüdisch-Liberale Zeitung* were no longer representative of the full gamut of Liberal ideological views but only of the most radical anti-Zionists. Although it is hard to evaluate this statement, it seems to me that Barkai's evaluation of the newspaper and the Vereingung as no longer interested in religious matters but only in the political power struggles in the community is one-sided at best. In any case, in a speech to the conference of Liberal rabbis in May 1929, Caesar Seligmann states that the disagreements (*Unstimmigkeit*) about relations to Zionism between the editors of the *Jüdisch-Liberale Zeitung* and the Liberal rabbis had been settled (*beigelegt*). *Jüdisch-liberale Zeitung*, May 31, 1929.

31. Rabbi Fuchs of Chemnitz replied to warnings that the Jewish community was moving toward the right by stating, "Was man heute den Zug nach rechts nennt, ist in Wahrheit: Zug nach Innen, in die Tiefe der Seele" ("Expressionistisches Judentum," *Jüdisch-Liberale Zeitung*, March 1, 1924). At the 1928 World Union conference, Professor Ismar Elbogen pleaded with his audience, "Lassen Sie uns paar Leute, die wir die Tradition halten wollen, ruhig die Tradition halten, solange wir die Tradition nicht als autoritatives Gesetz auslegen." *Jüdisch-Liberale Zeitung*, August 31, 1928.

32. The opinions were published in *Jüdisch-Liberale Zeitung*, February 22, 1929. Among Liberal Berlin rabbis, Rabbis Blumenthal, Galliner, and Weyl came out clearly in favor of the innovation; Rabbis Bergmann, Lewkowitz, and Warschauer clearly opposed it; and Rabbis Leo Baeck and Max Wiener called for compromise solutions. Naturally, the Orthodox rabbis of Berlin opposed the innovation. It is quite striking that some of the Liberal rabbinic opponents of the change considered it radical and dangerous.

33. See, e.g., *Jüdisch-Liberale Zeitung*, December 7, 1928, and January 4 and March 29, 1929. The use of the term *religiöse Feierstunde* instead of *Gottesdienst* (religious service) and the centering of the service on a religious lecture or discussion were all ways of stating that the solemnities were not Sabbath services despite their inclusion of prayers and organ music.

34. Besides frequent calls for Sunday services and the end of the separation of men and women in the synagogue, the columns of the *Jüdisch-Liberale Zeitung* also called for much greater use of the German language in the services, and even the transformation of the traditional

mourning for the destruction of the Temple on the ninth of Av into a festival celebrating the political emancipation of the Jews. *Jüdisch-Liberale Zeitung*, August 14, 1929.

35. Compared to other youth organizations appealing to non-Orthodox, non-Zionist, German Jewish youth (like the association of neutral Jewish youth organizations or youth organizations associated with the Central-Verein or of a more right-wing orientation like Schwarzes Fähnlein), the ILI remained a small organization. An article in *Jüdisch-Liberale Zeitung*, July 24, 1929, attempts to give an evaluation of the organization. It described the branches of the youth movement in the large cities of Breslau, Berlin, Magdeburg, and Frankfurt am Main as active and successful. Smaller branches in the Silesian towns of Ratibor, Liegnitz, and Oppeln were also very active. There had been much less success in other urban communities.

The *Jüdisch-Liberale Zeitung* contained several articles (for instance June 13, 1924, and July 24, 1929) explaining why it was important for Liberal youth to join a society based on Liberal ideology (*Gesinnungsverein*) rather than a neutral youth association, but the arguments they contained seemingly had little success.

36. Two militant Liberal laymen who are worthy of detailed study are Bruno Woyda, longtime editor of the *Jüdisch-Liberale Zeitung*, and George Goetz, executive director (*Syndic*) of the Vereinigung für das liberale Judentum. Both took consistently militant anti-Zionist positions and criticized those who favored a more moderate stance toward Jewish nationalism. Avraham Barkai, who stresses Woyda's affiliation with the Berlin *Reformgemeinde*, sees both men as "dangerously close" to Max Naumann's German nationalist Verband nationaldeutscher Juden. Barkai, "Between *Deutschtum* and *Judentum*," 84–87. Yet the *Jüdisch-Liberale Zeitung* strongly criticized Naumann and his movement. In their discussion of the Central-Verein and its compromises with Zionism, they not only stress their opposition to the Jewish national aspects of Zionism but also criticize Zionism and even the Central-Verein for a secular rather than religious approach. (E.g., George Goetz' article "'Deutsch-jüdische Probleme der Gegenwart' Ludwig Holländers neue Schrift," *Jüdisch-Liberale Zeitung*, April 12, 1929.) To my mind this emphasis on religion is not a mere tactic against Jewish nationalism but an appeal for a deep, if ill-defined, Liberal Jewish religiosity. (Some similar motivations may have animated Hans-Joachim Schoeps, usually seen merely as an extreme right-wing German nationalist.) Another reason not to group Woyda with the right wing of German Jewish politics is the strong support for the religious peace movement found in the *Jüdisch-Liberale Zeitung* as well as a warm article in the paper by Woyda about the Jewish anarchist thinker Gustav Landauer.

| 5 |

THE EVOLVING LEGACY
OF MOSES MENDELSSOHN

18

Moses Mendelssohn's
Dreams and Nightmares

SHMUEL FEINER

The life work of Michael Meyer, one of the leading historians in our generation, is in its entirety a profound cultural and intellectual journey that observes and interprets the various transformations of modern Jewish identity. His journey to investigate the intersection between Jews and modernity began in a book that appeared forty years ago—*The Origins of the Modern Jew: Jewish Identity and European Culture in Germany 1749–1824*—but that only came to my attention years later when I was a graduate student of Jewish history at the Hebrew University of Jerusalem in 1983. It was not included in my reading assignments, and I found it just by chance in a small Jerusalem bookshop. I took the book with me to my four weeks' *milu'im* (reserve army service) and in the cold, dark nights in the field I read about the prominent Jewish-German intellectuals Mendelssohn, Friedländer, Zunz, and others, so out of my then-Israeli experience context. I must confess that the book made an enormous impression on me, and from that day on it has been for me one of the most important keys to my understanding of basic issues in critical trends such as the Haskalah, the Reform movement, and *Wissenschaft des Judentums* that emerged among German Jews in the eighteenth and the early nineteenth centuries, which marked a great revolution in the way Jews related to their ancient culture and in their encounter with modern European culture.

Today I seem to have a better understanding of why I was so enthralled by this book. I was brought up on a school of historiography that related mainly to the big questions of the transformation of the Jewish people as a whole in the modern age, for example, the changes engendered by the great emigration from eastern Europe, the appearance of mass movements such as Hasidism and Zionism, and the tension between emancipation and antisemitism. In contrast, Michael Meyer touched with great sensitivity on a more intimate, more internal history, although one with enormous significance: on dilemmas of identity of those Jewish men and women whose European education and modern values conflicted with the heritage of their forefathers' tradition.

The first among them was the eminent Berlin philosopher Moses Mendelssohn (1729–86). Consequently, the first two chapters of Meyer's *The Origins of the Modern Jew* deal with him. Mendelssohn's name is already well known worldwide, and no one in Jewish historiography would omit writing about him, but in the expert hands of the historian Michael Meyer he is stripped of all the frills of the myth and restored to his historical dimensions as a Jew of his time who experienced a cultural conversion to Enlightenment without abandoning his religion or the Jewish community. Meyer characterized him, in a sentence I marked in red ink upon first reading it twenty-four years ago: "Inwardly he is torn between identification with the universal community of humanity, which now seems only a dream, and the more limited Jewish community."[1] When I approached the task of writing a biography of Mendelssohn, I saw myself following in Meyer's footsteps—to see Mendelssohn first of all as a man of his time and place, to listen to his authentic voice, to understand his frustrations, to interpret his thought from within the course of his life and the historical contexts.[2] I wanted to expose the dilemmas the philosopher was confronted with, as a man for whom questions such as religious tolerance versus religious coercion, for example, were truly existential issues for a Jew deprived of civil rights in Frederick the Great's Prussian kingdom, on the one hand, and an enlightened Jew in the Berlin community, on the other.

In 1770 Rochus Friedrich of Lynar wrote to Mendelssohn asking his opinion about the possibility of establishing a state for the Jews in Palestine. Mendelssohn replied firmly in the negative: just as it was impossible to expect the Jews to convert to Christianity, it was also unthinkable that they would return to their homeland. Not only were there too many obstacles to the implementation of such an plan, but in his view, the Jewish nation lacked the activist mentality to undertake such a national enterprise.³ Moreover, although throughout his life he had suffered the pain of the civic oppression of the Jews, his major concern had always been to ensure the existence of a tolerant society that would enable the Jews to live in dignity. And after all, why ask him? A project of national revival that would address the very problem of the Jews living in the Diaspora was beyond the scope of his thinking. As a philosopher, he could not provide practical ideas. He had not even considered establishing the Jewish Enlightenment movement. Indeed, although Mendelssohn had increasingly acquired the image of a leader of the Jews, owing to the public fame he had gained, he did not believe that he possessed qualities and talents in areas outside of his much loved field of philosophy.

The circumstances of his life, however, did not allow him to philosophize in solitude.⁴ On the contrary, Mendelssohn was the Jew most exposed in his time to the limelight of public opinion. He did not think of himself as an historical hero and hesitated to take his place in the public sphere, but he cared very much for the future of the Jews in emerging modern Europe.

In this essay, I should like to share with you some of Mendelssohn's dreams and nightmares, and would like to listen with you to the voice of that Jewish humanist from Berlin who was so sensitive and so attuned to slight shifts in the culture, thought, and politics of his time. What do I mean by dreams and nightmares? Let us look at some of the significant stations in Mendelssohn's intellectual life.

The year is 1754. Gotthold Ephraim Lessing has just published his play *Die Juden* (The Jews), and Mendelssohn, only twenty-five years old, is enraged by a review written by Johann David Michaelis claiming that outside of Lessing's imagination, no virtuous Jews exist in reality. In his reaction, Mendelssohn adopted the position of an intellectual demanding that the principle of religious tolerance be applied to his fellow Jews and putting this notion to the test of public opinion. But despite his self-confidence, it is actually a sense of humiliation that is strongly projected in this letter. "Such thoughts cause me to blush with shame. . . . What a humiliation for our hard-pressed nation! What an exaggerated contempt!" Mendelssohn wrote with pain. "The common Christian people have always regarded us as the scourge of humanity, but from learned men I would have expected a fairer judgment. . . . Is it not enough that we must suffer in so many cruel ways, from such bitter hatred of the Christians, must these wrongs also be justified by slander? . . . Allow us within this oppression and darkness at least the possibility to improve ourselves as individuals," Mendelssohn cried out in his letter.[5]

He would have liked at least to be able to build a private sphere in which the Jew could develop as an individual and even gain recognition as a learned, virtuous European Jew. But Michaelis in his review had cast doubt on the existence of Mendelssohn and his like as learned, enlightened Jews. It became an existential issue for him. Indeed, from this moment in 1754, when Mendelssohn first had to struggle with the conflict between prejudice and religious tolerance, he understood that he should not only engage in philosophical speculation but that he had to fight for what he believed was the obvious conclusion to be drawn from reason, natural rights, and humanism—that the Jew too is a human being.

The Enlightenment enabled the Jews to dream about an improvement of their relations with the non-Jewish world.[6] Obviously, as long as they had no cause to dream or to hope, they also experienced no great disappointments. Moses Mendelssohn was not a naive optimist, but he was one of those Jews who wanted to hope that the culture of the Enlightenment would free the Jews of the humiliating restrictions. Hence, he was also so sensitive to the voices in public opinion relating to the Jews, and each time the values of the Enlightenment were put to the test and failed, he took this as a personal affront.

If Mendelssohn had summed up his position in society and his literary achievements by the time he reached forty, he could have been very satisfied—many people sought his company, read his books, and valued his talents. He was known far and wide as the German Socrates; the Jewish community took pride in his public prestige, and his family grew and prospered. But again, a private letter shows that under the thin outer cover of personal and public success, Mendelssohn was sorely troubled by a sense of frustration.

In March of 1768 the educator Johann Bernhard Basedow asked Mendelssohn to help him promote the "elementary book" he had written. Mendelssohn's reply provides another glimpse into his troubled, embittered, and rebellious consciousness in view of his civil status as a Jew in Prussia, a self-awareness that differed widely from the optimistic messages he had been spreading during those years. "If you believe that your book is also suitable to us Jews," Mendelssohn wrote, "then you do not know the true situation of our nation." Because "the more noble your intentions, the wiser your principles and the more correct the means you wish to adopt are, the less able we are to make use of them. While your programs strive to educate rational persons, upholders of justice and humanism, lovers of truth and freedom who serve their country, the Jew cannot be part of this ideal." Here, Mendelssohn's suppressed sense of inferiority erupted, and he asked, "Should a Jew learn to respect human rights? If the Jew does not want to be more miserable within his condition of civil oppression, it would be better if he knew nothing of these rights. Should he love the truth and freedom that lies in reason in order to totally despair? In fact, all the civil arrangements in many places have but one intent—to keep him away from these two!"[7]

To Mendelssohn, the gap between the restricted status of the European Jew and the innovative changes inspired by the Enlightenment culture seemed so vast, so sorely offensive and intolerable, that he preferred to keep that culture hidden from the Jews to prevent them from being even more miserable and frustrated. The internal contradiction between the humanistic values of the Enlightenment culture and the "civil oppression" of the Jews continued to trouble him. He ended his letter to Basedow with an attempt at repressing his gloom: "But enough of that, these thoughts oppress me too much, so that I cannot think them without a sense of revulsion."[8]

However, hardly a year had passed before these frustrating thoughts resurfaced. A very unpleasant surprise, which only increased his depression and revulsion, awaited him at the end of the summer of 1769, forcing him to cope for the first time in the public arena with the question of his dual identity—the Enlightenment philosopher and the Jew. I refer, of course, to the polemic with Johann Kaspar Lavater, who demanded that Mendelssohn publicly explain why he should not convert to Christianity. Mendelssohn's reply is full of personal remarks and provides one more glimpse into his frustrated thoughts. In particular, Mendelssohn gave expression to his feeling of weakness as a Jew: "I am a member of an oppressed people which must appeal to the benevolence of the government for protection and shelter—which are not always granted, and never without limitations. Content to be tolerated and protected, my fellow Jews willingly forgo liberties granted to every other human being. Barred even from temporary residence in many countries, they consider it no small favor when a nation admits them under tolerable conditions. As you know, your circumcised friend may not even visit you in Zurich!"[9] It took a long time for Mendelssohn to recover from the Lavater affair before he could allow himself to continue fostering his dream of enlightenment and tolerance. The document most revealing of his dreams at the time is a personal letter to the educator and principal of the Philanthropin school, Joachim Campe of Dessau, written early in the spring of 1777. Mendelssohn's optimism was then growing stronger. He felt that, despite everything, the Enlightenment might yet weaken the strong grip of "prejudice."

Campe's willingness to admit Jewish students to the school and to appoint outstanding Jewish graduates to teaching positions seemed to be a step in the right direction.[10]

Three years later, on a summer evening in 1780, Mendelssohn was taking a stroll in the company of his wife and their children in the streets of Berlin. A gang of boys attacked the family, yelling, "Jews! Jews!" and throwing stones at them. The children, stunned and frightened, did not understand what was happening. "What have we done to them, Papa? Yes, dear Papa . . . they are always chasing after us in the streets, cursing us—Juden! Juden! Is just being a Jew enough reason for those people to curse us?" And their father, frustrated and helpless, unable at that moment to find any comforting words of explanation, could only mutter to himself with suppressed rage: "People, people, when will you stop doing these things?" Mendelssohn repressed this experience and never mentioned it publicly. Only in a letter to the young Benedictine monk Peter Adolph Winkopp, one of Mendelssohn's admirers, did he relate this terrifying and humiliating experience of his family.[11] This was one of those momentary flashes that tore aside the respectable thin veneer of his life, a moment that affronted his self-dignity and shook his faith in religious tolerance.

In the early 1780s, however, Mendelssohn's optimism was again on the rise. Christian Wilhelm von Dohm had published his book *Ueber die bügerliche Verbesserung der Juden* (On the civil improvement of the Jews), and Joseph II issued his Edict of Tolerance to the Jewish communities in the Habsburg Empire. Mendelssohn could not remain indifferent to these developments. He reacted to them early in 1782 in the "preface" to the German translation of Menasseh ben Israel's *Vindiciae Judaeorum*.[12] Mendelssohn's moods varied. At first, he allowed himself to be swept up by the rising wave of enthusiasm caused by the new developments in the public discourse relating to the Jews and to dream that the ardent wishes of the humanists were actually being realized. Unable to foresee that he would die within less than four years, Mendelssohn opened his preface with these words: "Thanks be rendered to a kind Providence for having allowed me to reach at the end of my days, this happy season in which a beginning has been made to consider human rights from a truly universal aspect."[13] But he also revealed his doubts about the possibility of introducing the much desired substantive change. Was the Enlightenment capable of ever erasing the traces of fanaticism and barbarism insofar as the attitude toward Jews is concerned? Was religious fanaticism diminished? In a renewed burst of pessimism, Mendelssohn informed his readers that the eighteenth-century Enlightenment had not yet succeeded in erasing "the traces of barbarism in history."[14] In certain cities in Germany,

Shmuel Feiner

the Jews were still not permitted "to walk out in daylight without a guard, for fear they might kill a Christian child or poison the wells. And at nighttime, even the strictest guard cannot be relied upon, because of the Jew's well known dealings with evil spirits." Is there any way of correcting this situation? Is there any way of successfully fighting against these "rude accusations" and "barbaric laws"? Even if we chop off the roots of these prejudices against the Jews they will continue to suck from the air and exist. And if that is the case, perhaps "in vain do reason and humanity raise their voice, for prejudice that has aged no longer has a sense of hearing."[15]

But in the very same breath in which he spoke these gloomy words, Mendelssohn began once again weaving the threads of his liberal dream. In it, the process of civil admission of the Jews would be successfully fulfilled if only the modern centralized state would adopt a pluralistic approach. This dream of civil admission, however, could only be realized if a higher obstacle were overcome—the autonomous communal organization of the Jews. In contrast to Dohm, Mendelssohn regarded this autonomy as an impossible situation that was contrary to the Enlightenment, to religious tolerance, and to the freedom of the Jews in the ideal state he dreamt of. Hence he came out decisively in favor of abolishing the right of excommunication, while outlining in detail his liberal approach that was opposed to the power and authority of any religious institution. From the unprecedented passion and zeal with which he battled against the position that permitted any church to use the force of threats, excommunication, and punishment "to expel rebels from its midst and to restore deviants to the straight path," it was obvious that this issue touched upon the very fiber of his being:

> I do not recognize any right over people that is anchored in and based upon doctrines and views . . . and even less do I recognize any right or control over opinions by the religion. . . . True, divine religion does not arrogate to itself any power over opinions and propositions. . . . True, divine religion needs neither arms nor fingers to be effective; it is all mind and heart. . . . With what kind of a heart can we lock the door before the dissident, the separatist, the unbeliever or the sectarian, and deny them freedom. . . . I remain silent on the danger involved in allowing this right of excommunication, the danger that it will be abused, which cannot be avoided if this right of religious coercion is granted, or in the case of any ecclesiastical discipline or power. Ah! Even after hundreds of years, humankind will not be healed

from the whip lashes struck at it by these monsters! I see no possibility of blocking or restraining the fanaticism of false religion so long as this way is open to it.[16]

Did Mendelssohn think of himself as a nonconformist who might have to stand in judgment before the Jewish church like Spinoza 130 years earlier in Amsterdam? Did he fear that his dream of a liberal civil state was dissolving? It seems that a little of each of these fueled Mendelssohn's anxieties.

From this point, a new chapter opened in Mendelssohn's life. August Cranz challenged Mendelssohn and caused him a great deal of embarrassment.[17] How could Mendelssohn's claim that Judaism negates coercion in matters of beliefs be reconciled with the religious fanaticism of the rabbis? Mendelssohn's wounds were reopened, and it seemed to him that the issue raised in public opinion by the Lavater affair had not been settled. Once again, every word of his was being scrutinized in an attempt to back him against the wall and to force him to choose—Judaism or Enlightenment, if not Judaism or Christianity. This was the background to his book *Jerusalem*, which was written in a pessimistic, skeptical tone. Michael Meyer justly observed, "*Jerusalem* was above all a personal defense of Mendelssohn's own existence and the goals of his life. He sought to strengthen the universal bonds of reason against the pernicious influence of narrowing dogma and its coercive implementation."[18]

I will cite only one example of Mendelssohn's nightmare taken from this book. He was agitated by the recent discussion of a uniform religious faith for all citizens, as an ostensibly enlightened solution of universal brotherhood, to once and for all uproot fanaticism. In this matter, he once again showed himself to be a liberal advocate of pluralism and freedom of thought but also a critic, from within, of the Enlightenment itself, who, many years before the appearance of postmodern criticism, had warned against the danger of tyranny in the name of reason. "They speak of the union of faiths as a very desirable state of affairs,"[19] Mendelssohn wrote, but this utopian slogan bears catastrophic consequences for reason, freedom and true tolerance. As soon as the articles of faith of that uniform and universal religion are adopted, a modern form of fanaticism will spring up: "Beware, friends of men, of listening to such sentiments without the most careful scrutiny! They could be snares which fanaticism, grown impotent, wants to put in the way of liberty of conscience."[20] The imposition of a uniform faith would be a tyranny that is totally opposed to God's desire for a multicolored, multicultural humankind as well as to the principle of

Shmuel Feiner

true tolerance.

For Mendelssohn, the idea of a uniform faith threatened to destroy his belief that the modern state, guided by the desire to admit the Jews as citizens, would cancel the link between civil rights and religious affiliation and would enable them to achieve civil happiness. He made the following declaration: "If civil union cannot be obtained under any condition than our departing from the laws which we still consider binding on us, then we are sincerely sorry to find it necessary to declare that we must rather do without civil union."[21] In its historical context, and in the discourse being conducted in the German-speaking parts of Europe about the attitude of the Enlightenment culture and the state toward the Jews, this was an extremely pessimistic statement, which expressed a deep lack of faith in the Enlightenment's ability to bring about a real change in the Jews' situation of civil oppression.

Toward the end of his life, Mendelssohn continued to feel haunted by the demon of anti-Jewish prejudice. In one of his last letters, written only two and a half months before his death, he said, "The prejudices against my nation are too deeply embedded to be easily uprooted."[22] And the words he used in his 1784 letter to the Swiss physician Johann Georg Zimmermann were particularly skeptical: "We dreamt of nothing but the Enlightenment and believed that the light of reason would so intensely illuminate the environment that delusions and enthusiastic fanaticism could no longer be seen. But as we can see, from the other side of the horizon, the night with all of its ghosts and demons is already falling. More frightening than anything is that evil is so active and potent. Delusion and fanaticism are acting while reason contents itself with talk."[23]

The tension between his Jewish identity as "other" and his high public standing was one of the major experiences underpinning Mendelssohn's life. On more than one occasion, this "otherness" of his filled him with a sense of helplessness, insult, and vulnerability. But Mendelssohn's "otherness" as a Jew did not only mean that he was a victim, exposed to attacks; it also provided him with a special viewpoint. As a major player in the circles of the German Aufklärer and as a Jew, he could observe his surroundings from a double vantage point—both as a participant on the inside and as a critic on the outside. This kept him from being carried away by the belief that the culture of modern Europe would inevitably bring about the happiness of all human beings, and it made him skeptical about the Enlightenment's belief that humankind was making great progress. He had learned that there are boundary lines that he was not permitted to cross, that prejudice was not being uprooted, and that the traditional negative image of the Jews was an obstacle even to his fellow advocates of the Enlightenment. Moreover, it seemed to him that even from the Enlightenment itself tyrannical and destructive trends could develop, for example, "the union of religions," which to him was such a terrifying idea.

Mendelssohn's historical importance actually lies in the fact that he was not a naive representative of the Enlightenment. His dreams about the opportunities offered by the modern era were often disturbed by nightmares and anxiety about the failure of the Enlightenment. Mendelssohn, the sober Jewish humanist of the eighteenth century, posted his "humanistic injunction" as a warning sign in Berlin, the center of the German Enlightenment. From an historical perspective, looking at the tragic fate of European Jewry in the middle of the twentieth century, this warning sign and its humanistic messages is of enormous significance. If Mendelssohn had been able to foresee what the future held in wait for the Jews of Berlin about 150 years after his death, he might have tried to use his warning sign to cry out the words he muttered in anger and despair after the attack on his family while they strolled through the streets of Berlin: "People, people, when will you stop doing these things?"

NOTES

1. Michael A. Meyer, *The Origins of the Modern Jew: Jewish Identity and European Culture, 1745–1824* (Detroit: Wayne State University Press, 1967), 32.

2. Shmuel Feiner, *Moses Mendelssohn* [in Hebrew] (Jerusalem: Zalman Shazar Center, 2005).

3. Moses Mendelssohn, "An einen Mann von Stande [Rochus Friedrich Graf von Lynar]," *Gesammelte Schriften, Jubiläumsausgabe*, Bd. 12.1 (Stuttgart: Bad Cannstatt, 1976), 211ff. See Shmuel Feiner, "Stimmen der Furcht vor politisch-territorialer jüdischer Unabhängigkeit im neunzehnten Jahrhundert," in *Janusfiguren, Jüdische Heimstätte: Exil und Nation im deutschen Zionismus*, ed. Christian Wiese and Andrea Schatz, 25–41 (Berlin: Metropol, 2006).

4. The most comprehensive biography is still Alexander Altmann, *Moses Mendelssohn: A Biographical Study* (Philadelphia: Jewish Publication Society of America, 1976).

5. Mendelssohn's letter to Aaron Gumpertz, June 1754, *Gesammelte Schriften*, Bd. 12, pp. 9–14; Altmann, *Moses Mendelssohn*, 40–43.

6. See Meyer, *Origins of the Modern Jew*, 11–18; Shmuel Ettinger, "The Beginnings of the Change in the Attitude of European Society towards the Jews," *Scripta Hierosolymitana* 7 (1961): 193–219; Jacob Katz, *Out of the Ghetto: The Social Background to the Jewish Emancipation, 1770–1870*

(Cambridge: Harvard University Press, 1973); Adam Sutcliffe, *Judaism and the Enlightenment* (Cambridge: Cambridge University Press, 2003).

7. Mendelssohn, letter to Johann Bernhard Basedow, April 1768, *Gesammelte Schriften*, Bd. 12.1, pp. 159–60.

8. Ibid., 160.

9. Mendelssohn, "Schreiben an den Herrn Diaconus Lavater" (1770), *Gesammelte Schriften*, Bd. 7, pp. 14–15.

10. Mendelssohn, letter to Joachim Heinrich Campe, March 1777, *Gesammelte Schriften*, Bd. 12.2, pp. 85–88.

11. Mendelssohn, letter to Peter Adolph Winkopp, July 28, 1780, *Gesammelte Schriften*, Bd. 12.2, p. 200.

12. Mendelssohn, "Manasseh ben Israels Rettung der Juden, nebst einer Vorrede" (1782), *Gesammelte Schriften*, Bd. 13, pp. 1–25.

13. Ibid., 3.

14. Ibid., 7.

15. Ibid., 10.

16. Ibid., 16–25.

17. [August Friedrich Cranz], *Das Forschen nach Licht und Recht, in einem Schreiben an Herrn Moses Mendelssohn auf Veranlassung seiner Vorrede zu Menasse ben Israel* (Berlin, 1782).

18. Meyer, *Origins of the Modern Jew*, 49. See Moses Mendelssohn, *Jerusalem, or on Religious Power and Judaism*, trans. Allan Arkush (Hanover: University Press of New England, 1983); Allan Arkush, *Moses Mendelssohn and the Enlightenment* (Albany: State University of New York Press, 1994); David Sorkin, *Moses Mendelssohn and the Religious Enlightenment* (London: Peter Halban, 1996).

19. Mendelssohn, *Jerusalem*, 136.

20. Ibid.

21. Ibid., 135.

22. Mendelssohn, letter to Leopold von Hirschen, October 18, 1785, *Gesammelte Schriften*, Bd. 13, p. 316.

23. Mendelssohn, letter to Johann Georg Zimmermann, September 1, 1784, *Gesammelte Schriften*, Bd. 13, pp. 221–22.

The Construction and Deconstruction of a Jewish Hero

Moses Mendelssohn's Afterlife
in Early-Twentieth-Century Germany

MICHAEL BRENNER

THE ARCHETYPICAL GERMAN JEW

German historian Thomas Nipperdey opened his two masterful volumes of modern German history with the statements "In the beginning was Napoleon" and "In the beginning was Bismarck." If Nipperdey had written a modern Jewish history, he would have no doubt opened it with the sentence "In the beginning was Mendelssohn." Moses Mendelssohn was not only the "archetypal German Jew" and the "patron saint of German Jewry," as his biographer Alexander Altmann called him, but in fact he was the quintessential modern Jew of the eighteenth century: without giving up traditions and religious laws he became part of the larger culture and society.[1] He was seen as the first modern Jew to walk—perhaps not always too comfortably—in two worlds. One of the most highly regarded philosophers of his time, he also left his imprint as the first editor of a modern Hebrew journal and was the engine behind a translation project of the Hebrew Bible. This is, of course, not the place and time to add another analysis to Mendelssohn's impressive life as a German-Jewish thinker, which Michael Meyer has analyzed in detail.[2] The question we will turn to in this article might tell us more about later generations of German Jews than about Mendelssohn himself: it is the question of Mendelssohn's afterlife.

In the words of Christoph Schulte, Mendelssohn served as "the role model of a Jewish enlightener."[3] It is therefore hardly surprising that Moses Mendelssohn is the only figure from Jewish history to enter the German canon of *lieux de mémoire*—the most important terms, places, and persons belonging to the collective German memory—which appeared in three volumes in 2001. He did so as the "symbolic figure, which accompanies and towers above the life of the Jewish minority in Germany from the end of the 18th century until the destruction by the Nazis."[4]

Indeed, all modern Jewish denominations of nineteenth-century Germany hailed Mendelssohn for his philosophical innovations, his Bible translation into German, and his demand for a synthesis between Judaism and the non-Jewish surrounding culture. The modern Orthodox emphasized that he was faithful to the observance of Jewish laws (halakha), which he saw as based on divine legislation. The early Reform movement claimed Mendelssohn as the one who opened the doors to future reforms, even though he had adhered to practical observances that the reformers left behind. For both the neo-Orthodox and the reformers, Mendelssohn embodied the possibility of remaining Jewish while at the same time becoming German.

The first biography of Mendelssohn was published as early as 1788 by the maskil Isaak Euchel.[5] This Hebrew study constituted the basis for later glorifications. German Jewish historians of the nineteenth century contributed much to the creation of Mendelssohn as a modern Jewish hero. Thus, for the first modern Jewish historian, Isaak Markus Jost, Mendelssohn was "the third Moses [six centuries after Maimonides], whose calling was to take care of the languishing synagogue and lead it out of deep darkness into the light. With him, Judaism saw 'the dawn of a more beautiful day.'"[6] For Jost, Mendelssohn was a reformer and an "opponent of rabbinism."[7] Heinrich Heine went even further by claiming Mendelssohn as a Jewish reformer who—in blatant contrast to reality—had dismissed the Talmud as a relevant source for Jewish life: "Just as Luther dismissed the papacy, thus Mendelssohn dismissed the Talmud. He did so in the same way by disregarding tradition and declaring the Bible as the source of religion. . . . He destroyed Jewish catholicism just as Luther had destroyed Christian catholicism."[8]

The most famous Jewish historian of the nineteenth century, Heinrich Graetz, began his discussion on the modern period in Jewish history with the appearance of Mendelssohn, which he called "The Era of Rebirth." According to Graetz, Mendelssohn transformed the term Jew from an "abusive name into a name of honor."[9] The reformer and educator Sigismund Stern titled his own history published in 1857 *Ge-*

schichte des Judenthums von Mendelssohn bis auf die Gegenwart (History of Judaism from Mendelssohn to the present time). In his history of the Jews and their literature, written at the threshold of the twentieth century, Marcus Brann was following Jost's lead when he called Mendelssohn "a third Moses, with whom a new light rose among Israel," a new Moses who led the Jews "into a land of freedom, into an empire of learning [*Bildung*] and enlightenment."[10]

Moses Mendelssohn was, as far as we know, the first Jew whose hundredth birthday was celebrated by a broader non-Jewish public.[11] As Christhard Hoffmann notes, "the Mendelssohn festivities of 1829 were celebrated the same way as Goethe, Schiller, or Lessing celebrations, structured according to the rituals of the German civil religion of *Bildung*. They were not held in the synagogue but in 'neutral' celebration halls, and the circle of invited participants was not limited to the Jewish community."[12] The "third Moses" and the "German Socrates" was hailed in 1829 as the liberator of German Jews from the bonds of oppression, the enlightened philosopher, and the precursor of religious reform. The 1879 celebrations, in contrast, were more focused on Gotthold Ephraim Lessing's jubilee, and it was the message of religious tolerance, as expressed in his play *Nathan the Wise*, which became of central importance as a warning against intolerance. Mendelssohn was certainly present here too, as the figure of Nathan was partly based on Lessing's friend Moses Mendelssohn. But 1879 was also the year in which Wilhelm Marr began to use the term "antisemitism," when Adolf Stoecker brought anti-Jewish sentiments into clerical politics, and when Heinrich von Treitschke published his anti-Jewish tirades. Only seven years later, there were again numerous Mendelssohn celebrations, this time mostly through Jewish organizations, on the occasion of the centenary of his death, his *yorzeit*.

But Mendelssohn was not remembered everywhere as a hero. Traditional Jews during his own time and beyond remained suspicious of what they conceived as a path leading to complete assimilation. In eastern Europe, the Mendelssohn reception had been quite different from the outset. The influence of his ideas was regarded there as an irreparable damage to Judaism. As Polish historian Majer Balaban recalled, his Hebrew name, Moshe Dessau, was distorted to Moshe Fresser (Moses the Glutton) in Poland. The mere mentioning of Mendelssohn in a work of religious literature sufficed in certain circles to dismiss the work and its author. Jacob Katz has shown that the reactions of Hungarian Orthodoxy were not less severe. The Pressburg rabbi Moses Sofer, perhaps the most respected halakhic authority of his generation, declared categorically: "Do not touch the books of Rabbi Moses of Dessau." His most important spiritual heir, Rabbi

Akiva Yosef Schlesinger and his circle faithfully followed this advice.[13]

The Zionists had an ambiguous relationship toward Mendelssohn. On the one hand, they were deeply indebted to him and his circle of Berlin maskilim, who had marked the beginning of enlightened Jewish thought. On the other hand, they held Mendelssohn responsible for the dissolution of the Jewish community and Jewish national unity. They did not see in him the father of the first modern Hebrew journal but rather the father of children converted to Christianity, not the obstetrician of modern Jewish religion but the gravedigger of the Jewish nation.[14] In the State of Israel, this latter version was clearly dominant. Not even the smallest street is named today after Mendelssohn in the capital of the Jewish state. Jerusalem, the title of one of Mendelssohn's most acclaimed books, ignores the first modern Jewish thinker, as does official Israel. Much of the later Zionist criticism of Mendelssohn was based on the writings of the maskil Peretz Smolenskin. In various articles written in the 1870s, culminating in his notorious attack *Et lata'at* (Time of planting) of 1875, Smolenskin blamed Mendelssohn for "doubly ensnar[ing] our people by weakening its sense of national unity and insisting on the continued total obligation of the religious laws."[15] Smolenskin went so far as to accuse Mendelssohn of hiding his Jewishness in the presence of Christians, and perhaps most poignantly, of selling his and his children's Jewishness for material reasons: "Ben Menahem [Moses Mendelssohn] . . . was an accountant . . . and accounting is what he taught [his children]. . . . The word went forth from Ben Menahem that we must seek reward for our labor, and that it is therefore in vain to toil for the Torah."[16] Nathan Birnbaum was the first German-speaking Zionist to echo this rejection of Mendelssohn. He regarded him as the father of assimilation and accused neo-Orthodox and reformers alike of an uncritical adherence to Mendelssohn's ideas.[17]

It would be a mistake to simplify the Mendelssohn reception by a clear east-west or Zionist–non-Zionist divide. To be sure, he was never well liked by traditionalists in eastern Europe, and his deconstruction was continued by east European maskilim like Smolenskin. But we should not forget that among the maskilim of eastern Europe, there was also an enthusiastic Mendelssohn reception during his own life and in later generations. Thus, Moshe Leib Lilienblum and Eliezer Ben Yehuda strongly opposed Smolenskin's attitude toward Mendelssohn. For the great Russian-Jewish historian Simon Dubnow, Mendelssohn was still a heroic figure, albeit with more modest dimensions than for his German-Jewish predecessors.[18]

While all this is quite well known, the changing image of Mendelssohn in early-twentieth-century central Europe, where he had been the undisputed Jewish hero throughout the nineteenth century, has been less noticed by historians. Alexander Altmann was aware of "the limitations that Mendelssohn's archetypal function suffered in the very last phase of German Jewry. The rise of Zionism on the one hand and the emergence of existentialism on the other tended to render the Mendelssohnian pattern in its political and religious complexion obsolete."[19] He did not analyze this change further, however.

To be sure, in 1929 his two hundredth birthday was celebrated by numerous Jewish communities. In Dessau and Berlin, government ministers and the mayors of the two cities in which he was born and where he lived praised the Jewish philosopher. The Dessau celebration was characterized by the usual long and boring speeches common at anniversary celebrations. As the Berlin *Vossische Zeitung* wrote, this perspective included a condescending look at the provincial setting, "One should have borrowed one of the many bicycle bells for those speeches to abbreviate the ceremony and to expel the funeral atmosphere which is emanating from the hollow sound of the celebrations."[20] The official anniversary service in the Dessau synagogue seemed to be organized in the same spirit. After the Torah portion (*shoftim*) and the prayer for the fatherland, the worshippers listened to Felix Mendelssohn Bartholdy's "Engelterzett für drei Frauenstimmen" from his oratorium "Elija."[21]

German theaters staged special performances of *Nathan the Wise*, and museums arranged exhibits on Mendelssohn. The Prussian State Library in Berlin exhibited more than seven hundred objects related to Mendelssohn, and the Nicolai Haus arranged a musical performance called *Moses, the Model of "Nathan."*[22] As the most lasting contribution to his legacy, three eminent scholars (Ismar Elbogen, Julius Guttmann, and Eugen Mittwoch) began with the publication of the first critical edition of his collected writings. But it was already a sign of the changing spirit that the first volumes of this edition did not sell well. Thus, the annual report of 1931 noted, "The continuation of the Mendelssohn edition is confronted with serious problems, as the sales fell considerably short behind the expectations."[23] And whoever compares the speeches and articles at the bicentenary of his birth in 1929 with those of the centenary of his death in 1886 will note the reduced enthusiasm.

SPIRITUAL SUICIDE

Perhaps least surprising was the critical tone in the German-language Zionist publications of central-eastern Europe, such as the Czernowitz *Ostjüdische Zeitung:* "We know exactly that the ideas of assimilation lead directly to de-Judaization, alienation, and indifference toward everything Jewish, and in the final analysis, to disintegration, and because we know it, in our eyes the image of this noble man, whose 200th birthday is celebrated today, is darkened."[24] The Berlin *Jüdische Rundschau*, Germany's main Zionist voice, was more cautious. It tried to protect Mendelssohn against radical Zionist attacks and emphasized that he stood at the beginning of Jewish renewal. He was also characterized as a "Hebrew writer." Still, his image was a far cry from the heroic figure it had been one hundred, even fifty, years ago. Israel Auerbach's lead article starts by stating how much removed from the hearts of German Jews this important thinker had become during the past century: "He may not have been a great figure compared to the towering figures of history; but he was the greatest among our people on the threshold of new times!" Auerbach accused those closest to Mendelssohn of deviating from his path and falsifying his teaching—of using his name in order to lead German Jews to "spiritual suicide."[25]

Two Zionist-oriented popular histories of the Jews may reflect the changing spirit most clearly. The first one was written by the popular young Berlin rabbi Joachim Prinz just a year after the celebrations for Mendelssohn's bicentenary.[26] For Prinz, Mendelssohn was first and foremost a *Bürger*, a bourgeois spirit—in a context where it served hardly as a name of honor but rather as a synonym for the shallowness of an older generation. In the words of Prinz, Mendelssohn "wanted to become a bourgeois [*Bürger*] at any cost. Thus, everything he has written bears the mark of the bourgeoisie—with all its good and all its narrow elements." The narrow elements were quite visible for a youthful Zionist rabbi such as Prinz: "Mendelssohn became a philosopher of fashion [*Modephilosoph*], certainly also because his philosophy was pleasant [*gefällig*]. . . . His theory of Judaism never had any real impact. . . . The development passed over Mendelssohn. One cannot say that he made history. But one can say that through him his period received a specific character." In Prinz's account, Mendelssohn may have been the archetypical German Jew of the time of Enlightenment but no longer a figure of light for future generations, no longer a hero for young Jewish Germans, a place he reserved for Theodor Herzl.[27]

One year after Prinz's *Jewish History*, Josef Kastein published his *History of the Jews* (1931). Kastein was no rabbi or scholar but a very successful author of historical novels on Shabbetai Zevi, Uriel da Costa, and Süßkind von Trimberg. His Jewish history may not have been the most academic one, but it was certainly the most popular one in the waning days of the Weimar Republic. Let us recall the nineteenth-century depictions of Mendelssohn as the beginning of a new, brighter era, shared unanimously by historians, such as Isaak Markus Jost, Heinrich Graetz, Marcus Brann, and even Simon Dubnow. Kastein's judgment of Mendelssohn could not be further removed from this kind of iconography. He sets out by denying Mendelssohn's oeuvre "any specific originality or creative power." To be sure, Kastein would not doubt Mendelssohn's "most pure and clean intentions," but he disliked the results of his work: the Torah translation was "an enterprise doomed to fail from the outset," and Mendelssohn's definition of Judaism in his philosophic work, *Jerusalem*, had nothing in common with Jewish sources. According to Kastein, Mendelssohn grossly misinterpreted and distorted Judaism; his "product of the ghetto [referring to *Jerusalem*] led to an understanding of a Judaism that never existed." For Kastein, then, Mendelssohn was instrumental in creating a shallow version of a purely rational Judaism, which was disconnected from the depth of its mythical and mystical thought and led to a blind "adoration of ratio and rationalism." Adopting the language of his own time, he juxtaposed shallow civilization with profound culture—Mendelssohn was a typical representative of the first approach.[28] Along with many other German Zionists, Kastein was "awakened" by Martin Buber and identified "authentic" Judaism with east European Hasidism. Just like the historians of the nineteenth century, Kastein too juxtaposed Hasidism with the Berlin Haskalah. But while Mendelssohn and his followers had been their heroes and the Baal Shem Tov's circle their villains, Kastein's judgment was exactly the opposite. He included both groups in one chapter called "Heart and Brain"—and his sympathies went clearly with the heart.[29]

In the more difficult years after 1933, intellectuals with Zionist sympathies, ranging from Joachim Prinz to Hannah Arendt, would distance themselves even further from Mendelssohn's heritage, which by now had lost most of its attraction to a Jewish community not on its way out of the ghetto but on its return into the ghetto.[30]

"WOE TO HIM WHO IS NOTHING BUT A GRANDCHILD"

More remarkable was the development within the Orthodox camp. For most modern Orthodox in the nineteenth century, Mendelssohn was, as we have seen, still a celebrated hero. In Samson Raphael Hirsch's family in Hamburg, Mendelssohn was referred to with great admiration, and as Mordechai Breuer notes, "Hirsch, in his writings, invariably refers to Mendelssohn with emphatic esteem."[31] Indeed, Hirsch explicitly preferred him to the great Moses before him: the medieval philosopher Moses Maimonides. At the centenary of Mendelssohn's death in 1886, all major German-Orthodox journals, the *Israelit, Je-*

Michael Brenner

schurun, and *Die Jüdische Presse*, praised the man who had first lived what was to become their ideal: *torah im derekh eretz*, to observe the religious commandments but at the same time take part in the cultural life of the non-Jewish surroundings. The *Israelit* characterized Mendelssohn as a model for the Jews of today who should succeed in participating in the affairs of the general society while remaining loyal to Jewish religious laws. Its editor Marcus Lehmann was full of praise for Mendelssohn and emphasized that one has to distinguish between the thinker himself and his disciples.[32] *Jeschurun*, edited by Isaak Hirsch, the son of the founder of neo-Orthodoxy, celebrated Mendelssohn as "one of the sages of the world, of the teachers of truth, of the models of virtue. . . . For us, Moses Mendelssohn will always remain the great and noble Jew, to whom we will be forever grateful for what he has done for us."[33]

However, these grandchildren saw both Mendelssohn and their own grandfathers in a more critical light. Mordechai Breuer notes that already before World War I, "all of a sudden, there was talk that Mendelssohn's Bible translation had had bad consequences and had been discredited by East European rabbis. . . . Whereas Mendelssohn had previously been presented as the prototype of a thoroughly modern Jew despite his strict religious observance, he was now said to have been a philosopher rather than an enthusiastic Jew, and he became a liability chiefly for the modern Orthodox school in its capacity as transmitter of Jewish knowledge."[34]

How different from the earlier celebrations was the tone of the Orthodox press at the occasion of the two hundredth anniversary of Mendelssohn's birth. At the opening of the summer semester of 1929 at the Orthodox Rabbinical Seminary, Professor Joseph Wohlgemuth gave a notable speech that he printed in full length in *Jeschurun*, now edited by him. The comparison between Maimonides and Mendelssohn is now fully in favor of Maimonides, and there is not even the slightest mark of praise for Mendelssohn, who is called "a small figure when it comes to Talmudic-Halakhic knowledge." In contrast to the Rambam, Moses of Dessau has never become a "guide of the perplexed," but has been characterized by his enormous passivity when it came to saving Jewish souls. His works are of "average quality and were outdated shortly after their appearance." Mendelssohn is called a "German of Jewish faith," and thereby clearly identified by Wohlgemuth with the Liberal foes of Orthodoxy.[35]

The new leaders of Orthodox Jewry adopted a more critical stance not only toward Mendelssohn but also toward the founder of their movement, Samson Raphael Hirsch. Thus, Wohlgemuth called Hirsch's system "time-bound." First and foremost among those younger critics was Hirsch's grandson Isaac Breuer, whose father had succeeded Hirsch as rabbi in the Frankfurt secessionist community. Isaac Breuer integrated many of those elements that were taboo in nineteenth-century German Orthodoxy: messianic mysticism, Jewish nationalism, and a critical view of emancipation and German patriotism. While the spiritual as well as the physical heirs of Samson Raphael Hirsch claimed to be inheritors of his *torah im derekh eretz* idea, all of them modified this concept substantially. Breuer, Hirsch's physical grandson, expressed his consciousness of the new path he chose by slightly changing a famous quote of Goethe's *Faust*: "Woe to him who is nothing but a grandchild."[36]

"FROM MENDELSSOHN ON . . . THE JEWISHNESS OF EVERY INDIVIDUAL HAS SQUIRMED ON THE NEEDLE POINT OF A 'WHY'"

It seems that many Liberal German Jews in Weimar Germany adopted Breuer's saying when it came to their relationship toward their erstwhile hero. While the general tone among mainstream Liberal German Jews on the occasion of Mendelssohn's two hundredth birthday was respectful, it is impossible to overlook the critical strokes within the generally generous praise. On a popular level, Jewish writers produced anthologies, such as Bertha Badt-Strauss's *Moses Mendelssohn: Der Mensch und das Werk* (Berlin: Welt-Verlag, 1929) or biographies for Jewish youth, such as Jakob Seifensieder's *Moses Mendelssohn: The Fairy Tale of his Life,* which opens with the sentence "Once upon a time there was a poor, frail Jewish lad" ("Es war einmal ein armes, gebrechliches Judenknäblein"). Apart from these fairytale-style stories, no major popular biographies of Mendelssohn appeared in the Weimar years. This stood in striking contrast to the sudden fascination with messianic and mystical figures representing the "darker" and irrational sides of Jewish spirituality, such as David Reuveni or Shabbetai Zvi, or to the continued enthusiasm about Hasidic tales in the aftermath of Martin Buber's collections.

When asked to define Liberal Judaism in a short essay, the Leipzig Liberal rabbi Felix Goldmann wrote about Moses Mendelssohn that he had "contributed little to the religious development" of Judaism; and his friends and successors—much celebrated a generation before—were seen by Goldmann in 1919 as the representatives of "Protestantism in Jewish garb" ("ein jüdisch frisierter Protestantismus").[37] Thus, it may not come as a surprise that in the midst of the Mendelssohn festivities, some authors struck a slightly critical tone.

How does one account for the change of opinion among wide segments of German Jewry, both Liberal and Orthodox, in the less than fifty years between the two Mendelssohn celebrations in 1886 and 1929? Of course, hardly any new documents of the philosopher from Dessau came to light during this period, and the most significant Mendelssohn biography was published by Meyer Kayserling as early as 1862. What had changed was the spirit of the time. Zionism had emerged as a political movement, Orthodoxy had become a more politically oriented movement, and Liberal Judaism in 1929 distanced itself from much of its nineteenth-century tradition. Even the essays praising Mendelssohn as the hero of modern Jewish history emphasized the enormous difference in intellectual environment. Thus, an otherwise positive article by the Breslau Liberal rabbi Hermann Vogelstein stated, "Hardly any of his writings has today a living impact on us. The spiritual tendencies of our time are essentially different from those in Mendelssohn's time, and the greatness of Mendelssohn is not that towering that we could overlook this difference."[38]

One of the crucial differences was the growing distance among both Liberals and Orthodox toward rational thought, with which Mendelssohn was so much identified. Liberal Judaism had undergone a profound transformation since the nineteenth century. The most visible element of this transformation was the abandonment of the traditional liberal principle of belief in human reason and progress as guiding spirits of the time. In comparison to a society in which the ideals of nineteenth-century liberalism were rapidly waning and liberal parties gradually disappeared from the political scene, Weimar Jewry indeed appeared as one of the last strongholds of liberal traditions. Yet, certain fundamentals of Liberal Judaism such as the purely religious definition of Judaism, the dominance of rationalist thought, and "cultural optimism" were weakened during the two decades preceding the Nazi rise to power. When the Jews of Weimar Germany referred to themselves as Liberals they did not necessarily mean the same thing as their ancestors in imperial Germany.

The movement away from reason and rationalism was reflected among Liberal German rabbis during their annual conference in 1921, when one of their leading representatives, the Offenbach rabbi Max Dienemann, delivered a speech called "On the Importance of the Irrational for Liberal Judaism." In this lecture, which amounted to a systematic criticism of nineteenth-century religious Jewish liberalism, Dienemann confessed that the rationalization of Judaism by liberal Jews had torn the roots from the tree of Judaism and gradually dried it out. The time of rationalism belongs to the past, he continued: "it is characteristic of our time that the irrational is dominant, that one cannot answer questions—as has been done in the previous era—out of contemplation, cool examination, rational thought, explanation and scientific orientation, not at all out of clarity, but out of the dark, the instinctive, the inexplicable, the mystical forces." Dienemann, who later became the editor of the prestigious liberal German-Jewish journal *Der Morgen* and the last president of the Liberal rabbinical association in Germany, welcomed this development.[39]

In such an intellectual climate, it would have seemed strange to revere the ultimate rationalist, Moses Mendelssohn, as a hero of modern Jewry. In a contribution to the celebrations of Mendelssohn's two hundredth birthday, Dienemann was more outspoken: "And what is our present position toward [Mendelssohn's statements concerning Judaism and religion]? It is, let us say it openly, a critical position. To be sure, we still enjoy reading of his proud and self-conscious adherence to Judaism . . . , but we cannot overlook the faults inherent in his thoughts; we have come to other conclusions concerning the meaning of religion and Judaism."[40]

As Jost and Graetz had in the nineteenth century, twentieth-century German Jewish thinkers also dated the enormous transformation of Jewish society to the appearance of Mendelssohn. However, they no longer regarded it as the beginning of a rebirth but as the start of a disintegration and atomization.

In a special issue of the *Zeitschrift für die Geschichte der Juden in Deutschland* on Mendelssohn, the Liberal rabbi Max Wiener opened his essay with critical remarks on the transformation of Jewish thought in the Enlightenment. According to Wiener "this period of Jewish spiritual life was not caused by an inner-Jewish transformation, but by the intrusion of alien enlightened European ideas." In contrast to the more favorable judgment of Mendelssohn's ideas as a synthesis between Jewish and European thought, Wiener regarded this new philosophy as an element foreign to Jewish thought. While reserved in his direct criticism of Mendelssohn, Wiener made him responsible for the process of denationalization and depoliticization of Judaism, which ultimately rendered a collective Jewish existence impossible.[41] In an earlier essay, which was free of the aura surrounding Mendelssohn's bicentenary celebrations, Wiener had been more outspoken. Here he had characterized Mendelssohn as a mediocre philosopher but as a personality of lasting influence.[42]

Fritz Bamberger, then a twenty-seven-year-old scholar at the Akademie für die Wissenschaft des Judentums, contributed an important essay to the bicentenary. He analyzed more specifically Johann Georg Hamann's interpretation of his contemporary Moses Mendelssohn but allowed also for some general comments, which are not far removed from Wiener's conclusions. The real achievement of Mendelssohn, according to Wiener, was based on his *Wesen* rather than on his *Werk*—his nature rather than his work. The mere existence of a Jew who was at the same time a philosopher made for an enormous change and left a profound imprint on his surroundings and his heirs.[43]

Shortly before his death in 1929, philosopher Franz Rosenzweig composed a brief introduction to one of the many Mendelssohn celebrations, in which he made clear that, with all due respect, nineteenth-century Jews had already walked in "un-Mendelssohnian fashion" and that, therefore, "we, children of another changing era have to try out new paths."[44] Already in 1923, Mendelssohn's successor as the leading German-Jewish philosopher had noted, "From Mendelssohn on . . . the Jewishness of every individual has squirmed on the needle point of a 'why.'"[45]

This much more cautious evaluation of Mendelssohn was, as we have seen, part of a generally critical mood toward Enlightenment ideas. While Liberal thought was under fire among Jewish Germans, in the German intellectual and political world at large it more or less ceased to exist. Thus, it is hardly surprising that Mendelssohn's illustrious friend, the German philosopher and playwright Gotthold Ephraim Lessing, and especially his play of religious tolerance, *Nathan the Wise*, were seen with critical eyes.

The same year of Mendelssohn's two hundredth birthday, 1929, was also Lessing's two hundredth birthday. And as with Mendelssohn, Lessing too was received as anything but relevant for the new times. No one expressed this more eloquently than Thomas Mann: "A rationalist and enlightener. What does he have to say to us today. . . ? To us, who not only mistrust reason, but adore the irrational? . . . What does he have to say to you? I am afraid, nothing—disregarding the fact that he would have a lot to say to you, and especially to you today, if your ears were not too 'long' for a speech as his."

As Barbara Fischer shows in a recent study of the reception of *Nathan the Wise* in the German public before 1933, a broad variety of critics regarded Nathan's tolerance as outmoded.[46] Even the Jewish reception of Nathan began to change, and for the first time a skeptical undertone could be heard in the still predominantly positive reviews. Zionists, in particular, criticized the universalism of the Nathan parable. Nathan was seen more as a human being than a Jew, and the play was conceived as a prescription for assimilation. Those who still adhered to the spirit of Mendelssohn and Lessing now expressed their deep sorrow that the world around them had moved so far away from that of the two Enlightenment thinkers. Lessing's *Nathan the Wise*, a classic of the German theatrical repertoire, was banned to a spiritual ghetto: only in the Jewish *Kulturbund* could this play be performed, by Jewish actors and to an exclusively Jewish audience. What a tragic irony that 150 years after his death, the very person who had symbolized German Jewry's exodus from the ghetto and who had been immortalized in the figure of Nathan was now forced to return to the ghetto.

Notes

I would like to thank Professor Shmuel Feiner for his valuable comments on this essay.

1. Alexander Altmann, "Moses Mendelssohn as the Archetypical German Jew," in *The Jewish Response to German Culture: From the Enlightenment to the Second World War*, ed. Jehuda Reinharz and Walter Schatzberg, 17–31 (Hanover: University Press of New England, 1985), 18. There has recently been an increase in the literature on the Mendelssohn reception. See, e.g., David Sorkin, "Die zwei Gesichter des Moses Mendelssohn," in *Menora: Jahrbuch für deutsch-jüdische Geschichte* (Munich: Piper, 1993), 275–89; Jacques Ehrenfreund, "Moses Mendelssohn," in *Deutsche Erinnerungsorte*, vol. 3, ed. Etienne Francois and Hagen Schulze, 258–73 (Munich: C. H. Beck, 2001); Jacques Ehrenfreund, "Moses Mendelssohn: la construction d'un herós juif-allemand sous le second Reich," *Les cahiers du Judaisme* 13 (2003): 84–95; Christhard Hoffmann, "Constructing Jewish Modernity: Mendelssohn Jubilee Celebrations within German Jewry, 1829–1929," in *Toward Normality? Acculturation and Modern German Jewry*, ed. Rainer Liedtke and David Rechter, 27–52 (Tübingen: Mohr Siebeck, 2003); Guy Miron, "The Emancipation 'Pantheon of Heroes' in the German-Jewish Public Memory in the 1930s," *German History* 21, no. 4 (2003): 476–503; Christoph Schulte, "Herr Moses war kein Zionist. Zur Rezeption Moses Mendelssohns in Israel," *Mendelssohn-Studien* 14 (2005): 19–29; and Dominique Bourel, "'Mendelssohn ist kein Wunder.' Zur Ikonologie Moses Mendelssohns," ibid., 9–18. Still of fundamental value is Jacob Katz, "Moses Mendelssohns schwankendes Bild bei der jüdischen Nachwelt," in *Moses Mendelssohn und die Kreise seiner Wirksamkeit*, ed. Eva J. Engel and Norbert Hinske, 349–62 (Tübingen: Mohr Siebeck 1994).
2. Michael A. Meyer, *The Origins of the Modern Jew: Jewish Identity and European Culture in Germany, 1749–1824* (Detroit: Wayne State University Press, 1967), 11–56.
3. Christoph Schulte, *Die jüdische Aufklärung: Philosophie, Religion, Geschichte* (Munich: C. H. Beck, 2002), 204.
4. Ehrenfreund, "Moses Mendelssohn," 258.
5. Isaak Euchel, *Toldot rabenu he-ḥakham moshe ben menahem* (Berlin, 1788).

6. Isaak Markus Jost, *Geschichte des Judenthums und seiner Secten*, vol. 3 (Leipzig: Dörffling und Franke, 1859), 293–97.

7. See his *Geschichte der Israeliten seit der Zeit der Makkabäer bis auf unsere Tage*, vol. 8 (Berlin: Schlesinger, 1827), 65, 80.

8. Qtd. in Siegbert S. Prawer, *Heine's Jewish Comedy: A Study of His Portraits of Jews and Judaism* (Oxford: Clarendon, 1983), 416.

9. Heinrich Graetz, *Geschichte der Juden: Von den ältesten Zeiten bis auf die Gegenwart. Ausgabe letzter Hand*, vol. 11 (Leipzig: Oskar Leiner, 1908), 2.

10. Marcus Brann, *Geschichte der Juden und ihrer Litteratur*, vol. 2, 2nd ed. (Breslau: Jacobsohn, 1899), 379–80.

11. Ismar Elbogen, "Zum Geleit," in *Gedenkbuch für Moses Mendelssohn*, 7–10 (Berlin: Verband der Vereine für jüdische Geschichte und Literatur in Deutschland, 1929), 7.

12. Hoffmann, "Constructing Jewish Modernity," 39.

13. Katz, "Moses Mendelssohns schwankendes Bild," 358, 360. For a detailed analysis see Meir Hildesheimer, "The Attitude of the Hatam Sofer Toward Moses Mendelssohn," *PAAJR* 60 (1994): 141–87.

14. See Isaac E. Barzilay, "National and Anti-National Trends in the Berlin Haskalah," *Jewish Social Studies* 21 (1959): 166–92.

15. Qtd. in Isaac E. Barzilay "Smolenskin's Polemic against Mendelssohn in Historical Perspective," *PAAJR* 53 (1986): 11–48, quote on 12.

16. Ibid., 27

17. See the discussion in Dominique Bourel, *Moses Mendelssohn: La naissance du judaisme moderne* (Paris: Gallimard, 2004), S. 31.

18. Simon Dubnow, *Weltgeschichte des jüdischen Volkes. Von seinen Uranfängen bis zur Gegenwart*, vol. 7 (Berlin: Jüdischer Verlag 1930), 364–72.

19. Altmann, "Moses Mendelssohn," 30.

20. *Vossische Zeitung*, October 10, 1929. For an elaborate discussion of the official Mendelssohn celebrations see Ernst G. Lowenthal, "Vor fünfzig Jahren: Das erste große Mendelssohn-Gedenken/Versuch eines Rückblicks," *Mendelssohn-Studien* 4 (1979): 235–75.

21. I found this and other information on the Mendelssohn celebrations in the private archives of the late Professor Simon Rawidowicz. I want to express my gratitude to his son, Professor Benjamin Ravid of Brandeis University, who made these documents available to me. See, e.g., "Mendelssohn-Feiern," in *C.V.-Zeitung* 36 (September 6, 1929), 483.

22. Thomas Lackmann, *Das Glück der Mendelssohns: Geschichte einer deutschen Familie* (Berlin: Aufbau, 2005), S. 427.

23. Günther Holzboog, "Ur-Geschichte der Jubiläumsausgabe," *Mendelssohn-Studien* 4 (1979): 277–92, here 280.

24. Zitiert in Julius H. Schoeps, "Assimilant oder Präzionist? Zur Moses Mendelssohn-Rezeption im Zionismus," in *Deutsche Aufklärung und Judenemanzipation*, ed. Walter Grab, 299 (Tel Aviv: Universität Tel Aviv, 1980).

25. Israel Auerbach, "Zur Mendelssohn-Gedenkfeier," *Jüdische Rundschau*

70 (September 6, 1929): 459; S. Meisels, "Mendelssohn als hebräischer Schriftsteller," ibid.: S. 459–60.

26. Prinz's autobiography, *Rebellious Rabbi*, was edited by Michael A. Meyer (Bloomington: Indiana University Press, 2007).

27. Joachim Prinz, *Jüdische Geschichte* (Berlin: Verlag für Kulturpolitik, 1931), 201–3; on Herzl, 243–48. For Prinz's rejection of the bourgeois spirit, see also his characterization of the new bourgeois Jew as "Der Typus des Kommerzienrats mit der Sehnsucht nach den Offizierspauletten für den Sohn," ibid., 237.

28. Kastein, *Eine Geschichte der Juden*, 513–18.

29. Ibid., S. 519.

30. Christoph Schulte, "Herr Moses war kein Zionist. Zur Rezeption Moses Mendelssohns in Israel," *Mendelssohn-Studien* 14 (2005): 219–29, here 22–24. See Joachim Prinz's conclusion of Mendelssohn's influence on his chidren and pupils, summarized in the phrase: "getauft, getauft, getauft!" Joachim Prinz, *Wir Juden* (Berlin: Erich Reiss, 1934), 56.

31. Mordechai Breuer, *Modernity within Tradition: The Social History of Orthodox Jewry in Imperial Germany* (New York: Columbia University Press, 1992), 57–58.

32. "Moses Mendelssohn," *Der Israelit*, January 4, 1886, 1–4.

33. "Moses Mendelssohn," *Jeschurun*, December 31, 1885, 833–39, here 833 and 839.

34. Breuer, *Modernity within Tradition*, 356.

35. The quotes are taken from Joseph Wohlgemuth, "Moses Mendelssohn und das thoratreue Judenthum," in *Jeschurun* 16 (1929): 321–40, here 321, 331, and 322, consecutively.

36. Goethe's original is "Wehe dir, dass du ein Enkel bist." See *Der Israelit* 47, no. 41 (1906): 11; see also Breuer, *Modernity within Tradition*, 384. In another Orthodox paper, the *Jüdische Presse*, the young Breuer was attacked with the ironic question "Sollte er ein Enkel sein?" ("Should he be a grandchild?"). *Jüdische Presse* 34 (1903): 554.

37. *Das deutsche Judentum. Seine Parteien und Organisationen*, 19–20. In the same sentence Goldmann characterized the last remnants of nineteenth-century radical reform congregations in Germany as "neither able to live nor to die." See also Goldmann, "Taktik oder Prinzip?" *C.V.-Zeitung*, June 25, 1926, 345–46.

38. *Breslauer Jüdisches Gemeindeblatt*, August 1929, 131.

39. Max Dienemann, "Über die Bedeutung des Irrationalen für das liberale Judentum," in *Liberales Judentum. Monatsschrift für die religiöse Erneuerung des Judentums*, vol. 13, Heft 4–6 (1921), 27–32.

40. Max Dienemann, "Moses Mendelssohn's Gedanken über Religion und Judentum," *Israelitisches Gemeindeblatt Mannheim*, August 23, 1929, 7.

41. Max Wiener, "Moses Mendelssohn und die religiösen Gestaltungen des Judentums im 19. Jahrhundert," in *Zeitschrift für die Geschichte der Juden in Deutschland* 1 (1929): 201–12, here 201 and 209.

42. See his "Zur Würdigung der geschichtlichen Bedeutung Moses Mendelssohns," *Der Morgen* 5 (December 1926): 514–22.

43. Fritz Bamberger, "Die geistige Gestalt Moses Mendelssohns," *Monatsschrift für Geschichte und Wissenschaft des Judentums* 3 (1929): 81–92, esp. 92.

44. Franz Rosenzweig, "Vorspruch zu einer Mendelssohn-Feier," *Der Morgen* 4 (October 1929): 374.

45. Frank Rosenzweig, "Die Baulete," *Kleinere Schriften* (Berlin: Schocken, 1937), 110.

46. Barbara Fischer, *Nathans Ende? Von Lessing bis Tabori: Zur deutsch-jüdischen Rezeption von "Nathan der Weise"* (Göttingen: Wallstein, 2000).

Singing New Songs

Translation as a Metaphor for Modernity

RICHARD N. LEVY

Michael A. Meyer began his book *The Origins of the Modern Jew* with a discussion of the work of Moses Mendelssohn, arguably the first "modern" Jew, namely, one who sought to bridge the culture of the (German) Enlightenment with traditional Judaism. One of Mendelssohn's most important works was his translation of the Bible into "pure" (as opposed to Judeo-) German. "For the orthodox," Meyer argues, "it would open the door to culture; for the assimilated it would make possible a return to Torah." It would be, Mendelssohn claimed, "the first step toward culture, something from which my nation, sadly, is kept at . . . remove."[1] The editors of the 1917 Jewish Publication Society's (JPS) Bible translation, *The Holy Scriptures*, believed that Mendelssohn wished to bring Yiddish-speaking European Jews "into closer contact with their neighbours" through the use of his "pure" German text.

Mendelssohn wanted his Bible translation to introduce German Jews to higher culture, a goal shared by the Jewish authors of early English translations as well. Whether due to their translations or other causes, Jews in the West did acquire "culture"—but once they did, would Bible translations only become a means for non-Hebrew speakers to understand the holy text? Mendelssohn in some ways saw his translations as a means to higher cultural ends, but once those were met, would the Bible still have a role to play in the spread of modernity?

Mendelssohn's heirs, upon moving to America, saw the same needs he did: Isaac Leeser published the first widely read Jewish translation of the Hebrew Bible into English, followed by the 1917 JPS translation—both of which were more revisions of the King James Bible than completely new translations. Indeed, the towering place of King James in the English-speaking world threatened to make Jews unschooled in Hebrew believe that what King James said was what the Bible said. In Psalm 2:12, for example, King James translates, "Kiss the Son, lest he be angry, and ye perish from the way. . . . Blessed are all that put their trust in him." Still, the editors of the JPS translation chose to use the elevated, seventeenth-century language of King James rather than a twentieth-century idiom, just as Mendelssohn chose to use "pure" German rather than the "jargon" spoken by most German Jews.

Leeser's translation was very popular—why did the Jewish Publication Society feel the need, in 1892, to contemplate a new one? Several clues are offered in the introduction to the 1917 translation: the growth of the English-speaking Jewish population in the United States, the desire for a translation that would cross Jewish denominational lines, and the need for the "improvement and recasting" of Leeser's work in the light of "the advance of time and the progress made in almost all departments of Bible study." The last criterion suggests that the language of Leeser's translation was found to be a bit dated in an era that presaged the indication that "the English language, unless all signs fail, is to become the current speech of the majority of the children of Israel."[2]

These motives echo Mendelssohn's: to open the Bible to Jews unable to read it in the original and to make a contribution to Jews' appreciation of the vernacular of the country in which they were living, increasingly more securely. Were these motives contradictory? On the one hand, they wished to bring what Meyer identifies as "the assimilated" back to Torah; on the other, by reinforcing Jewish fluency in cultured German and English, it might be argued that they were in some ways contributing to assimilation. Reading through the 1917 JPS translation, one repeatedly senses that it offered Jews a way to appreciate the elegance of King James without the guilt that they might be betraying the Jewish meaning of the Hebrew Bible. Its title even echoed the King James edition, whose official name was "The Holy Bible."

Few of the Hebraically illiterate readers of the 1917 edition could have appreciated that the title was also a direct translation of the traditional Hebrew phrase *kitvei ha-kodesh.*

Translation from Hebrew into an elevated vernacular was in some ways a metaphor for the translation of European and later North American Jews into the refined culture of which they wished to partake, at the same time that they wished to hold on to some basic elements of Jewish tradition. When World War I brought an end to the optimistic reign of high culture in Europe, and the ravages of the Depression and World War II created a social leveling of Americans as well, the English language in America began to reflect this increased democratization. Ernest Hemingway did not write in the elevated style of Henry James, and Jewish writers like Abraham Cahan and Henry Roth joined gentile writers who reproduced the sounds of various forms of immigrant English in best-selling fiction. The committee that produced the Revised Standard Version understood that Protestant Americans no longer spoke the language of King James, and if the Bible was to remain relevant to them, it needed to be rendered in a language closer to the vernacular—without the encumbrances of "thee" and "thou," and verb endings like "eth" and "est."

What was to become of Mendelssohn's criteria now? By the 1950s and 1960s, an English Bible was no longer needed to "open the door to culture," and if such a translation was to bring Jews "into closer contact with their neighbors," how could a Jewish English translation be more useful in this aim than a Protestant one? The only criterion remaining was "for the assimilated, [to] make possible a return to Torah." The course the Jewish Publication Society would take when it convened in 1953 to discuss a new translation was not in doubt. "The proposed translation would reproduce the Hebrew idiomatically and reflect contemporary scholarship, thus laying emphasis upon intelligibility and correctness."[3] In that sense, its goals were similar to the 1917 translation, though this was a new work. A sign that it had closed the door on Mendelssohn's hope that a vernacular Bible translation would lead to a cultural elevation of its readers was this sentence: "The translators avoided obsolete words and phrases and, wherever possible, rendered Hebrew idioms by means of their normal English equivalents."[4] The word *normal* is revealing. Unlike King James, which had helped set a standard for literary English for generations to come, the new JPS translation, like the Revised Standard Version it seems to have emulated, was accessible but hardly elevating. If there was any intention in the minds of the translators to make a contribution to contemporary American literature, it was not apparent.

Richard N. Levy

It took JPS twenty-five years to issue the complete 1917 translation; it took them thirty years to produce three volumes of the complete Tanakh in 1985. But unhappiness with it had already begun to surface even before the second and third volumes were published. American Jews no longer needed a Bible translation to establish their place in American culture. By the time the new translation of the Torah appeared in 1962, writers like Saul Bellow, Bernard Malamud, Herman Wouk, and Arthur Miller were among those who defined what American literature was; in a decade Philip Roth would join them. American English began to embrace more and more Yiddish words; Leonard Bernstein was named conductor of one of the most important American orchestras and was writing music set to Jewish themes and Hebrew texts. Jews no longer had to take steps toward culture in this country; they were helping to shape it. The new JPS translation was at best an imitation of a bland Protestant work, but one done by Jews.

Somewhere in this period, awareness began to grow of a remarkable Bible translation that Martin Buber and Franz Rosenzweig had begun in the 1920s but which had faltered with Rosenzweig's fatal illness and Buber's immigration to Palestine after the Nazis' ascent to power. Unlike Mendelssohn's work, it was not an attempt to introduce Jews to literary German through the Bible but to bring German Jews and gentiles into a knowledge of biblical language through a translation that would re-create the biblical idiom in German. In a sense, they would create a new German idiom to express the Bible. Rosenzweig even created new German words or borrowed from earlier works of German literature "to find forms suitable for rendering certain Hebrew expressions."[5] Writing in 1930, Buber argued that even the Septuagint, Vulgate, and Luther translations "do not aim principally at maintaining the original character of the book as manifested in word choice, in syntax, and in rhythmical articulation [but] rather at transmitting to the translators' actual communities—the Jewish diaspora of Hellenism, the early Christian *oikumene*, the faithful adherent of the Reformation—a reliable foundational document. They accordingly carry over the 'content' of the text into another language" but not reliably the peculiarities of its constituent elements.[6]

In 1983 Everett Fox published an English translation of Genesis based on the Buber-Rosenzweig principles in the Jewish countercultural magazine *Response*. Turning his back on the "normality" principle of the New JPS translation, Fox claimed that heretofore "the premise of almost all Bible translations, past and present, is that the meaning of the text should be conveyed in as clear and comfortable a manner as possible in one's own language. I have sought primarily to echo the style of the original, believing that the Bible is best approached, at least at the beginning, in its own terms." Perhaps alluding to Isaac's famous description of his younger son covered with hair like Esau but with Jacob's speech, Fox adds, "I have presented the text in English dress but in a Hebrew voice."[7] In other words, as Jacob's hairy hands were the means by which Isaac could listen to the voice, Fox's English translation is the means by which a Hebraically ignorant reader can hear the voice of the original. Echoing Buber and Rosenzweig, Fox believes that the text was meant to be read aloud and listened to. He has tried to be faithful to the Buber-Rosenzweig principles that "the translation of individual words should reflect 'primal' root meanings; translation of phrases, lines and whole verses should mimic the syntax of the Hebrew; and that the vast web of allusions and wordplays present in the text should be somehow perceivable in the target language."[8]

In a sense, then, Fox tried to do what the King James translation did in an earlier age: to create a new language in which English speakers (and listeners) could read Biblical Hebrew in their own tongue. The question remains, though: did he succeed?

In Fox's 1995 introduction to his translation of all five books of the Torah, he associated the work with the "explosion of 'literary' study of the Bible," as "numerous scholars have turned their attention to the form and rhetoric of the Biblical text."[9] Nine years later, in 2004, one of the leading proponents of biblical literary criticism, Robert Alter, published his own translation of the Five Books, utilizing some of the Buber-Rosenzweig principles but some of his own as well. While Alter praises Fox's faithfulness to the Hebrew idiom, he faults him for having emphasized the "strangeness of the Hebrew original . . . at the cost of often being not quite English."[10] While Rosenzweig hoped that his and Buber's German translation would expand the boundaries of the German vernacular, Alter seems to suggest that Fox's English version of their work has produced something that is not even in the English vernacular. Alter approves of "giving the English a certain Hebrew coloration" by "imitating many Hebrew idioms"—as William Tyndale did in the translation that led to King James—but in a much more limited fashion than Fox did.[11] He agrees with Fox that "there is no good reason to render Biblical Hebrew as contemporary English," but hopes to forge "a language that is stylized yet simple and direct, free of the overtones of contemporary colloquial usage but with a certain timeless homespun quality."[12] In terms of how to render the endlessly recurring Hebrew letter *vav* (simply, "and"), he would avoid transforming biblical repetitiveness into "elegant synonymous variation"; he also opposes changing the translation of recurring words depending on their context.[13]

Fox's and Alter's groundbreaking works have, in a sense, turned the Mendelssohnian principles on their head. On the one hand, they endeavored to "make possible a return" not only to the content of Torah but its language; on the other, they recognized that contemporary "normal" English is not a language that elevates culture but flattens it, and so they try to create an English garment for biblical Hebrew that will reveal the unique qualities of the Hebrew. The vernacular for them, as opposed to Mendelssohn, is not an end in itself, to whose lofty reaches the Bible should help the newcomer gain access, but it is rather a means to encounter a language that really will elevate them, namely, the Hebrew of the Hebrew Bible. They have also returned to Mendelssohn's practice of writing a translation by one author, able to imprint his own stamp on the work without having to compromise principles to gain the approval of a committee, as the Revised Standard and Jewish Publication Society editorial boards did.

The inadequacy of merely "normal" English for a biblical translation raised its head at least twenty years before Alter's translation appeared. Non-Orthodox American Jews began applying the feminist critique to religious language in general, particularly the use of the masculine gender for God and other entities not necessarily masculine. Reform, Reconstructionist, and Conservative prayerbooks dealt with the issue in the next decade in different ways: choosing gender neutrality over literalness by rendering "He" as "You," repeating the word "God" in place of "He," or combining phrases to eliminate these endless repetitions of "God." But for a long time it was believed that what could work in a prayerbook could not work in a Bible translation, which is not a devotional text where "You" could be appropriate but rather a narrative in which addressing God as "You" would change the entire context of a God described in the third person. In 2001 Rabbi Chaim Stern completed a revised edition of Genesis taking the gender issue into account, and in 2005 the Union for Reform Judaism Press issued a gender-sensitive translation of the complete Five Books of Moses and Haftarot, edited by David E. S. Stein. As Stein describes their method: "We re-examined the Hebrew text's nouns, verbs, inflections, and phrasing in order to determine the (social) gender sense in context. . . . The question became: Is this the sort of thing that the original audience would have presumed that women were (or were not) engaged in? . . . The resulting translation may best be termed "gender accurate." Technically speaking, it is not "gender neutral" because that would have been unfaithful to the biblical text."[14]

For example, the New JPS renders Exodus 16:16 as

This is what the Lord has commanded: Gather as much

as each of you requires to eat, an omer to a person for as many of you as there are, each of you shall fetch for those in his tent.

Fox's translation reads:

This is the word that YHWH has commanded: Glean from it, each-man according to what he can eat, an *omer* per capita, according to the number of your persons, each-man, for those in his tent, you are to take.

Alter's translation reads:

This is the thing that the Lord charged: 'Gather from it each man according to what he must eat, an *omer* to a head, the number of persons among you, each man for those in his tent he shall take.

The New URJ translation reads:

This is what the Eternal has commanded: Gather as much of it as each of you requires to eat, an *omer* to a person for as many of you as there are; you shall each fetch for those in your tent.

The New JPS begins with the nongender-specific "you," but concludes by being faithful to the Hebrew "in his tent." Alter maintains the Hebrew masculine throughout; the New URJ is gender-inclusive throughout. These translations make it clear that if one is to adhere to the Buber-Rosenzweig principles of translation, gender-inclusive translations are hard to come by ("you" is very different from "he"). In a sense, therefore, the New URJ translation has also produced a contribution to English language Bible translation, demonstrating how biblical language can be rectified with the contemporary principle of gender inclusiveness or "gender-appropriateness." And while as the Alter translation makes clear, to do this violates the language of biblical Hebrew (which divides almost all words and particles into masculine or feminine), it does not violate the meaning of it, which seldom intends for words to be understood as intrinsically masculine or feminine. This issue of the form and content of gender, of course, points up one of the fallacies of the Buber-Rosenszweig approaches.

The contemporary concern about gender language reminds us of other contemporary concerns, particularly the concern for recovering the spiritual power of religious texts. Buber, Rosenzweig, and Fox argued that the Bible was meant to be heard, but there is at least one book of the Bible that includes many pieces intended to be sung: the Book of Psalms. The songs proclaiming God's royalty, the psalms of Hallel, the fifteen Songs of Ascents, which the rabbis argued were intended to be chanted as the Levites ascended the fifteen steps of the Temple, are the most obvious ones, but from the model of David strumming his harp to soothe the anguished King Saul, it may be that some of the psalms that articulate the agonies of an ill or terrified person were also intended to be sung. With the knowledge of the musical values of the trope marks in Psalms long forgotten, non-Hebrew speakers are dependent on translations to convey the diverse emotions represented in the book.

But how does one best carry over emotions from one language into another? Buber and Rosenzweig created new words in German, and Fox forged new linguistic combinations in English, but at the beginning of the twenty-first century we can consider another way to expand the vernacular to embrace biblical Hebrew: the rendering of well-known Hebrew words in transliterated Hebrew rather than in translated English. In Psalm 95, for example, one of the psalms the Lurianic kabbalists chose to welcome the Shabbat bride, the Hebrew of verse 1 reads: "L'khu n'ran'nenah l'Adonai, nari'ah l'tzur yishenu." The New JPS renders this: "Come, let us sing joyously to the Lord, raise a shout for our rock and deliverer." But what leader, trying to inspire a chorus, would speak in such formal terms as "let us sing joyously"? And wouldn't it be nice to reproduce the repetition reflected in the "n" sounds in *n'ran'nenah?*

I would suggest this translation: "Come, let's sing to God! / Let's make a *t'ruah* sound before the Rock of our triumph!" There is no rule that translations need to be so formal as to rule out contractions. "Let's" conveys a spontaneity that might encourage joyful singing by the group the speaker is addressing. And while *Adonai* is generally translated "the Lord" or "the Eternal," the single syllable "God" conveys the enthusiastic spontaneity more than the multisyllabic translations for *Adonai.* To reproduce the root of the Hebrew *nari'ah* through the well-known shofar sound *tru'ah* is more evocative than "raise a shout." And while we have not echoed the repeating "n" sounds of *n'ranenah,* to combine *tru'ah* with "triumph" creates a new alliteration in the latter half of the verse.

Another use of Hebrew in translation can be found in the next psalm, 96, verse 11: "Yism'hu ha-shamayim v'tagel ha-aretz; yir'am ha-yam um'lo-o." The New JPS renders this: "Let the heavens rejoice and the earth exult; let the sea and all within it thunder." I would suggest instead: "Make a *simḥa* in the heavens, let earth rejoice, / Let the waves thunder, and all sealife sing!" Again, by using a word with the same root as *yism'ḥu*, which is well-known to Jewish readers, one can get closer to the meaning of the Hebrew word. "Make a *simḥa*" may thus be more evocative of the mood than an English substitution. "Let all sealife sing" is an attempt to echo the alliteration of *yiram ha-yam* with a repetition of different sounds.

To introduce Hebrew roots into the translation is a mark of how far we have come from the translation criteria of Moses Mendelssohn. The culture that contemporary Bible translations reflect is one in which Yiddish participates for American Jews and, to some extent, for non-Jews, and a Jewish translator is not afraid to introduce a Hebrew word (*tr'uah*) that large numbers of Jews know, and which other Jewish and non-Jewish readers may come to know through a commentary. A contemporary translation may take into account the fact that some Hebrew words have become part of the vocabulary of ordinary Jews, and that to use them can evoke richer meaning than some English equivalents. Jews who attend Rosh Hashanah services (a large number) will hear a sound in the word *t'ruah*, which will help them understand the meaning of a verb with the same root even more easily than they would understand Fox's method of creating an artificial mixture of two English words that do not relate to each other (a kind of lexical *shaatnez*).

Furthermore, when trying to echo a mood in Hebrew through the very different language of English, some playfulness (like using contractions) may well be in order. The 1917 JPS translation reflected a time when English was a much more formal language; by its surrender to "normality," the New JPS translation also surrendered formality. The psalm translations, like the translations in the Buber-Rosenzweig spirit, do not attempt to reproduce "normal" English. Rather, they introduce the reader not only to the meaning of a psalm but also to its mood, so that the person reading it can echo the mood of the writer (or singer). Exclamation points can help too. These translations are meant not only to be read but also to be applied—to be taken up as a vehicle for celebration or for commiseration.

Using a well-known Hebrew variation of an otherwise unfamiliar Hebrew root is only one way of conveying meaning of an original text. A more controversial solution is to explain the meaning by adding words to the text. The New JPS translation of Psalm 96:1 is "Sing to the Lord a new song, / sing to the Lord, all the earth." But what is a "new song"? Kohelet (1:9) argues that there is nothing new under the sun—that is, in the human sphere. Every human melody must be merely a reworking of previously created notes. If it is to God that we are to sing this song, this injunction would seem to call for a radically innovative human creation—but given the limitation of existing musical notation, how is this possible? (One thinks of the attempts of the serialists like Arnold Schoenberg or minimalists like John Cage). Here is an attempt to deal with these questions:

> Sing to God a new song,
> Sing all earth,
> As though Song itself were new!

To approach composition not only as though this particular melody were unprecedented but as though the whole genre of song were coming into being with this composition is to suggest that if indeed the whole earth were to break forth into song, that would be something that had never existed before—and it calls upon the reader of the psalm to imagine what such a radically new song might sound like.

Another advantage of adding explanatory words to the translation can be found in Psalm 96:5:

> What the nations allow to rule them Are empty clods,
>   mere godlets—
> But Adonai made the very heavens above!

A literal translation of the first line would be "For all the gods of the nations are *elilim*," a word the New JPS translation renders as "mere idols." But this translation limits the first line to its own time in the Bible when the non-Israelite nations worshiped a pantheon of deities and often made little statues to represent them. But the "new song" of this psalm seems intended to apply to all times, so a translation is called for that would attack contemporary practices as well as ancient ones. From the writings of Karl Marx and Erich Fromm (*You Shall Be as Gods*), we know that a false god is something to which a person or a nation has given power, hence the translation, "What the nations allow to rule them." The word *elilim* is a mocking diminutive of *El* (God) in the plural, describing idols often made of earth, compared with the God who made heaven and earth—hence the coined translation "godlets."

We have thus come to a remarkable place in the life of English Bible translations in the United States. The early translations, following Mendelssohn's principles, were attempts to uncover the mysteries of the Bible in a vernacular whose elevated style would in turn elevate the Jewish reader new to the Enlightenment (or to American shores). Now, however, we have reached a place where some parts of biblical language itself have woven themselves so thoroughly into the vernacular that they do not need translation. In addition, rather than elevating readers through the quality of the vernacular translation, translators attempt to elevate them through the biblical language itself, in Buber-Rosenzweig Hebrew-English, in the use of Hebrew words, or in a vernacular style that conveys the mood of the Hebrew. Far from being a vehicle for elevation, the contemporary American English vernacular has become a language in *need* of elevation. It is biblical Hebrew that is charged with elevating it, as it elevated Jacobean English three hundred years ago. It is as though Hebrew—which, as the language of Creation, the rabbis considered the mother of all the seventy languages humans speak—is reclaiming its parentage, giving nurture to one of its youngest offspring, American English. One of the clues that we may have moved beyond modernity is that the quintessential languages of modern culture are now being expanded by the ancient language of Hebrew, much as the rediscovery of ancient Greek and Latin moved the Western world beyond the Middle Ages into the Renaissance.

A major part of Michael A. Meyer's life-work has been the translation of German Jewish culture to an American, and particularly an American Jewish, audience. Sublimely fluent in German, English, and Hebrew, Meyer has worked for forty years to acquaint American Jews with the noble culture that we thought the Nazis had destroyed. How fitting that as we celebrate the fortieth anniversary of *The Origins of the Modern Jew*, German Jewish culture is on the rise again in the land that originally nurtured it, and American Jews familiar with Meyer's oeuvre are able to embrace that culture and the promulgators of it in large part because he has prepared us. To paraphrase Meyer's description of Mendelssohn, quoted at the beginning of this essay, "Meyer has opened the door to German Jewish culture for us, even as the assimilated heirs of Mendelssohn have returned Torah to their homeland."

Notes

1. Michael A. Meyer, *The Origins of the Modern Jew: Jewish Identity and European Culture in Germany, 1749–1824* (Detroit: Wayne State University Press, 1967), 42–43.
2. Preface, *The Holy Scriptures* (Philadelphia: Jewish Publication Society, 1955), vi.
3. Hebrew-English Tanakh, preface to the 1985 English edition, *The Holy Scriptures* (Philadelphia: Jewish Publication Society, 2003), xxiii.
4. Ibid., xxiv.

Richard N. Levy

5. Everett Fox, trans. *The Five Books of Moses* (New York: Schocken, 1995), xxi.
6. Martin Buber and Franz Rosenzweig, *Scripture and Translation*, trans. Laurence Rosenwald with Everett Fox (Bloomington: Indiana University Press, 1994), 74.
7. Fox, *Five Books*, ix.
8. Ibid., x.
9. Ibid., xxiii.
10. Robert Alter, trans. *The Five Books of Moses* (New York: Norton, 2004), xix.
11. Ibid., xxxvi.
12. Ibid., xxxii.
13. Ibid., xxiv–xxv.
14. David E. S. Stein, ed. *Five Books of Moses and Haftarot* (New York: Union for Reform Judaism Press, 2005), xxviii–xxix.

| 6 |

Cultural Explorations
in Modern Jewish Life

Reflections on Jewish Nostalgia in the Era of Globalization

RICHARD I. COHEN

Modern Jews have been challenged repeatedly in the last centuries by ideological, political, and cultural tendencies and have responded in myriad ways. Much of Michael Meyer's esteemed career as a historian has been devoted to studying the preoccupation of European and American Jews from the eighteenth century onward with these modern challenges and looking at their reconfigurations in the areas of Jewish religion and culture. He has constantly tried to decipher what it meant for the modern Jew to fashion an existence within these turbulent currents, often turning to some of the most creative minds in German-Jewish history to uncover the parameters of their identity. Indeed, the sifting process of modern Jewry is what has urged Michael on and on, as a prolific and insightful historian of modern Jewry and as a wonderful human being and committed Jew, whose underlying credo from *The Origins of the Modern Jew* until today has remained firm: "to be a Jew vigorously in the modern world will continue to mean confronting new external enticements, sorting them out, and seeking to integrate those that do not contradict the fundamental principles of the Jewish tradition."[1] Globalization is one of the newest "external enticements" and deserves to be looked at from its challenge to the modern Jew and how it is being confronted. Within the perspective of the last centuries, globalization in its present varieties appears to be less dramatic than some earlier developments that rocked Jewish life from their basic moorings, but it shares some of the potential for future upheavals.

By way of contrast, no one looking at Jewish life in 1789, on the eve of the French Revolution, could imagine how the emancipation process would affect the lives of Jews in most countries. In every possible field of endeavor, Jews were transformed by the change in their legal status. Simon Dubnov was correct in seeing the revolution as a cataclysmic moment that augured well for the Jews but also threatened to disrupt their internal unity were they not prepared to assert their communal needs. Stereotypical images of Jews fell by the wayside, and new ones emerged as Jews developed new relationships with the countries in which they resided; emerging from their "ghettolike" existence into citizens deeply involved in the countries they inhabited, Jews in Europe redefined their attachments to Judaism and the state. Characteristic of their new sense of affiliation was the notion of being "Germans of the Mosaic faith," a form of identification that emerged in Germany at the beginning of the nineteenth century but had close parallels in other central and western European countries.

Whereas in Europe it was emancipation that contributed significantly to the tremendous upheaval in Jewish identification, it was the effect of westernization during the nineteenth and twentieth centuries that ruptured the apparent unity of Jewish communities in Islamic countries and resulted in the changing terrain of the nature of belonging to Jewish religion and the resident country. Jews in Islamic countries gravitated to the urban centers as they did in Europe, and their presence in Baghdad, Casablanca, and Tunis was no less impressive than what it became in Odessa, Prague, and Vienna. They became diversified in belief, political identification, and social and economic class and took an active role in the changing ideological and political philosophies that emerged during these centuries. True, in Europe and under Islam, they often gave these currents a certain spin, adjusting and molding them to unique forms, but large elements of Jewish society responded to these challenges by drafting them into their personal and communal existence. Yet these encounters with the ever-developing terrain of politics and culture that often modified the sense of attachment to Judaism or transformed it completely (what Meyer has called the "reconceptualization of Judaism") tended to create a certain longing for the world that was, prior to that transformation. One particular expression of that longing, nostalgia, took on diverse forms in the last two centuries and became a creative cultural mode that existed side by side with the developments in modern society and affected

Richard I. Cohen

Jews in various contexts. Forms of nostalgia in the age of globalization will engage us in this essay in the spirit of Meyer's continued search to unravel "the complex grappling with modernity."[2]

Scholars of nostalgia, and the phenomenon does exist, have detected two kinds of nostalgia in one's relationship to the past, to the "imagined community," to home, to one's own self-perception—restorative and reflective nostalgia. According to Svetlana Boym, "Modern nostalgia is a mourning for the impossibility of mythical return, for the loss of an enchanted world with clear borders and values; it could be a secular expression of a spiritual longing, a nostalgia for an absolute, a home that is both physical and spiritual, the edenic unity of time and space before entry into history."[3] In the era of globalization, where virtual reality allows one to be seemingly drawn into feeling part of a global village, nostalgia is no less powerful. Following Boym and others, it appears that in such situations nostalgia emerges and helps recreate the lost home and reconstitute gaps in memory, though the agents involved in this process would not consider themselves to be engaged in nostalgia but in creating truth. This is rampant among national and nationalist revivals all around the world. They engage in the antimodern myth-making of history by means of returning to national symbols and myths that often manifest themselves in reconstructions of monuments of the past. Physical objects are invoked to compensate for the sense of loss. The imperfect process of remembrance evokes expressions of nostalgia—dreams of another place and time and even a certain longing on ruins, on physical authenticity in the past.

Boym's appreciation of the need to find solace from the vacuum created by modern life seems to apply admirably to the quest of many contemporary Jews. It is not the individual psyche that I am interested in pursuing but the ways in which Jewish individuals and Jewish collective remembrance interrelate with one another. Jews, who underwent tremendous cataclysms in the last century, and I am not alluding to the Holocaust alone but also to mass dislocations from their homeland (be it from Islamic countries or from Europe), have had to find ways to explore the incongruities of the past and present, and no less now in the era of globalization. Jewish individual and collective memory meet and unfold in this longing for the lost home and the desire to fill in the lost memory.

I will begin by looking briefly at three short literary vignettes of the last decade that appeared in Israel and America that appear to me relevant to this phenomenon. The first is Amoz Oz's epic quasi-autobiographical *A Tale of Love and Darkness*.[4] My interest here is to relate to the resounding success of the book in Israel. It is not my concern whether Oz (the agent in this case) was trying to provoke nostalgia among his readers but rather the way they have read it. Its appearance in Israel sparked immediate involvement of the readers. They reveled in its detailed descriptions of Jerusalem in the forties before the creation of Israel, found themselves passionately absorbed in the sensitive and imaginative reconstructions of Oz's east European roots and moved by the tragic elements of the family saga. Oz delved into his own autobiography, his experiences as a city teenager on the kibbutz, his family's failures and tragedy, and the quest for connection and identification with the world of his forefathers. He touched a sensitive nerve among the contemporary Israeli reading public—especially among the Ashkenazic public. He revived in them something of their past and captured the longing of at least two generations for their lost past, for the sense of an imagined homeland. *A Tale of Love and Darkness* engaged these generations of Israelis especially as it was the creation by the Sabra, par excellence, who while depicting premodern Israel through his own autobiography, shorn of the heroism associated with the mythic Sabra, penetrated deeply into the recent *galut* experience, sensitively and tenderly. It resonated among his generation, now seeking the "authentic" past, and a younger generation, already looking for the link to the previous world. The penultimate Sabra, Amos Oz, was no longer *creatio ex nihilo*. He emerged from the *galut* and accorded it and the vicissitudes of life in the *galut* (in Poland, Ukraine, Russia, and Germany) a veritable legitimacy. Both worlds—the local and the global—resonated in this epic; they seemed to reside together in harmony, upsetting neither the "here" nor the "there."

Oz created the link between the world that was and the present in an integral way, touching the ambiguities of the collective sensibility of many Israelis, arousing in them a profound sense of identification and nostalgia—and possibly a longing for their own childhood. It was also the language that had a message—a clearer and more modern Hebrew than that of Agnon, free of the constant intimations and allusions to Jewish sources but not free from the past. Israeli readers, increasingly dependent upon globalized fibrespace, were transformed temporarily into a community awash in nostalgia, open to allowing different worlds to cohabit together.

Baghdad Yesterday, a slim collection of autobiographical memoirs by Professor Sasson Somekh, illuminates the life of bourgeois Jews in Baghdad prior to their immigration to Israel with the creation of the state. Born in Baghdad in 1933, Somekh immigrated to Israel in 1951 and pursued a career in contemporary Arab literature. Poignantly, Somekh gives vent to his profound attraction to the world that was his childhood, sensing that if his generation will not reveal it, the world of his forefathers would be lost to future generations. His genre is very different from that of Oz's—he is explicit about his purpose. Here too the nostalgic rendezvous with the past is not a private affair; voluntary and involuntary recollections intertwine with collective memories of Jews from an "eastern" (in particular, Iraqi) background who have allowed their past to be hidden, clouded by certain distressing events. Reliving summer nights on the Euphrates, remembering his high school literature teacher, recalling the sounds and smells of the street they lived on, Somekh gave pride of place to the profound and intimate connection to the physical place and the human contact. Baghdad comes alive in a different veneer from its role in the apparent global confrontation between west and east, and Baghdad Jewry emerges as a thriving Diaspora at the cusp of modernization, secular and western in orientation and proud of its historic connection.

Without glorifying the world that disappeared, Somekh was concerned that the succeeding generations "would also hear of the story of the remarkable partnership that characterized the life of Jews in the Arab world for 1500 years." Perhaps, what Somekh and others (e.g., Naim Kattan's *Farewell, Babylon: Coming of Age in Jewish Baghdad* [2005]) missed most as a result of the historical cataclysm and exile was not simply the past and the homeland but rather this potential space of cultural experience that one has shared with one's friends and compatriots that is based neither on nation nor religion but on elective affinities. The desire to retrieve that world in some fashion and overcome the overriding, conflictual image of Jews and Arabs lay at the basis to Somekh's memoirs.

Susan Rubin Suleiman's autobiographic memoir of Budapest provides a powerful response to the question under study—does globalization and postmodernism transcend history and memory or does it provoke the desire to engage in the memories of the past?[5] She writes, "One is the child not only of one's parents. History too nourishes us or deprives us of nourishment."[6] She left Hungary in 1949 at the age of ten, became an American, and forgot Budapest, though her native tongue, Hungarian, was never forgotten, even if it was "frozen in time." She spoke little of her past to her children, "as if my past had never existed."[7] Prior to her mother's death, she took her children to Budapest for two weeks, a visit that began the rekindling of a relationship with Budapest and the Hungarian language, and a certain reliving of her childhood. Suleiman summarizes in a postmodern vein her own appreciation of the diary she herself wrote in large part in 1993 after the fall of communism:

> It's the story of a woman's return, after many years of forgetfulness, to a city she once called home. Her peculiar rela-

tion to the city is best summed up as a relation to language: she speaks its language like a native, but with an accent. In the process of rediscovering the city as an adult—unforgetting what she once knew, learning what she never had a chance to know—she comes to experience it as home; but not *the* home, sentimentalized, found again at last. Rather, Budapest becomes one of the places where she feels at home, a city with a river running through it.[8]

The breakdown of communism—a central peg in globalization—brought with it the breakdown of boundaries and the physical and emotional accessibility to the past. Suleiman controls her memoir carefully, never allowing it to fall into a narcissistic preoccupation, but allows the reader to gain the sense of how she gradually reclaimed the city of her birth.

Preoccupation with the past is common to these three literary vignettes. In the face of succumbing to the worship of modernity and its obliteration of the past, these authors all evoke a profound association with a physical territory that is not part of their daily life. Their personal life stories cannot be molded or framed within their national existence alone, almost as if a certain codependency exists between their new lives and their past ones. But this expression did not come in their earlier years. All three of the authors are in their sixties or early seventies and had accomplished themselves in their respective fields prior to delving openly into their private realm. To my mind they, and many of their readers, reflect a broader phenomenon that encompasses many individuals, Jews and others, which Erik Erikson has described as "the collective need of human adults, between the complex process of having been 'brought up' and a certain terminal 'decline,' to affirm ceremonially with whom they have grown up and whose standing in the world they now share."[9] Erikson points to a moment in an adult's life when the individual is urged to find some contact with the past and overcome the sorrow accompanying the passage of time.

Clearly, Jews who have witnessed and were at the centers of wars, cataclysms, dislocations, and catastrophes in the twentieth century are inevitably drawn into this process that is usually accompanied by a modicum of nostalgia. Globalization threatens to level experiences and erase the difference between phenomena. But it apparently does not nullify this personal, and collective, search but possibly magnifies it, or at least sharpens the contradiction between the local and the global. At the least, its breakdown of barriers and borders lends itself to giving expression both to the local and the more global experience. The plethora of memoir literature in the last two decades, a sample of which I have discussed here, is evidence of the recurrent need to reattach oneself to a distinctive past, notwithstanding virtual reality.

But as a result of the physical and political developments of the end of the century the physical visit to the homeland, or to the home now disappeared or destroyed, is even more widespread than memoir literature. No virtual reality can replace this longing for something tangible. The last decade has seen a tremendous rise in the reencounter with the "homeland"—be it Poland, Germany, Morocco, Ukraine, and so on—not necessarily by the native sons and daughters themselves but by their offspring and descendants. Certainly the ability to reach these countries has changed dramatically over the last two decades and with it a cottage industry has emerged, encompassing many elements, around the visit to the homeland. Its "popularity," and I should say, public utilization, has occasioned criticism from different circles, especially with regard to organized visits to the concentration camps. Bernard Wasserstein has characterized the involvement by contemporary Jews as "an almost necrophiliac obsession." Polemic writers like Norman Finkelstein have treated many of these trips as serving the "Holocaust industry," largely trumped up to serve Zionist machinations, while the popular Israeli satiric ensemble known as the *chamishiya hakameri* lampooned these visits on public television by presenting them, *inter alia*, as a ploy by travel agents to attract business.

Yet, notwithstanding some of their more crass aspects, the visits to the death camps, to sites of destruction, to towns and cities once populated with vibrant and extensive Jewish communities, endow the visitor with the ability to reimagine the world that was, preoccupy oneself with personal and collective memory, and create a nostalgic bond, in the restorative sense, with the past. The renewed physical presence of the "home country" in the lives of immigrant and native Jews, in Israel and elsewhere, has given greater legitimization to that past, and has endowed the former world with a certain aura that often overshadows its more variegated nature. One's national existence, be it Israeli, American, French, or other, is no longer sufficient—one yearns for some mechanism in which the attachment to and nostalgia for the past cohabits with the present. Selectivity of the past dominates this form of nostalgia. A sense of sacred that seems to be missing from the modern world is restored, even if momentarily.

Distinctive Jewish museums have joined memoir literature and travels to the homeland as expressions of the nostalgia for the world that disappeared. Certainly many other cultural and ideological tendencies joined hands in the creation of the plethora of Jewish museums across the world, but nostalgia has its specific contribution. Part of the extensive phenomenon of museum building in western society, Jewish museums often resonate with a certain apologetic, enabling the visitors, Jews and non-Jews, to sense that they are encountering a unique culture that needs to be granted its due in the historic process, notwithstanding the homogenizing ideology of globalization. Couched in terms such as "precedence," "antiquity," "continuity," "coherence," "heroism," and "sacrifice," exalting the unique heroes and virtues, and celebrating success (in some cases), stability, and progress, Jewish museums have asserted their presence in the public space. Providing a neutral territory, where Jews and non-Jews of all backgrounds can mingle and interact, the Jewish museums have struggled to grant Jews and Judaism an entity that is not easily confined to one element or another of their identity.

Museum curators are often bent on different agendas from those of their visitors, especially of their Jewish visitors, who commonly seek in the museum a vehicle through which they can remember (often nostalgically) a certain past. The objects are granted a symbolic role in this process. Marc Chagall's paintings are exemplary of this. Many become attached to them for the associations alluded to: refugees, observant Jews, beggars, rabbis, butchers, lovers, roosters, simplicity, snapshots of the old world and the new, are celebrated as connections to roots—far from the global erasure of distinction. It is part of the internal dialogue that Jews have created with eastern Europe—wanting to preserve artificially the sense of its pristine nature and traumatic element—almost to preserve the mythic story of "from rags to riches." That nostalgic image has recently been seriously and cogently challenged by Ben Nathans in his book on Jews in late imperial Russia, in which he describes the rise of a very visible Jewish element that integrated impressively into the higher echelons of Russian society. Wealth, education, mobility marked their lives.[10] Yet the nostalgic drive will not easily succumb to scholarship. The "successful" Jews are not part of Chagall's baggage; neither are they part of the nostalgic memory of the past; yet they were very much part of the Russian-Jewish experience of the turn of the century. Celebration of that aspect of the Jewish past is not a common museological agenda in Jewish museums, neither in those organized by Jews nor in those organized by non-Jews, as it does not seem to feed on the restorative nostalgia of the post-Holocaust generation.

Finally—and here I am going out on a limb and into troubled waters, but I will do so nonetheless and only telegraphically—as we witness a significant, and surprising (contradicting most theorists of modernization), upsurge of ultra-Orthodox communities in Europe, America, South Africa, and Israel, among which one finds individuals who have acculturated dramatically to globalization in some respects, we are struck by the apparent attraction to and return of the external appearance of the ultra-Orthodox among new age Jews. Whether they be youthful, right-wing fanatics in the hills of the West Bank—the *naarei hagvahot* (youth of the hills)—or enthusiastic followers of R. Nachman of Bratslav, who join the pilgrimage to his grave in Uman for *Rosh Hashana*, or hard-core offspring of Orthodox families, the external appearance seems to create a nostalgic link to the apparent, authentic Jew of the past. The contradictions seem to be in themselves appealing. Cellular phones, digital cameras, laptops, sidecurls, large white *kippot*, and *tallit katan* (though by no means small) worn as an outer garment, as if to say to the global community—we are distinct—are the male aspects of this counter-culture; the females present a similar throwback to the nostalgic image of the eastern European Jewish housewife. This nostalgic admiration for paradise lost in an attempt to retrieve paradise is one of the more fascinating acts of cultural resistance to the hegemonic ideology of globalization.

To conclude, the cultural expressions that I have alluded to—memoir literature, travel to the "homeland," Jewish museums, and forms of Jewish religious behavior—have certainly many sources other than nostalgia, but they all share a common longing to return to the pristine, authentic, and distinct past. In the era of globalization, bent on heralding the mutual and universal features of society, these cultural developments emphasize the luring attraction to upset the homogenizing ideology of universalism and globalization. They bring us back to, and confirm, the quest for survival within modernity that Michael Meyer has labored so creatively to illuminate within modern Jewish history: "that, even as it [modernity] threatens to swallow up the faith of a diminishing minority, [it] also offers the possibility for differentiation, development, and renewal."[11]

Notes

1. Michael A. Meyer, *Jewish Identity in the Modern World* (Seattle: University of Washington Press, 1990), 85.
2. Michael A. Meyer, *Judaism within Modernity: Essays on Jewish History and Religion* (Detroit: Wayne State University Press, 2001), 11.
3. Svetlana Boym, *The Future of Nostalgia* (New York: Basic Books, 2001), 8.
4. Amos Oz, *Sippur al ahava vaḥoshekh* [A tale of love and darkness] (Jerusalem: Keter, 2002).
5. Susan Rubin Suleiman, *Budapest Diary: In Search of the Motherbook* (Lincoln: University of Nebraska Press, 1996).
6. Ibid., 7.

7. Ibid., 9.

8. Ibid., 14.

9. Erik H. Erikson, ed., *Adulthood* (New York: Norton, 1978), 20.

10. Benjamin Nathans, *Beyond the Pale: The Jewish Encounter with Late Imperial Russia* (Berkeley: University of California Press, 2002).

11. Meyer, *Judaism within Modernity*, 10.

From Klausner to Oz and Back

Arnold J. Band

As early as his first book, *The Origins of the Modern Jew* (1967), it was clear that Michael A. Meyer was not restricting himself to the actual topic of research, modern German Jewry, but was rendering a coherent formulation of a broader experience, the modernization of the Jews. The modern Jewish experience in its totality has been his obsession throughout his productive career, and those who have known him since the early days of his emergence as a Jewish historian have understood that this preoccupation was not merely academic. The child of German Jews who found refuge in Los Angeles, he personally experienced one of the landmark events in modern Jewish history. He was fortunate to find in that city a mentor, the charismatic rabbi Max Nussbaum, who embodied a rare combination of several of the most attractive features of German Jewry: a profound erudition in Jewish history, a commitment to Jewish communal life, and a deep love of Zion. Unlike his mentor, however, Meyer went on to become one of the leading Jewish historians of his generation; he wrote and made Jewish history.

The generation of Jews who fortunately escaped Europe when it was still possible to do so invites more intense historical scrutiny than it has received to date. I offer here in honor of Michael Meyer a study of an amazing book by a Jewish writer whose parents also fled Europe in those perilous days and found refuge not in Los Angeles but in Jerusalem. I refer to Amos Oz and his novel *Sipur al ahavah vaḥoshekh* (*A Tale of Love and Darkness*). Meyer and Oz were born about the same time to parents who were displaced by the rise of fascism in Europe. Their lives, of course, were radically different: Meyer grew up in America, while Oz was raised in the Yishuv, later Israel, and Meyer did not undergo the personal family trauma Oz did when he was twelve years old. Nevertheless, while Meyer writes history and Oz ordinarily writes fiction, in this book Oz transgresses the boundaries between history and fiction and recreates the early days of his life in Jerusalem. To do so, he has both availed himself of historical sources and generated quasi-historical scenes. A study of the portrait he has achieved invites serious speculation on the very act of historiography.

"The portrait of the artist as a young man" is such a pervasive paradigm in modern literature that it needs no theoretical elaboration or justification. The category that interests us most here is the time perspective. We ask: Is the supposed self-portrait primarily looking forward toward future adventures or writing, or backward to past experiences often described or understood for the first time? Joyce's *Portrait of the Artist as a Young Man* is a classic example of the first, while Amos Oz's novel *Sipur al ahavah vaḥoshekh*, is the second. For the literary critic, the very existence of such a hybrid document—part history, part fiction, part verifiable fact, and part the author's interpretation of fact—is always intriguing. It raises all sorts of interpretive possibilities and sheds light on the author's other works, usually openly declared works of fiction.

In a densely wrought work like *Sipur al ahavah vaḥoshekh*, which covers roughly the first seventeen years of the author's life (1939–56) but was written more than fifty years and many books later, the interwoven narrative strands invoke all sorts of interpretive strategies. By titling this essay "From Klausner to Oz and Back," I obviously refer to the dual movement of the book; we have the plot line through which the author tells us of his childhood as Amos Klausner and his break with the world of "the Klausners"—his father and his renowned grand-uncle Joseph Klausner ("Hadod Yosef"). It continues when he joins the kibbutz and changes his name to Amos Oz, then revisits this life through the narrative of the mature author around the year 2000, who reexamines and tries to make peace with this fracture. This dual movement generates and shapes the pervasive ambivalence of the book, certainly one of its most intriguing characteristics. There are, to be sure, many other motifs, including the desultory powerful meditation on his mother's suicide, but few, we would argue, are so dominant as the author's interpretation of his own intellectual development.

The most dramatic way to enter this world is not from the opening or the closure of the novel, but rather from the climactic chapter 52 [51] (474–84 [423–37]) in which, according to the author, "It was at this point that it happened. The Fall. The expulsion from Paradise" (479 [429]).[1] The scene described after this retrospective announcement is the high comic speech of Menahem Begin during which the author, then a boy of twelve years, explodes in uncontrollable laughter, embarrassing the family and all their friends and bringing upon him the sharp slaps of his ordinarily gentle paternal grandfather. The mock-serious introduction to the now famous Begin passage is crucial for two seemingly contradictory reasons: it is ironic and yet it introduces and highlights what turns out to be the ideological climax of the entire novel. To understand it and its relevance, the reader should have already grasped both the historic background that precedes it and the ambivalent tenor of the discourse in which it is conveyed. This clearly delineated scene, after all, appears well into the book. By then, the reader has read many pages of discourses about the author's childhood in Kerem Avraham, about the family (especially Hadod Yosef) and his father's Revisionist friends, about long digressions through family histories, both paternal and maternal, his childhood education and fantasies, and the first agonized reference to the traumatic suicide of his mother (245 [201]). His ambivalence suffuses the entire novel, with the possible exception of more straightforward historical passages dealing with the history of the family (105–235 [81–201]). Even the opening sentence, "Noladti vegarti bedirat-karka ketana me'od" (I was born and bred in a tiny low-ceilinged, ground floor apartment), can be read as both a statement of fact and the parodic opening of the autobiographical novel. The author, after all, has written a series of sophisticated novels and a critical study, *Shetikat hashamayim* (The silence of heaven). Very early in the narrative, he draws a clear distinction between the cloistered life of his Jerusalem petit-bourgeois neighbors and family friends, mostly members of the Revisionist Party, and the wider heroic world of the halutzim of "hayishuv hame'urgan" (the organized yishuv) of the Labor Party in Tel Aviv and the Galilee.

To lend coherence to the Klausnerism against which the narrator revolts after the climactic Begin scene, he wisely focuses not on his father, who is both a frustrated minor scholar and a failed father figure, but on his father's famous uncle, Joseph Klausner. By describing Sabbath pilgrimages to the home of the elderly scholar in Talpiot, the assemblage of late Saturday afternoon guests with their reverence of the scholar and his platitudes, the author satirizes the pretensions and self-righteousness of the Zionist right wing of the period through ideological clichés conveyed in bombastic Hebrew rhetoric. Joseph Klausner, after all, was one of the icons of this Zionism: he attended the First Zionist Congress, came to Palestine on the historic steamer *Russlan* in 1918, and was one of the most published scholars of the Mandatory period, known for such political tracts as *Keshe'uma nilhemet al heruta* (When a nation fights for its freedom) and his autobiographical *Darki likrat hatehiya vehage'ula* (My road toward the revival and the redemption). Following his lead, the author's father, Yehudah Aryeh Klausner, preferred the "masculine, Greek" poet Saul Tchernichowski over the "Jewish, exilic, feminine" Hayyim Nahman Bialik. For Oz, a passionate admirer of the writer S. Y. Agnon, the latter's disdain for Joseph Klausner (which was concretized in the figure of Professor Bakhlam in Agnon's novel *Shira*) only corroborated his impression that intellectual sincerity was to be found not in the world of the Klausners but in Agnon and the writer Yosef Hayyim Brenner.

These themes and many more coalesce in the Begin chapter (52 [51]), whose very structure reveals its purposefulness. While the central part, the scene of Begin in the Edison Theatre, takes place about 1951, the first section (not found in the English translation) takes place in 1949, and the last section is set in 1955 or 1956. The disruption of the time sequence in order to compose a unit with greater ideational coherence is paradigmatic of the entire novel. In mid-1949, we are told in the section missing from the English translation, the young author went with his father and his friend Y. D. Abramsky to visit the writer Yehoshua Heshel Yeivin. The group there was apparently disgusted with the terms of the truce that was in effect and all blame was directed at the Mapai (Labor) leaders: at Ben-Gurion, Golda Meir, and the soldiers from the kibbutzim. With his customary ferocity, the poet Uri Tzvi Greenberg, also present, cried out: "They simply don't want the Temple Mount! They don't want Anatot and Shiloh! They could have liberated them—but they didn't liberate them! . . . Lost! Lost! Everything is lost! From the heavens they offered us the third Kingdom of Israel . . . but we again preferred the Golden Calf over the sparks of Kingdom" (473).

Before placing Begin on the stage in the center of the chapter, the author digresses to admit that in his childhood he too wrote wildly nationalistic stories, in which he, in the heroic spirit of Jabotinsky and the songs of the partisans, of Tchernichowski and Avraham Stern, imagined his falling repeatedly in bloody battles with the enemy. This admission is related in a rush of self-parody designed to undermine both the pathos of Uri Zvi Greenberg that preceded it and Menahem Begin that follows it.

The scene of Begin haranguing his admirers at the Edison Theatre sometime in 1951 is carefully staged both for its comic effect and
for its dramatic implications in the life of the author. Begin's dema-
goguery is undercut by his use of an obsolescent Hebrew word for
armament. Deploring the difficulty the Ben Gurion government was
having in securing proper arms for its war with the Arab states, Begin
called for a change of government in which he, as savior to the nation, would secure the proper arms. In saying "to arm," Begin used
the word *lezayen*, which also meant "to have sexual intercourse" and,
in its pejorative sense, "to screw," instead of *lehamesh*, the word used
for armament by a younger generation of Hebrew speakers in Israel.
The author, brought there by his father and grandfather, exploded in
laughter at the absurdity of Begin's diction. Laughter generated by mistakes in the understanding of words is a venerable comic ploy, and Oz
exploits this stratagem to good effect. First, although Begin presents
himself as the new, nonghetto Jew who will fight for his freedom, he
still uses the language of the European Jew, not the young Israeli. Second, the speech is delivered in obvious demagogic clichés designed
to incite the audience. Third, the entire assembly is staged with the
pageantry of fascist parties; youths in uniform, rousing songs, warm-
up speeches, exaggerated rhetoric. The dramatic scene, the boy's disruptive laughter, and his punishment by his embarrassed grandfather
lead up to the anguished explanation (481–82 [431–32]) of his reasons
for leaving the world of the Klausners for the kibbutz.

The explanation offered for his flight from the world of Begin's
Herut Party and from Jabotinsky's "Revisionism" warrants scrupulous
attention since it combines many of the themes of this autobiographical novel. The dominant verb is *barahti* ("I fled"). His choices were
dominated by flight from, not attraction toward, an object of desire.
The Herut ideology is conveyed by key symbols: the ancient heroic cities Yotapata, Masada, and Beitar; the two key concepts, *oz* ("strength"—
ironically, the author's adopted name), and *hadar* ("glory"). All this
Betar ideology is found not in his father's books but in that of Hadod
Yosef, Joseph Klausner, whose autobiographical book, *Darki likrat
hatehiya vehage'ula*, contains both the history of the Klausner family
and the author's Revisionist ideology. The mature Oz, looking back at
the day of the Begin speech, can declare, "On that day I seem to have
begun to run away from resurrection and redemption. I am still running" (482 [431]).

Oz also declares in the subsequent emotional passage, "But that
was not the only thing I ran away from. The suffocation of life in that
basement, between my father and my mother and between the two of
them and all those books and their ambitions, the repressed, denied

nostalgia for Rovno and Vilna . . . failures that I was tacitly charged with converting into victories in the fullness of time" (482 [431]). This flight from his parents and their failures drove him to the kibbutz, the normal refuge in those days from depressing family circumstances. "I wanted to be like them [the halutzim] in order not to be like my father and my mother and all the dejected refugee-intellectuals who filled Jewish Jerusalem." Here we find the most open and clear delineation of the intersection between the personal and ideological axes of the novel. These two axes become the parallel vectors that motivate his life and energize each other in a complex reciprocating field of energy. The reader is thus impelled to note, for instance, the relationship in the mind of the young artist between the fall from grace in the Begin scene and the mother's suicide.

Even before this connection is made, however, we should note the dramatic structure of the last segment of chapter 52 [51], which has as its epicenter the Begin scene in the Edison Theatre. We are then shifted to the kibbutz several years later, after the mother's death and the father's remarriage. The scene is staged like an old film: Two men in a kibbutz are talking to each other as they stand on top of ladders picking apples. The author, now fifteen or sixteen, is talking to Efraim Avneri, one of the founders of the Ḥulda kibbutz. The young author told Avneri the story of the Begin scene with the use of *lezayen* that was so comic to him. Avneri understands the author's story but tells him that he really missed the point.

Avneri declares,

> The thing that is so funny about them, about Begin and his entire noisy crew, is not their use of the word "arm" but their use of words in general. They divide everything up into "obsequious, Diaspora-Jewish," on the one hand, and "manly Hebrew" on the other hand. They don't notice how Diaspora-Jewish the division is. Their whole childish obsession with military parades and on hollow machismo and weapons comes straight from the ghetto. . . . He believes that if we Jews start shouting at the top of our voices that we're no longer the ways Jews used to be, we're not longer sheep for the slaughter . . . but we are now dangerous . . . they'll let us have the whole land. (483 [433]).

This seemingly simple explanation on top of a ladder stands in contrast to the author's pervasive use of parodic language throughout the novel, especially when he is describing scenes of his father or his father's uncle, Hadod Yosef. This, it appears, is Klausnerian language, which one must avoid at all cost.

Similarly, in the next section, Avneri teaches the young author his first non-Klausnerian, non-Herut political lesson. As they are on guard duty one night, Avneri presents a moderate political position that shocks the young man brought up on Herut extremism. He explains that he actually can sympathize with the Arab marauders against whom they are defending the kibbutz since they had lost their homes in the 1948–49 war and are dispossessed. This simple fact of political existence surprises Oz, who had never considered that there might be another side to the Arab-Israeli conflict. This section thus balances the first section of the chapter in which Uri Zvi Greenberg presented an uncompromising, apocalyptic position. The differences between the two positions are exemplified, furthermore, in the language used to convey them. The extreme nationalistic ideas of Greenberg or Begin are conveyed in flowery, apocalyptic Hebrew, while Avneri's discourses are presented in a common, everyday language, always spoken while he is in the process of work, either picking apples or standing on guard duty.

The complex of ideas and attitudes so exquisitely woven together in chapter 52 [51] informs much of the book and, by extension, much of Oz's fiction. Shortly after this, in chapter 55 [54], the author surveys the books that had made an impression on him in his childhood. Here too the chapter is structured to emphasize the ideational positions of the book. Toward the end of the chapter, for instance, he tells of his childhood love of the book *Me'al haḥorovot* (Over the ruins), by Zvi Lieberman Livneh, which he had read many times (514 [463]). It takes place in a small mountain village during the wars against the Romans in the days of the Second Commonwealth. The Romans came, slaughtered all the adults, and ravaged the village. Before the slaughter the adults hid the children, who escaped the destruction. After the Romans left, the children emerged and created their own new society—an ideal society of young heroes. The mature author writing of his childhood fascination with the book realizes that the book contained a "dark Oedipal sweetness." All the children there had buried their parents. "And so," he explains, "a well-repressed desire of the Zionist ethos and of the child I was at the time was miraculously fulfilled: that the grownups should be dead [*sheyamutu kevar*]. Because they are so alien, so burdensome. They were always full of demands and commands, they never let you breathe" (515 [463]). Oz concludes the chapter with the terrifying insight: "The death of all the grown-ups concealed a mysterious, powerful spell. And so, at the age of fourteen and a half, a couple of years after my mother's death, I killed my father and the whole of

Jerusalem, changed my name and went on my own to Kibbutz Hulda in order to live there over the ruins" (516 [464]).

This dense passage is crucial for any understanding of the rich oeuvre of the author Amos Oz. It is illuminated by the explication of chapter 52 [51] presented earlier and comprises an insight into the psychodynamics of Zionist youth, the children of the Third and Fourth Aliyah (the eastern European Jews among them, not the German Jews).[2] Here, however, the object of disdain and anger is not the Labor Party, Ben-Gurion, or Golda Meir but the Zionist narrative as embodied in the essays of the seminal figure of Joseph Klausner, abetted by all his Revisionist admirers and advanced by Begin and other Herut ideologues. One finds here, furthermore, echoes of the arguments of *Hahistoriyonim hatzeirim* (the young historians) of the past twenty years with one significant difference: here the personal psychological aspects are not latent or deliberately hidden but rather laid out in a bold, compelling, sustained narrative. The portrait of this artist as a young man includes both public and private domains, often intertwined, illuminating and giving meaning to each other.

This realization allows us to move to the third part of my title: "From Klausner to Oz and Back." By saying "and back," I am by no means suggesting that the author Amos Oz shows any sign of becoming a Klausner again but rather that through the process of writing this rich autobiographical novel he returns as a mature writer to the period of his youth to come to terms with it in one sense or another. This, like all returns, is belated and does not purport to be a return to previous existence. And, like many returns, it produces much interesting ambiguity. The author's attitude toward the naive Zionist ethos of his childhood years is mostly negative, but he still recalls his childhood fantasies as a great warrior warmly. Joseph Klausner is mostly portrayed as a pompous, self-righteous scholar and ideologue, but the history of the Klausner family going back to the eighteenth century is reproduced as an article of pride. The author's father, Aryeh Yehudah Klausner, usually appears ridiculous in both his rigid behavior and his artificial Hebrew diction, yet he evokes our sympathy in touching scenes that describe his excitement over the appearance of his first book or his attempts to cultivate a garden with inadequate tools in the hard-scrabble soil of Jerusalem.

There is even ambiguity in the portrayal of the mother, Fanya, which is arguably the emotional center of the book. For while all the portrayals of her are loving, Oz still cannot stifle his hurt and anger that she abandoned him by committing suicide shortly before his Bar Mitzvah. In the novel we find movement from a description of childhood fury (244 [211]) to a mature understanding in the last chapters of the novel, especially in the ultimate chapter 63 [62], which is mostly a fictional account of her last days, of what he imagines his mother might have suffered. Describing his feelings as a child at the time of her suicide he can say, "In the weeks and months that followed my mother's death, I did not think for a moment about her agony. . . . I was angry with her for leaving without saying good-bye, without a hug, without a word of explanation. . . . Is that the way to leave, rudely, in the middle of a sentence? . . . How could she? I hated her" (245–46 [211–12]). But as he matured, he realized how much she had suffered. Coming from a middle-class background in Rovno and a year's study at the university in Prague, she arrived impoverished with her family in Palestine in 1933. Marrying Aryeh Yehudah Klausner, a frustrated scholar with the position of a minor librarian, she spent her prime years in the crowded basement apartment in Kerem Avraham, far from the expansive world of her dreams. Memories of her suffering evoke in him passages from Agnon's novel *Bidemi yameha* (In the midst of her days). The gap between the soaring rhetoric of Zionist propaganda and the crushing reality of life lived on the ground, here not on the soil but in streets and dingy Jerusalem apartments, evoke echoes of the stark insights of the novels of Yosef Hayyim Brenner, one of Oz's favorite writers.

As he nears the end of his narrative, the author explains how the discovery of Sherwood Anderson's stories "freed his writing hand" (544 [490]). Until then, he had found writing daunting since he could not match in his personal experience the heroic deeds of the young Israeli writers. Anderson's stories of the daily lives of ordinary people liberated him from this misconception, that only heroic deeds are worthy of serious narrative treatment. He confesses: "Thus the stories of Sherwood Anderson brought back what I had put behind when I left Jerusalem, or rather the ground that my feet had trodden all through my childhood and that I had never bent over to touch: the tawdriness of my parents' lives [*hamerupatut she'afefa et ḥayei horay*]" (545 [492]). The possibility of narrating the mundane aspects of a person's life, his frustrations and failures, liberated him. Through this liberation he could perceive for the first time the true nature of his parents' lives and his own origins: "a dreary tangle of sadness and pretense, of longing, absurdity, inferiority and provincial pomposity, of sentimental education and anachronistic ideals, of repressed traumas, resignation, and helplessness" (546 [492]). This realization allowed him to return to the lost world he had left by moving to the kibbutz. He tried to recapture this world in words and to give it dignity by attempting to understand the unbridgeable gap between the soaring Zionist dreams of his parents and the coarse reality of their daily existence in the Jerusalem of his childhood.

The recuperation of his childhood world did not take place in the 1950s when Oz first began to write. It obviously took him almost a half century to deal in detail with the trauma of his mother's suicide. In his efforts to understand why she did commit suicide, he had to immerse himself in a study of his family by using both personal interviews and written sources. The mature writer realized that the problem began not in Jerusalem but back in Rovno, just as the problems and achievements of the State of Israel began not in Jerusalem or Tel Aviv of 1948 or 1917 but in Europe going back several generations. In this daring enterprise of reconstructing his own past, Oz becomes a learned historian, a virtual Klausner—but still only a virtual one. He will not change his name back to Klausner. He is Amos Oz, the writer of fictions.

The reader, finally, cannot escape an inherent analogy in the *Tale of Love and Darkness*. The boy described in the novel has two parents and much of the novel is devoted to describing the world of both parents, their families, their cultural milieux. The father, a Klausner, stemmed from a learned family and was a Revisionist admirer of Menachem Begin. The mother came from a solid Jewish bourgeois family, who were impoverished in the antisemitic turmoil of 1930s Poland. The mother's suicide seems to be paralleled by the collapse of whatever world of ideals the father represented in Jerusalem. After the mother's death, the father remarries and the son leaves that world entirely by joining the kibbutz, the world of the mainstream Labor Party. By changing his name, joining a kibbutz, and becoming a writer, the young artist becomes a new person; he remakes himself. Fifty years later, by writing this quasi-historical book, he can chronicle and interpret this crucial development in his life.

NOTES

1. The English translation by Nicholas de Lange appeared in 2003 (New York: Harcourt). Since the translator omitted several passages, the chapters of the English translation do not always correspond to those of the Hebrew original. In our text, pages and chapters refer to the original, but they are followed by the English citation in brackets.
2. As described, for instance in Oz Almog's *Hatzabar: deyokan* (The sabra: a portrait), or in Tom Segev's various books.

Stumbling Stones

Marks of Holocaust Memory on German Streets

MONIKA RICHARZ

In front of more than ten thousand buildings in Germany there are little brass memorial plaques set in the pavement. They are square and no bigger than the palm of a hand or a cobblestone, so they are not very conspicuous and can easily be overlooked. Yet from time to time, when their eyes fall on the pavement, passers-by notice the plaques and stop to read the inscriptions engraved in the brass surface. The text generally begins with "Here lived," followed by a person's name in capitals, then the year of birth and the place and year of death, sometimes with one or two other details. These details always refer to the violent death of the individual named, in the years between 1933 and 1945. In this modest, unobtrusive form, victims of National Socialism are commemorated directly in front of their last voluntary place of residence. These little commemorative plaques are continuously increasing in number and by the end of 2006 could be found in more than 190 cities, towns, and villages in Germany. They also have a name: *Stolpersteine* (literally, "stumbling blocks," "stumbling stones"). The name does not imply physical stumbling—after all, the plaques are set flush with the pavement. It is rather meant symbolically: the plaques catch the attention of people passing by more or less by chance and cause them to suddenly stop, which is precisely what the initiators intended.

To stumble upon something does not necessarily have to have positive connotations; symbolically speaking, one stumbles upon something that stands out, something that is in one's way and needs to be dealt with or negotiated somehow. In other words, one does not stumble voluntarily. Those who lay such "stumbling stones," therefore, want to achieve something with them.

This essay examines the origin, the motivation, the meaning, and the political significance of the memorial stones. The laying of these commemorative plaques has become a kind of mass remembrance movement, which is also spreading in other countries. Although the original idea was conceived by an artist, who still today produces and lays the stones himself, the small stones have now taken on an astonishing dynamic of their own, without the patronage of a central organization behind them. Thousands of people have carried out research and made donations for the stones, thus trying to pin down for posterity the remembrance of the life and death of those who were murdered. The results go far beyond what is inscribed on the little plaques. They were used for countless events and press reports on the ceremonial laying of the stones, for exhibitions, city tours, and documentation on the Internet. Even after they have been laid, the stumbling stones often arouse in the public a deeper interest in those named, giving rise to further historical research and publications. Assistance has been provided by dozens of archives, history workshops, local history museums, citizens' initiatives, schools, and private individuals. The creation of the small, visible memorial stone thus has a much broader historical background than is evident in its modest form. Each is a memorial to one murdered individual, but many individuals have been involved in the work behind it and have learned from this. Some have criticized the stones as being undignified, since the name is trodden underfoot. And a very small minority have denied the existence of victims of National Socialism altogether and have torn up stones.

The stumbling stones are the creation of the Cologne-based sculptor and performance artist Gunter Demnig, who was born in Berlin in 1947.[1] After creating various political art projects that revolved around the idea of laying traces, in 1990 he made a trail through Cologne using chalk, which marked the starting point of the route along which Cologne's Sinti and Roma were deported in 1940. When the chalk trail faded, he replaced several lengths of it with an inscribed brass ribbon. It was while he was working on this in 1993 that the idea of the memorial stones was born. Working together with the Cologne Roma Association, which provided names and details, Demnig created the first 250 stones, which he laid in 1995 after they had been exhibited. From the very beginning, however, the project was not designed to be restricted to Sinti and Roma victims but was to include all the different groups of victims of National Socialism. Today the vast majority of stones are dedicated to murdered Jews, some are dedicated to members of the political resistance, especially Communists and Social Democrats, and a small number are dedicated to euthanasia victims, homosexuals, and Jehovah's Witnesses. By the end of 2006, Demnig had produced around nine thousand memorial plaques and laid them in over 190 German cities, towns, and villages.[2] They consist of a concrete base covered with a sheet of inscribed brass measuring ten by ten centimeters. All the stones are donated by sponsors, who pay ninety-five euros for the stone and its installation. In the last few years the project took on such large dimensions that it was necessary for Demnig to employ Uta Franke as coordinator, as well as an assistant. In larger cities Demnig sometimes lays several dozen stones together, and he gives lectures about the project in the districts where he is working.

The inscriptions that Demnig engraves in the brass sheet can only be very short. They include up to eight lines, each containing a maximum of three words. The place reference "Here lived" is followed by the name of the victim, sometimes spread over two lines, and for women including the maiden name; the next line contains the year of birth. The lines that follow contain information about the persecution and death of the victim. For example:

DEPORTED IN 1941
LODZ GHETTO
MURDERED

If the date of death is known, this is given precisely:

DEPORTED IN 1941
MINSK
MURDERED
22.1.1945 IN
KZ FLOSSENBÜRG

Sometimes all the stages of the ordeal are given:

KZ FUHLSBÜTTEL
KZ SACHSENHAUSEN
DEPORTED 1942
AUSCHWITZ
???

Some stones, for example, that of Martha Liebermann in Pariser Platz in Berlin, have the inscription "Suicide before deportation." At first Demnig used the official expression "Missing without trace" (*verschollen*) when the date of death was unknown, but later he started using "Murdered" or the three question marks, for instance, after "Deported to Auschwitz."

Demnig has often been asked about his motivation and about the intentions behind the memorial stones. In an interview in 2002 he said:

> The well-known central memorials can only commemorate the victims on a general level, and in addition, many of them are dedicated only to particular groups of victims. On a memorial stone each victim gets their name back again — their identity and their fate, as far as this is known, can be read. I originally imagined that the stones would be polished again and again through being walked on — and the memory would thus be renewed each time. However, experience has shown that it doesn't always work like that. In smaller streets people tend not to step on the memorial stones. They seem to be evocative of small gravestones, although this association was never intended. On the other hand, though, it can be assumed that most of the victims do not have a gravestone. As a result of commemorating these people on a personal level in front of the houses they lived in until they were deported, their remembrance becomes a concrete feature of our daily lives. At the same time, each personal stone itself functions as a symbol for the victims in their entirety, as all the stones that would actually be needed can never be laid. . . . Ultimately, the project can only be a gesture.[3]

Demnig is quite right when he points out that the little memorial stones fulfill quite different needs than a traditional monument does. Indeed, the contrast between a traditional monument and these little plaques could hardly be starker. In the first place, visibility is the essential prime characteristic of a monument. And this can lead to an extreme of monumentality, as can be seen with the Berlin memorial for the murdered Jews. In contrast, the small stones can only be seen with some effort — and they may remain unseen for a time, until they are discovered anew. Their very principle lies in the fact that they become visible again and again. The memorial stones also differ from a traditional monument in that they are decentralized. There are thousands of them, spread out over many streets and towns, so one can stumble upon them quite by chance, whereas a traditional monument remains at its central, prominent location and the visitor goes to see it deliberately. And yet a single small memorial stone can still act as a symbol for them all.

Above all, however, the decentralized memorial of the small plaques enables the victims to be commemorated individually, as their names and details are inscribed. This is evidently the most important point for all those concerned, for real individual people are involved here, their homes, their lives, and their death. Even some of the conceptions for the Berlin Holocaust memorial included attempts to visibly include the names of the victims, but this proved to be an impossible undertaking, given their sheer number. Demnig wanted to create a kind of "antimonument," commemorating the victims on a concrete and individual level rather than an abstract and monumental one. The stones mark everyday places of everyday life—yet these are places in which people who were neighbors became victims. They, therefore, also point directly to the question of who were the perpetrators and who stood by and watched.

The memorial plaques are the only public sign of remembrance for many of the victims, as they have no graves. The stone is laid where their life took place, but like a gravestone it shows the date of birth and death. The association with a gravestone is, therefore, a very obvious one to make. This is especially highlighted by the fact that an increasing number of family members from all over the world have stones laid for their relatives. Some also travel to witness the stone being laid; there is a small ceremony, and often a relative will say Kaddish. For many relatives the setting of this physical sign fulfills a strong psychological need. According to one elderly Jewish lady who had nineteen stones laid for deported relatives, "Nothing remains of the deported— no place where they are buried, no gravestone, nothing. They have simply disappeared. With these memorial stones a piece of remembrance returns. They lie where they used to live. With the help of the memorial stones, something of them remains: a sign of their lives."[4]

The Hamburg coordinator of the project, Peter Hess, says in an interview:

> I personally am most touched by the reaction of the relatives who want to have stones laid for murdered family members. The ceremony is very, very important for them. They come from Australia, from America, from Israel to witness the ceremony. . . . Other relatives, who live here, or sponsors regularly go to visit the stones on the victims'

birthdays or the anniversaries of their death; they clean them, lay a flower on the stone, or silently commemorate their murdered relatives. . . . That's why it is so important that the project is happening now: in ten to fifteen years' time, none of the generation of the victims' children will be alive any longer.[5]

It can also happen that the family of a victim discovers by chance—sometimes from the Internet—that unbeknownst to them a stone has been laid for their relative.[6] This gives rise to great astonishment. Naturally it is only possible to make inquiries with descendants when there has already been some contact with them and their address is known. In most cases, therefore, the memorial stones are laid on the initiative of local sponsors. However, the son of a South African exile made a decisive contribution to the laying of the first memorial stones in Berlin. In 1996 Demnig had just laid the first few stones in Kreuzberg as part of an exhibition with the New Art Society (Neue Gesellschaft für Bildende Kunst), where they were seen by Steve Robins, a visiting professor. After a decision by the Kreuzberg district council and with the help of the Kreuzberg Museum, he had stones laid for his uncle and aunt. This marked the real beginning of the regular laying of stones in Berlin, the organization of which was taken on by the Kreuzberg Museum. By the end of 2006 there were thirteen hundred of the small memorial stones in front of buildings in Berlin. The whole selection procedure and public debate surrounding the Berlin Holocaust Monument, as well as the process of building it, was thus accompanied all along by the simultaneous creation of this memorial of the smaller stones.

A comparison of the two memorials is also revealing from a political point of view. The monument for the murdered Jews started out as one citizen's initiative and ended up as a national project, with the federal parliament ultimately taking the decision to have it built. The memorial stones project, however, emerged on the initiative of one single artist, who has been supported over the years by dozens of citizens' initiatives. It never became a state-run undertaking and never received public funding but instead has remained a "grassroots memorial," sponsored and financed by many individuals. In contrast to the Holocaust Monument, the memorial stones project received little public attention, and as a work in progress, which it always will be, it has never been the subject of spectacular headlines. The Central Committee of the Jews in Germany (Zentralrat der Juden in Deutschland) expressed its support for the project in 2003. However, on a local level the memorial plaques have certainly given rise to a great deal of controversy and have had to face considerable opposition.

Demnig laid the first memorial stones "illegally," but it soon became clear that to set the stones in the pavements of public streets would require authorization from the relevant municipal authorities. This means that town and city councils, and also district councils in the larger cities, have to think about the project and debate the issue publicly and controversially in order to reach a decision. It would be interesting to read the minutes of these debates. In Hamburg, for example, one district council initially rejected the project on the grounds that it would have a negative effect on the value of properties involved—but they were later successfully persuaded to allow it to go ahead after all.

There are some cities, most notably Munich, whose city councils decided against the memorial stones. The mayor of Munich said he was afraid of "memorial inflation" and considered it to be a humiliation of the victims for them to have their names trodden underfoot. This opinion is shared by the president of the Jewish community in Munich, Charlotte Knobloch, who became the chairperson of the Jewish Central Committee in 2006; she also probably fears that the stones could be the target of vandalism. Instead she had the names of the Munich Jewish victims engraved on a tablet in Munich's new synagogue. There they are protected from too much public exposure to a certain extent, but they no longer have any function in the everyday life of the neighborhoods where the victims used to live. When Demnig laid two stones without official authorization at the request of a relative of the victims, the Munich city council had them removed and taken to the Jewish cemetery.[7] However, a citizens' initiative, "Memorial Stones for Munich too" (Stolpersteine auch für München), was formed, which commissions Demnig to produce stones and have them laid on private land. This shows the strength with which the concept of local remembrance has taken off on a nationwide level. By the end of 2006, around 190 local councils had voted to allow the laying of memorial stones.

Applying for authorization from so many local councils might be a time-consuming process, but still the main task of the sponsors and helpers consists of reconstructing the biographies of the victims. This often proves to be difficult, even though a good aid to research exists for Jewish victims in the form of the four-volume *Memorial Book of the Federal Archive*.[8] However, this memorial work does not contain addresses; these are to be found, for example, in the files of the tax offices or in the restitution files. Researching the details thus involves a considerable amount of work with the archives and study of National Socialist policy, not least the whole process behind the deportations and the sites of the mass murder. Without the help and knowledge of historians, this research would hardly be possible. For instance, small work-groups have often been formed under the guidance of a historian, which have taken one individual life as a starting point but ended up delving deeper into the history of National Socialism than originally expected. This, of course, provides an ideal pedagogical situation for learning through one's own research. It is therefore not surprising that an increasing number of teachers and pupils are involved in this research, which brings with it benefits that can hardly be stressed enough. Peter Hess reports on his experiences working with schools:

> Young people, schoolchildren, have a particularly strong interest. They ask if there had been any Jewish teachers or pupils in their school. Even today, this issue has still not been dealt with in most schools. The pupils then form a research group. I get them access to the State Archive and they work on reconstructing the biographies of the victims. After that, the money needed for sponsoring a stone is collected. The memorial stones for murdered teachers are laid in front of the school, and those for victims who had been pupils are laid outside their former homes. At the ceremony when the stones are laid, pupils report about the life of the victim.[9]

The learning process is incredibly intense when pupils work on a task of their own choosing, dealing with a person from their own neighborhood and possibly being confronted with the last handwritten signs of life of a victim. The document in question might be, for example, the forced declaration of the victim's property and effects, written with painstaking detail just before deportation, thus granting a very personal insight into their life. There might also be documentation about what happened then to the victim's possessions—records of auctions or the accommodation in the victim's apartment of people whose homes had been bombed. Two pupils, whose names would suggest they are from immigrant families, close their research report with the following words: "Working in the State Archive enabled us to gain some insight into the personal situation of one single victim. As a result of this, the monstrousness of the Nazi atrocities really became clear to us."[10] Developing empathy with one individual is clearly beneficial for the pupils' broader historical understanding and perception.

Apart from studying such dreadful documents, when possible the pupils also interview contemporary witnesses of events and victims' relatives. With the help of this information, along with more general information about the history and persecution of the Jews, they try to piece together a picture of the life of the person in question, which they then present when the memorial stone is laid. The pupils also learn other useful skills for communicating with the public, when they are collecting the money needed, when they invite the press, other pupils, and neighbors to the laying ceremony, and when they make presentations or school exhibitions and explain the project. In the course of all of this it can certainly happen that they are confronted with and thus have to react to right-wing extremist views. One teacher in Kreuzberg, Berlin, who was the first to work with schoolchildren on the memorial stones project, emphasized the strong motivation of the pupils. As she put it, "The questions which arose in the course of the project sent them far beyond the bounds of the school, out into various institutions and to the public at large. Presenting the results of the project outside the school framework made many pupils conscious for the first time of what it means to be politically active."[11]

Today, numerous young people are committed researchers for the small memorial stones. But they are by no means the only ones. In Hamburg, for instance, lawyers, judges, and doctors with the help of their professional associations, researched the names of fellow professionals who were murdered and sponsored memorial stones for them.[12] Elsewhere, church parishes have taken up the search, or former classmates of victims have laid stones for them. It also happens that, having got to know about the stones, individual citizens get involved by finding out whether Jews from their own building or street were deported, in which case they might form a small work-group, debate the project with opponents, collect money, and have a stone laid. In Hamburg in particular there are residential areas in which virtually every building was the home of a victim. For example, in the Isestraße alone, 121 memorial stones have been laid.[13] One reason for the striking commitment of Hamburg's citizens might be the fact that from the nineteenth century Hamburg had Germany's highest number of marriages between Jews and Christians, and so numerous Hamburg families have Jewish ancestors whom they want to commemorate. The research involved for non-Jewish victims of National Socialism is by no means easier. This is usually based on the research carried out by the associations of Sinti and Roma, the homosexual associations, the memorial archives of the German Resistance (Gedenkstätte deutscher Widerstand) in Berlin, or on the documentation concerning euthanasia. Political parties and the Association for the Victims of the Nazi Regime (Verband der Verfolgten des Naziregimes) also get involved for those victims who were politically persecuted. These memorials are almost always for little-known resistance fighters, above all Communists and Social Democrats. In an interview, Peter Hess comments on this: "We are not only commemorating Jews; we might also be approached by someone, a worker or a trade unionist, whose father or grandfather was a Communist. They are proud that their family has collected the money. At the laying ceremony, one of them once said, 'It used to be only the rulers who got memorials. Now we simple people are getting a stone too.'"[14]

Up to the end of 2006 most of the memorial stones had been laid in Hamburg (1,600), Cologne (1,400) and Berlin (1,300). This is not only because of the large number of Jewish victims in the big cities but is also because of the particular commitment of institutions and individuals who are prepared to devote their time and energy as coordinators for the project. These are not only volunteers, such as Peter Hess, but most of all qualified employees in the city or state archives who have acquired a special knowledge of Jewish local history. In Cologne, the National Socialism research department of the city archive (NS-Dokumentationszentrum) itself took on the coordination for the project. The coordinators give advice to interested parties, offer help with research, and look for new sponsors. In Berlin there are district-based initiatives that act as contact points for the project, chiefly local history museums and teachers, but in 2005 a city-wide coordination office was created for the memorial stones, financed by the senate. In the states of the former GDR the project is spreading more slowly. Here the district councils have often taken on the coordination and indeed the sponsorship themselves, like in Leipzig, for instance, where the city council had initially rejected the project. The delay in eastern Germany might be a result of the fact that the official memorial culture of the GDR always commemorated the victims of the "fight against fascism," but on the other hand the Jews, as the largest group of victims of National Socialism, are not so prominent in the minds of the population. What is more, the danger of vandalism is higher in the states of the former GDR, as the right-wing extremist groups there tend to riot more violently.

The small memorial stones have indeed been the target of acts of vandalism in both eastern and western Germany. Public opposition to the local laying of memorial stones is generally verbal opposition, expressed in letters of complaints or even in lawsuits. While laying stones, Demnig often hears antisemitic remarks from passers-by or residents of the building in question. Once an indignant house-owner shouted, "Now I have two gravestones on my doorstep. If I'd known that Jews had lived here, I'd never have bought the house in the first place!"[15] A lawyer in Cologne went to court about the laying of a stone in front of his building, with the argument that this would give rise to "considerable difficulties in selling or letting the flat." A similar argument was used by a house-owner in a small Rhineland town, in response to which the town council decreed that memorial stones

Monika Richarz

could only be laid in the pavement with the consent of the owners of the buildings. One passer-by, on seeing a group of memorial stones, was heard to say loudly "Anyway, at least these five Jews won't be able to murder any Arabs in Lebanon."[16] Others demanded that there should finally be an end to all this commemoration and complained that money was being spent on Jews. These blatantly antisemitic comments demonstrate yet again that a latent antisemitism is still present in one part of society and this can come to the surface at any time.

When it comes to right-wing extremist acts of vandalism, the little memorial stones are really too small to be smeared with paint or graffiti, so instead they are sometimes pulled up altogether and stolen. When asked about the worst things he had experienced, Demnig once replied, "In Halle eight stones were dug up, presumably by right-wing extremists, straight after they had been laid. That was terrible, since the relatives of the victims were still there. In Wedding, Berlin, eight stones were also dug up once, probably by Islamist extremists this time. All in all, though, the amount of vandalism is fairly limited: around 20 of the 3,700 stones have been attacked."[17] In Halle, citizens collected money for new stones in 2004. In 2006 stones also disappeared in Henningsdorf near Berlin and in Cottbus, also in the east, but they were quickly replaced, with the help of donations.[18] It turned out that in fact such acts of vandalism triggered an increase in solidarity.

The small memorial plaques evidently provoke strong reactions, whether positive or negative. Their effect goes far beyond the remembrance of the names and fate of the victims. The place where they are laid is what gives rise to emotions and also to reflection among those who see them. Here it is clear for all to see: the victims lived as citizens "in our midst"; the crime against them was perpetrated in the course of what seemed to be normal life, and nobody put a stop to it. Seeing this documented thousands of times in the streets today is and will remain horrific, and also engenders resistance. The time of the events is becoming ever more distant, now two to three generations past, but the familiar locality, having a stone in one's own neighborhood, in front of one's own home, has a historical effect that creates a sense of immediacy and present relevance. This is one possibility to bridge the temporal gap and also to involve the next generation in the process of remembrance. This becomes an increasingly important task as the generations of the victims and their children die out, for remembrance cannot be sustained by ritualization alone. As Berlin's undersecretary for cultural affairs, Andre Schmitz, put it at the stone-laying ceremony for Martha Liebermann, "The remembrance of the Shoah should not be banished from everyday life and only commemorated in ritualized forms at particular places. People must have access to it, on a personal level, everywhere."[19]

Demnig's initiative has gained public recognition, and there is an international interest in the memorial stones project. Demnig has won several awards, for example, the German Jewish Obermayer Award from the United States in 2005, and in October 2005 he received the Bundesverdienstkreuz (Medal of Honor) from the German president. The international press, among others the *New York Times*, is reporting increasingly on the project.[20] The first memorial stones have been laid in Austria, in the Leopoldstadt district in Vienna in 2005, and in Braunau, Hitler's birthplace, in 2006. Preparations are being made to lay stones in Hungary in 2007, and requests have come in from Poland, as well as from Odessa, Paris, and other foreign cities. Demnig's remark "The more stones are laid, the more inquiries I receive" is thus becoming a self-fulfilling prophecy.[21] It seems that on seeing individual memorial stones, many people are won over to this form of remembrance spontaneously.

As has been shown here, the memorial stones project has a striking pedagogical and psychological dimension to it. It can also be interpreted as an attempt at self-therapy by the descendants of the perpetrators. Of the uncountable number of victims, it is possible to get closer to single individuals and their life and death can be shown in an exemplary fashion. This self-chosen task leads the researcher closer to the victim as a person and makes it possible to empathize. By the same token, conversations about the individual victims can take place between those who were involved in the laying of the stone and those who later see the stone. The act of remembrance can thus adopt a concrete and everyday form, which at the same time reaches beyond the remembering of the one individual.

It might be true that every monument is to a certain extent a memorial to the person who has it made, yet it is still first and foremost a memorial to the person named on it. The memorial stones, therefore, have an effect in two directions: on the descendants of the victims and those of the perpetrators. Peter Hess has this to say about the strong effect that the small stones can have on the families of victims:

> One woman wrote and told me that as the last surviving family member, it was very important to her to know that a stone had been laid, and that with it "the stone I have carried in my heart can also be laid to rest." The knowledge that stones have been laid for their relatives and that money has been raised for this locally does people a lot of good. I am always getting inquiries from people about who has

paid for their relative's stone. It is of no small importance for them to see that there is another, democratic Germany, which faces up to the task of remembering.[22]

For some of the descendants, the little memorial stone can thus ease the burden and change their perception of modern-day Germany. At the same time it also enables today's Germans to engage positively with the biggest crime against humanity in their history.

NOTES

1. For more on Demnig, see "Am treffendsten lässt sich meine Berufs-bezeichnung mit Bildhauer umschreiben," Uta Franke interview with Gunter Demnig, in *Stolpersteine: Dokumentation—Texte—Materialien* (Berlin: Neue Gesellschaft für Bildende Künste e.V., 2002), 9–22. Current information can be found on the project's website: www.stolper-steine.com.

2. Information from www.stolpersteine.com (accessed December 2006).

3. *Stolpersteine*, 13–14.

4. *Tageszeitung* (Berlin), May 15, 2006.

5. "'Ein Mensch ist erst vergessen, wenn sein Name vergessen ist': Die Aktion Stolpersteine," Beate Meyer interview with Peter Hess in *Die Verfolgung und Ermordung der Hamburger Juden, 1933–1945*, ed. Beate Meyer (Göttingen: Geschichte, Zeugnis, Erinnerung, 2006), 167

6. This, e.g., happened to Jackie Kohnstamm (London), whose parents had been deported from Berlin. She came across photos of the memorial stones for Amalie and Max Rychwalski on the Internet just four days after they had been laid on November 30, 2005, and traveled to Berlin in January 2006. See her report, Jackie Kohnstamm, "The Responsibility of Remembering," *Second Generation Voices* (London, 2006).

7. On the controversy in Munich see *Süddeutsche Zeitung*, June 13, 2004; *Spiegel*, September 30, 2005; and the website www.stolpersteine.com.

8. *Gedenkbuch: Opfer der Verfolgung der Juden unter der nationalsozialist-ischen Gewaltherrschaft in Deutschland 1933–1945*, 2nd revised and improved ed., 4 vols. (Koblenz: Bundesarchiv, 2006).

9. Meyer, *Verfolgung*, 169

10. Ibid., 82. See also Monika Ebertowski, "Hinweise zur pädagogischen Begleitung," in *Stolpersteine*, 74–105, here 82.

11. Monika Ebertowski, "Projekt Stolpersteine," *Pädagogik* 6 (2006): 82. For more detail, see also Ebertowski, "Hinweise zur pädagogischen Begleitung." Several reports by young people from Turkish and other immigrant families can be found here.

12. Meyer, *Verfolgung*, 169.

13. Ibid. The appendix contains an address list for all the stones laid in Hamburg up to February 2006, arranged according to street names.

For Isestraße, 216–18.

14. Ibid., 168.
15. *Spiegel* online, September 30, 2005, www.spiegel.de.
16. Qtd. from a speech by Wolf Biermann, *Die Zeit*, October 26, 2006, 63.
17. Interview with Gunter Demnig in www.projekt-gegen-antisemitismus.de/Inhalte.
18. *Bild* (Berlin), November 25, 2006, 11. For further examples of removed and replaced stones, see www.stolpersteine.de.
19. *Berliner Zeitung*, October 15–16, 2005.
20. Kirsten Grieshaber, "Plaques for Nazi Victims Offer a Personal Impact," *New York Times*, November 29, 2003, late ed., section B.
21. *Stolpersteine*, 18.
22. Meyer, *Verfolgung*, 167–68.

Is Literary History Possible?

Reflections on Literary History

GERSHON SHAKED

Professor Gershon Shaked passed away in December 2006, only weeks after completing this essay, and days after last seeing his longtime friend Michael Meyer. While his contribution differs from other articles here in both its subject and its highly theoretical emphasis, Dr. Shaked's essay offers an important example of the diversification that Jewish studies has experienced in recent decades. Though this essay is a distillation and summation of his masterful five-volume work of literary criticism *Hebrew Narrative Fiction, 1880–1980,* Dr. Shaked clearly deemed it appropriate for a collection that focuses on Jewish history. In his opinion, as he notes here, "literature is unable to disconnect itself from history." In this sense, the appearance of Shaked's essay—which may well be the last he ever wrote—in a collection honoring a historian is eminently fitting, and validates the ethos of multidisciplinary study that inspires so much of the work included in this volume.

In this essay I wish to present the theoretical background to my five-volume work *Hebrew Narrative Fiction, 1880–1980.* This theoretical outlook was for me a post-facto development. I did not approach the facts with ready-made assumptions, but rather they slowly consolidated during the course of the work, and as far as I can tell have undergone certain changes over the course of the twenty years (1977–98) during which I labored over the five volumes.¹ The diachronic description of the issues of Jewish heritage and the impact of Europe and the processes of secularization and sanctification in literature was the major goal of my history of modern Hebrew fiction. The following pages are an attempt to elucidate the methodology of my work and to discuss the important issue of whether and to what extent historical context should be considered in literary criticism. This, of course, is particularly relevant in the case of modern Hebrew literature.

The theoretical approach to the history of literature has endured many changes between nineteenth-century positivism and the twenty-first century's increasing repudiation of any type of criticism that involves an all-inclusive literary-historical worldview and its restriction to sectorial narratives alone. Literary history attempts to describe the development of literature or one of its genres over a period of time, based on a particular combination of its smaller units into a larger whole. This simplification is, of course, a definition that was never accepted in this form and over the last hundred years has undergone far-reaching changes. The positivist approach was widespread during the nineteenth and early twentieth centuries, and successors have appeared over the past few generations as well. It sought to reveal non-literary factors that left their mark on texts, as well as the channels of influence of those factors.² The weakness of positivism's external description lies in its mechanical linking of cause and effect. Scholars of this persuasion believed that they could achieve a measure of objectivity that no other type of description (including traditional literary criticism) could possibly hope to attain. In their opinion, a review of historical and biographical events might aid in the interpretation of literary texts, as it is through them that the scholar ascertains the parameters out of which all possible understandings of the text are constructed. In the study of Hebrew literature, Yosef Klausner and ensuing generations of his students tended toward this approach.³

An alternative extraliterary approach was based on the claim that every cultural epos is controlled by the dominant spirit of the age, with the scholar's task the definition of the Zeitgeist. Such scholars attempted to define literature and its development in homogenous and monolithic terms, offering evaluation as well as diagnosis, and to a certain extent they silenced dissenting voices. In general this outlook was primarily of German origin, influenced by philosophical idealism during the period of German national consolidation.⁴

As far as Hebrew literature is concerned, it was Baruch Kurzweil who formulated the basic spiritual assumptions and described and evaluated literature accordingly. The Marxist school of thought also viewed the social and economic framework as the foundation revealed by its symptomatic literary superstructure. George Lukács held that not only does literature reflect the tensions of the ruling society of a given period; it must contain a corresponding tension of its own if it wants to earn the great prize in his eyes—a realist literature worthy of the name. Such an assumption is an evaluative prognosis as well as a diagnosis, in that it sought to dictate to Marxist believers how to write and which material to work with in order to fashion that ideal realism of Lukács's vision.[5] The Israeli critic whose theories most closely match those of Lukács is David Canaani. He was the most complex and subtle of the Marxist critics (Uchmani, Rozenzweig, Ben-Nahum) of his day.[6]

Perhaps I should make the point explicitly before I continue with my survey of the various approaches to historical description: literature is unable to disconnect itself from history. Language is an historical creation, and this fundamental tool of literature is subject to continual historical upheavals. Modern Hebrew literature had its beginnings at the end of the eighteenth century. During the nineteenth century it was a literature of Enlightenment fighting against the rabbinic establishment and trying to enable Jews in western Europe (mostly in Germany and the Habsburg Empire) and later in eastern Europe (the Russian Empire, including Poland, Lithuania, etc.) to be "Jews at home and human beings on the outside." The novels and poems of Enlightenment (Haskalah) in the 1860s and 1870s tended to be both melodramatic and didactic and called for the reform of Jewish society, which in the view of the writers, had become petrified and stagnant. As faith in the Haskalah weakened, and as the literature opened itself to new theories of literary production, so too did its concerns and modes of representation undergo transformation. From its beginnings in the eighteenth century, Hebrew literature was influenced by European literatures. The major sources were nineteenth- and early-twentieth-century Russian literature; in the early twentieth century western European literature dominated, and since the establishment of the Jewish state American literature has been the model.

Literary criticism of the first half of the twentieth century formulated a dialectical response to the hegemony of the discipline of history. The counterassumption was that a focus on literature alone might prove no less precise than historical research. This was the basic position of Russian Formalism. In 1921 Roman Jakobson compared the positivistic historian to a policeman who wants to arrest a certain person and to that end grabs hold of any person who crosses his path. The literary historian can turn to all disciplines—anthropology, psychology, politics, philosophy—rather than deal with literature itself. Jakobson claims that these scholars have failed to notice that due to their recourse to secondary disciplines the literary text has become the handmaid of many masters.[7]

Jakobson wanted to save literature from the clutches of those historians who had made it subservient to another framework. The Formalists rejected the connection between literature and history. In their eyes these were two separate disciplines. Wimsatt, a "New Critic," formulated the idea of the literary product as increasing the distance between the text-as-world and the world itself. The historical document receives its authorization and influence from the event about which it testifies. It should not be viewed as a work of art that establishes its own laws but rather as geared toward practical aims. Consequently, the Formalist emphasis on literary self-referentiality prevents it from seeing literature through the *writer's* historical intentions. The New Criticism removed literature from its social roots in order to fashion for it a different world from the historical one. These schools of Formalism and Structuralism were introduced into the study of Hebrew literature mainly by Benjamin Harshav, who founded the Department of Poetics and Comparative Literature at Tel Aviv University, and by the scholarly journal *Ha-Sifrut* (Literature).[8]

The internal examination of the history of literature typifies post– World War II historical research whose basic assumption is that the subject of criticism is literature itself. Thus, the history of literature must adjust itself to the historical periods and genres by which the texts define themselves. In this view, literary history must make reference to the historical context of literature, as its organizational principles are based on the relationship between text and context. Yuri Tynyanov's article "Literary Evolution" (1927) is a key one in the diachronic development of literature and can be seen as an inspiration for the Tel Aviv school of literary theory, which pursued similar lines of thought. Itamar Even-Zohar can be seen as a sort of successor to Tynyanov.[9] This theory encounters difficulties when it tries to distinguish pure literary texts from others. Likewise, it struggles to understand literary activity as social behavior and as part of the cultural and material activities of a specific historical moment.

Such assumptions were swept aside by deconstructivist approaches based on the philosophical activity of Jacques Derrida, a kind of extreme version of New Criticism that nonetheless led to almost contradictory results. The deconstructivist movement has shown that the range of humanistic scholarship, ostensibly based on a referential relationship with reality, was actually composed of discourses that relied on the most basic literary devices and merely retold the truths concealed in the forms of the story through which they disclosed their

Gershon Shaked

message.[10] Hayden White and similar scholars claimed that all history is make-believe and that the nature of its inventions is in accordance with the particular ideology through which it interrogates reality. If this is true of an historian it is all the more so of the literary historian, who sifts not through facts but among fictions, and who attempts to establish connections and highlight advances within variously related fictions.[11]

In the Jewish context, we see that Hebrew writing adopted ideas and techniques from the canon of European literature while it simultaneously drew on its own reserves of Jewish history and culture. Indeed, from the *Haskalah* to the present, Hebrew literature has evidenced the conflict between ancient Jewish sources and the humanist secular culture of Europe. Most of the fiction is, to be sure, more imitative of European than Jewish forms. However, quite a number of texts stay fairly close to traditional Jewish narrative structures such as tales of piety and Midrashim.[12] To a large extent, this incorporation of an old religious tradition into a new secular literature is what gave Hebrew writing its distinctive character. Indeed, it is possible to say that the greater the tension between traditional and contemporary elements, the more complex and interesting the fiction became.

The renewed historicization of literature was to a certain measure accomplished through theories of reception that emphasized the relativity of interpretation and literary evaluation on the one hand, while on the other formulated the concept of "horizon of expectations," referring to limitations in the recognition and evaluation of various social groups and generations. In other words, criticism is legitimized through a metadiscourse when it openly refers to some grand narrative such as the dialectic of the humanities, a revelation of meaning, the liberation of the rational, the status of the worker, the accumulation of property, or even the metanarrative of Zionism or its counternarratives. To present its new Jewish reality, Hebrew writing secularized traditional materials and celebrated secular ones, often using religious motifs and themes to infuse secular values with religious significance. Bialik, Berdyczewski, and Agnon sanctified art; many other writers did the same with nature, labor, and love. The Zionist imperative supplanted the religious commandments, and even atheism was perceived by some writers as a form of religious expression.

As literary critic David Perkins observes, "The writing of literary history involves selection, generalization, organization, and a point of view. It selects for representation only some of the texts and relevant events in the track of past time it supposedly describes; it collects these into general entities, it adopts a point of view toward them; and it makes them constituents of a discursive form with a beginning, a middle, and an end, if it is Aristotelian narration, or with a statement, development and conclusion, if it is an argument."[13]

Revolutionary and superior works usually speak to the "literary republic," which at times also constitutes the cultural vanguard and whose long-term influence is perhaps greater than that of the best sellers. The creative cultural vanguard treats its addressees as the spiritual pioneers of their society. In Israel, it was Moshe Shamir who in the 1970s noted the limited political influence of literature. In the wake of his political conversion to the right, he claimed the following in an article in the newspaper *Ma'ariv*: "Two or three (perhaps five or six) politically left-wing Israeli writers can boast of tens of thousands of readers—the majority of whom are really young. Some achieved this status because they are genuinely good writers while others because they are bad writers (the two most accepted reasons for best-seller billing). I have no doubt that tens of thousands of youngsters love these writers' works, admire them as artists—and are also enriched on a personal level from their reading, a matter of importance in its own right. Yet all this does not add up to political opinions, worldviews or social commitments, certainly not when it comes to voting."[14]

In light of all of this, it seems to me that although diverse narratives endure side by side synchronically, a dominant narrative exists with its own structure, to which other narratives have to refer, deal with, or undermine. Often the subversive (such as feminist, postcolonial, or minority narratives) can only be understood in the context of its confrontation with the narrative at the top of the hierarchy. When the balance of power changes and the lower orders overturn the higher ones, the victorious narratives refer to the earlier or contemporary vanquished narrative.

This brings me to a different aspect of the subject, which for convenience I will call the mythic viewpoint, although it can also be termed a metapsychological outlook. I am referring to a basic set of relationships that frame our historical thinking because they shape the fundamental processes of our existence. These mythological depictions express basic collective processes on both the individual and communal levels. What I refer to here as myths leave their mark on those processes and the way we consider them, consciously or otherwise. For reasons I will not go into here, human thought is subject to them to a greater degree than the rational reader is prepared to admit.[15] Numerous scholars (whose names I will not list here; the most well-known of them is certainly Harold Bloom) have discussed at length the oedipal factor in the development of literature, which is also significant in certain forms of modern Hebrew literature. Sons rebel against their fathers and return to their grandfathers. Scholars made much of the seminal family in their description of cultural developments and the relationship between writers and creativity. The diachronic system was portrayed as a continual uprising of one generation against the other, with social, historical, and even political implications.[16]

Terms such as "deautomatization," "defamiliarization," "changes in the horizon of expectations," and "the dominant" are associated with the oedipal model, as the agents in question shape literature in the same way that they influence historical events. Those scholars shared the fate of literature itself. Just as literature developed diachronically along oedipal lines, so literary criticism evolved by way of a similar dialectical process. The historical movement we have traced from biographical positivism through the turn to the text itself in a (usually futile) effort to detach it from its context, until the emphasis on various thematic connections of more importance to scholars than the text itself (such as feminism, minority and postcolonial discourses, or Mao Tze-Tung's permanent revolution) becomes a characteristic trend in the history of culture. To speak of the literature closest to us, namely, Hebrew literature, its territorial adjustments, the compression of its historical events, and the ever-changing demographics of its target audience have caused the speeding up of these processes in Hebrew literature. In almost every decade a fresh Abraham is bound upon the altar, and an Isaac exalts himself as king, to use the phrases of our myths. Moreover, the myth usually uses the singular—historical myths speak in the singular—yet the reference is to the plural.

Cultural progression is invariably at once diachronic and synchronic. Developments do not only occur in the context of a father-son relationship but also as a result of sibling rivalry. Even before Noah's sons uncovered their father's nakedness, Cain and Abel had fought over their father's recognition and honor, with Seth eventually emerging as the victorious third party. Literary development is an outcome of a confrontation of brothers. Siblings are interlocked in a permanent struggle, and the conflict between brothers is no less a factor in literary development than the clash of sons and fathers.[17]

In addition to sibling rivalry nowadays, we have the war between genders. Here too a great transformation is emerging in the balance of power, but familiarity with the rival agents is needed in order to appreciate this change. Feminist literature is characterized by its struggle with the opposing force, just as feminist criticism is based on a comparison with those other disciplines. In every generation we find the polarization of various central discourses along ideological, stylistic-methodological, or personal lines—or all three at once—as they draw planets into their orbits. The creative tension between these agents generates their works and those of the artists caught between them.

Thus, for example, Lukács tended to emphasize the naturalism-realism dichotomy, as well as others such as appearance versus essence, or the abstract as opposed to the material. In his opinion, Mann and Kafka represent the two poles—the first incorporating all the positive aspects of the dichotomy, the second all its negative ones.[18]

Our own sages' system of pairs, from Shemaya and Avtalyon through Hillel and Shammai and Abaye and Raba, is a version of the same intragenerational polarization that typifies Hebrew literature as well as all literatures with which I am familiar. The development of pairs into foursomes and groups of eight only increases the pluralistic richness. Every description of literary development requires a double presentation—a certain writer differs from his father or grandfather so-and-so and is similar or different from one or another of his analogous brothers or sisters.[19]

One further observation appears pertinent to me: history (literary history included) is certainly not only a linear, sequential progression. Of necessity it bears linear characteristics, but as an entity in its own right it also boasts various cyclic features. Such theories were developed in the field of historical studies, first and foremost by Hegel, Spengler, Toynbee, and the like, yet a number of historians from the same school also spoke of a cyclic historical pattern in the cultural realm as well.[20] Postmodernists can disparage this idea as they will, but certain things remain true with or without their consent.[21]

The picture I have sketched here portrays the construction of historical thought, without which no description is possible. It is this very reflection on events that makes literary history possible. Every historian must determine the active agents of the cultural arena—undoubtedly a matter disputed among his colleagues—as well as provide different names to the recurring features. Yet, without an understanding that the process develops through a series of actions on the historical stage and in the relations between changing times and varying spaces, no description can be offered for a particular event, *as the isolated event is always the product of these processes.*

The comparison with corresponding social processes is a fruitful one, as it reveals parallels to literary phenomena from outside the literary realm. Such determinations are at times arbitrary, and radical Marxists or post-Zionists (or both) will associate cultural events with literary features of different currents of thought. Consequently, they will select and emphasize material that is more relevant to what they consider to be the significant social processes, and a different overall picture will emerge from that of scholars who approached the subject from a dissimilar starting point. Yet even those who choose other features and material, and as a result sketch out other processes, cannot escape the dialectical mode of thought on which I have focused. While the particular dominant force might change, the kaleidoscope will still be formed synchronically and diachronically according to an historical mode of thought that crosses ideological borders.

My ideas might sound abstract, but if I may say so, they are in large part a summary of my painstaking work over the years 1977–98, during the preparation of the five volumes of *Hebrew Narrative Fiction, 1880–1980*. I do not know if I have consistently pointed out the correct groups or the agents that were active in the same time and place—those who read (or do not read) this text are free to agree or disagree with me. I assume that in light of the process I myself have just described, those who take issue will outnumber those who concur, and this is apparently part of the process itself. Yet it remains clear that from the very beginning of Hebrew literature, from one version to its counterversion, from one genre to the antigenre, from traditional literature to the modernism of the interwar years, and from the generation of the land and the generation of the state, we have seen a procession of rival groups fighting for hegemony—both between biological generations and within individual generations themselves.

NOTES

1. Gershon Shaked, *Hebrew Narrative Fiction, 1880–1980*, 5 vols. (1977, 1983, 1988, 1993, 1999).
2. An example of positivistic historical research is the work of the German researcher, Herman Hettner, *Literaturgeschichte des achtzehnten Jahrhunderts*, 6 vols. (1836–1970).
3. Yosef Klausner, *History of Modern Hebrew Literature*, 6 vols. (Jerusalem, 1952–).
4. A central figure in this movement was the Hegelian Wilhelm Dilthey. "What actually interests Dilthey is not what makes literature 'graphic' but how he can extract from literature a world view, a wisdom, an ideal of life." Rene Wellek, *A History of Modern Criticism*, vol. 5, *The Twentieth Century* (New Haven, 1965), 327. Israeli critic Baruch Kurzweil comes close to a similar outlook in his books of criticism. See his framing work, *Our New Literature: Continuity or Revolution?* (Tel Aviv, 1959); Stanley Nash, "Criticism as a Calling: The Case of Baruch Kurzweil," *Prooftexts* 5, no. 3 (1985): 281–87.
5. Georg Lukács's (1885–1971) best known work is *The Historical Novel* (Russian, 1938; German, 1954). It appears that his theory is connected to Augustin Thierry's basic axiom that history involves a passage from innocence and perfection to a situation that involves conquerors and conquered—the move from Rousseau's natural state to civilization. The

source of history is conflict, and the story (or narrative) of history lies in the understanding or pursuit of these conflicts. Lukács did not mean reflection (he termed this naturalism, and objected to it) but rather a proper summary of the basic structure of the period. This structure is concealed between the lines of the material and its plots, and it is the task of criticism to reveal the hidden secret and solve it. The problem was that critics often ended up with that self-same solution.

6. David Canaani, *Between Them and Their Times* (Tel Aviv, 1955).

7. The most important arguments for the Formalist tradition can be found in Victor Erlich's book *Russischer Formalismus* (München, 1964; German translation).

8. See Allen Mintz, "On the Tel Aviv School of Poetics," *Prooftexts* 4, no. 3 (1984): 213–35. Also compare Chayyim Nachman Bialik, "Revelation and Concealment in Language," *Complete Works of C. N. Bialik* (Tel Aviv, 1947), 191–93. In Jerusalem, the late Joseph Even and I wrote a number of books closely aligned with this critical school of thought.

9. See I. Even-Zohar, "The Function of the Literary Polysystem in the History of Literature," *Papers in Historical Poetics* (Tel Aviv, 1978), 11–14.

10. Derrida proved that philosophy is a form of writing rather than a method of thinking, one that oppresses other activities in the name of absolute reason. Not only has philosophy hidden its dependence on those very same rhetorical forms that it accuses literature of using, but it has also been able to repress its involvement with language itself. Derrida presented his ideas in an interview with Houdebine and Scarpetta. See Jacques Derrida, "Positions: Interview with J. L. Houdebine and G. Scarpetta," *Positions* (1981): 37–96. On the literary implications of Derrida's theory see Vincent B. Leitch, *Deconstructive Criticism* (New York, 1983).

11. Hayden White, "The Historical Text as Literary Artifact," *Topics of Discourse: Essays in Cultural Criticism* (Baltimore, 1986), 81–100.

12. For instance, S. Y. Agnon's midrashic tale "Forsaken Wives" (*Agunot*) and Mendele Moykher Sforim's parody of the allegorical interpretation of Canticles (Song of Songs) in his story "The Nag" (*Susati*).

13. David Perkins, *Is Literary History Possible?* (Baltimore, 1993), 19.

14. Moshe Shamir, "Literature as 'Happening,'" *Ma'ariv*, October 6, 1977.

15. Lacan, e.g., describes all sense of loss as a yearning for primary androgyny, based on Plato's *Symposium*, an idea that can also be found in our sources.

16. Bloom is the theorist of the oedipal nature of literary dialectics. See Harold Bloom, *A Map of Misreading* (New York, 1980).

17. As Foucault remarked in an interview, "Who fights against whom? We all fight each other. And there is always within each of us something that fights something else." *Power/Knowledge: Selected Interviews and Other Writings, 1972–1977*, ed. C. Gordon, 207–8 (Brighton, 1977). And as Althusser said, "The struggle between classes can be summed up as a clash of words."

18. From "Peter v. Zima," *Textsoziologie* (Stuttgart, 1980).
19. Lacan claims that subjectivity is always relative, and its realization occurs in opposition to and in spite of the self (of the other). Subjectivity is not essence but a relationship that works only through a symbolic system that existed before the subject and determines its cultural identity.
20. Hegel deploys his master-slave parable of history as the slaves' increasing negation of their slavery. Eventually the thesis of the master and the antithesis of the slave are dialectically cancelled out in the synthesis, a cyclical dialectic position that influenced Marx and Foucault.
21. Fritz Strich is merely one of a number of scholars who portrayed the recurring changes among literary schools. In his book *German Classics and Romance (Deutsche Klassik und Romantik)* he claims that the cyclical revolutions in schools of art should be viewed as transformations of dialectically related similar and associated phenomena, Fritz Strich, *Deutsche Klassik und Romantik, Oder Vollendung und Unendlichkeit, Ein Vergleich* (München, 1924). Northrop Frye tried to build a synchronic model of the structure of literature (models, symbols, myths, and genres) whose diachronic development typically follows Vico's five stages: Myth, Romance, High Mimetic, Low Mimetic, Irony. He views the history of western culture as a recurring downward spiral. Frye's theory is both cyclical and mythic at once. Northrop Frye, *Anatomy of Criticism: Five Essays* (Princeton, 1957).

SELECTED BIBLIOGRAPHY OF THE WORKS OF MICHAEL A. MEYER

With the exception of Michael A. Meyer's books, which are listed here in their entirety, this bibliography includes a selection of his published works. In the interest of space, I have chosen not to include his more than 230 book reviews.—LBS

BOOKS

The Origins of the Modern Jew: Jewish Identity and European Culture in Germany, 1749–1824. Detroit: Wayne State University Press, 1967.

    Hebrew: *Tsemiḥat ha-yehudi ha-moderni: zehut yehudit ve-tarbut eropit be-germanyah, 1749–1824.* Jerusalem: Carmel Publishing House, 1990.

    German: *Von Moses Mendelssohn zu Leopold Zunz: Jüdische Identität in Deutschland, 1749–1824.* Munich: C. H. Beck, 1994.

Ideas of Jewish History, ed. Michael A. Meyer. Detroit: Wayne State University Press, 1987. First published 1974 by Behrman House.

Jewish Identity in the Modern World. Seattle: University of Washington Press, 1990.

    German: *Jüdische Identität in der Moderne.* Frankfurt am Main: Jüdischer Ver-lag, 1992. Includes a German translation of "The German Jews: Some Perspectives on Their History," a lecture delivered at Syracuse University, 1990.

Hebrew Union College-Jewish Institute of Religion: A Centennial History, 1875–1975. Cincinnati: Hebrew Union College Press, 1992. Originally published as "A Centennial History," in Samuel E. Karff, ed., *Hebrew Union College–Jewish Institute of Religion at One Hundred Years,* 3–283. Cincinnati: Hebrew Union College Press, 1976.

Response to Modernity: A History of the Reform Movement in Judaism. Detroit: Wayne State University Press, 1995. First published 1988 by Oxford University Press.

    Hebrew: *Ben masoret le-kidmah: toldot tenu'at ha-reformah ba-yahadut.* Jerusalem: Zalman Shazar Center, 1989.

    German: *Antwort auf die Moderne: Geschichte der Reformbewegung im Judentum.* Vienna: Böhlau, 2000.

German-Jewish History in Modern Times. 4 vols. Ed. Michael A. Meyer, Michael

Brenner, assistant editor.

Vol. 1: *Tradition and Enlightenment, 1600–1780,* by Mordechai Breuer and Michael Graetz. New York: Columbia University Press, 1996.

> German: *Tradition und Aufklärung: 1600–1780.* Munich: C. H. Beck, 1996.

> Hebrew: *Toldot yahadut germanyah ba-et ha-khadashah,* vol. 1. Jerusalem: Merkaz Shazar, 2000.

Vol. 2: *Emancipation and Acculturation, 1780–1871,* by Michael Brenner, Stefi Jersch-Wenzel, and Michael A. Meyer. New York: Columbia University Press, 1997.

> German: *Emanzipation und Akkulturation 1780–1871.* Munich: C. H. Beck, 1996.

> Hebrew: *Toldot yahadut germanyah ba-et ha-khadashah,* vol. 2. Jerusalem: Merkaz Shazar, 2000.

Vol. 3: *Integration in Dispute, 1871–1918,* by Steven M. Lowenstein, Paul Mendes-Flohr, Peter Pulzer, and Monika Richarz. New York: Columbia University Press, 1998.

> German: *Umstrittene Integration 1871–1918.* Munich: C. H. Beck, 1997.

> Hebrew: *Toldot yahadut germanyah ba-et ha-chadashah,* vol. 3. Jerusalem: Merkaz Shazar, 2005.

Vol. 4: *Renewal and Destruction, 1918–1945,* by Avraham Barkai and Paul Mendes-Flohr. New York: Columbia University Press, 1998.

> German: *Aufbruch und Zerstörung 1918–1945.* Munich: C. H. Beck, 1997.

> Hebrew: *Toldot yahadut germanyah ba-et ha-chadashah,* vol. 4. Jerusalem: Merkaz Shazar, 2005.

The Reform Judaism Reader: North American Documents, ed. Michael A. Meyer and W. Gunther Plaut. New York, UAHC Press, 2000.

Judaism within Modernity: Essays on Jewish History and Religion. Detroit: Wayne State University Press, 2001.

> Hebrew: *Yahadut b'tokh ha-moderniyut.* Tel Aviv: Am Oved, 2006.

Leo Baeck Werke. 6: Briefe. Reden. Aufsätze. herausgegeben in Zusammenarbeit mit Bärbel Such. Gütersloh: Gütersloher Verlagshaus, 2003.

Joachim Prinz, Rebellious Rabbi: An Autobiography—the German and Early American Years, ed. Michael A. Meyer. Bloomington: Indiana University Press, 2007.

Selected Articles

"Samuel S. Cohon: Reformer of Reform Judaism." *Judaism* 15 (1966): 319–28.

"Great Debate on Antisemitism: Jewish Reaction to New Hostility in Germany, 1879–1881." *Leo Baeck Institute Year Book* 11 (1966): 137–70.

"The Problematics of Jewish Ethics." In *Judaism and Ethics,* ed. Daniel Jeremy Silver, 113–29. New York: Ktav Publishing House, 1970.

"Caesar Seligmann and the Development of Liberal Judaism in Germany at the Beginning of the Twentieth Century." *Hebrew Union College Annual* 40–41 (1969–70): 529–54. Abbreviated German version: "Caesar Seligmann und die Entwicklung des Liberalen Judentums in Deutschland zu Beginn des 20. Jahrhunderts." In *Caesar Seligmann, 1860–1950. Erinnerungen,* ed. Erwin

Seligmann, 17–33. Frankfurt am Main: Waldemar Kramer, 1975.

"Jewish Religious Reform and *Wissenschaft des Judentums:* The Positions of Zunz, Geiger, and Frankel." *Leo Baeck Institute Year Book* 16 (1971): 19–41.

"Christian Influence on Early German Reform Judaism." In *Studies in Jewish Bibliography: History and Literature in Honor of I. Edward Kiev,* ed. Charles Berlin, 289–303. New York: Ktav Publishing House, 1971.

German: In *Judaica: Beiträge zum Verständnis des jüdischen Schicksals in Vergangenheit und Gegenwart* 38 (1982): 164–77.

Encyclopaedia Judaica (Jerusalem, 1971) articles on Lazarus Levi Adler, Bernhard Beer, Harry Bresslau, Bemhard Brilling, Nathan Michael Gelber, Gesellschaft zur Förderung der Wissenschaft des Judentums, Joseph I. Gorfinkle, Hochschule für die Wissenschaft des Judentums, Institutum Judaicum Delitzschianum, Jüdisch-Literarische Gesellschaft, Julius Landsberger, Isaac Last, Fürchtegott Lebrecht, Leopold Loewenstein, Oesterreichische Nationalbibliothek, and Edmund Silberner.

"Rabbi Gedaliah Tiktin and the Orthodox Segment of the Breslau Community, 1845–1854." *Michael* 2 (1973): 92–107.

"The Jewish Synods in Germany in the Second Half of the Nineteenth Century" [in Hebrew]. *Studies in the History of the Jewish People and the Land of Israel [Meḥkarim]* 3, 239–74. Haifa: University of Haifa, 1974.

"Where Does the Modern Period of Jewish History Begin?" *Judaism* (Summer 1975): 329–38.

"Abraham Geiger's Historical Judaism." In *New Perspectives on Abraham Geiger: An HUC-JIR Symposium,* ed. Jakob J. Petuchowski, 3–16. Cincinnati: Hebrew Union College Press, 1975.

"Differing Views of Modern Rabbinical Education in Germany in the XIXth Century" [in Hebrew], *Proceedings of the Sixth World Congress of Jewish Studies* 2, 195–200. Jerusalem: World Union of Jewish Studies, 1975.

"Universalism and Jewish Unity in the Thought of Abraham Geiger." In *The Role of Religion in Modern Jewish History,* ed. Jacob Katz, 91–107. Cambridge: Association for Jewish Studies, 1975.

"The Refugee Scholars Project of the Hebrew Union College." In *A Bicentennial Festschrift for Jacob Rader Marcus,* ed. Bertram W. Korn, 359–75. Waltham, Mass.: American Jewish Historical Society, 1976.

"Reform Judaism." In *Movements and Issues in American Judaism: An Analysis and Sourcebook of Developments since 1945,* ed. Bernard Martin, 158–70. Westport, Conn.: Greenwood Press, 1978.

"Jews in America—Jews in Israel: How Shall We Understand Our Relationship?" In *Jews in a Free Society: Challenges and Opportunities,* ed. Edward A. Goldman, 71–83. New York: Hebrew Union College Press, 1978.

"Toward a Definition of Jewish Studies." Tenth Annual Conference Address. *Association for Jewish Studies Newsletter,* March 1979, 1–4.

"The Religious Reform Controversy in the Berlin Jewish Community, 1814–1823." *Leo Baeck Institute Year Book* 24 (1979): 139–55.

"Ambiguity and Ambivalence: The Plight of Eighteenth-Century Jewry in Western Europe." In *Religion in the 18th Century,* ed. R. E. Morton and J. D. Browning, 117–35. New York: Garland, 1979.

"The Question of Continuity in Jewish History" [in Hebrew]. *Gesher* (Spring–Summer 1979): 14–21.

Introduction to *Selected Writings on Religious Reform* [in Hebrew], by Abraham Geiger, v–ix. Jerusalem: Zalman Shazar Center and Dinur Center, 1979.

"Jewish Studies and Jewish Commitment" [in Hebrew]. *Gesher* (Spring–Summer 1980): 24–31.

"The Establishment of the Hamburg Temple" [in Hebrew]. In *Studies in the History of Jewish Society in the Middle Ages and the Modern Period Presented to Professor Jacob Katz*, 218–24. Jerusalem: Magnes Press, 1980.

"The Orthodox and the Enlightened—An Unpublished Contemporary Analysis of Berlin Jewry's Spiritual Condition in the Early Nineteenth Century." *Leo Baeck Institute Year Book* 25 (1980): 101–30.

"German-Jewish Social Thought in the Mid-Nineteenth Century—A Comment." In *Revolution and Evolution: 1848 in German-Jewish History*, ed. Werner E. Mosse et al., 329–35. Tübingen: J. C. B. Mohr, 1981.

German Political Pressure and Jewish Religious Response in the Nineteenth Century. Leo Baeck Memorial Lecture no. 25. New York: Leo Baeck Institute, 1981.

"Ob Schrift? Ob Geist?—Die Offenbarungsfrage im deutschen Judentum des neunzehnten Jahrhunderts." In *Offenbarung im jüdischen und christlichen Glaubensverständnis*, ed. J. J. Petuchowski and Walter Strolz, 162–79. Freiburg im Breisgau: Herder, 1981.

"Am ve-emuna—le'an? Ideological and Historical Perspectives." *Central Conference of American Rabbis Yearbook* 91 (1981): 98–103.

"Alienated Intellectuals in the Camp of Religious Reform: The Frankfurt Reformfreunde, 1842–45." *AJS Review* 6 (1981): 61–86.

Foreword to the new printing of *Abraham Geiger and Liberal Judaism*, by Max Wiener. Cincinnati: Hebrew Union College Press, 1981.

"American Reform Judaism and Zionism: Early Efforts at Ideological Rapprochement," *Studies in Zionism* 7 (Spring 1983): 49–64.

"The German Model of Religious Reform and Russian Jewry." In *Danzig between East and West: Aspects of Modern Jewish History*, ed. Isadore Twersky, 67–91. Cambridge: Harvard University Press, 1985.

"Reform Jewish Thinkers and Their German Intellectual Context." In *The Jewish Response to German Culture*, ed. Jehuda Reinharz and Walter Schatzberg, 64–84. Hanover: University Press of New England, 1985.

"Heinrich Graetz and Heinrich von Treitschke: A Comparison of their Historical Images of the Modern Jew." *Modern Judaism* 6 (1986): 1–11.

"Aron Bernstein—The Enigma of a Radical Religious Reformer." In *Proceedings of the Ninth Congress of Jewish Studies.* Division B, vol. 3:9–16. Jerusalem: ha-Igud ha-Olami le-Madae ha-Yahadut, 1986.

Introduction to *The German Rabbinical Conferences, 1844–46* [in Hebrew], v–viii, 7–22. Jerusalem: Dinur Center, 1986.

"German-Jewish Identity in Nineteenth-Century America," in *Toward Modernity: The European Jewish Model*, ed. Jacob Katz, 247–67. New Brunswick, N.J.: Transaction Books, 1987.

"The Emergence of Modern Jewish Historiography: Motives and Motifs." *History and Theory* 27, no. 4 (Beiheft 27): 160–75.

"Reform Judaism." In *Contemporary Jewish Religious Thought*, ed. Arthur A. Cohen and Paul Mendes-Flohr, 767–72. New York: Scribner's, 1987.

"The Particular Significance of the Holocaust for Jews." In *Assessing the Significance of the Holocaust*, ed. Abie I. Ingber and Benny Kraut, 15–18. Cincinnati: University of Cincinnati Judaic Studies Program, 1987.

"On Being a Rebbitz." *Journal of Reform Judaism* (Summer 1987): 538.

Contribution to "American Jews and Israel—A Symposium." *Commentary*, February 1988, 54–55.

"Modernity as a Crisis for the Jews." *Modern Judaism* 9 (1989): 151–64.

"Anti-Semitism and Jewish Identity." *Commentary*, November 1989, 35–40.

"A Heritage Freighted Across the Abyss." In *The German-Jewish Legacy in America 1938–1988*, ed. Abraham J. Peck. Detroit: Wayne State University Press, 1989. Reprinted from *American Jewish Archives*, November 1988, 297–301.

"Toward a Unity-Oriented Jewish Historiography." *Association for Jewish Studies Newsletter* (Spring 1989): 8–9.

"*Berit Mila* within the History of the Reform Movement." In *Berit Mila in the Reform Context*, ed. Lewis M. Barth, 141–51. N.p.: Berit Mila Board of Reform Judaism, 1990. First published in Hebrew in *Shalhevet* 35 (September 1989): 31–35.

The German Jews: Some Perspectives on their History. B. G. Rudolph Lecture at Syracuse University, 1990.

"Recent Historiography on the Jewish Religion." *Leo Baeck Institute Year Book* 35 (1990): 3–16.

"Jews as Jews versus Jews as Germans: Two Historical Perspectives." *Leo Baeck Institute Year Book* 36 (1991): xv–xxii.

"'Ganz nach dem alten Herkommen'? The Spiritual Life of Berlin Jewry Following the Edict of 1823." In *Bild und Selbstbild der Juden Berlins zwischen Aufklärung und Romantik*, ed. Marianne Awerbuch and Stefi Jersch-Wenzel, 229–43. Berlin: Colloquium Verlag, 1992.

"Jüdische Wissenschaft und jüdische Identität." In *Wissenschaft des Judentums: Anfänge der Judaistik in Europa*, ed. Julius Carlebach, 3–20. Darmstadt: Wissenschaftliche Buchgesellschaft, 1992.

"Tradition and Modernity Reconsidered." In *The Uses of Tradition: Jewish Continuity in the Modern Era*, ed. Jack Wertheimer, 465–69. New York: Jewish Theological Seminary, 1992.

Preface to *The Merit of Our Mothers*, by Tracy Guren Klirs et al., ix–x. Cincinnati: Hebrew Union College Press, 1992.

"On the Slope Toward Syncretism and Sectarianism." *CCAR Journal* (Summer 1993): 41–44.

"Salomon Ludwig Steinheim and the Reform Movement." In *"Philo des 19. Jahrhunderts": Studien zu Salomon Ludwig Steinheim*, by J. H. Schoeps et al., 143–58. Hildesheim: Georg Olms, 1993.

"Liberal Judaism and Zionism in Germany" [in Hebrew]. In *Tsiyonut vedat*, ed. Shmuel Almog et al., 111–26. Jerusalem: Merkaz Shazar, 1994.

"Should and Can an 'Antiquated' Religion Become Modern? The Jewish Reform Movement in Germany as Seen by Jews and Christians." In *The Jews in European History: Seven Lectures*, ed. Wolfgang Beck, 57–72. Cincinnati: Hebrew Union College Press, 1994. Also published in German and French.

"Changes in the Relationship of Liberal Judaism to Jewish Law and Custom" [in

Hebrew]. In *Proceedings of the Eleventh World Congress of Jewish Studies*. Division C, vol. 1:243–49. Jerusalem: ha-Igud ha-Olami le-Madae ha-Yahadut, 1994.

Foreword to *The State of Israel in Jewish Public Thought: The Quest for Collective Identity*, by Yosef Gorny, ix–xii. London: Macmillan, 1994.

"Jenseits und diesseits des Abgrundes. Die Aufgaben des Leo Baeck Instituts." *LBI Information* 4 (1994): 6–12.

"Von Moses Mendelssohn bis Leo Baeck: Die Bedeutung Berlins für die jüdische Reform," in *Jüdische Geschichte in Berlin*, ed. Reinhard Rürup, 37–51. Berlin: Edition Hentrich, 1995.

"Setting Zion Before Us." *Journal of Reform Zionism* 2 (March 1995): 4–8.

"From Cincinnati to New York: A Symbolic Move." In *The Jewish Condition: Essays on Contemporary Judaism Honoring Rabbi Alexander Schindler*, ed. Aron Hirt-Manheimer, 302–13. New York: UAHC Press, 1995.

Contribution to "What Do American Jews Believe?—A Symposium." *Commentary*, August 1996, 72–73.

"'How Awesome Is This Place!' The Reconceptualization of the Synagogue in Nineteenth-Century Germany." *Leo Baeck Institute Year Book* 41 (1996): 51–63.

"Abba Hillel Silver as Zionist within the Camp of Reform Judaism." *Journal of Israeli History* 17 (1996): 9–31.

"The Thrust of My Work as an Historian of Jews and Judaism." *CCAR Journal* (Spring 1997): 71–73.

"Maimonides and Some Moderns: European Images of the Rambam from the Eighteenth to the Twentieth Century." *CCAR Journal* (Fall 1997): 4–15.

"Reflections on Jewish Modernization." In *Jewish History and Jewish Memory: Essays in Honor of Yosef Hayim Yerushalmi*, ed. Elisheva Carlebach, John M. Efron, and David N. Myers, 369–77. Hanover: University Press of New England, 1998.

"*Gemeinschaft* within *Gemeinde*: Religious Ferment in Weimar Liberal Judaism." In *In Search of Jewish Community: Jewish Identities in Germany and Austria 1918–1933*, ed. Michael Brenner and Derek J. Penslar, 15–35. Bloomington: Indiana University Press, 1998.

"Juden-Deutsche-Juden. Wandlungen des deutschen Judentums in der Neuzeit." In *Deutsch-Jüdische Geschichte in der Neuzeit: Zwei Vorträge*, with Michael Brenner, 5–16. Frankfurt am Main: LBI Information Sonderheft, 1998.

Foreword to the paperback edition of *State of Israel, Diaspora, and Jewish Continuity: Essays on the "Ever-Dying People,"* by Simon Rawidowicz, 5–8. Hanover: University Press of New England, 1998.

"Jewish Religious Reform in Germany and Britain." In *Two Nations: British and German Jews in Comparative Perspective*, ed. Michael Brenner et al., 67–83. Tübingen: Mohr Siebeck, 1999.

"Scripture in Modern Judaism." In *Living Traditions of the Bible*, ed. James E. Bowley, 191–206. St. Louis: Chalice Press, 1999.

"'God of Abraham and Sarah': The Status of Women in Non-Orthodox Judaism" [in Hebrew]. In *Barukh she'asani isha*, ed. David Yoel Ariel et al., 179–88. Tel Aviv: Yediot Aharonot, 1999.

"Being Jewish and . . ." In *National Variations in Jewish Identity: Implications for Jewish Education*, ed. Steven M. Cohen and Gabriel Horencyzk, 21–33.

Albany: State University of New York Press, 1999.

"The Thought of Leo Baeck: A Religious Philosophy for a Time of Adversity." *Modern Judaism* 19 (1999): 107–117.
    Hebrew: "A Religious Philosophy for a Time of a Time of Adversity." In *Leo Baeck: Manhiguto ve-haguto, 1933–1945,* ed. Avraham Barkai, 73–82. Jerusalem: Merkaz Shazar, 2000.

"Zur deutschen Gedächtnisliteratur oder das Ringen um adäquate Museumskonzepte." In *Ein Jüdisches Museum für München,* ed. Kulturreferat der Landeshauptstadt München, 43–60. Munich, 2000.

"Jewish History and Israeli History: The Problem of Distinguishing between Them." In *The Margins of Jewish History,* ed. Marc Lee Raphael, 95–101. Williamsburg, Va.: College of William and Mary, 2000.
    Hebrew: In *Gesher* (Winter 2001): 13–23.

"The Study of Judaism in Modern Germany: Some *Desiderata.*" *Leo Baeck Institute Year Book* 45 (2000): 218–19.

Preface [in German] to *Judentum und religiöse Reform: Der Hamburger Israelitische Tempel 1817–1938,* by Andreas Brämer, 6–8. Hamburg: Dölling und Galitz Verlag, 2000.

"Denken und Wirken Leo Baecks nach 1945." In *Leo Baeck 1873–1956. Aus dem Stamme von Rabbinern,* ed. Georg Heuberger and Fritz Backhaus, 129–46. Frankfurt a/M: Jüdischer Verlag im Suhrkamp Verlag, 2001.

"'Eine bestimmte Seelenhaltung': Leistungen, Grenzen und Erbschaft des liberalen Judentums in Deutschland." *LBI Information* 9 (2001): 104–17.

"Ludwig Meidner (1884–1966): Künstler und Jude." In *Vorträge aus dem Warburg-Haus,* Band 5, 121–64 (Berlin: Akademie Verlag, 2001).

"Will the Center Hold? Conservative Judaism Re-examined." *Conservative Judaism* 54, no. 1 (2001): 5–16.

Foreword [in German] to *Der jüdische Jesus und das Christentum: Abraham Geigers Herausforderung an die christliche Theologie,* by Susannah Heschel, trans. Christian Wiese, 9–11. Berlin: Jüdische Verlagsanstalt, 2001.

"Our Collective Identity as Reform Jews." In *Platforms and Prayer Books: Theological and Liturgical Perspectives on Reform Judaism,* ed. Dana Evan Kaplan, 93–96. Lanham, Md.: Rowman and Littlefield, 2002.

"Rivkin on Jewish Modernity and Continuity." In *Structural Analysis: The Historiographic Method of Ellis Rivkin,* ed. Allen Podet, 218–39. Diepenau: Göttert, 2002.

"Streitfragen in der zeitgenössischen jüdischen Historiographie." In *Jüdische Geschichtsschreibung heute: Themen, Positionen, Kontroversen,* ed. Michael Brenner and David N. Myers, 36–43. Munich: C. H. Beck, 2002.

"Leo Baeck: A Sense of Duty." *CCAR Journal* (Spring–Summer 2002): 11–16.

"The Imagined Jew: Heinrich Heine's 'Prinzessin Sabbath.'" In *History and Literature: New Readings of Jewish Texts in Honor of Arnold J. Band,* ed. William Cutter and David C. Jacobson, 209–21. Providence: Brown Judaic Studies, 2002.

"Reflections on the Educated Jew from the Perspective of Reform Judaism." In *Visions of Jewish Education,* ed. Seymour Fox, Israel Scheffler, and Daniel Marom, 149–77. New York: Cambridge University Press, 2003. First published as "Reflections on the 'Educated Jew' from the perspective of Reform

Judaism." *CCAR Journal* (Spring 1999): 7–20.

"German Jewry's Path to Normality and Assimilation: Complexities, Ironies, Paradoxes." In *Towards Normality? Acculturation and Modern German Jewry,* ed. Rainer Liedtke and David Rechter, 13–25. Tübingen: Leo Baeck Institute, 2003.

"'Most of My Brethren Find Me Unacceptable': The Controversial Career of Rabbi Samuel Holdheim." *Jewish Social Studies* 9, no. 3 (2003): 1–19.

"The Place and Identity of the Non-Jew in the Reform Synagogue" [in Hebrew]. *Gesher* 48, no. 146 (2003): 66–74.

"Two Persistent Tensions within *Wissenschaft des Judentums.*" *Modern Judaism* 24, no. 2 (2004): 105–19.

"Without Wissenschaft There Is No Judaism"—The Life and Thought of the Jewish Historian Ismar Elbogen. Braun Lectures in the History of the Jews of Prussia no. 11. Ramat Gan: Bar Ilan University, 2004.

Foreword to *Preserving the Legacy of German Jewry: A History of the Leo Baeck Institute, 1955–2005,* ed. Christhard Hoffmann, v–ix. Tübingen: Mohr Siebeck, 2005.

"Heinrich Zirndorf (1829–1893): Writer, Rabbi, Historian." *Jüdische Welten* (2005): 207–24.

"Ismar Schorsch, the Historian: A Critical Appreciation." In *Text and Context: Essays in Modern Jewish History and Historiography in Honor of Ismar Schorsch,* 3–23. New York: Jewish Theological Seminary, 2005.

"The Establishment of Rabbinical Seminaries in Germany: A Comparative View" [in Hebrew]. In *Yeshivot uvatei midrashot,* ed. Emanuel Etkes, 199–207. Jerusalem: Merkaz Shazar, 2006.

"Liberal Judaism in Nazi Germany." In *On Germans and Jews under the Nazi Regime: Essays by Three Generations of Historians,* ed. Moshe Zimmerman, 281–95. Jerusalem: Hebrew University Magnes Press, 2006.

"Rabbi L. Baeck's Legacy to Progressive Judaism." *European Judaism* 39, no. 2 (2006): 70–79.

"German Jewish Thinkers Reflect on the Future of the Jewish Religion." *Leo Baeck Institute Year Book* 51 (2006): 3–10.

"'Ich bin der Ewige, Dein Gott, Du sollst'" das Vermächtnis Leo Baecks für das Progressive Judentum heute." In *Leo Baeck: Philosophical and Rabbinical Approaches,* ed. Walter Homolka, 37–48. Berlin: Frank and Timme, 2007.

"Toward a Reform Jewish Vision for Zion." *CCAR Journal* 54, no. 2 (2007): 98–112.

"Jüdischer Geistiger Widerstand während der NS-Zeit. Die Rabbiner Leo Baeck und Joachim Prinz." *LBI Information* 12 (2007): 6–16.

Translations

Leo Baeck. "Theology and History." *Judaism* 13 (1964): 274–78.

Martin Buber. "The Election of Israel: A Biblical Inquiry," 80–92; "Samuel and the Ark," 131–36; and "Biblical Humanism," 211–16. In *On the Bible: Eighteen Studies,* by Martin Buber. New York: Schocken, 1968.

Ten essays in Gershom Scholem, *The Messianic Idea in Judaism and Other Essays on Jewish Spirituality.* New York: Schocken, 1971.

Contributors

Arnold J. Band is professor emeritus of Hebrew and comparative literature at the University of California, Los Angeles. His major works include *Nostalgia and Nightmare: Studies in the Fiction of S. J. Agnon* (1968), *The Tales of Rabbi Nahman of Bratzlav* (1978), *Studies in Modern Jewish Literature* in the JPS Scholars of Distinction series (2003), thirty-six literary introductions to Psalms in *I Wake the Dawn* (2007), and a selection of Hebrew essays in *She'elot nikhbadot* (2007).

Avraham Barkai is a fellow of the Leo Baeck Institute in Jerusalem and served as its chairman from 1995 to 1998. Among his publications on German-Jewish history of the nineteenth and twentieth centuries and on National Socialism are *Das Wirtschaftssystem des Nationalsozialismus* (1977; English edition: *Nazi Economics: Ideology, Theory, and Policy* [1991]), *From Boycott to Annihilation: The Economic Struggle of German Jews 1933–1943* (1989), *Wehr Dich! Der Centralverein deutscher Staatsbürger jüdischen Glaubens, 1893–1938* (2002). He is the coauthor, with Paul Mendes-Flohr, of *Aufbruch und Zerstörung, 1918–1945*, vol. 4 of *Deutsch-Jüdische Geschichte in der Neuzeit* (*German-Jewish History in Modern Times*), edited by Michael A. Meyer (1997; English edition: *Renewal and Destruction: 1918–1945* [1998]).

Michael Brenner is professor of Jewish history and culture at the University of Munich, Germany. He serves as chairman of the Wissenschaftliche Arbeitsgemeinschaft des Leo Baeck Institute in Deutschland. His books include *The Renaissance of Jewish Culture in Weimar Germany* (1996), *After the Holocaust: Rebuilding Jewish Lives in Post-war Germany* (1997), and *Zionism: A Brief History* (2003). He also served as assistant editor to the four-volume *German-Jewish History in Modern Times* (with Michael A. Meyer, editor, 1996–98).

Elisheva Carlebach is professor of history at Queens College and the Graduate Center, CUNY. Among her publications are *The Pursuit of Heresy* (1990; 1994) and *Divided Souls: Converts from Judaism in Germany, 1500–1750* (2001). She is also a coeditor (with John M. Efron and David N. Myers) of *Jewish History and Jewish Memory: Essays in Honor of Yosef Hayim Yerushalmi* (1998).

RICHARD I. COHEN is the Paulette and Claude Kelman Professor in French Jewry at the Hebrew University of Jerusalem. He is the author of *Jewish Icons: Art and Society in Modern Europe* (1998) and *Burden of Conscience: French-Jewish Leadership during the Holocaust* (1985). Among his edited volumes are *Diary of a Witness, 1940–1943*, by Raymond-Raoul Lambert (2007), *Image and Sound: Art, Music, and History* [in Hebrew] (2007), and, with Jeremy Cohen, *The Jewish Contribution to Civilization: Reassessing an Idea* (2007).

DAVID ELLENSON is the president of Hebrew Union College–Jewish Institute of Religion, where he is also the I. H. and Anna Grancell Professor of Jewish Religious Thought. He is the author of *Tradition in Transition: Orthodoxy, Halakhah, and the Boundaries of Modern Jewish Identity* (1989), *Rabbi Esriel Hildesheimer and the Creation of a Modern Jewish Orthodoxy* (1990), *Between Tradition and Culture: The Dialectics of Jewish Religion and Identity in the Modern World* (1994), and *After Emancipation: Jewish Religious Responses to Modernity* (2004).

SHMUEL FEINER is professor of modern Jewish history at Bar Ilan University, Israel, and the chair of the Leo Baeck Institute, Jerusalem. Among his publications are *Haskalah and History: The Emergence of a Modern Jewish Historical Consciousness* (2002), *The Jewish Enlightenment* (2004), and *Moses Mendelssohn* (2005).

EVYATAR FRIESEL is professor emeritus of modern Jewish history at the Hebrew University of Jerusalem. He served as state archivist of Israel from 1993 to 2001. He has written extensively on the history of Zionism, American Jewish history, and European Jewish history.

KARLA GOLDMAN is historian in residence at the Jewish Women's Archive in Boston. She is the author of *Beyond the Synagogue Gallery: Finding a Place for Women in American Judaism* and of articles on such subjects as black-Jewish relations, the development of American Judaism, and American Jewish women's history.

SUSANNAH HESCHEL is the Eli Black Professor of Jewish Studies in the Department of Religion at Dartmouth College. She is the author of *Abraham Geiger and the Jewish Jesus* (winner of the National Jewish Book Award) and of the forthcoming book *The Aryan Jesus: Nazis, Christians, and the Bible*. She has coedited a number of books, including *Betrayal: German Churches and the Holocaust* (with Robert P. Ericksen), *Insider/Outsider: American Jews and Multiculturalism* (with David Biale and Michael Galchinsky), and *Moral Grandeur and Spiritual Audacity: Essays of Abraham Joshua Heschel*, and edited the classic collection *On Being a Jewish Feminist*.

CHRISTHARD HOFFMANN is professor of modern European history and head of the Department of Archaeology, History, Cultural Studies, and Religion at the University of Bergen, Norway. His books include *Juden und Judentum im Werk deutscher Althistoriker des 19. und 20. Jahrhunderts* (1988; repr. 2007), *Juden und Judentum in der Literatur* (coeditor, 1985), *Exclusionary Violence: Antisemitic Riots in Modern German History* (coeditor, 2002), and *Preserving the Legacy of German Jewry: A History of the Leo Baeck Institute, 1955–2005* (editor, 2005).

PAULA E. HYMAN is the Lucy G. Moses Professor of Modern Jewish History at Yale University. She is coauthor of *The Jewish Woman in America* (1976), and author of several books, including *From Dreyfus to Vichy: The Remaking of French Jewry, 1906–1939* (1979), *The Emancipation of the Jews of Alsace* (1991), *Gender and Assimilation in Modern Jewish History* (1995), and *The Jews of Modern France* (1998). She also coedited *Jewish Women in America: An Historical Encyclopedia* (1997) and the multivolume *Jewish Women: An Historical Encyclopedia* (2006).

MARION KAPLAN is the Skirball Professor of Modern Jewish History at New York University. She is author or editor of several books, including *Jewish Daily Life in Germany, 1618–1945* (2005), *Jüdische Welten: Juden in Deutschland vom 18. Jahrhundert bis in die Gegenwart* (2005), *Between Dignity and Despair: Jewish Life in Nazi Germany* (1988), *The Making of the Jewish Middle Class: Women, Family, and Identity in Imperial Germany* (1991), and *The Jewish Feminist Movement in Germany: The Campaigns of the Juedischer Frauenbund, 1904–1938* (1979).

RICHARD N. LEVY is the director of the School of Rabbinical Studies and lecturer in rabbinics at HUC-JIR, Los Angeles. He is the author of *A Vision of Holiness: The Future of Reform Judaism*, the editor and principal contributor to *On Wings of Awe: A High Holyday Prayerbook* and *On Wings of Freedom: A Passover Haggadah*, and the author of articles on spirituality, liturgy, and Reform Judaism. He is currently working on a translation of the Book of Psalms with a textual and spiritual commentary.

STEVEN M. LOWENSTEIN is the Isadore Levine Professor of History at the American Jewish University (formerly the University of Judaism). Among his books are *Frankfurt on the Hudson: The German Jewish Community of Washington Heights, 1933–83, Its Structure and Culture* (1989), *The Berlin Jewish Community: Enlightenment, Family and Crisis, 1770–1830* (1994), and *The Jewish Cultural Tapestry: International Jewish Folk Traditions* (2002), and chapters of *German-Jewish History in Modern Times*, vol. 3 (1998).

DAVID N. MYERS is professor of Jewish history and director of the Center for Jewish Studies at the University of California, Los Angeles. His books include *Re-Inventing the Jewish Past: European Jewish Intellectuals and the Zionist Return to History* (1995) and *Resisting History: Historicism and its Discontents in German-Jewish Thought* (2003), as well as several edited volumes.

PETER PULZER is the Gladstone Professor Emeritus of Government at Oxford University, England, and chair of the London chapter of the Leo Baeck Institute. He is the author of *The Rise of Political Anti-Semitism in Germany and Austria* and *Jews and the German State: The Political History of a Minority, 1848–1933*, and he was a contributor to volume 3 of *German-Jewish History in Modern Times* (1998).

MONIKA RICHARZ is professor emerita at the University of Hamburg, Germany, and former director of the Institute for the History of German Jewry, Hamburg. Her books include *Der Eintritt der Juden in die akademischen Berufe: Jüdische Studenten und Akademiker in Deutschland, 1678–1848* (1974) and *Jüdisches Leben in*

Deutschland: Selbstzeugnisse zur Sozialgeschichte, 1780–1945, 3 vols. (1976–82). She edited *Die Hamburger Kauffrau Glikl: Jüdische Existenz in der Frühen Neuzeit* (2001) and was a contributor to *German-Jewish History in Modern Times: Integration in Dispute, 1871–1918*, vol. 3 (1998).

DAVID B. RUDERMAN is the Joseph Meyerhoff Professor of Modern Jewish History and director of the Center for Advanced Judaic Studies at the University of Pennsylvania. His books include *The World of a Renaissance Jew* (1981), *Kabbalah, Magic, and Science* (1988), *A Valley of Vision* (1990), *Jewish Thought and Scientific Discovery in Early Modern Europe* (1995, 2001), *Jewish Enlightenment in an English Key: Anglo-Jewry's Construction of Modern Jewish Thought* (2000), and *Connecting the Covenants: Judaism and the Search for Christian Identity in Eighteenth Century England* (2007). He also coedited the source reader for the series Heritage: Civilization and the Jews (1984).

JONATHAN D. SARNA is the Joseph H. and Belle R. Braun Professor of American Jewish History at Brandeis University and director of its Hornstein Jewish Professional Leadership Program. He is author or editor of more than twenty books on American Jewish history and life, including *Jacksonian Jew: The Two Worlds of Mordecai Noah*, *The Jews of Boston* (coauthor), *JPS: The Americanization of Jewish Culture*, *The American Jewish Experience* (editor), and *Women and American Judaism* (coeditor). His most recent book, *American Judaism: A History*, won the 2004 Jewish Book of the Year Award from the Jewish Book Council.

ISMAR SCHORSCH is chancellor emeritus of the Jewish Theological Seminary of America and the Rabbi Herman Abramovitz Professor of Jewish History at JTS. He is the author of *From Text to Context: The Turn to History in Modern Judaism* (1994) and of several collections of articles and sermons that he wrote during his years as chancellor. These include *The Sacred Cluster: The Core Values of Conservative Judaism* (1995), *Polarities in Balance* (2004), and *Canon without Closure* (2007).

GERSHON SHAKED was professor emeritus of Hebrew literature at the Hebrew University of Jerusalem. Among his many books published in Hebrew are *The Narrative Art of S. Y. Agnon* (1973), *Hebrew Narrative Fiction 1880–1980*, 5 vols. (1977–98), *No Other Place* (1983), *S. Y. Agnon—A Writer with a Thousand Faces* (1989), and *Identity: Jewish Literatures in European Languages* (2006). He was also the author of more than thirty books of criticism in several languages, including *The Shadows Within: Essays on Modern Jewish Writers* (1987) and *Shmuel Yosef Agnon: A Revolutionary Traditionalist* (1989). Shaked received the Bialik Prize (1986), the Israel Prize for Literary Scholarship (1992), and the Bahat Award for Non-Fiction (2004).

MICHAEL STANISLAWSKI is the Nathan J. Miller Professor of Jewish History at Columbia University. His books include *Tsar Nicholas I and the Jews* (1983), *For Whom Do I Toil* (1986), *Psalms for the Tsar* (1986), *Zionism and the Fin-de-Siecle* (2001), *Autobiographical Jews: Essays in Jewish Self-Fashioning* (2004), and *Murder in Lemberg: Politics, Religion, And Violence in Modern Jewish History* (2006). He also coedited the source reader for the television series *Heritage: Civilization and the Jews* (1984).

Lauren B. Strauss is a lecturer in Modern Jewish history and literature at the George Washington University and the American University in Washington, D.C. She has published articles on American Jewish journals, women, and artists, and in 2004 she served as a historical consultant for the Library of Congress exhibition From Haven to Home: 350 Years of Jewish Life in America. Her doctoral dissertation, "Painting the Town Red: Jewish Visual Artists, Yiddish Culture, and Progressive Politics in New York, 1917–1939," is being prepared for publication.

Ernst-Peter Wieckenberg is the former head of the Humanities Editorial Department at C. H. Beck Publishing House in Germany. He is the author of *Anton Reiser: ein psychologischer Roman* (coauthor, 1961), *Zur Geschichte der Kapitelüberschrift im deutschen Roman vom 15. Jahrhundert bis zum Ausgang des Barock* (1972), and *'Die tausend und eine Nacht. Johann Heinrich Voß als Übersetzer Antoine Gallands* (2002), among other publications.

INDEX

Cahan, Abraham, 292
calendar. *See* Jewish calendar
Calvin, John, 172
Campe, Joachim, 267, 268
Canaani, David, 341
capitalism: development of, and
    Puritanism, 172; effect on German
    Jews, 176–79; identification of Jews
    with, 169–70
Cardoso, Abraham, 36
Carigal, Raphael Haim Isaac, 189
Cassirer, Ernst, 69n18
Central Committee of the Jews in
    Germany (Zentralrat der Juden in
    Deutschland), 330
Central-Verein, 207, 218, 244n53, 249,
    254, 258n36
Chagall, Marc, 312
chamishiya hakameri, 311
charity Judaism *(Wohltätigkeitsjudentum)*,
    249
Charlemagne, 12
chiliastic ideas, 64
Christian European anti-Judaism, 57,
    168; defined the Jew as masculine,
    210; negative image of Jewish
    merchants and tradesmen, 171. *See
    also* antisemitism
Christian Hebraists, 38, 39, 189
Christian humanism, 78
"Christianity of virtue," 57
"Christian Jews," 38
Christian West, and the Jewish State,
    138–39
Churchill, Winston, 153, 166n35
Cincinnati Jews, 7; creation of first
    successful national institutions
    of Jewish life, 195–203; dream
    of rabbinical school, 200–202;
    fund-raising for Hebrew Union
    College, 202; high sense of civic
    and social status, 197–98; hope
    that synagogues and rabbis would
    secure the regard of non-Jewish
    neighbors, 198; singular American
    contributions, 203; synagogue
    dedications, 198–99
Cohen, Aharon, 149
Cohen, Gershom, 127
Cohen, Hermann, 127, 258n27
Cohen, Jeremy, 76

Cohen, Steven, 20
Cologne, 326, 334
Cologne Roma Association, 326
colonial American Jews: engagement in
    mystical practices in private lives,
    189; messianic hopes and mystical
    devotions, 186–90; messianic
    speculation, 189–90; "port Jews,"
    185
colonialist fantasy of seduction of alien
    female, 82, 211
communal structures, decline of in
    modern period, 33
Communist Party (MaKI), 149
Communist victims of National
    Socialism, 327, 333
Conservative prayerbook, 295
Constantinople, sack of, 172
constructionism, 135
conversion: of Jewish women, 82; for
    purpose of enabling intermarriage,
    216; as response to antisemitism,
    216; during the 1920s, 256n8
Conversos: entrance of into university,
    35; merchant colonies of, 33;
    messianism, 36; mobility of, 32;
    reintegration into Jewish life, 38;
    and Sabbateanism and Spinozism,
    37; shaping of personal identity
    from both Judaism and Christianity,
    39
Cosmann, Carl, 228
court Jews, 124
Cranz, August, 270
cultural Zionism, 234

D'Acosta, Uriel, 45, 279
Davar, 150
deconstructionism, 135, 342–43
dehiyyot, 45
Deir Yassin, 165n24
Demnig, Gunter, 7, 326–31, 334–36
Der Große Herder, 129
Der Jude, 129
Der Morgen, 284
De' Rossi, Azariah: *Matsref la-kesef*, 45;
    Me'or Eynaim, 45
Derrida, Jacques, 74–75, 342, 348n10
Diaspora journalists, silent consent to
    Israel's treatment of Arabs, 154–55
Diaspora nationalism, 2

160; role of for younger American Jews, 20; suppression of memory of by survivors, 151
"homeland," reencounter with, 311
homiletics, 94
homosexual victims of National Socialism, 327, 333
"horizontal tolerance," 66, 67, 72n68
Hoshana Rabbah, 45
HUC Chronicle, 17
Hulda kibbutz, 320
Humboldt, Wilhelm von, 122
Hungarian Orthodoxy, 276

Idel, Moshe, 32
Iggeret Ha-Kodesh ("The Holy Letter"), Hebrew version, 96
Iggeret Ha-Kodesh ("The Holy Letter"), Yiddish translation of, 96–100, 103; advice for women's behavior in the home, 100; concept of *tsnies* (sexual modesty), 98; discussion of foods to be eaten before sex, 99; discussion of Friday night as best time for sexual intercourse, 99–100; ideas not accessible from rabbinic sources of sexuality, 98–100; omission of kabbalistic references, 97–98; sex manual aimed exclusively at men, 97
Ihud Association, 150
Il Pecorone, 75
Industrial Revolution, 176
intermarriage, 216, 240–41, 249, 255n5, 333
internal colonialism, 211
internationalization, 114
Irgun, 80
Irving, Henry, 79
Isaac of Aachen, 124
Islamic countries, effect of westernization on Jewish communities in, 306
Israel, Jonathan, 29–30, 33
Israel, State of: and the Christian West, 138–39; debate over expulsions of Palestinian Arabs, 148–52; debates regarding status of Arab residents, 139, 145, 151, 161; efforts to institutionalize memory of Holocaust, 151–52; establishment of

in spite of destruction of European Jewry, 140; Land Acquisition Law, 154; representation of adaptation of Jews to modernity, 137; role of for younger American Jews, 20; suppression of memory of Arab expulsion, 151
Israel Defense Force, 149
Israeli-Arab confrontation, 137–38
Israeli intellectuals, concern over relationship between Jewish power and morality, 160
Israelit, 280, 281
The Israelite, 201, 202
itinerant preachers, 32

Jabotinsky, Vladimir Zev, 165n24, 318, 319
Jakobson, Roman, 341–42
James, Henry, 292
Jehovah's Witnesses, victims of National Socialism, 327
Jerusalem school of historiography, 27
Jeschurun, 280–81
Jeshuat Israel, Newport, 188, 190
Jesus, 84, 86
Jewish Agency, 254
Jewish calendar: and dispute over revival of rabbinical ordination, 44; rationalist critique, 46–47; sixteenth-century challenge to, 44–45; traditionalist view of, 47–51
"Jewish Christians," 38
Jewish Committee to Combat White Slavery, 217
Jewish culture. *See* early modern Jewish culture
Jewish Emancipation, 14, 86, 114, 207, 306
Jewish Enlightenment. *See Haskalah*
Jewish fraternities, 215
Jewish historical consciousness, in the nineteenth century, 109
Jewish identity: effect of political antisemitism on, 207, 218–19; in the fin de siècle, 206, 207, 218–19; and rise of racist conceptions of Jews, 207–9
Jewish *Kulturbund*, 286
Jewish labor movement, 140
Jewish medical community, 35

Jewish men: establishment of own organizations to display their masculinity, 215; fin de siècle references to "feminization" of, 208–9; internalization of antisemitic stereotypes, 214; response to disparagement of masculinity, 213–16

Jewish museums, 311–12

Jewish nationalism, 253, 254

Jewish Publication Society, 295; 1917 Bible translation, 290, 291, 298; 1953 Bible translation, 292; 1985 Bible translation, 293, 296, 298

Jewish scholarship, and personal involvement of scholars, 2

Jewish student clubs, 215

Jewish studies, 6, 75; feminist theory and women's history, 94; modern, 29

Jewish Theological Seminary of America, 5, 17

Jewish trade, negative attitudes toward, 171

Jewish women: antisemitic caricature depiction as grotesque, 212; assertion of political rights within the community, 216–17, 219; conversion of, 82; danger associated with seductive female connected to antisemitic elements, 210, 211; depiction of as purveyors of disease, 211–12; disabilities suffered in divorce law and secondary status, 206; fin de siècle image of, 210; negative images appeared with rise of modern antisemitism, 212–13; Orientalization of, 211

Jews: effect of capitalism on, 176–79; entrance of into university, 35; idea of "return to history," 136–37; internal dialogue with eastern Europe, 312; self-consciousness, 205; self-definition in early modern Europe, 38; self-hatred, 209; view of as the Other, 211. *See also* Ashkenazic Jews; Cincinnati Jews; colonial American Jews

The Jew Within (Cohen and Eisen), 20

Jodensavanne, 188

Joseph ben Gershon (Yosel of Rosheim), 124

Joseph II, 268

Jost, Isaac Marcus, 3, 28, 125, 275, 280

Joyce, James: *Portrait of the Artist as a Young Man*, 316

Jubilees, 46

judenrein Vienna, 77

Jüdischer Frauenbund, 217

Jüdische Rundschau, 279

Jüdisch-Liberale-Jugendverein (ILI), 254, 260n35

Jüdisch-Liberale Zeitung, 250, 253, 254, 258n30, 259n34, 260n35, 260n36

Jüdisch-religiöse Mittelpartei für Frieden und Einheit in der Gemeinde, 258n27

Jud Süß, 77

kabbalah, 32, 39, 94, 189, 190

Kafka, Franz, 346

Kafr Kasem, 151

Kameralismus, 173

Kant, Immanuel, 15

kapparot, 94

Karaites, 45, 51

Kastein, Josef: *History of the Jews*, 279–80

Kattan, Naim: *Farewell, Babylon: Coming of Age in Jewish Baghdad*, 309

Katz, Jacob, 27, 44, 276; *Out of the Ghetto*, 143

Kayserling, Meyer, 283

Kean, Edmund, 78

Keren Hayesod, 254

kevi'ot, 46–47, 50

King James Bible, 291, 292, 294

Klausner, Fanya, 322–23

Klausner, Joseph, 316, 317, 318, 322, 340; *Darki likrat hatehiya vehage'ula*, 319

Klausner, Yehudah Aryeh, 318, 322, 323

Klemperer, Victor, 129, 227, 228–30, 231, 236, 240–41

Klimt, Gustav, 210

Knesset, 153, 154

Knobloch, Charlotte, 331

Kober, Adolf, 129

Kohelet, 298

Kohler, Kaufmann, 202–3

Kohn, Hans, 146

Kohnstamm, Jackie, 337n6

Kol ha'am, 150

Kol Nidre prayer, 94, 171–72

Kol Sakhal (Voice of a Fool), 45

konfessionslos, 216
Königsberg choir, 255n2
Kornick, Meyer Moses, 47–51, 54n37;
    Davar be-itto, 47; *System der*
    Zeitrechnung in Chronologischen
    Tabellen, 53n21
Kors, Charles, 63
Korshin, Paul J., 63
Krauss, Werner, 77
Kreuzberg Museum, 330
Kristallnacht, 77
Krochmal, Nachman, 28
"Kurgäste," 212
Kurzweil, Baruch, 347n4
Kuznets, Simon, 176, 180n29

Labor Zionists, 158
Lacan, Jacques, 349n19
Ladino, printed books in, 35
Lampert, Lisa, 81
Land Acquisition Law, 154
language: as historical creation, 341;
    of modern culture, expansion by
    Hebrew language, 300
Lasker, Eduard, 254n1
Lavater, Johann Caspar, 125, 267, 270
Law of Return, 151, 153
League of Nations, 136
Leß, Gottfried: *Wahrheit der Christlichen*
    Religion, 62–63, 66
Leeser, Isaac, Jewish translation of
    Hebrew Bible into English, 291
Lehmann, Behrend, 124
Lehmann, Marcus, 281
Leibniz, Gottfried Wilhelm, 60, 61
Leibowitz, Yeshayahu, 146, 160, 167n46
Leo Baeck Institute, 6, 12, 129
Lessing, Gotthold Ephraim, 61, 62; *Die*
    Juden, 56–57, 60, 265; "Leibnitz
    von den ewigen Strafen," 60;
    Nathan the Wise, 78, 79, 125,
    276, 278, 285; *Zur Geschichte*
    und Litteratur: Aus den Schätzen
    der Herzoglichen Bibliotek zu
    Wolfenbüttel, 60
Lessing, Karl, 60
Levi Ibn Haviv, 44–45
Levush, 50
Liberale Synagoge Norden, Berlin,
    257n23
Liberal German prayer book

(Einheitsgebetbuch), 252
Liberal Jewish Movement of England,
    253, 258n26
Liberal Judaism. *See* German Liberal
    Judaism
Lichtheim, Richard, 214
Lieberman, Livneh: *Me'al hahorovot*
    (Over the Ruins), 321
Liebermann, Martha, 328, 335
Lilienblum, Moshe Leib, 277
Lilienthal, Max, 197–98
Lipman ben Juda, 124
literary criticism, dialectical response to
    hegemony of history, 341–42, 345,
    347
literary history, 339–47; defined, 340;
    Marxist school, 340–41; must refer
    to historical context, 342; positivist
    approach, 340, 345
literature: Hebrew, 340, 341, 343, 345,
    346; historicization of, 341, 343;
    image of Jew in, 6
Lithuania, 94
Livnat, Limor, 163n7
Löhr, Max, 128
London, Shlomo Zalman: *Hinnukh*
    Katan, 100; *Kohelet Shelomoh*, 100,
    102; Passover Haggadah, 100–101;
    Zoker Ha-Berit, 100–104
Lopez, Rodrigo, 76
Lost Ten Tribes, 187
Loth, Moritz, 202
Lukács, George, 341, 346; *The Historical*
    Novel, 347n5
Luria, Isaac: *Tikkunei Shabbat*, 101
Lurianic kabbalah, 36
Lutheran Orthodoxy, 57–58, 62, 63, 64,
    66
Luxon, Thomas, 75
Luzzatto, Moses Hayyim, 37
Lydda, 149, 150, 164n13
Lyotard, Jean Francois, 89

Ma'ariv, 344
Magen Abraham of Mauricia, 187
Maharil, 102
Mahler, Raphael, 2
mahzor katan, 46–47
Maimon, Salomon, 125, 206
Maimonides, 50, 280
MaKI, 150

Malamud, Bernard, 293
Mann, Golo, 129
Mann, Thomas, 285, 346
"Ma'oz Tzur," 255n2
Mapai party, 150, 159
Mapam, 149
Mappa, 33
Marcus, Jacob Rader, 185
Marmontel, Jean François: *Bélisaire,*
     58–59
Marr, Wilhelm, 276
Marranos, 45, 74, 81, 86
Martyrs' and Heroes' Remembrance
     Authority, 151
Marx, Hugo, 227
Marx, Karl, 169–70, 172, 179, 299,
     349n20; "On the Jewish Question,"
     169
Meidner, Ludwig, 15
Meir, Golda, 318
Menasseh ben Israel: *The Hope of Israel,*
     186–87, 190; insistence that
     Indians of New World descended
     from Adam and Eve, 187; *Mikveh
     Israel,* 188; millenarian belief, 188;
     Nishmat Hayyim, 186; *Vindiciae
     Judaeorum,* 268
Mendelssohn, Dorothea, 205
Mendelssohn, Moses, 4, 72n62, 78;
     as "archetypical German Jew,"
     274–78; changing image of among
     Liberal German Jews, 282–86;
     changing image of in early
     twentieth-century Europe, 277–82;
     concept of the Jew as German, 125;
     criticism of in German-language
     Zionist publications, 277, 278–80;
     dream of civil admission of Jews,
     269; dreams about opportunities
     of modern era and anxiety about
     failure of Enlightenment, 266,
     267, 268, 272, 290; embodiment
     of possibility of remaining
     Jewish while becoming German,
     275; favored abolishing right of
     excommunication, 269–70; feeling
     of weakness as Jew, 267; first
     biography of, 275; first Jew whose
     hundredth birthday was celebrated
     by non-Jewish public, 276; haunted
     by anti-Jewish prejudice, 271;
on idea of uniform faith, 271;
     Jerusalem, 270, 280; and Orthodox
     Judaism, 280–81; on possibility
     of establishing a state for Jews in
     Palestine, 264–65; reception by
     traditional Jews, 276–77; struggle
     with conflict between prejudice and
     religious tolerance, 266; tension
     between Jewish identity as "other"
     and high public standing, 271–72;
     terrifying experience of family with
     antisemitism, 268; translation of
     Bible into "pure" German, 290–91;
     two hundredth birthday celebration,
     278; view of as philosopher rather
     than enthusiastic Jew, 281
mercantilism, 29
The Merchant of Venice (Shakespeare):
     associations of with the Holocaust,
     81; can be read as anti-Jewish
     or anti-Christian, 90; and the
     Christian as Jew, 83–86; concern
     with presence of Jews in Christian
     society, 76; cross-dressing of
     Portia in courtroom scene, 83–84;
     failure of church to convert Jews,
     90; interrogation of nature of
     the Christian, 81–83; Israeli
     productions of, 80–81; and the Jew
     in the Christian, 86–89; Jew of
     the Christian imagination, 75–76;
     Jewish portrayals of, 79; Nazi use
     of, 77; notion that Christianness
     requires both nationality and race,
     81–82; pairing of Christian man
     and Jewish woman, 82; problem
     of forgiveness, 87; productions of
     during Third Reich, 77; productions
     of in the Yishuv, 80; question
     of transubstantiation, 85–86;
     scholarship on attitude toward Jews,
     74; Shylock as polysemic figure,
     89–90; undermining of theology
     of Christian anti-Judaism, 89. *See
     also* Shylock
Meyer, Eduard, 174
Meyer, Michael A., 75, 129, 186;
     on American Judaism and
     individualism, 20–21; association
     with Hebrew Union College—
     Jewish Institute of Religion, 18;

biographical context of work, 3, 316; characterization of Moses Mendelssohn, 263; commitment to Zionism and State of Israel, 144; on complementarity of contemporary Zionism and Reform, 22–23; contributions to formation and growth of junior scholars, 144; on ethnic Judaism, 22; experience of dislocation, 13–14; history of request for tolerance of Jews, 56; on Jewish integration in nineteenth century, 130; and Leo Baeck, 15; on Mendelssohn, 270; participation in modern Jewish institutions, 6; on phenomenon of "salon Jewesses," 205–6; on Rawidowicz, 145, 147, 160; "reconceptualization of Judaism," 306; and Reform Judaism, 5, 13, 17, 18, 19, 144; and return of the Jews to history, 133; on role of early Cincinnati institutions in Reform Judaism, 195; study of intersection of Judaism and modernity, 3–4, 15, 19–20, 144, 263, 305; study of Ludwig Meidner, 15; on tasks of Jewish education, 19, 21–22; teaching of rabbinical students, 18; translation of German Jewish culture to American audience, 300; on United States as "galut-exile for the Reform Jew," 22–23; and universalism, 20

Meyer, Michael A.—WORKS: editor of German-Jewish History in Modern Times, 144; "Gemeinschaft within Gemeinde: Religious Ferment within Weimar Liberal Judaism," 257n23; German-Jewish History in Modern Times, 3, 12–13; Ideas of Modern Jewish History, 1, 2, 23, 28; Jewish Identity in the Modern World, 121, 144, 313; "Jewish Political Leadership in Nazi Germany," 11–12; Judaism within Modernity, 13, 144; The Origins of the Modern Jew, 11, 13, 109, 121, 143–44, 205, 206, 263, 264, 290, 300, 305, 315; "Reflections on the 'Educated Jew' from the Perspective of Reform Judaism," 2019; Response to

Modernity, 5, 11, 12, 13, 14, 121, 144; "Where Does the Modern Period of Jewish History Begin?", 3, 27–28, 43, 144; "Will the Center Hold?", 20
Meyerhof, Hans, 230
Michaelis, Johann David, 56, 57, 125; review of Die Juden, 265, 266
Midrashim, 343
migrations, large-scale, 32
Miller, Arthur, 293
Milman, Henry Hart: The History of the Jews, 126
Miranda, Isaac, 190
mistanenim, 153
Mittelpartei, 251, 253, 256n15
Mittwoch, Eugen, 278
mixed seating, 252–53
mobility, and early modern Jewish culture, 32–33
Modena, Leon de: critique of Jewish calendar, 45; Zeli esh, 101
"modernist" German-Jewish historians, identification of modern age as "Jewish," 109–10
modern Orthodox Judaism, 4
mohelim, 81, 101, 103
moladot, 49, 50
Moldenhawer, Johann Heinrich, 63
Momigliano, Arnaldo: "Popular Religious Beliefs and the Late Roman Historians," 93
Monis, Judah, 190
Montagu, Lily, 253
Montefiore, Claude, 253
Moravia, 94
Moroccan Jews, 142
Morris, Benny, 146–48, 163n7, 164n13, 164n23, 165n28
Mosaic principle, 116
Moshe Dessau. See Mendelssohn, Moses
Mosse, George: German Jews beyond Judaism, 143
muskeljudentum (muscular Jewry), 215

Nachmanides, 96–97
Nachman of Bratslav, 313
Nachshon Gaon, Rabbi, 47
Nathan of Gaza, 36
Nathans, Ben, 312
Nationality Law, 151, 153, 154, 165n27
National Socialism, victims of,

www.ingramcontent.com/pod-product-compliance
Lightning Source LLC
Chambersburg PA
CBHW070439100426
42812CD00031B/3337/J